Reinterpreting Rahner

Reinterpreting Rahner

A CRITICAL STUDY
OF HIS MAJOR THEMES

Patrick Burke

Fordham University Press
New York • 2002

Library of Congress Cataloging-in-Publication Data

Burke, Patrick, 1964–
    Reinterpreting Rahner : a critical study of his
  major themes / Patrick
Burke.—1st ed.
     p. cm.
    Includes bibliographical references and index.
    ISBN 0-8232-2218-7—ISBN 0-8232-2219-5 (pbk.)
    1. Rahner, Karl, 1904– I. Title.
BX4705.R287 B87   2002
230′.2′092—dc21   2002007506

Printed in the United States of America
02 03 04 05 06   5 4 3 2 1
First Edition

CONTENTS

INTRODUCTION

PROBABLY NO THEOLOGIAN exercised so profound an influence on Catholic theology during the last half of the twentieth century as Karl Rahner. By his historical and theological research before the Second Vatican Council, he contributed mightily to the foundations of the so-called new theology that was finally to win acceptance from the Council Fathers. During the council, he actively participated as a *peritus* in the drafting of many conciliar decrees, and in the years subsequent he tirelessly interpreted the council's intentions to the world in books, articles, and lectures translated into innumerable languages. He was undoubtedly one of the great synthetic thinkers of the twentieth century, and his theology was and remains an outstanding achievement.

Although the vast majority of his work consisted in individual articles and lectures that were only subsequently collected and published together, Rahner's theology is rightly recognized as a theological system because of the fundamental unity that runs throughout his writings. The key to this unity of approach lies in a foundational structure of thought that is revealed in the philosophical works with which he began his intellectual career and that is apparent throughout his theological development. His early philosophical works *Geist in Welt* and *Hörer des Wortes*[1] are

---

[1] *Geist in Welt,* 2d ed., edited by Johannes Baptist Metz (Munich: Kösel, 1957), henceforth referred to as *Geist.* Because of the substantial changes made to the text by Metz in the second edition of *Hörer des Wortes,* almost all references will be to the first edition (Munich: Kösel, 1941), henceforth given as *Hörer 1.* When necessary, references to the second edition (edited by J. B. Metz, 1963; rpt. Munich: Kösel, 1985) are given as *Hörer 2.* References to Rahner's work in the notes are to the original German editions, but for quotations I use published English translations where such translations exist and cite them in the notes. Those texts for which I do not cite a specific translation have not been translated officially yet. Quotations of *Geist in Welt, Hörer 1,* and *Hörer 2* come from the following translations: *Spirit in the World,* revised by J. B. Metz, translated by William Dych (London: Sheed and Ward, 1968); *Hearer of the Word,* translated by Joseph Donceel (New York: Continuum, 1994); and *Hearers of the Word,* revised by J. B. Metz, translated by Ronald Walls (London: Sheed and Ward, 1969).

therefore absolutely intrinsic to a correct understanding of his theology. Those who attempt to interpret Rahner without reference
to these early philosophical writings or who dismiss them as un-
connected to his later theology not only misunderstand him but
also run the risk of distorting his remarkably nuanced and bal-
anced system of thought.

Through his analysis of Thomistic epistemology, which is the
subject of *Geist,* Rahner uncovered a fundamental structure in
human knowing. According to this structure, human knowledge
consists in a dynamic oscillation or *Schwebe* between the horizon
of all being and the sensible singular, within which dynamic
movement there is always and simultaneously a static conceptualizing moment. But, according to Rahner, being is knowing, and
so through the same analysis the structure of man is revealed as
similar: man himself is the *schwebende Mitte,* the dynamic oscillating midpoint between God and the categorical world, but also
and always a pure static nature.

This structure of dynamic oscillation, within which there is always and simultaneously a static conceptualizing moment, is basic
to Rahner's understanding of reality. I call this structure *dialectical
analogy* because through it Rahner oscillated constantly between
unifying dynamism and conceptual distinction and therefore
united dialectically while still holding in distinction the traditional
antinomies of Christian thought—God and the world, spirit and
matter, grace and nature. This complex and nuanced structure
gave Rahner's thought remarkable balance and flexibility, allowing him to develop a theological system that was both new and
dynamic and that also maintained all the distinctions necessary for
orthodox Christianity.

However, despite its originality and brilliance, there is a foundational weakness in Rahner's system. The role of the concept in
his epistemology is weak. Rahner, recognizing the importance of
conceptual knowledge in distinguishing his position from modernism, insisted doggedly on both the necessity and validity of the
concept within the knowing process. Nevertheless, it is difficult
to ground the claim within his own system. Because the passive
intellect is reduced within his analysis to a mere name *(Titel),* the
place of the concept is unclear. Often it seems to be imposed on
the system and therefore relativized within the dominant dynamic

Schwebe that constitutes human being and knowing. Because of the fundamental unity of Rahner's thought, it is unsurprising that this epistemological weakness is reflected in his metaphysics and in his theology. It is this weakness that accounts for the progressively stronger emphasis on the dynamic, unifying side of his thought in his later works. It is also the reason why so many commentators have pushed Rahner's system further than Rahner himself either went or would have gone. Sensing the inconsistency of the conceptualizing moment within the knowing process and also the priority of the dynamism in his later development, these commentators all too often have interpreted Rahner according to only one side of his thought. In doing so, they not infrequently have lost the balance and nuance of Rahner's original perspective.

In this analysis of the principal elements of Rahner's philosophical and theological synthesis, therefore, I examine the structure of dialectical analogy as it appears in each of the major themes of his theology, showing that it is an indispensable hermeneutical key to the correct interpretation of his thought. But I also expose a very real tension within the system, which needs to be addressed by Rahnerian scholars if the complex and profound balance of his theological vision is not to be endangered or even lost.

Reinterpreting Rahner

1

Foundational Thought

IN HIS EARLY AND FOUNDATIONAL WORKS *Geist in Welt* and *Hörer des Wortes,* Rahner attempted to elaborate a metaphysics of knowledge based on an interpretation of St. Thomas's understanding of man. With this epistemological metaphysics, Rahner wanted to establish the possibility of metaphysics as the elaboration of the a priori conditions of possibility of all knowledge as such. To this end, he took as his basis *Summa Theologiae* I, q. 84, a. 7, maintaining that this article reveals the basic structure of St. Thomas's epistemology.[1]

For Thomas, as indeed for Rahner, man is primarily and always in the world, and it is from this man that any attempt to understand man must begin.[2] Indeed, the whole of *Geist in Welt* is devoted to establishing the conditions of possibility of the objective knowledge of the world that man is found already and always possessing. For Thomas, all knowing is to be understood as intuition:

> There lies at the basis of the Thomistic metaphysics of knowledge, as in every metaphysics of knowledge, the view that the act which is the primary foundation of all knowing is to be understood as intuition, as an immediate grasping of what is known in its own real and present self.[3]

---

[1] Rahner's use of Thomas's texts has been criticized heavily by C. Fabro, *La Svolta antropologica di Karl Rahner* (Milan: Rusconi, 1974), 97–121, 169–77, 217–26, who rejects Rahner's claim to have interpreted Thomas legitimately. See also G. Vass, *A Theologian in Search of a Philosophy,* vol. 1 of *Understanding Karl Rahner* (London: Christian Classics, Sheed and Ward, 1985), 43; S. De h-Ide, "Rahner and Lonergan," *Studies* 65 (1976), 65; J. Knasas, "'Esse' as the Target of Judgment in Rahner and Aquinas," *The Thomist* 51 (1987): 230–45. P. Eicher, *Die Anthropologische Wende* (Freiburg: Universitätsverlag, 1970), 72–78, also notes Rahner's departure from traditional Thomism, interpreting it positively, however, as a sign of Rahner's originality and genius.

[2] *Geist,* 47, 53, 75, 79, 89, 127, 129, 232, 244, 404–5; *Hörer 1,* 202–3.

[3] *Geist,* 39, 40 n. 8.

But man in the world has no purely intellectual intuition. Man's only intuition is sensible intuition, and such sensible intuition is not capable of objectifying knowledge.[4] The objectification of sense knowledge is what is called "thought," and such thought is attributed by Thomas to the intellect. Thus, for Thomas what is specific to human knowing—as opposed to angelic knowing, which knows through intellectual intuition—is an intellect that acts through sensibility to know the sensible singular other. It is Rahner's thesis that *Summa Theologiae* I, q. 84, a. 7, reveals that for Thomas there is only one unified act of knowing, namely the judgment, which ultimately can be identified with the emanation of sensibility from the spirit and which logically precedes and includes the moment of abstraction. Abstraction itself, which allows what is sensibly apprehended to be objectified, is made possible only by the spirit's permanent preapprehension of being as such, which enables the recognition of the limitation of the sensibly given object and therefore the formation of the universal. Abstraction and conversion together, therefore, exist in a relationship of mutual priority, and metaphysics is in fact nothing other than the reflexive elaboration of the conditions of possibility of this one knowing that man already finds himself possessing when he begins to question.[5] Human knowing consists in a dynamic oscillation or *Schwebe* between the sensible singular and the preapprehended horizon of all being. However, lest all objective human knowledge threaten to dissolve in this dynamic oscillation, Rahner insists that there is simultaneously within the *Schwebe* a moment of conceptualization. Translated into Thomistic terms, this means that there is no knowledge without a conversion to the phantasm that precedes and includes the abstraction.

In *Hörer,* Rahner sought to develop a metaphysical anthropology based on the epistemological foundations that he had laid in *Geist.* Through his interpretation of the metaphysical question that he believes defines the being of man, he posits man as "spirit in the world," as that being who is with all of being and yet also

---

[4] *Geist,* 40, 51, 220–21, 266, 269, 395.

[5] The unity of the knowing process: *Geist,* 41 n. 8, 46, 57 n.1, 60, 62, 79–80, 90, 130, 143, 192, 215, 219, 233, 243, 247, 278–79. See also J. McDermott, "The Analogy of Knowing in Karl Rahner," *International Philosophical Quarterly* 36 (1996), 210–12.

with matter and therefore not with being. It is my contention that from this foundational analysis of man as the oscillating mid-point of sensibility and intellect, within which there is always a moment of conceptualization, Rahner developed a subtle, flexible doctrine of the analogy of being that is not only central to these two foundational works but that in fact provides the key to his whole theology. In this first chapter, therefore, I trace Rahner's analysis of human being and knowing before moving on to look specifically at how this dialectical analogy informs the rest of his theology.

1. The Unity in Diversity of the Foundational Question

A. Being as the Unifying Unity of Being and Knowing

Borrowing from Heidegger, yet with an anchoring in St. Thomas, Rahner took as his point of departure the statement "man questions."[6] This is something final and irreducible. The question is the only "must," the only necessity, the only thing beyond question to which man is bound.[7] But this necessity can be grounded only in the fact that being is accessible to man at all only as something questionable, that he himself is insofar as he asks about being. For not just any question can ground the necessity of questioning as such: man can turn away from this or that question.

---

[6] Heidegger's influence in Rahner's writings has been noted extensively: A. Carr, *The Theological Method of Karl Rahner* (Missoula, Mont.: Scholars Press, 1977), 18–35, 259; J. B. Lotz, "Zur Thomas-Rezeption in der Marechal-Schule," *Theologie und Philosophie* 49 (1974), 388; D. Bradley, "Rahner's *Spirit in the World*: Aquinas or Hegel?" *The Thomist* 41 (1977), 194; B. Girotto, "Il problema dell'essere nel pensiero di K. Rahner," *Filosofia* 30 (1979), 555–56, 562, 564; J. Honner, "Unity-in-Difference: Karl Rahner and Niels Bohr," *Theological Studies* 46 (1985), 505–6; G. McCool, "The Philosophy of the Human Person in Karl Rahner's Theology," *Theological Studies* 22 (1961), 547; R. Lennan, *The Ecclesiology of Karl Rahner* (Oxford: Clarendon Press, 1995), 7; T. Sheehan, "Metaphysics and Bivalence: On Karl Rahner's *Geist in Welt*," *Modern Schoolman* 63 (1985), 22 ff. T. Sheehan, *Karl Rahner: The Philosophical Foundations* (Athens: Ohio University Press, 1987), 311, 314–17, passim, interprets Rahner in almost exclusively Heideggerian terms.

[7] *Geist,* 71–72; *Hörer 1,* 46–48. See D. Bradley, "Religious Faith and the Mediation of Being: The Hegelian Problem in *Hearers of the Word*," *Modern Schoolman* 55 (1978), 137–38, who criticizes Rahner's starting point in the question.

However, the question about being in its totality is the only question from which he cannot turn away, which he must ask if he wants to be at all. Man exists as the question about being and in the being of the question that man is, "being as that which is questioned both reveals itself and at the same time conceals itself in its own questionableness [*Fragwürdigkeit*]."[8]

Every question has a point of departure, but the metaphysical question can take a point of departure for its questioning and thus for the content of its answer only from itself, from the compelling necessity to ask about being in its totality.[9] The metaphysical question also reveals itself, however, as a knowledge of man about his questioning essence. He is already with being because otherwise he cannot ask about it, yet in asking about it he reveals that he is not with being. He is already *quodammodo omnia,* yet he is still tabula rasa.[10] "But this first starting point of all metaphysical enquiry turns out to be a *Schwebe,*"[11] which gives the starting point of metaphysics a peculiar duality and a unity at once: the starting point is questioning man, who is already at the goal of his inquiry when he begins and yet is himself not the goal, but a finite man. This peculiar *Schwebe* is also apparent in Thomas's formulation of the problem of the conversion to the phantasm: all knowledge is linked to the phantasm, but by the fact that there is a return to the phantasm we have to recognize that the mind has returned from being in its totality to this here and now.

When man begins to inquire about everything (by the very fact that he is inquiring about everything), he starts out from "nothing."[12] And yet this "nothing" cannot be an empty void (in view of the fact that he is summoned to ask about being in its totality). So what is this existent "nothing" with which man always and

---

[8] *Geist,* 71–72. See also Jacynthe Tremblay, *Finitude et devenir* (Montreal: Fides, 1992), 181.

[9] *Geist,* 73.

[10] *Geist,* 74, 192, 195, 284–85, 407; *Hörer 1,* 89.

[11] *Geist,* 74, 77, 78. This German word *Schwebe* can hardly be translated: it denotes a suspension or a hovering, a trembling in the balance or a hanging in suspense, a swaying or an oscillation. Vass and Carr also note the importance of the *Schwebe* as the starting point of all metaphysics: Vass, *A Theologian in Search of a Philosophy,* 35, 35 n.12; A. Carr, "Starting with the Human," in *A World of Grace: An Introduction to the Themes and Foundations of Karl Rahner's Theology,* edited by L. J. O'Donovan (New York: Seabury Press, 1980), 29.

[12] *Geist,* 75.

necessarily is and at which point he is called into the presence of being in its totality? For Rahner, as for Thomas, it is the reality of this world. "Man is in the presence of being in its totality insofar as he finds himself in the world."[13] In this knowledge of the world, man has already and always comprehended being in its totality when he asks about it. Hence, a relationship between being and knowing is already understood simultaneously in the most general question of metaphysics. Now, if man, in order to come to a knowledge of an existent here and now, is already and always with being in its totality, then in the necessity by which he dwells with the individual existent in his knowledge he affirms the questionability *(Fragbarkeit)* of being in its totality. And hence we come upon, says Rahner, a fundamental determination of being as such: being is being-able-to-be-known *(Sein ist Erkanntseinkönnen).*[14]

Now one cannot affirm the questionability of being without also affirming its fundamental knowability, for what is absolutely unknowable cannot be asked about. Thus, in view of the reality of the question about being, the concept of a being, unknowable in principle, is in fact a contradiction. Whatever can be, can be known. But this fundamental relationship between being and knowing can be grasped in its possibility only if it is not added as a relationship established subsequent to being, for, according to Thomas, the intellect and the intelligible must be proportional. "Thus, being and knowing exist in an original unity."[15] Knowing does not come upon its object by chance. Thomas explicitly rejects the commonsense conception of knowing as a coming upon something.[16] Rather, being and knowing are the same. "Knowing is the being-present-to-self of being, and this being-present-to-self is the being of the existent [*Erkennen ist Beisichsein des Seins, und dieses Beisichsein ist das Sein des Seienden*]."[17] Therefore, the

---

[13] *Geist,* 76.

[14] *Geist,* 81.

[15] *Geist,* 82; *Hörer 1,* 50. See the following articles for a critical perspective on this Rahnerian identification of being and knowing: W. Kern, "Einhert in Mannigfaltigkeit," in *Gott in Welt: Festgabe für Karl Rahner zum 60. Geburtstag,* edited by J. B. Metz, W. Kern, A. Darlap, and H. Vorgrimler (Freiburg: Herder, 1964), 207–30; De h-Ide, "Rahner and Lonergan," 65.

[16] *Geist,* 82, 83, 96; *Hörer 1,* 55, 57, 146.

[17] The luminosity of being: *Geist,* 40 n. 8, 49 n.1, 82–83, 87, 88 n.15, 91, 93,

beingness *(Seiendheit)* or the intensity of being *(Seinsmächtigkeit)* of the being of an existent is determined by the degree of possibility of being able to be present to itself (Thomistically by the *reditio super seipsum*).[18] Being is the one ground that lets knowing and being known spring out of itself as its own characteristics and thus grounds the intrinsic possibility of an antecedent, essential, intrinsic relation of both of them to each other. Knowing is the subjectivity of being itself. Indeed, "being itself is the original, *unifying* unity of being and knowing in their *unification* in being known."[19] In this, the two are not brought together accidentally but are actualized in their original relatedness to each other.

If being able to know and knowability are thus intrinsic characteristics of being itself, then an actual, individual knowing cannot be conceived definitively in its metaphysical essence if it is understood merely as the relationship of a knower to an object different from him, as intentionality. Rather, knowing must be understood as the subjectivity of being itself, as the being-present-to-self *(Beisichsein)* of being. "Being itself is already the original unifying unity of being and knowing, it is onto-logical; and every actual unity of being and knowing in the actualization of knowledge is only raising to a higher power that transcendental synthesis which being is 'in-itself.'"[20]

B. Matter and the Analogy of Being

If being is defined as being-able-to-be-known and if man necessarily questions being, then we arrive at an apparent contradiction, for why must being be asked about if being is already and

---

95–96, 110, 141–43, 191–92, 222, 234, 238, 371; *Hörer 1,* 50, 52, 57, 86, 88, 91, 103, 107, 116, 122, 146, 151, 183, 201, 206. R. Hurd, "Being Is Being-Present-to-Itself: Rahner's Reading of Aquinas' Metaphysics," *The Thomist* 52 (1988): 65–71; Bradley, "Religious Faith," 136; M. Hines, *The Transformation of Dogma: An Introduction to Karl Rahner on Doctrine* (New York: Paulist Press, 1989), 13. All of these writers maintain that this notion of *Sein* as *Beisichsein* is the hermeneutical key to all of Rahner's thought.

[18] The intensity of being is determined by its degree of presence to self *(reditio)*: *Geist,* 84, 85, 86–87, 146, 221–22; *Hörer 1,* 52, 57, 61, 91–92, 128, 146, 153, 157.

[19] *Geist,* 82. See Vass, *Theologian in Search of a Philosophy,* 36.

[20] *Geist,* 83.

always being-present-to-self? The question discovered in the nature of man reveals that man is already with being in order to ask about being, yet he is not with being in its totality because he still questions being. Thus, the being who must ask is nonbeing, is deficient in the innermost ground of being. "But then the concept of being itself and its content begins to fluctuate [sway]."[21] It is not a univocally definable quantity from which something unambiguous can be drawn about its content, about knowing as the presence-to-self of being. Rather, our original insight concerning the presence-to-self of being has been transposed into a formal scheme—namely, that the intensity of knowledge is parallel to the intensity of being and, vice versa, that the degree of this subjectivity is the measure of an existent's intensity of being.

Knowability, therefore, does not mean the indifferent being-there of an essence in itself with the indifferent possibility of being known by another. Rather, the knowability of an existent is originally being-able-to-be-present-to-self and this, as an intrinsic determination of the essence of being, itself varies with a being's intensity of being. Now if the being-able-to-be-present-to-self of being is an essentially indeterminate and variable quantity, and if according to experience there is a being that does not know in any way and hence is in no way present-to-self, then the being of this existent itself cannot be present-to-itself; it cannot belong to itself; it must be the being of "another."

> This other must on the one hand be real, but on the other hand it cannot have being in itself and of itself. This empty, in itself indeterminate "wherein" [*Worin*] of the being of an existent, in which being is in such a way that it is not for itself but for that and so is not "present-to-itself," is called Thomistically prime matter.[22]

It is therefore self-evident that knowing and knowability as presence-to-self and as being-able-to-be-present-to-self are in a fixed

---

[21] "Damit aber gerät mit seinem Inhalt der Begriff des Seins selbst ins Schwanken." *Geist,* 85, 87, 401; *Hörer 1,* 61, 63, 146, 152, 217. See Hurd, "Being Is Being-Present-to-Itself," 71–78, and J. Conlon, "Karl Rahner's Theory of Sensation," *The Thomist* 41 (1977), 403, for accurate summaries of Rahner's understanding of the analogous nature of *Beisichsein.* Also see Tremblay, *Finitude et devenir,* 76, 82.
[22] *Geist,* 87, also 58, 93, 110, 127–28, 153, 159–60, 163, 343–44, 347, 371; *Hörer 1,* 153, 159–60.

relationship to the relation of being to matter. The intensity of being can be determined formally from the relationship of being to matter and then be transposed materially into knowledge and knowability. Thus, an essence that has no intrinsic relatedness to matter is by this very fact already actually present-to-self: it is knowing and actually knowable. The actually knowable by no means expresses in the first instance a relation to another knowing but is a determination of the essence of being in itself.[23]

It is also self-evident that if being is primarily presence-to-self, then the real and original object of a knowing being is that with which it originally is: itself.[24] Thus, concludes Rahner, the real epistemological problem does not lie in bridging the gap between knowing and object. Such a gap is merely a pseudoproblem.[25] The real problem is how a gap is possible at all, how the known, which is identical with the knower, can stand over against the knower as "other," or, more profoundly, how a being can ever have a proper object of knowledge that is anything other than itself. This, according to Rahner, is precisely the problem of sensibility.[26]

2. SENSIBILITY

The Dialectical Nature of Sensibility

The problem of sensibility—namely, how there can be a knowledge of another as such in which this other is the proper object of the knowledge—seems to be insoluble, for if something is present-to-itself, then its own intensity of being, its own "subjectivity," seems essentially and necessarily to be the first object known, the proper object. The knowledge of another is therefore possible only "by the fact that *the knower itself is the being of the other*."[27] The

---

[23] *Geist*, 87, 371–72.

[24] *Geist*, 88, 91; *Hörer 1*, 158.

[25] *Geist*, 88, 141–42.

[26] See Conlon, "Karl Rahner's Theory of Sensation," 407–16, for an excellent summary of Rahner's theory of sensibility.

[27] *Geist*, 92, also 104, 107, 138, 142–43, 157, 252, 254; *Hörer 1*, 157, 208. Emphasis in quotations from Rahner's work is in the original unless otherwise indicated.

being of what intuits receptively must be the being of another as such. That means that "antecedent to any apprehension of a definite other, the knower of itself must have already and always entered into otherness."[28] Only if a being is ontologically separated from itself by the fact that it is not the being of itself, but the being of what is absolutely other, can it have the possibility of possessing a foreign ontological actuality as its own in such a way that everything that is its own is by that very fact another's because the being of the knower in question is not being for itself, but being for and to another. *That real nonbeing, as the being of which a being is separated from itself, is called Thomistically prime matter. Thus receptive knowledge is essentially conceivable only as the being of something material, it is sensibility.*"[29]

But this conclusion seems to lead us into another fundamental contradiction, for earlier prime matter was seen precisely as the reason why there could be an existent that is not a knower; it was seen as that which gives an existent the possibility of being without retaining the meaning of being—namely, being-present-to-self. Thus, intuition of another as proper object seems to presuppose an intensity of being of such a kind that this being is not its own, but that of matter, and intuition as knowledge seems to demand a potency for being that excludes materiality. If, however, sensibility does exist as the receptive intuition of another as such,[30] it is clear from the paradoxical nature of such an intuition that the essence of sensibility can be apprehended "only by defining it dialectically from two sides."[31] That holds for the determination

---

[28] Being has entered into otherness already and always: *Geist,* 92, 107–8, 115, 127, 129, 130, 141, 167, 235, 268–69, 288, 298, 379; *Hörer I,* 161. See G. Vass, *The Mystery of Man and the Foundations of a Theological System,* vol. 2 of *Understanding Karl Rahner* (London: Christian Classics, Sheed and Ward, 1985), 37; T. Allik, "Karl Rahner on Materiality and Human Knowledge," *The Thomist* 49 (1985), 371–72; Girotto, "Il problema dell'essere," 572–73.

[29] *Geist,* 93. See Tremblay, *Finitude et devenir,* 351–62.

[30] *Geist,* 40, 41 n. 8, 51, 220–21, 266, 269, 395.

[31] *Geist,* 93–94, 129. The dialectical nature of Rahner's theory of sensibility has been well noted: E. Simons, *Philosophie der Offenbarung* (Stuttgart: Kohlhammer, 1966), 39–41; Allik, "Karl Rahner on Materiality," 367–86; Bradley, "Rahner's *Spirit in the World,*" 117; Conlon, "Karl Rahner's Theory of Sensation," 407–12; McDermott, "Analogy of Knowing," 204–6; A. Tallon, "Spirit, Matter, Becoming: Karl Rahner's *Spirit in the World,*" *The Modern Schoolman* 48 (1971), 162. I maintain that this dialectical understanding is grounded in Rahner's foundational structure of thought as dialectical analogy.

of the intensity of being of a sentient knower as well as for the peculiarity of the presence-to-self that belongs to sense knowledge, for

> if knowing is the being-present-to-itself of being, but knowing the other as proper object means essentially and ontologically being-away-from-self-with-the-other [*Weg-von-sich-beim-andern-Sein*], then the being of the sentient knower can only be understood as the oscillating midpoint [*die schwebende Mitte*] between a real abandonment to the other of matter and an intrinsic independence of being over against matter, so that the sensible act is in undivided unity material *(actus materiae)* and, as material, the act of the assertion of being (of form) over against matter *(actus contra materiam)*.[32]

Likewise, the conscious being-present-to-itself of the sentient knower can be defined only negatively from two sides. It is neither a presence-to-self that can possess itself as set over against the other nor the being-with-the-other in such a way that it would have lost itself utterly in this other with the elimination of any consciousness. The being of the sentient knower is present-to-itself, but this being is precisely the oscillating undivided midpoint *(die schwebende ungeschiedene Mitte)* between a total abandonment to the other and an intrinsic independence over against this other.[33] Thus, Rahner concludes that it is not relevant to ask whether sensibility really perceives the "outside world" or only its own "affections." It does neither one nor the other because "the interiority of sensibility as the act of matter is precisely its exteriority, and vice versa, and every separation between the two requires an act which would not be material."[34] Therefore, if there is to be any knowledge at all of another as the fundamental and first knowledge, if the world is to be the first and only intu-

---

[32] *Geist,* 93–94. Rahner often asserts this dialectical nature of sensibility as simultaneously *actus materiae* and *actus contra materiam: Geist,* 107, 110, 111–13, 127, 129, 233. His strange identification of being with form is made a number of times in *Geist* and *Hörer* and seems to imply a certain relativization of the essential order (*Geist,* 94, 110, 132, 146, 151, 233, 234, 249, 360, 371; *Hörer 1,* 184, 208); see P. Burke, "Conceptual Thought in Karl Rahner," *Gregorianum* 75 (1994), 72–73, 73 n. 27; Bradley, "Rahner's *Spirit in the World,*" 181, 183, 185; Vass, *Theologian in Search of a Philosophy,* 59–61, 127; Eicher, *Die Anthropologische Wende,* 186 ff.

[33] *Geist,* 67–68, 93–94, 406.

[34] *Geist,* 94.

ition of man, then human intuition must be sensible, the being of the one intuiting must be the being of the other, of matter.

> In the final analysis, therefore, the sensible object does not pene-trate into the interior of sensibility, but sensibility as the act of mat-ter has already moved out into the exterior of the world, and as act over against matter is always of such an intensity of being that what enters into its medium is by that fact already reflected upon itself, is already conscious, and only means a formal delimitation of that possession of the world that sensibility already and always is through its being.[35]

3. ABSTRACTION

We have seen that when man begins to ask about being in its totality, he finds himself already and invariably away from himself, situated in the world, in the other through sensibility. But his very ability to question means that man is not lost in the other. By questioning, he places himself in sharp relief against the other, objectifies the other, and thus achieves in his thought a subject/object distinction for the first time. This means that "he returns from 'outside' to where he already and always was."[36] It is not until then that man stands in the world as man, not until then that he is on that ground on which he found himself situated at the beginning of his metaphysical inquiry. This capacity of the one human knowledge to place the other—which is given in sensibil-ity, away from itself and in question, to "return" to self—is called thought or intellect. It is first through thought that the human experience of an objective world becomes possible. If the one human knowledge of the world is of such a nature, then the grasping of its possibility must take place in two phases: first, in the self-liberating return from his abandonment in the subject-object unity of sensibility the knower acquires his position as man; second, he possesses himself as the one who has really become a subject only when he places himself over against himself and turns

---

[35] *Geist,* 107. Sheehan, *Karl Rahner,* 311, 314–17, seems to stop here in his analysis of Rahner's epistemology, wrongly reducing knowing in Rahner to sensibility alone.
[36] *Geist,* 129.

again to this world. These two "phases," which are treated in Thomistic metaphysics under the titles *abstractio* and *conversio,* of course are not to be thought of as coming one after the other; "they mutually condition each other and in their original unity form the one human knowledge."[37] Before, however, attempting to demonstrate the intrinsic unity of these two phases, we first of all must look at the structure of the abstractive return in which this subject/object distinction is achieved initially. We will do this by examining first the characteristics of abstraction and then the conditions of its possibility.

A. The Characteristics of Abstraction

(i) The Universal Concept

If the differentiation of subject and object is accomplished initially in abstraction, then the first indication of what this means is given in the universal concept,[38] for the formation of the universal signifies precisely the capacity to objectify the "other" and to return to self. Rahner defines a universal concept as "a known intelligibility that exists in many and can be predicated of many."[39] In the universal concept, therefore, a being as such is apprehended as capable of being predicated of many possible existents. It follows that it would no longer be a universal concept if its content could

---

[37] *Geist,* 130, 289–90, 382–83.

[38] The importance and the necessity of the concept in Rahner's epistemology should not be underestimated and has been noted: Lotz, "Zur Thomas-Rezeption," 389; R. Moloney, "Seeing and Knowing: Some Reflections on Karl Rahner's Theory of Knowledge," *Heythrop Journal* 18 (1977), 406; Honner, "Unity-in-Difference," 498, 502; W. Dych, "Theology in a New Key," in O'Donovan, ed., *A World of Grace,* 4–5. K.-H. Weger, *Karl Rahner: An Introduction to His Theology,* translated from German by D. Smith (New York: Seabury, 1980), 68, fails to note this Rahnerian insistence on the concept, arguing that according to Rahner when we verbalize our experience, we necessarily falsify it. There is, however, a distinction between falsification and conceptualization. The following writers also fail to pay sufficient attention to Rahner's concept: M. J. Buckley, "Within the Holy Mystery," in O'Donovan, ed., *A World of Grace,* 46; T. O'Meara, "A History of Grace," in O'Donovan, ed., *A World of Grace,* 87.

[39] The concept as repeatability: *Geist,* 132, 114, 134, 147, 181, 184, 197, 221, 351; *Hörer 1,* 160. See Carr, *Theological Method of Karl Rahner,* 73–74; McCool, "The Philosophy of the Human Person," 540.

be separated completely from its reference to possible subjects that could be determined by it.[40] However abstract from possible subjects it might be conceived, the reference to possible subjects belongs to the universal essentially.

This characteristic of the universal is important for our understanding of human thought in general, for Rahner insists that *all* our known intelligibilities are similarly formed and that they are distinguished as universal or concrete only by the fact that they are related either immediately, and as such to the concrete thing given in sensibility, or only mediately. The singular concept always contains in itself a universal ("this thing of this kind"), and the universal as such is still related to a "this" ("the kind of this thing"). Even if the nonconcrete as such is made an object of thought, then by this very fact it functions as a concrete, for then one thinks something about it, and this "it" is related to this "something" as a concrete to its universal. Thus, what was at first apparent as a characteristic of the universal concept as such turns out to be an expression of the essential mode of human knowing altogether: something is always known about something. In fact, it is here that the return of the subject to himself becomes manifest.

Every objective knowledge is always and in every case the reference of a universal to a "this." The "this" appears as the reference point standing over against the knowing to which the knower refers what is known (universally) by him. But then the subject with the content of his knowledge already stands to some extent at a distance from the "this" to which he refers the content of the knowledge. "This content of knowledge is universal precisely because it stands on the side of the knowing subject in its opposition to the 'this' and therefore can be related to any number of 'this's.' "[41] Precisely by disengaging the content of knowledge from the subject/object unity of sensibility, the subject returns to self, and thereby the universal is "liberated." The return of the knowing subject to himself and the liberation of a universal from its subjects are therefore one and the same process and to-

---

[40] That the universal is always related to a "this": *Geist,* 132–33, 135, 138, 142–43, 148, 150, 158, 166, 167, 172, 176–77, 199, 233; *Hörer 1,* 160.
[41] *Geist,* 134.

gether indicate the opposition between subject and object that first makes possible an objective experience of the world.

(ii) The Judgment

If the universal concept is essentially the "what" of a possible something, a known intelligibility able to be synthesized with a possible subject, this means that the universal concept is distinguished from the judgment, in which it is the predicate, not as a part from the whole, into which the concepts are pieced together only subsequently to their own intrinsic constitution, but as a possible from an actually realized synthesis of subject and predicate, for the reference to a possible subject already belongs to the universal concept as such. "But at the same time this means that the proposition is *prior* to the universal concept, since the realized synthesis is prior to the possible."[42] It therefore becomes clear that every universal concept is apprehended with and in a concretion that is necessarily conceived simultaneously, and every individual is conceived objectively in a concretion that already contains in itself a universal differentiated from the "this."

Usually the judgment is understood as the synthesis of the two concepts of subject and predicate. This is true, says Rahner, as long as we bear in mind the intrinsic structure of the concept that in every case is a concretizing synthesis itself. The synthesis of the two concepts of a proposition must be understood, therefore, as the synthesis of the universal contained in both concepts with the same supposite. "In the judgmental synthesis, therefore, it is not at all a question of the synthesis of two quiddities of the same order with each other, but the reference of two quiddities to the same 'this.'"[43] Whereas the predicate as such in the concretizing synthesis is the possible synthesis of a universal with any "this" at all, now the subject determines unambiguously what "this" is meant. This is called Thomistically the *affirmative synthesis,* and, if looked at correctly, objective knowledge is not reached until this affirmative synthesis. Expressed another way, "a concretizing synthesis occurs in real thought only as an affirmative synthesis."[44]

---

[42] *Geist,* 135, 137, 141.
[43] *Geist,* 135–36, 140.
[44] *Geist,* 136–37, 141.

There is no knowing by human consciousness at all, therefore, except in an affirmative synthesis, and this judgment is not connecting concepts, as though these concepts were the fundamental elements of thought and the only role of judgment were to connect them subsequently, but it is referring knowing to an in–itself *(Ansich)*, and in this reference concepts are present as moments possible only in the judgment.[45] Concepts occur either in a judgment about things, or as objects of a judgment about concepts. This also says, to anticipate slightly the development of Rahner's thesis, that "the opposition between object and subject, which takes place in the abstractive return of the subject to himself, which return forms universal concepts, is as a matter of fact [*tatsächlich*] the affirmative synthesis."[46]

(iii) Truth

Finally, there already has followed from this discussion the third indication of the complete return of the subject to himself— namely, truth. It is not that the concretizing synthesis as such is true or false but that its successful or unsuccessful reference to the thing itself in the affirmative synthesis is true or false. Accordingly, insofar as truth means a relation of knowing to a reality existing in itself, and insofar as the return takes place in this affirmative synthesis, truth creates this opposition between subject and object for the first time, and this opposition is not possible at all without truth.[47]

B. The Conditions of Possibility of Abstraction

(i) The *Vorgriff*

How then are we to grasp the possibility of the abstractive return that is the constitutive element of the affirmative synthesis? From what has been said about sensibility, it follows first of all negatively

---

[45] *Geist,* 136, 140, 141–42, 200–209.

[46] *Geist,* 137. The abstraction is a moment within the conversion: *Geist,* 41 n. 8, 61–62, 131, 134–37, 141, 163–64, 202 n.11, 215, 215 n. 20, 230, 233, 242, 244, 270–71, 282, 284, 288, 407.

[47] *Geist,* 137, 140–42.

that sensibility as such cannot accomplish this return, for sensibility is precisely the being-away-from-self with the other of matter. The return must be, therefore, the achievement of a spontaneous activity of the intellect that sets the knower over against what exists in itself *(das Ansichseiende)* by the abstraction of being from an existent. If, therefore, we are inquiring about the conditions of possibility of the abstractive return, we are in fact inquiring into what Thomas refers to as the *agent intellect.*[48]

Rahner insists that when Thomas speaks of the agent intellect's "liberating" an intelligible species, impressing it on the possible intellect, and so on, such images are to be understood metaphorically and not literally. The figurative expressions in which the activity of the agent intellect is described should not mislead us to the assumption that in human knowing the sensible form as such in its qualitative content is brought to another "level." But what, then, is it supposed to mean when it is said that the form becomes actually intelligible insofar as it becomes universal, and vice versa? Certainly it can be said first of all, and provisionally, that the form becomes "liberated" *(abgelöst)* from the matter in which and by which it is individuated. But the real questions are how this liberation *(Loslösung)* of the material form from matter, by which its referability to many "this's" is known, is to be understood and how it can be grasped in its possibility, for if we were to assume a literal liberation of the form from matter, then abstraction would become intrinsically contradictory. As we have seen, "the form of a material thing as being and as known is intrinsically and essentially related to a 'this.' "[49] How, then, is it to be detachable either as being or as knowing? Or still more simply: How can the form and the "this," being and an existent, be differentiated from each other at all, considering that they are always given in sensibility only as one, that being always occurs and can occur only as an existent?

The factual accomplishment of the liberation is grounded, Rahner argues, in the antecedent, although not independent, knowledge of the contingency of the sensible concretion, which is always already accomplished antecedent to sense knowledge

---

[48] *Geist,* 153, 210; *Hörer 1,* 83.
[49] *Geist,* 150.

and in which alone the sense possesses being. Such contingence, of course, is not a sensibly intuited datum, is not one thing among other things in the form, but is the mode of being of the form itself, its limitedness in matter ("contraction," "confinement"), which of its essence is hidden from sensibility. Therefore, the form must be known as limited by the "this" whose form it is; only then can it be known that it is "broader" in itself and so able to be related to other "this's" and then for the first time can it appear as ontologically different from matter, from its supposite, and as universal in itself. "Hence the intellectual element in abstractive thought is the knowledge of the confinement of form by matter and only that; a qualitative content of the sensible is not transferred to the level of the intellect."[50] Just from this conclusion it follows that abstraction cannot be thought of, in a naive interpretation of the figurative formulations in Thomas, as a production in the intellect of an intellectual "double" of what is given sensibly in intuition, as an "image" *(Bild)* that the intellect looks at as sensibility looks at its objects. "Intelligible species" as such, in spite of the Platonic origin of the terminology, does not have the character of an image in Thomas.[51] Only the sensibly intuited has the character of an image.

The function of the agent intellect is, therefore, not the power to imprint on the possible intellect a spiritual image of what has been sensibly intuited. Rather, it is the capacity to know the sensibly intuited as limited, *as* a realized concretion, and only to that extent does it "universalize" the form possessed sensibly, only to that extent does it liberate the form from its material concretion. How is this possible? Only if, antecedent to and in addition to apprehending the individual form, it comprehends of itself the whole field of these possibilities and thus, in the sensibly concretized form, experiences the concreteness as limitation of these possibilities, whereby it knows the form as able to be multiplied in this field. This transcending apprehension of further possibilities Rahner calls the "preapprehension" *(Vorgriff)*. Although this term is not to be found in Thomas, its content, Rahner asserts, is con-

---

[50] *Geist,* 151, 153, 156, 397; *Hörer 1,* 75, 77.
[51] *Geist,* 152, 83–84, 96, 97, 109, 171 n. 39, 200, 243, 292, 371, 377; *Hörer 1,* 56.

tained in what Thomas, using a similar image, calls the *"excessus.*"[52] It is this a priori preapprehension that offers the possibility of experiencing the forms of sensibility as limited, of differentiating them from the ground of their limitedness, the sensible "this," and thus of creating for knowing the possibility of a complete return.[53]

From the previous description of the preapprehension, it is already clear that the preapprehension does not, as such, attain to an object. By its very essence, it is one of the conditions of possibility of an objective knowledge. On the other hand, the essence and the breadth of the preapprehension can be determined only by establishing that to which it attains. From this it follows that:

a. This "whither" [*Worauf*] of the preapprehension as such is not a humanly conceivable object.
b. The "whither" nevertheless must be designated after the manner of a human object although not affirmed as such.
c. Although the "whither" of the preapprehension as such is not an object, yet it can disclose objects beyond the one for whose apprehension the preapprehension occurred in a definite act. This disclosure is not meant as a presentation of the object in its own self, but it comes about in that the preapprehension implicitly and simultaneously affirms the real possibility of these other objects within the scope of its "whither."
d. Thus, human knowledge always falls short essentially of its complete fulfillment, which fulfillment is designated by the breadth of its preapprehension. Nevertheless, this preapprehension toward this ideal with all that it simultaneously affirms as really possible is not an inconsequential supplementation, but the condition of possibility of any objective knowledge at all.

Thus the "whither" of the preapprehension can reveal itself only in the consciousness of the preapprehension itself as such, although the preapprehension can only be made thematic in the assertion of a "whither." But that means nothing other than that the preapprehension (and its "whither") is known insofar as knowledge, in the apprehension of its individual object, always experiences itself as

---

[52] *Geist,* 153, 153 n. 14; *Hörer 1,* 94.
[53] The *Vorgriff* as the condition of possibility of all objective knowledge: *Geist,* 115, 155, 165, 190–91, 192, 390, 397; *Hörer 1,* 77, 81, 84–86, 94, 99, 129, 179–80, 184–85.

already and always moving out beyond it, insofar as it knows the
object in the horizon of its possible objects in such a way that
the preapprehension reveals itself in the movement out toward the
totality of the objects.[54]

There follows the task of determining the scope of the a priori
preapprehension of the intellect, but in order to address this question we need to ask first what it is that actually is "liberated"
through this preapprehension, or *Vorgriff*, that reveals limit.

α. What Is "Liberated" by the *Vorgriff*?

We are interested in establishing the scope of the preapprehension. To do this, we still need to bring out more clearly what
actually is "liberated" in the abstractive preapprehension. What
"form" is it whose limitation is to be apprehended by the preapprehension? It is obviously a question of a liberation from that
subject that is given in sensibility as something real and concrete,
for it is of this subject that something is first affirmed. It is over
against this subject that the knower who knows objectively first
sets himself. That is to say that what is "form"—in other words,
predicate in the affirmative and not merely concretizing synthesis—is what is liberated first and fundamentally. Thus, there is
question of the abstraction that is, as it were, the negative phase
of the affirmative synthesis. The "concrete" that arises through a
merely concretizing synthesis as such or, more correctly, that
would arise if it could take place by itself is not yet an object, as
we have already seen. Hence, the form of such a synthesis in itself
can in no way reveal what was liberated in the decisive abstraction
as an abstraction from a genuine, unique "this" that was given in
sensibility as real.

What is the form in the affirmative synthesis that as such was
also the form of the fundamental abstraction? If we go back to
what was said about the essence of the affirmative synthesis, we
must say first of all that what was meant in the affirmative synthesis was what-is-in-itself *(das Ansichsein),* which belongs of itself to
the thing designated by the subject of a proposition, independently of the realization of the affirmative synthesis. Thus, an al-

---

[54] *Geist,* 156.

ready realized synthesis *(complexio)* is always given prior to the affirmation of the judgment. What is given antecedent to thought and yet really given to human knowing is this already realized synthesis in sensibility. "We can therefore say that what the abstractive preapprehension attains to as unlimited is what was affirmed as limited in the synthesis *(complexio)*, the objective in-itself [*Ansich*] of the known. Hence, what-is-in-itself as such [*das Ansichsein überhaupt*] is apprehended in the preapprehension."[55] This "in-itself" that is apprehended in its formal universality in the preapprehension is what Thomas calls *esse.*

β. The Concept of *Esse*

If the first object of human knowledge is the world received in sensibility, then human knowledge can know *esse* as the real and only being-in-itself *(Ansichsein)* only insofar as *esse* is given to it in sensibility in its concrete, limited self. Thus, when we ask what *esse* is, we also must refer always to the *ens* (being) that is had in its own self in sensibility; without this sensibly given *ens*, absolutely no knowledge of what *esse* can mean is possible. But the question still emerges as to how this *ens* can be known objectively, something that sensibility cannot achieve. Abstraction is necessary to achieve this objective knowledge, and therefore we need to look first at the abstraction of *esse* and then at the understanding of *esse* revealed in abstraction. Furthermore, if human knowledge is an objective knowing of the other in differentiation from the knowing subject, then it can know this *esse* objectively as the being-in-itself *(Ansichsein)* of the definite other only insofar as this *esse*, given in sensibility as limited, is apprehended as unlimited in itself in a preapprehension attaining to *esse* as such.

Now what is this *esse*? For Rahner, *esse* is identical with what he has defined as the in-itself, *Ansich*. It means to-be-actual *(Wirklichsein)*, to-be-real *(Realsein),*[56] and he argues that for Thomas *esse* as *Wirklichsein* is the only fundamental in-itself. "Thus for him [Thomas] the judgment, which attains to an in-itself *(applicatio ad rem)*, attains to *esse*, which in Thomas always expresses to-be-

---

[55] *Geist*, 166.
[56] *Geist*, 167–68, 172, 186.

real."[57] Thought attains to being, not to propositions valid in themselves; therefore, the idea of eternal truths, of ideal validities has no place in Thomas's metaphysics of knowledge. The only in-itself that Thomas knows is real being.[58]

To-be-in-itself *(Ansichsein)* and *esse* as to-be-actual *(Wirklichsein)* coincide. Objective knowing, therefore, attains to real being in principle, and "essences" can be the in-itself of objective knowledge only in an ordination to *esse*. "Essence" is never, says Rahner, a "pattern" that dwells in an ideal in-itself, indifferent of itself to real being, but is only the potency for *esse* and can be conceived objectively in its own self only as such. "Thomas knows essences only as the limiting potency of *esse,* as the real ground and expression of the fact that *esse* in the individual 'this' is not given in its unlimited fullness. Beyond that they are nothing."[59] Therefore, further determinations are not added to *esse* in the sense that it would be perfected by them; rather, that which is most formal is *esse* itself.[60] In fact, form, species, and so on limit *esse* only as every potency limits its act.[61]

This means, however, that we require a radical revision of the common concept of *esse. Esse* is no longer mere presence (*Vorhandensein*), the indifferent ground, as it were, upon which different essences must stand, if in addition to their real ideal being they also wish to be really. "*Esse* is not a 'genus,' but appears rather as intrinsically variable, not as statically definable, but oscillating [*oszillierend*], as it were, between nothing and infinity."[62] The essences are only the expression of the limitation of this *esse,* which is limitless in itself, to a definite degree of the intensity of being in this or that definite being. Thus, essences no longer stand unrelated one after another but are related to the one *esse,* "and *esse* is not the emptiest, but the fullest concept."[63]

---

[57] *Geist,* 168.

[58] *Geist,* 169, 170, 173–74, 226; *Hörer 1,* 168.

[59] Essence as the limiting potency of *esse: Geist,* 159, 161, 170–71, 171 n. 39, 172, 180, 182 n. 27, 184, 216–18.

[60] *Geist,* 171, 184–85, 186.

[61] *Geist,* 171, 187, 216.

[62] *Geist,* 172. Other writers have noted this very strange concept of *esse* oscillating between nothing and infinity, which is characteristic of Rahner's whole dialectical view of reality: Bradley, "Rahner's *Spirit in the World,*" 183; Conlon, "Karl Rahner's Theory of Sensation," 406.

[63] *Geist,* 172.

(ii) The Scope of the *Vorgriff*

We are now in a position to inquire directly into the scope of the intellect's preapprehension. We have seen that objective knowledge is possible only by the knowledge of the intrinsic limitedness of the object with which the judgment is concerned. We have concluded that this intrinsic limitedness of the definite individual, in which the universal affirmed of it is found to be limited, is knowable only in a preapprehension reaching beyond the limited. This "more" has appeared so far as the negative (formal) infinity of "form" in itself. Now, on the other hand, we also have concluded that the judgment as affirmative synthesis attains to an in-itself that ultimately is always *esse*. We have seen, in this respect, that essences are apprehended as potencies for and limitations of *esse,* but we have not yet demonstrated that *esse* itself, as unlimited in itself, is apprehended in an abstractive preapprehension and not merely in essence alone. When we show this, then the connection between the abstraction of form and that of *esse* will necessarily follow: "the abstraction of *esse* is the condition of the possibility of the abstraction of form."[64]

The preapprehension of *esse* must be able to be apprehended in a way similar to the way that the preapprehension of the form as in itself negatively unlimited appeared: the form as content of the predicate of the proposition appeared, with respect to the concrete thing to which the judgment relates it, as broader in itself, as universal, because it is able to be affirmed of many possible concrete things. This is also the case with *esse.*

> To-be-in-itself [*Ansichsein*] as *esse* can be affirmed of many individuals. In the individual judgment, an *esse* is ascribed to (or at least implicitly affirmed of) the object of the judgment designated by the subject, which does not necessarily belong precisely to this object alone but is in itself broader, universal and unlimited. This is shown in the apprehension of the *esse* of many of the same thing: such an *esse* is itself one and many.[65]

From this statement, it follows necessarily that the one *esse* that bestows reality upon the essence and its accidents must have the

---

[64] *Geist,* 180, 214. See Bradley, "Rahner's *Spirit in the World,*" 183.
[65] *Geist,* 181.

intrinsic freedom and infinity to bestow reality as much upon one quiddity as upon another. But this means that in every essential judgment (for example, the tree is green) a universal *esse* also is affirmed simultaneously, which, as one, is able to include in itself the quiddity of the subject and that of the predicate (being tree and being green) and to that extent is one and universal (that is, it is the being of many determinations).

The affirmative synthesis, therefore, attains to the one *esse* insofar as the quiddities of the subject and of the predicate have their unity in it as one. Thus, the affirmative synthesis attains to something that is always already realized, to a synthesis "in itself." But this in-itself is precisely *esse*. Insofar as an existent has *esse,* the plurality of its determinations is unified into a synthesis that is always already realized and given prior to the affirmative synthesis—that is, into a really existing essence. "And insofar as *esse* is apprehended in the judgment as something of many quiddities, it is essentially apprehended as universal."[66]

α. The Universality of *Esse*

To avoid misunderstanding, we must define this universality of *esse* more precisely. *Esse* has a formal (negative) infinity.[67] The affirmative synthesis attains to an in-itself that is being *(ens).* Expressed in another way, this means that the concretizing synthesis of the subject and predicate of the proposition as concepts becomes something objective existing in itself by the affirmation of *esse.* But *esse* has been shown to be universal itself in the judgment, to be the ground of the reality of all possible quiddities.[68] The concrete essence of something is, therefore, the expression of the extent to which, in a definite existent, *esse,* the ground of reality for an existent can let such an existent really exist. This brings out already the peculiarity of the universality of *esse.* The universality of a material, essential form consists in the fact that it can be repeated in many material subjects as the same form:

---

[66] *Geist,* 183.

[67] *Geist,* 187, 192, 193, 195.

[68] *Geist,* 183–84, 186, 187, 187 n. 40, 192, 216. Knasas, " 'Esse' as the Target of Judgement," 224–26, notes the peculiarity of Rahner's notion of a universal *esse* and questions its validity.

universality as the repeatability of the same. The universality of *esse* also appears as repeatability, insofar as many of the same really can be, insofar as many concrete instances of the same quiddity are apprehended as existing. "The universality of *esse* is only another expression for the universality of form insofar as this is conceived as the quiddity of many existing things."[69]

But the universality of *esse* manifests itself in still another way that is proper to itself: it is the one realizing ground of many essential determinations. Hence, it is universal as the unified fullness that releases out of itself the essential determinations of an existent as those of a single thing and holds them together in itself, for *esse* was called precisely that being-in-itself *(Ansichsein)* in which the determinations affirmed in the judgment are one. Hence, *esse* does not mean the empty indifference of a mere existence that prescinds completely from what exists by it. *Esse* is not something that, after the manner of a potency bereft of determination, is filled and determined by determinations that are added to it, for these determinations are real and so determine precisely through *esse*. *Esse* is "formal" in the sense that it is that which is affirmed of something, that it is thus what determines this something, although in another way than is the case with the form in respect to its subject because it is not one determination among many but the one ground of all real determinations. "Therefore, it possesses with respect to every such determination the character of what determines, of an 'agent,' not that of a passive receiver."[70] From this, it follows that the universality of *esse* in itself is transcategorical, for it is the one ground of all categorical determinations.

Esse cannot be understood as though it were present in its whole fullness in the individual object of our judgments as the ground of its being. Then the fullness of all determinations would have to belong to each object, and *esse* would no longer be the "whither" of the preapprehension, but rather an object of the first order for knowledge. Rather, the judgment that ascribes certain quiddative determinations to something that exists is implicitly and precisely a judgment that *esse* does not belong in all its fullness to this thing that exists in itself. This also means, however, that

---

[69] *Geist,* 184.
[70] *Geist,* 187.

the real objects of our judgments are not distinguished merely by their quiddative determinations but precisely in their *esse* as the ground of these latter. "Thus every judgment is precisely a critique of the object, an evaluation of the measure of *esse* which belongs to what is judged."[71] Therefore, the objects of possible judgments are distinguished in their *esse* as such, and *esse* can be affirmed of them only analogously insofar as the determinations in each of them are related in the same way to the ground of their reality—that is, to the *esse* proper to each—and insofar as the *esse* of each of these objects as limited by its essence must be understood as a partial realization of *esse* in itself. In summary, we can say that in every judgment and thus in every abstraction a universal *esse* is grasped simultaneously in a preapprehension.

β. *Esse Commune* and *Esse Absolutum*

Thus far, the discussion has shown *esse* to be the "whither" *(Worauf)* of the preapprehension that is the condition of the possibility of the abstraction and hence of the complete return that makes possible an objective human knowledge. It follows that the whither of the preapprehension as such is not an object; neither is it the object of a metaphysical "intuition." For the *esse* apprehended in the preapprehension is known implicitly and simultaneously *(mitgewusst)* as able to be limited by quiddative determinations and as already limited because the preapprehension *(Vorgriff)*, if it is not to be a "grasp" *(Griff)*, can be realized only in a simultaneous conversion to a definite form limiting *esse* and in the conversion to the phantasm. The fullness of being that *esse* expresses, therefore, is never given objectively. If *esse* is made objective in order to be thematically known itself, then that can be done only insofar as it is itself concretized again by a form. Either this is a definite form and then it limits *esse* to the fullness of a definite degree of being, or it represents every form; it is the form of *ens commune* (any quiddity), and then its *esse* indeed is not limited to any definite degree of ontological actuality but for that reason completely reduced to the empty void of *ens commune*.

---

[71] *Geist,* 188, 195. See also 168, 170, 172–73, 175–76, 179, 182, 186, 208, 214, 216.

Hence, insofar as this *esse* simultaneously apprehended in the pre-apprehension is able to be limited, it shows itself to be nonabsolute because an absolute necessarily excludes the possibility of a limitation. "This *esse* apprehended in the preapprehension is therefore in itself *esse 'commune'* ('common' *esse*), although this must not be equated with *ens commune*."[72]

But in this preapprehension as the necessary and always already realized condition of knowledge (even in a doubt an in-itself and thus *esse* is affirmed), the existence of an Absolute Being is also affirmed simultaneously *(mitbejaht)*,[73] for any possible object that

---

[72] *Geist*, 190. Here Rahner designates the "whither" of the preapprehension as *esse commune*. However, throughout *Geist*, the "whither" or term of the *Vorgriff* is described variously as, for instance: *esse schlechthin*, 208, 210, 218, 232, 244, 247, 272, 287, 315, 390, 398; *Sein überhaupt*, 282, 287, 288, 296, 394, 405; *Sein im ganzen*, 287, 288, 299; *Sein schlechthin*, 287, 288, 296, 395–96, 397, 399; *Sein als solches*, 395. Only once in *Geist* is the term of the *Vorgriff* referred to as *"absolute Sein"* (287), and only once does Rahner say that *"der Vorgriff geht auf Gott"* (190). All these subtle distinctions seemed to be dropped in *Hörer*, where the *Vorgriff* is referred directly to God: *Hörer 1*, 82, 85, 110, 130, 206. The following commentators incorrectly refer the *Vorgriff* in *Geist* directly to God: J. H-P. Wong, *Logos-Symbol in the Christology of Karl Rahner* (Rome: LAS, 1984), 99; Lennan, *Ecclesiology of Karl Rahner*, 50; and Carr, *Theological Method of Karl Rahner*, 76–77. Carr does this (77 n. 1) with a reference to *Geist*, 190, which is fully out of context in that it is the only place in the whole of *Geist* where the term of the *Vorgriff* is referred to God. On the other hand, other commentators have noted and criticized this reference of the *Vorgriff* to *esse commune*, as opposed to God, on the grounds that such a term of transcendence prevents man's ever getting beyond time: B. Lakebrink, *Klassische Metaphysik: Eine Auseinandersetzung mit der existentialen Anthropozentrik* (Freiburg: Rombach, 1967), 61 f.; W. Hill, *The Three-Personed God: The Trinity as a Mystery of Salvation* (Washington, D.C.: Catholic University of America Press, 1982), 13–35; Vass, *Theologian in Search of a Philosophy*, 51–52. Sheehan, *Karl Rahner*, 192, 198, 236, notes this limitation favorably, arguing that this is precisely what Rahner intended. J. McDermott, "The Christologies of Karl Rahner," *Gregorianum* 67 (1986), 93 n. 40, offers an alternative interpretation of the distinction between *esse commune* and *esse absolutum*.

[73] *Geist*, 189–90, 191, 232, 390; *Hörer 1*, 81–82, 84, 87, 93. P. Molnar, "Is God Essentially Different from His Creatures?" *The Thomist* 51 (1987): 575–631, questions this notion of human transcendence to *esse commune* in which God is affirmed simultaneously. Because of the plurality of terms that Rahner uses in German when writing about being and God, it is sometimes difficult to render the text accurately in English. For instance, to translate both *schlechthin* and *absolut* as "absolute" would be to miss a subtle distinction in the text. For Rahner deliberately refers the term *absolut* only to God, so that *esse absolutum* and *absolute Sein* always mean God, whereas *esse schlechthin* and *Sein schlechthin* seem to refer to *esse commune* and *not* to God. From this point on, I refer to what

can come to exist in the breadth of the preapprehension is affirmed simultaneously. An absolute being would completely fill up the breadth of this preapprehension; hence, it is affirmed simultaneously as real. "In this sense, but only in this sense, can it be said: the preapprehension attains to God,"[74] not because it attains to the Absolute Being immediately in order to represent it objectively in its own self, but because the reality of God as absolute *esse* is affirmed implicitly and simultaneously by the breadth of the preapprehension, by *esse commune or being as such*.[75] This is in no sense, Rahner argues, an a priori proof of the existence of God, for the preapprehension and its "whither" can be proved and affirmed as present and necessary for all knowledge only in the a posteriori apprehension of a real existent and as the necessary condition of the latter.

The structure of the agent intellect is, therefore, the *Vorgriff* to the negative infinity of being as such. This structure is the a priori structure of the mind but is known only in the a posteriori knowledge of the sensible other, the world. With this conclusion, we have discovered a decisive characteristic of human knowing, which is the basis of one side of Rahner's dialectical analogy—namely, a *Schwebe* between the horizon of all being and the sensible singular. Human knowledge as preapprehending is ordered to being as such, and for that reason man is spirit. He always has this infinite only in the preapprehension, and for that reason he is finite spirit.[76]

C. The Agent Intellect as the Power of the Excessus to Esse

The agent intellect is, then, the power of the human spirit to preapprehend being as such. But this agent intellect is not itself known as an object; rather, it is known only as the condition of possibility of objective knowledge. Just as light is not seen except

---

Rahner terms *Sein schlechthin* and *esse schlechthin* as "being as such," presuming that the reference is to *esse commune* and not to God. When quoting, I leave the original German untranslated.

[74] *Geist,* 190.

[75] This rather odd concept of God as existing within the horizon and yet transcending it is a point to which we will have to return. Molnar, "Is God Essentially Different?" 591, also notes this oddity.

[76] *Geist,* 195.

in seeing that which it makes visible, so the light of the agent intellect is known simultaneously with and in the object known. It is apprehended by thought insofar as it is known simultaneously as the ground of the visibility of the object.[77] This, Rahner argues, clarifies Thomas's understanding of Aristotelian aposteriorism. For Thomas, there are no innate ideas, but there is an a priori structure of the human mind, which is the condition of possibility of all human knowledge.[78] This a priori structure is not an innate idea because it is known only and simultaneously as the condition of possibility of the intellectual apprehension of what is given sensibly, namely then, when it exercises a "formal" function in respect to the material of sensibility. Therefore, the light of the agent intellect also can be designated as form in respect to the sensibly given, which functions as the "material element" of knowledge. "*Spirit* and *sensibly given* are related in the constitution of the intelligible as act and potency."[79] Consequently, we must say that the light of the agent intellect is itself the form of the sensibly given:

> In abstraction, the light of the agent intellect is known simultaneously [*miterkannt*] in the universal object, and this light is the actuality of the knower himself, from which it follows again that this actuality is such that of itself it has its knowableness [*Erkanntheit*] in itself when it becomes the form of the sensible content.[80]

But how is it possible that the actuality of the knower is the actuality of the known? For Rahner's Thomas, the answer is clear: the intellect and the actually intelligible are the same.

The agent intellect is, then, the spontaneity of the human spirit, which is dynamically ordered to the totality of possible objects. As such, this agent intellect already anticipates in its dynamic orientation the totality of all objects according to their most universal metaphysical structure and yet still needs the determinations of sensibility in order to present an object to the possible intellect.

---

[77] *Geist,* 224–26, also 155–56, 190–91, 216–17, 389 n. 9, 390; *Hörer 1,* 77, 82–83, 100, 183.

[78] *Geist,* 147, 226–27.

[79] *Geist,* 227.

[80] *Geist,* 226–27, 228, 230, 270, 282, 294, 296, 297, 315, 321, 323, 325, 377–78.

Thus, it apprehends the individual determination of sensibility (phantasm) in its dynamic ordination to the totality of all possible objects, to *esse,* and hence it apprehends this determination as being. Insofar as the agent intellect apprehends this material as sensibility within its anticipatory dynamism to *esse,* it "illuminates" this material; its actuality becomes that of the actually intelligible and thus lets the universal be known in the sensible.

Thus far, the discussion has established that the essence of human knowledge is a coming-to-self in a coming-from-the-other, or, in other words, a return of the knower to himself. In sensibility, the spirit goes out of itself in order to be with the other. In the abstractive return, the other is distinguished from the subject and objectivized. This is possible only because the agent intellect is oriented spontaneously toward being as such, which it preapprehends. This preapprehension, or *Vorgriff,* is the essence or ontological structure of the agent intellect. It apprehends the sensible object within its dynamism, "illuminates" it according to its ontological structure, recognizes it as limited and therefore as repeatable or universal and passes on in its dynamic striving for being as such. The species, therefore, by which the sensible object is known as "other" is simultaneously the ontological determination of both the knower and the known, and the *abstractio* of this species or form, occurring through the turning of the intellect toward the sensible singular, does not actually precede the *conversio* but is a constitutive moment within it.

Material being is not present-to-self but is given-over-to-the-other. Immaterial being, on the other hand, is essentially present-to-self. What is peculiar to human knowing, therefore, is the continual coming to self from sensibility. The return is never a complete separation from matter; it is a constant coming from matter. Thus, the question of human knowledge is how and why all intellectual knowledge is known only insofar as it is apprehended in the sensibly known. This question, argues Rahner, is nothing other than the question about the *conversio ad phantasma.*

4. THE CONVERSION

A. *The Point of Departure*

The phantasm, according to Rahner, cannot be considered a "thing." It is, rather, just the key word designating sense knowledge as such.[81] When, therefore, it is asserted in the proposition about the conversion to the phantasm that human intellectual knowledge takes place essentially in a turning to the phantasm, this statement does not mean that intellectual knowledge is accompanied by phantasms. Rather, it says that intellectual knowledge is possible only with a simultaneous realization of sense knowledge, that sense intuition and intellectual thought are united in the one human knowledge. "Being-present-to-oneself and abstraction are intrinsically and essentially a knowing-something-of-another and therefore are already themselves a conversion to the phantasm."[82] Just from this it follows that our task is not to prove that the conversion to the phantasm is a factual characteristic of human knowledge; this conclusion has been affirmed already. Rather, our task now is to grasp it in its possibility.

From the question about the conditions of a receptive, intuitive knowledge, we arrived at the essence of sensibility and thereby at the essence of man as a sentient knower: act of matter, form of body. From the insight into the possibility of a judgmental, universal knowledge attaining to the in–itself of the object differentiated from the subject, we arrived at the essence of thought and thereby at the essence of man as spirit: *excessus* to being as such, a form subsisting in itself.

But this leaves the ontological constitution of man, which manifests itself in his knowledge as the possibility of this knowledge, in a peculiar duality that seems almost contradictory: man is at once "subsisting in himself" and "actuality of the other." Thus, the question necessarily follows: How is this duality of determinations in the ontological constitution of man to be grasped from a more original unity without the duality being eliminated? Conversion to the phantasm is the expression designating the essential unity of the one human knowledge, and therefore it requires that the unity of this knowing be grasped from the unity of the ontological constitution of man as its origin, for only then can it be grasped in itself. This original unity of man's being as the ground of his knowledge, therefore,

> must manifest itself in the very thing which is to be unified, not as
> a subsequent bond, but as the one essence unified in itself which,

[81] *Geist,* 243.
[82] *Geist,* 244.

in order to come to itself, lets what is distinct from itself come forth from itself, and which therefore also holds together in unity that which is distinct as the fulfillment of its own essence: the essence of man unifying itself into its own unity [*sich zu seiner Einheit selbst einigendes Wesen*].[83]

Spirit, although blind without the intuition of sensibility, is the more original element in man, and therefore it is our task to ground the plurality and unity of man's cognitive powers in the light of the original essence of human intellectuality. As *agent intellect* was the Thomistic term under which we had to look for that which enables us to grasp human knowledge as spiritual, so, too, *possible intellect* will be the key word that enables us to grasp this spirit as human. We must show, therefore, that the possible intellect, in virtue of its being potency to be present to self, must produce the means to achieve this self-presence, namely sensibility. We must then proceed to show that because sensibility and intellect exist in an original and unifying unity in the spirit, the production of sensibility is in fact an emanation from the spirit, which constitutes itself insofar as it allows its powers to emanate. We must then recognize this emanation of sensibility from the spirit as the decisive turning of the intellect to the other of matter and therefore as the fundamental *conversio ad phantasma*. Finally, because the abstraction is a moment within the conversion, as we have seen already, the emanation of sensibility from the spirit reveals itself to be the fundamental abstractive conversion in which all human knowledge occurs and that occurs as a moment within the spirit's dynamic striving toward being as such.

B. *The Possible Intellect as the Origin of Sensibility*

(i) The Nature of the Possible Intellect

However much Thomas maintains the real distinction between the agent and possible intellect, they form just as much an essential unity as complimentary moments of the one knowing.[84] If the

---

[83] *Geist,* 245, 251, 261–62, 265–66.

[84] *Geist,* 146, 247, 323–24. Rahner's understanding of the possible intellect has been criticized widely as inadequate and untrue to Thomas: Fabro, *La Svolta antropologica,* 35, 45, 53 f., 66–69, 162; Eicher, *Die Anthropologische Wende,* 125–

agent intellect is the spontaneous, dynamic ordination of the human spirit to being as such, then the possible intellect as intellect is the potentiality of the human spirit to comprehend *esse* absolutely in receptive knowledge. The one knowing follows from both functions, and the receptive breadth of the possible intellect is the same as the apprehensive breadth of the active intellect. The possible intellect is possible in the sense that it is being—that is to say, being-present-to-oneself, complete return—but it is not of itself already and always present to itself.[85] By itself, it cannot give itself immediately to itself; it comes to itself only insofar as it receptively allows another to encounter it, and without this receptive letting-self-be-encountered by another it is not present to itself. Thus, Rahner concludes that "the possible intellect as possible comes to exist at the midpoint between a separated form and a form whose ontological actuality exhausts itself in the determination of matter, and this midpoint is ontologically definable only by being distinguished from these two extremes." Indeed, the essence of the possible intellect can be defined relatively simply from the way that it knows: "it is that being which is present to itself in the knowledge of another." But as soon as this definition is to be translated into ontological terms, it can be discovered only as the midpoint between two different definitions: "in its being-present-to-itself the possible intellect is a form subsisting in itself; in its drive [*Zwang*] to let itself be encountered by another it is sensibility: form of matter, form of body." Only in this duality, in which both definitions intrinsically modify each other, is the possible intellect grasped ontologically.

> Insofar as the drive to let itself be encountered by another, in order to be present to itself, is derived from the fact that the intellect indeed really is intellect, that is, the intellect is able to be present to itself, but it is not present to itself through its mere existence [*Dasein*]—which is precisely what is said by the term *possible intellect*—*possible intellect is the most adequate and most simple conception for human knowledge and for human being altogether.*[86]

33, 159–63, 328–32; Burke, "Conceptual Thought in Karl Rahner," 65–93; J. McDermott, "Karl Rahner on Two Infinities," *International Philosophical Quarterly* 28 (1988), 445–47; De h-Ide, "Rahner and Lonergan," 65; J. Speck, *Karl Rahner's theologische Anthropologie* (Munich: Kösel, 1967), 182–84.

[85] *Geist,* 249, 250–51.
[86] *Geist,* 249–50.

According to Rahner, the possible intellect is a spirit that of itself exists in potency actually to be present to itself. In virtue of its being, it must of itself place itself in the possibility by which it is enabled to come to itself. Insofar as this essentially does not happen by the fact that it is already of itself always present to itself, this coming-to-itself is possible only by the fact that it comes to itself in the receptive letting-itself-be-encountered by another as what is immediately and first apprehended. "Therefore, in virtue of its being, the (possible) intellect must of itself create the possibility that another can encounter it objectively as its first-known."[87] Now we have seen that a knowledge that receptively accepts what is other than itself as its first and immediately apprehended object is essentially sensibility and is conceivable only as the act of matter. It follows from this that the possible intellect can establish itself in the real possibility of being spirit only by becoming sensibility, and this becoming sentient [*sinnlichwerden*] of the possible intellect can be understood only in such a way that it lets sensibility emanate [*Entspringen*] from itself as its power, without losing itself completely in it.[88] This emanation of sensibility is in fact, according to Rahner, the decisive turning of the intellect toward matter, the fundamental conversion to the phantasm:

> Thus the (possible) intellect appears as the origin of sensibility in such a way that it is a power in its own right alongside of it, but sensibility, since it emanates from the possible intellect and thus is its actuality, is the already realized [*schon vollzogene*] turning of the intellect itself to the other, is the conversion to the phantasm.[89]

(ii) Emanation

In order to understand the nature of emanation correctly, Rahner argues, we have to realize that in the question of the origin of one power from another and from the substantial ground of the spirit we are not at all dealing with the relationship between a finished complete existent as an efficient cause and an effect pro-

---

[87] *Geist,* 252.

[88] *Geist,* 220, 229, 246, 252–54.

[89] *Geist,* 252. The emanation of sensibility constitutes the fundamental *conversio: Geist,* 41 n. 8, 252, 268, 270, 282, 288, 289–90, 292, 294, 382–83.

duced by it, which remains extrinsic to it. Rather, we are dealing with the intrinsic metaphysical constitution of an individual essence in itself as a single being in the plurality of its powers. The plurality of powers that intrinsically constitute an existent, therefore, can be conceived as those of a single existent only if the plurality to be unified is conceived as arising out of a single origin in which the plurality, antecedent to itself, is already and always one.[90] Thomas calls this "emanation," and it is situated, says Rahner, at the midpoint, hardly able to be defined further, among an efficient causality, a simple essential determination and an accidental determination. We consequently are dealing here with "the unfolding, which is essentially given simultaneously with a unified existent, of its essence from its innermost core into the plurality of its powers in which it is first itself."[91]

The plurality of powers that constitute an existent can be conceived of as those of one existent only if the plurality to be unified is conceived of as arising out of a single origin in which plurality is already and always one, for unity must be found before multiplicity.[92] It necessarily follows that the relationship between the essential core of an existent and the powers emanating from it can be conceived of only as a dialectical relationship of unity and plurality. "The origin is the end (finis) of what emanates."[93] The

---

[90] Geist, 96, 25, 258, 260, 292.

[91] Geist, 259.

[92] Geist, 217–18, 258; Hörer 1, 51–52, 147.

[93] Geist, 260–62. This dialectical notion of " 'one' becoming 'other' in order to be itself" is, as we will see, central to Rahner's thought and foundational to his notions of "symbol" and "becoming": K. Rahner, "Zur Theologie des Symbols," in Schriften zur Theologie, vol. 6 (Einsiedeln, Zürich, Cologne: Benziger, 1965), 279–81. In order to simplify the footnotes, henceforth all references to Schriften are made with the title of the particular article (or a shortened title) followed by Schriften and the volume number. Translations of the Schriften come from Theological Investigations, 23 vols., translated by C. Ernst, K. H. Kruger, B. Kruger, K. Smith, D. Bourke, D. Morland, E. Quinn, H. Riley, and J. Donceel (vols. 1–6, Baltimore: Helicon, 1961–69; vols. 7–10, New York: Herder and Herder, 1970–73; vols. 11–14, New York: Seabury, 1974–76; vols. 15–21, New York: Crossroad, 1979–88; vols. 22–23, London: Darton, Longman, and Todd, 1991–92). K. Rahner and J. Ratzinger, Episkopat und Primat, Quaestiones Disputatae no. 11 (Freiburg, Basel, Vienna: Herder, 1961), 97; translations from The Episcopate and the Primacy, translated by K. Barker, P. Kearns, R. Ochs, and R. Strachan (Edinburgh and London: Nelson, 1962). K. Rahner, Sendung und Gnade (Innsbruck, Vienna, Munich: Tyrolia, 1959), 58–59. Rahner uses this dialectical idea to ground the relationship of spirit and

origin lets itself flow out into its powers in order to be itself, for there is question not of producing a separate other, which producing already presupposes the producer as complete, "but of the origin itself coming-to-its-end [*Zu-ende-Kommen*], of its unfolding out into its own essence *(ad completionem subjecti)*." Thus, the origin that lets emanate reveals itself as a receptive origin.

> The origin as receptive receives in itself what emanates as its fulfillment; it would be less perfect without the emanation which it retains in itself; it is related to it as being in potency for it; it grows to its fulfillment only through less perfect stages.[94]

This unfolding of an essence from its central point into the plurality of its powers takes place in a definite order. It is conceivable only as a plurality of partial moments in the one movement toward a goal, and this goal assigns its definite place in this movement to everything that emanates.[95] Thus, the series of origins begins with the emanation of the most perfect and ends with the less perfect, and the whole process occurs in virtue of the ground striving for its fulfillment. It is also clear that this whole relationship of origin among the powers cannot be thought of as a process that happens once and for all, that ran its course perhaps at the temporal beginning of a human existence and then ceased. Rather, the powers are held constantly in this relationship of emanation from the substantial ground and from one another. "The human spirit exists permanently in letting its powers emanate and only in this way."[96] Finally, because the process of emanation is *one,* the emanation of several powers can be understood only as partial moments of the one movement of the self-realization of the one human spirit, and because the intellect is more perfect in relation to sensibility, because it is more present-to-self, the intellect is the primary emanation from the spirit, and sensibility is metaphysically, not temporally, subsequent. Conversely, sensibility as the less-perfect power is the first to be received in the receptive origin.

---

sensibility (*Geist,* 79–80, 220, 283), cogitative sense and imagination (*Geist,* 308–11), knowledge and love (*Hörer 1,* 127–28).

[94] *Geist,* 262.

[95] *Geist,* 262, 265–66, 267.

[96] *Geist,* 264–65, 283, 314, 324–25.

C. The Emanation of Sensibility from the Spirit Is the Fundamental Abstractive Conversio

It is now clear that the origin of sensibility from the intellect is to be understood as the fundamental and decisive conversion to the phantasm. We have established that the abstraction of the universal is itself but a moment within the conversion to the phantasm because the "intelligible" in the strict sense is nothing other than the light of the agent intellect preapprehending being as such, the a priori structure of the spirit itself, which when turned to the phantasm becomes conscious as the "form" of what is sensibly known. Thus, the emanation of sensibility from the intellect *is* the conversion to the phantasm, which *itself is* the illumination of the phantasm by the light of the agent intellect, through which illumination the abstraction is already accomplished. Conversion to the phantasm and abstraction therefore are moments of the single process of the emanation of sensibility from the intellect and are inseparably related to each other in a relationship of reciprocal priority.

We also have seen that sensibility and intellect exist antecedent to any knowledge in an original unity in the spirit, which is in fact a "unifying unity," for the spirit constitutes itself insofar as it lets its powers emanate.[97] The spirit constitutes itself insofar as it lets sensibility emanate through the intellect, and the sensible act of apprehension is an actualization of the spirit itself.[98] In the one process of the emanation of sensibility from the spirit, therefore, the abstractive conversion takes place, and the unity of human knowing is revealed.[99]

What are the conditions of possibility of this emanation of sensibility from the spirit? How does it take place? In our examination of the process of abstraction, we saw that it was, on the one hand, to be grounded and accomplished in an *excessus* to being as such and, on the other hand, as the becoming conscious of the a priori structure of the spirit itself in the sensibly given content that it informs. Therefore, "the essence of the spirit is the '*quo est*

---

[97] *Geist,* 263, 265–66.
[98] *Geist,* 257, 265, 267–68, 270, 273, 283–84, 287, 289, 293, 300, 311, 314, 379, 382–83; *Hörer 1,* 176–77, 208.
[99] *Geist,* 41 n. 8, 270, 287–90, 292, 294, 382–83.

omnia fieri': spirit is in potency for *Sein schlechthin*. It is 'in a certain way (that is, in potency and in ordination toward) every-thing.'"[100] Its becoming conscious of its a priori reality is the pre-apprehension of all being and vice versa. As transcendent apprehension of being as such, moreover, this actuality of the spirit is a becoming, a dynamic orientation to the totality of its objects.[101] As such, the human spirit is desire *(Begierde)*, striving *(Streben)*, action *(Handlung)*. Desire, therefore, is a characteristic of knowledge, in that the intellect also has a desire in itself as its own intrinsic drive.[102]

Insofar as every being tends toward its own fulfillment, the human spirit, being appetite in itself, is in movement toward its end and goal. It also can be said that a nature tends toward only one end. Therefore, any movement of the spirit, wherever it is directed, occurs in virtue of the desire for the one end and goal, for every act of a power is also caused by its final end. And the final end of the one desire of the spirit, expressed formally, is the "good of the intellect," truth as such.[103] This truth that is the good of the intellect is being as such, for spirit is the potentiality for the reception of all being *(alles Sein)* and the active desire for it. Therefore, every movement of the spirit, including the pro-duction of sensibility, occurs as a moment in the spirit's desire for being as such.

> Thus, in its preapprehension, the spirit already and always possesses in every act *Sein im Ganzen* and seeks to fill up the formal emptiness of the being given in the preapprehension through the object of every individual act. *Sein überhaupt* in this material fullness, *absolute Sein,* is therefore the end and goal of the spirit as such. Every opera-tion of the spirit, whatever it might be, can therefore be understood only as a moment in the movement toward *Sein schlechthin* as toward the one end and goal of the desire of the spirit.[104]

---

[100] *Geist,* 284–85.

[101] *Geist,* 263, 265–66, 285, 315; *Hörer 1,* 101.

[102] *Geist,* 285, 397; *Hörer 1,* 108, 119, 125, 127. Vass, *Theologian in Search of a Philosophy,* 82–84, is critical of this Rahnerian identification of knowing and willing.

[103] *Geist,* 286–87.

[104] *Geist,* 287. Every act of the spirit occurs in virtue of the desire for *esse: Geist,* 263, 265–66, 287, 291, 296, 397, 406; *Hörer 1,* 177, 181.

Now, the origin of sensibility from spirit has been defined by the fact that in producing the complete constitution of its own essence toward which it tends, spirit lets sensibility emanate from itself, bears sensibility permanently in itself as its power, and informs sensibility from the outset with the laws of its own essence because it produces sensibility in its striving toward its own fulfillment. But the desire of the spirit for its own fulfillment, which produces sensibility, has shown itself to be a desire for absolute being, which was shown earlier to be the fundamental abstraction. "Consequently, the spirit produces its sensibility in this desire for being which constantly preapprehends absolute being, and this is abstraction."[105] The spirit comes to its own essence—that is, to itself as the power that preapprehends being as such—and to the actual apprehension of being, only insofar as it continually lets sensibility emanate from itself as the antecedent condition for this apprehension, in such a way that spirit and sensibility are reciprocally the receptive origin of each other.[106] Thus,

> insofar as the spirit is the origin that lets sensibility emanate, the sensibly known is always *abstracted*, since it is apprehended within *Sein überhaupt* toward which the spirit is tending in the production of sensibility. Insofar as sensibility is the receptive origin of the spirit, a conversion to the phantasm is always already accomplished, since *Sein im Ganzen* is only had in a sentient, intuitive possession of the world. With that we have acquired a conception of the possibility of an abstractive conversion to the phantasm from the emanation of sensibility from the spirit.[107]

5. THE POSSIBILITY OF METAPHYSICS

According to Rahner, being as such, or *ens commune*, is the object of metaphysics. God is not the object of metaphysics but is known as the ground of the object and therefore is affirmed simultaneously with *ens commune*.[108] God is known, therefore, only insofar as the "object" of metaphysics already presupposes him as its

---

[105] *Geist*, 288, 292, 294, 382–83.
[106] *Geist*, 289, 379.
[107] *Geist*, 289–90.
[108] *Geist*, 232, 387–92; *Hörer 1*, 15.

ground, without this ground itself being an object that might be investigated by itself. Knowledge of God in this way is in a certain sense the "ultimate end" of metaphysics but not in such a way that one comes upon God "at the end," after one has apprehended the intrinsic essence of what is grounded, taken by itself and without its ground. God is "known later with regard to us," later than what can be known otherwise. But what this does not mean is that we grasp God subsequently to another knowledge that is grounded in itself, so that the object we know "subsequently" would be the ground only of the object known first, not the ground of the knowledge of what is known first; hence, it would only as a matter of fact be prior in itself to what is known first. Quite the contrary, "what is prior in itself is also prior in human knowing, not as a known object . . . but as a 'principle of knowledge.' "[109] Thus, God is apprehended simultaneously and implicitly with the preapprehension of being as such, and because all knowledge is possible only within this preapprehension, it is possible to conclude that the implicit affirmation of God is the condition of the possibility of any knowledge.[110] Metaphysics is therefore the reflexive elaboration of the ground of human knowledge. It is opened up to man as the condition of the possibility of the objective knowledge of the world that he finds himself already and always possessing.

The question of the conversion to the phantasm has revealed itself to be, therefore, the essential question concerning the possibility of metaphysics for a mode of thought whose only intuition is sense intuition. And despite the necessary conversion of human thought to the imagination, metaphysics is shown to be possible through the *excessus*. The *excessus* is the first and primary act that, as a condition of the knowledge of the world, is what makes both physics and metaphysics possible. The *excessus* attains to *esse*—that is, not merely to the totality of what is representatively imaginable in sensibility, but to being as such. Insofar as the *excessus* affirms the condition of its own possibility, and insofar as the "whither" of this *excessus* belongs to this condition, it affirms being as such

---

[109] *Geist*, 389.

[110] *Geist*, 232, 387–92; *Hörer 1*, 15, 87, 110, 187. See also Tremblay, *Finitude et devenir*, 289–90.

as possible and real beyond the world. We have seen that this *excessus* essentially takes place only in the judgment, so the judgment is the only expression of the dynamic desire of the spirit for being as such. Metaphysics does not consist in the vision of a metaphysical object, perhaps of being as such, but in the transcendental reflection upon that which is affirmed implicitly and simultaneously in the knowledge of the world, in the affirmation of physics.

If the possibility and the limit of metaphysics consist only in the reflection on the *excessus* to being as such, which makes physics possible, then the only metaphysical statements of a fundamental kind that can be made about an object beyond the realm of our objects—that is, beyond the realm of the imagination—are the intrinsic moments of the concept of being itself. These moments are known as the transcendentals, and the essential ones are being, true, and good. We do not possess, therefore, a knowledge of the quiddity of "separated things." We know only of their existence; of their essence we know only what is necessarily given implicitly in the knowledge of their existence—that is, the transcendental determinations in that intensity of being in which they necessarily belong to an existent or to absolute being as such without material limitation. But that defines the metaphysical object only from the empty concept of being. Although *esse* is in itself the full ground of every existent, this fullness is given to us only in the absolute, empty infinity of our preapprehension or, what is the same thing, in *ens commune* with the transcendental modes intrinsic to it. Hence, it remains true that "the highest knowledge of God is the 'darkness of ignorance.' "[111] The analogy of being is not, therefore, merely a construction designed to help toward the conceptual, negative definition of the essence of God, but already has its starting point where the experienced world is transcended in a preapprehension through *excessus* and negation. In fact, the concept of being is not first of all univocal, in order to be expanded analogously afterward, but as the form of the preapprehension it is analogous and becomes univocal in the conversion to the phan-

---

[111] *Geist,* 401.

tasm as the being of material things. "The analogous is the ground of the univocal, and not vice versa."[112]

In conclusion, a correct understanding of St. Thomas will not lead toward a type of formal apriorism. Every genuine metaphysical a priori does not simply have the a posteriori "alongside" of or "after" itself, but holds it in itself. Not as though the a posteriori, the "world" in its positive content, were able to be resolved adequately into pure, transcendental apriority, but in such a way that the a priori of itself is referred to the a posteriori that in order to be really itself it cannot keep itself in its pure transcendentality but must release itself into the categorical.

> Hence the openness of the a priori for the a posteriori, of the transcendental for the categorical, is not something secondary, perhaps merely a subsequent piecing together of two completely separable contents of reality and of knowledge, but it is the fundamental definition of the contents of the one metaphysics of man.[113]

6. Spirit in the World

Thomas's whole metaphysical inquiry begins from man's situation and simultaneously places man in question. Although the basis of all his philosophizing from the outset is the world, it is precisely the world into which the spirit of man—in turning to the phantasm—has already entered. Thus, the first thing confronting man is not the world, but rather the world transformed by the light of the spirit. The world as known is always the world of man, is essentially a concept complementary *(Komplementärbegriff)* to man. And the last known, God, shines forth only in the limitless breadth of the preapprehension, in the desire for being as such by which every act of man is borne and that is at work not only in

---

[112] *Geist,* 401, 209; *Hörer 1,* 62–63, 217; "Über den Begriff des Geheimnisses in der katholischen Theologie," *Schriften* 4: 70, 73. See also Carr, *Theological Method of Karl Rahner,* 114, 170; Molnar, "Is God Essentially Different?" 599; Buckley, "Within the Holy Mystery," in O'Donovan, ed., *A World of Grace,* 43–44.

[113] *Geist,* 404, 405–406; *Hörer 1,* 82–83, 94–96, 101–2, 125–26, 174, 178, 181, 183, 184–85, 189, 202–3, 208.

man's ultimate knowledge and in his ultimate decisions, but also in the fact that the free spirit becomes and must become sensibility in order to be spirit and thus exposes itself to the whole destiny of this earth.

> Thus, man encounters himself when he finds himself in the world and when he asks about God; and when he asks about his essence, he always finds himself already in the world and on the way to God. He is both of these at once and cannot be one without the other.[114]

Therefore, man is, according to Rahner, fundamentally ambivalent; he is *Schwebe*. He is simultaneously in the world and yet, by the fact of his questioning, already and always beyond it. Each side of this ambivalence calls the other forth; we seem to know God only as the necessary horizon of the experience of world that is possible only in this way. Thus, every venture into the world has shown itself to be borne by the ultimate desire of the spirit for being as such, and every entry into sensibility, into the world and its destiny, shows itself to be only the coming to be of a spirit that is striving toward the absolute. "Thus man is the midpoint [*schwebende Mitte*] suspended between the world and God, between time and eternity, and this boundary line is the point of his definition and his destiny."[115]

It is upon this notion of man as the midpoint, or the *Schwebe*, between being as such and the material world that Rahner builds his theological anthropology. In order to be able to hear whether God is speaking or not, man must know that God is; however, in order that it be necessary for God to speak, he must be hidden from man. Insofar, therefore, as man enters into the world by turning to the phantasm, the revelation of being as such and in it the knowledge of God's existence have been achieved already, but even then this God who is beyond the world is always hidden from man. "Abstraction is the revelation of being as such which places man before God; conversion is the entrance into the here and now of this finite world, and this makes God the distant Unknown."[116] Abstraction and conversion are ultimately the same

---

[114] *Geist,* 405.
[115] *Geist,* 406; see also 67–68, 93–94.
[116] *Geist,* 407.

thing: man. Man, who can listen to hear whether God perhaps has not spoken because he knows that God is; man, who must listen for the word of God because God is the Unknown.

7. CONCLUSION

Rahner's metaphysical starting point in the ultimate and irreducible nature of the original question led him, as we have seen, to a number of fundamental conclusions. The question revealed firstly, and most importantly, is that man (because he must necessarily ask about being) is simultaneously present to all of being and yet not present to being. Man is in himself an oscillation, a *Schwebe;* he stands already at his goal, which is also his beginning, being, and yet he is not there. This notion of *Schwebe* dominates Rahner's vision of reality and is the basis for the further development of his thought.[117]

From this understanding of man as *Schwebe,* Rahner was able to deduce two foundational metaphysical principles concerning being and matter. First, he was able to deduce the primordial unity of being and knowing. Because being can be questioned, it must be knowable. The necessity of man's question can be grounded, therefore, only if knowing is not something extrinsically added to being but rather is itself the presence-to-self of being *(Beisichsein des Seins).* Knowing is the subjectivity of being. It is important to notice, however, that this postulated unity of being and knowing is not in itself a simple unity of identity. The very term that Rahner uses to describe it, *Beisichsein des Seins,* seems to imply self-presence, a duality in unity rather than an absolute and simple identity. In fact, in the paradoxical but important affirmation that "Being itself is already the primordially unifying unity of being and knowing," Rahner himself seems to deny a simple identity, implying instead that being has a certain primacy within the being-knowing unity.[118] Clearly for Rahner

---

[117] See J. McDermott, "Dialectical Analogy: The Oscillating Center of Rahner's Thought," *Gregorianum* 75 (1994): 675–703, and "Analogy of Knowing," 201–16; McDermott exhaustively analyzes Rahner's understanding of dialectical analogy as the oscillating center of Rahner's thought.

[118] *Geist,* 83.

there is an oscillation at the most fundamental level even within being itself.[119]

Second, the *Schwebe* of man reveals the existence of matter: If being is presence-to-self, how does a question ever arise? Only if the being of the questioner involves a certain nonbeing, or prime matter, which hinders its complete self-reflection or self-mastery. According to the extent of matter's composition with being, grades of self-possession—that is, of being—are recognized. A finite being is being to the extent that it is free of matter. On the one hand, matter is that which prevents self-consciousness, yet, on the other hand, insofar as matter enters the composition of a being that is self-reflective, matter can become the knowing being's proper object. Being and matter appear to constitute, therefore, another diversity in unity, and man is revealed as that being whose presence-to-self is in itself a presence-to-the-other.[120] This union of being with nonbeing in fact is implied by the original diversity in unity of being and knowing and explains how being's presence-to-self involves primordially a distance from self. Inversely, because from the beginning the distance belongs to being, matter belongs to being in its self-possession, and what in its diversity is not the proper object of intelligence becomes in unity its proper object. Again we see Rahner holding together unity and diversity within a mobile union of opposites.

The foundational question reveals, therefore, that man is that being who exists as a *schwebende Mitte* between the total presence-to-self of independent being and actual abandonment to matter.[121] This is possible only because knowing being, in its dynamic desire for the preapprehended horizon of being as such, in sensibility has entered, already and always, into "otherness" in order to receive the "other" into itself. Because, therefore, the knowing being is itself the being of the other, the primary object of knowing is both the material other and its own being, and the problem of the "bridge" between knower and known is overcome.[122] Sensibility thus is grasped dialectically as both *actus materiae* and *actus contra materiam,* and the sensible species, by which the sensible

---

[119] *Geist,* 236 f.; *Hörer 1,* 55–57, 60–61.
[120] *Geist,* 87, 89, 92, 389, 391, 405; *Hörer 1,* 151–54.
[121] *Geist,* 67–68, 93–94, 406.
[122] *Geist,* 88, 141–42.

object is known, is simultaneously both the self-realization of the sensible object and the self-realization of the sensible knower. Man is present to himself insofar as he stretches out to the other, for "the very being of a limited being must be the being of an "other.'"[123] So we see the epistemological consequence of the metaphysical union of being and nonbeing worked out in that knowing as presence-to-self is always and simultaneously a knowing the other, a presence-to-the-other.

This similarity between the structure of man as *Schwebe* and the structure of knowing should not surprise us because for Rahner, as we have seen from the beginning, knowing is but the subjectivity of being. Knowing consists ultimately in a dynamic *Schwebe* between the categorical singular possessed originally and always in sensibility and the preapprehended horizon of being as such. However, within this dynamic *Schwebe* of being and knowing there is always and simultaneously a static moment of conceptualization.[124] This abstraction or conceptualization, which is made possible by the *Vorgriff* or preapprehension of all being, consists in the recognition of limitation and hence of possible repetition. Logically preceding the affirmative synthesis, or *conversio*, which is itself identified as the emanation of sensibility from the spirit, this abstraction is interpreted by Rahner as a moment within the spirit's dynamic desire for being as such. The concept that emerges from this dynamic *Schwebe* of knowing is therefore weak, itself oscillating between nothing and infinitude.[125] It is relativized in that it is always referred to as "this" *(Diesda)* and also to the infinite horizon of *esse*, toward which the abstractive movement of the intellect tends. Nevertheless, Rahner insists that this mo-

---

[123] *Geist*, 31, 49, 53, 89, 91–93, 104, 107, 405; *Hörer 1*, 151–52.

[124] Rahner's commentators often overlook the importance of this moment of conceptualization within the knowing process: see, for instance, T. Pearl, "Dialectical Panentheism: On the Hegelian Character of Karl Rahner's Key Christological Writings," *Irish Theological Quarterly* 42 (1975), 125, and Hines, *Transformation of Dogma*, 6–7, both of whom note Rahner's understanding of knowing as *Schwebe* between the sensible singular and the horizon of being, but who also fail to see the importance of the concept within the dynamism of the *conversio*.

[125] This weakness of the concept is reflected in Rahner's reduction of the passive intellect, which in traditional Thomism received the *species impressa* that became the concept, to a mere name *(Titel)*, indicating that the spirit for itself effects and then possesses the receptive faculty of sensibility (*Geist*, 146, 323–24).

ment of conceptualization is intrinsically present within the knowing process, and he never abandons either its necessity or its validity.

Thus, beyond the original *Schwebe* of being and its presence-to-self, or being and nonbeing, we have seen emerging in Rahner's foundational epistemology a secondary *Schwebe* or double emphasis. On the one hand, human knowing appears to be an oscillation between two unconceptualizable poles, God and matter, and, on the other hand, human knowing never occurs without a moment of conceptualization. The dynamic oscillation of the judgment and the static moment of the abstraction exist themselves in a relationship of mutual priority, and Rahner himself seems to alternate between the two in his explanation of the unity in diversity of the knowing process. This double emphasis or *Schwebe* between unifying dynamism and conceptual distinction constitutes, in fact, a remarkably flexible structure of thought that I call *dialectical analogy* and that, I maintain, is the hermeneutical key to the correct interpretation of Rahner's theological system.[126] Through this structure of thought, Rahner is able to oscillate between unity and diversity as necessary: when he needs to, in line with the dynamic unifying side of his thought, he can stress the unity of God and the world, the transcendental and the categorical, grace and nature, but when necessary, in line with the conceptualizing side of his thought, he equally can stress the distinction between these polarities. This constant changing of perspectives is not, for Rahner, contradictory but is precisely dialectical analogy. The contradiction might emerge only if the two positions were held as statically opposed to one another, but, for Rahner, the analogous structure of man is itself precisely the constant oscillation among these perspectives. Man is the creature on the edge between spirit and matter, God and world, grace and nature. All the distinctions must be preserved, but they are preserved properly only in the constant *Schwebe* that is true dialectical analogy.

---

[126] A number of commentators have recognized partially this structure of dialectical analogy, although they have not perceived its importance and centrality in Rahner's thought: Vass, *Theologian in Search of a Philosophy,* 58, and *Mystery of Man,* 20; Molnar, "Is God Essentially Different?" 603, 607, 623–624; Honner, "Unity-in-Difference," 480–82, 485–89, 503–6; Sheehan, "Metaphysics and Bivalence," 21–43; Tremblay, *Finitude et devenir,* 277, 339 ff., 366 ff.

2

Nature and Grace

THROUGH AN ANALYSIS OF Rahner's epistemological metaphysics, we have uncovered a foundational structure to his thought, which I call *dialectical analogy*. The essence of this dialectical analogy is twofold and is seen most clearly in Rahner's analysis of human knowing as, first, an oscillation or *Schwebe* between the horizon of being and the sensible singular, and second, simultaneously, a moment of conceptualization in relation to the movement of the judgment. This twofold structure of dynamic transcendence and *Schwebe,* emphasizing unity and based in the judgment, and of static conceptualization, emphasizing diversity and based in the abstraction, provides Rahner with a remarkably flexible structure through which he can hold together and dialectically unite polarities.

Turning our attention now to Rahner's treatment of the traditionally difficult problem of nature and grace, we find operative the same structure of dialectical thought present in his earlier writings. However, we also see for the first time an important development in his thought that will have repercussions throughout his theology. In his earlier work and in line with the conceptualizing and distinguishing side of his thought, Rahner sees divine revelation as coming to man's elevated subjectivity from without. He is concerned with the conditions of possibility that enable man to hear this word of divine self-communication. However, by the early 1960s a change of emphasis appears. Now, in line with the dynamic and unifying side of his thought, Rahner, although never actually denying the grace-nature distinction, stresses ever more their existential unity and by interpreting transcendentally given grace as revelation in itself (a real novelty in Catholic theology), which is expressed categorically in history even outside of official revelation, begins to see categorical revelation as only the posterior explicitization of what man always and originally is, the clearest expression of grace and the final cause to which all grace tends.

In this chapter, therefore, we shall see the application of Rahner's dialectical analogy to the conundrum of grace and nature, through which he holds both the dynamic orientation of nature to grace and their existential unity, without thereby sacrificing the all-important distinction between them. I first review his early treatment of quasi-formal causality and the relation of created and uncreated grace, then look at his treatment of the specific problem of nature and grace and at his theory of the supernatural existential, before finally examining how within a Scotist perspective on incarnation and grace he continues to insist on the double gratuity of grace and therefore on the necessity of the concept of pure nature, notwithstanding the difficulty in both defining and grounding such a concept.

1. CREATED AND UNCREATED GRACE

One of the notable features of Rahner's theology is its lack of emphasis on the distinctions, so common in scholastic thought, between the various "types" of grace. This shift of emphasis was due, at least in part, to his reinterpretation of the traditional understanding of the relationship between created and uncreated grace. In a very early article, dating from 1939, Rahner proposes a realignment of the common understanding of this relationship. Because his new theory of "quasi-formal" causality throws light on his subsequent theory of the "supernatural existential," it will be helpful to examine this article carefully.[1]

In the "textbook" theology of grace so common before the Second Vatican Council, heavy emphasis was laid on the role of created grace as that which qualitatively modified man, enabling him to receive the divine indwelling, known as uncreated grace. Whatever the differences between the various scholastic theories, "in each case the indwelling of the Spirit in the justified man by grace is seen merely as a *consequence* of the bestowal of created

---

[1] "Zur scholastischen Begrifflichkeit der ungeschaffenen Gnade," *Schriften,* 1: 347–75.

grace, as the end-term of a (categorical) relationship of man to God given with created grace."[2]

Rahner points out that although this position is reasonable and has a venerable tradition in the scholastic theology, it seems to contradict the evidence of Scripture and the witness of many Church Fathers. After a brief overview of the patristic and scriptural evidence, Rahner concludes that for St. Paul and St. John it is the indwelling of the Holy Spirit that produces in the justified man a created effect. This perspective, taken up by many of the Church Fathers (especially the Greek Fathers), suggests that

> man's inner sanctification is first and foremost a communication of the personal Spirit of God, that is to say, in scholastic terms a *donum increatum;* and that every created grace, every way of being *pneumatikos,* is a consequence and a manifestation of the possession of this uncreated grace.[3]

Rahner begins his attempt to harmonize this apparent contradiction by analyzing the scholastic teaching that the closest of relations holds between grace (as a whole) and the ontological presuppositions of the beatific vision.[4] If it is accepted that the life of glory is the definitive flowering of the life of grace, then grace, as the basis of the supernatural life, must also be an entitative principle of the vision of God. In other words, "there is at least no objection in principle to applying to an ontology of grace a set of concepts which have proved themselves objectively valid in an ontology of the immediate vision of God."[5]

Having established this continuum between grace and glory, Rahner analyzes the life of glory, or beatific vision, in order to throw light on the true nature of grace. Presupposing his own epistemology, he begins his analysis by trying to uncover the real

---

[2] "Zur scholastischen Begrifflichkeit," *Schriften,* 1: 353.

[3] "Zur scholastischen Begrifflichkeit," *Schriften,* 1: 349–51.

[4] Rahner later found confirmation of the validity of this starting point in the encyclical *Mystici Corporis* of Pius XII; see "Natur und Gnade," *Schriften,* 4: 220. Rahner continued to use this starting point in his future work; see, for example, "Über den Begriff des Geheimnisses," *Schriften,* 4: 84, and *Sacramentum Mundi IV,* 1969 ed., s.v. "Selbstmitteilung Gottes," by Karl Rahner, 522, 524. Translations of articles by Rahner in *Sacramentum Mundi* are by W. O'Hara and come from *Sacramentum Mundi,* 6 vols. (London: Burns and Oates, 1968–1970).

[5] "Zur scholastischen Begrifflichkeit," *Schriften,* 1: 354.

meaning of the Thomistic teaching that in the immediate vision of God, God's essence itself takes the place of the *species impressa* in the created mind. This presupposition is both necessary and problematic. It is necessary because an immediate, nonontological vision of God cannot be based on a created species; such a species would reveal its object—that is, God's infinite being—only in the measure of its own entitative capacity, as a finite determination of the knowing subject. However, the presupposition is also problematic: when it is said that God's own being appears in the place of the created species of the finite mind, this asserts a real "relation" between creature and God that is not founded upon a real, absolute modification of one of the related terms in itself and with regard to itself.

Rahner contends that such a new "relationship" of God to the creature in the beatific vision cannot be brought under the category of efficient causality. It can be explained only through the idea of formal causality. Such formal causality is able to transcribe the concept of supernatural being in its strictly mysterious character, "for all the strictly supernatural realities with which we are acquainted . . . have this in common, that in them there is expressed a relationship of God to a creature which is not one of efficient causality (a production *out* of the cause), and which must consequently fall under the head of formal causality (a taking up *into* the ground)."[6] Such formal causality is also conceptually possible, in the case of the Hypostatic Union for instance, even if it is not known to us in the realm of nature and so cannot be ascertained, as regards its actual realization, without revelation.

In order to draw attention to God's absolute transcendence and immutability, God's formal causality should be prefixed by *quasi*. Thus, in the beatific vision, God's being exercises a *quasi-formal* causality on man.[7] Thus,

---

[6] "Zur scholastischen Begrifflichkeit," *Schriften,* 1: 357–58.

[7] The notion of quasi-formal causality is, as we shall see, a central Rahnerian notion. "Natur und Gnade," *Schriften,* 4: 220–21; "Zur Theologie des Symbols," *Schriften,* 4: 287–88; "Über den Begriff des Geheimnisses," *Schriften,* 4: 90; "Dogmatische Erwägungen über das Wissen und Selbstbewusstsein Christi," *Schriften,* 5: 234; *Sacramentum Mundi II,* 1968 ed., s.v. "Jesus Christus," by Karl Rahner, 942–43; "Christologie im Rahmen des modernen Selbst- und Weltverständnisses," *Schriften,* 9: 237.

in the beatific vision there is present, as its ontological presupposition, a "relation" between creature and God which is not a categorical one, resting upon an accidental absolute modification, but is a quasi-formal causality of God himself upon the created spirit so that the reality of the mind in the beatific vision, so far as such a reality in itself is due to a species as the means of knowledge, is the very being of God.[8]

How this quasi-formal causality functions is seen more clearly in the relationship between God's formal causality on the spirit and the *lumen gloriae*. Within Thomistic thought, the *lumen gloriae* is a *dispositio* of the spirit for the reception of the formal causality of God's intelligible being upon it. In God's immediate conjunction with the spirit, the *lumen gloriae* is described in the category of material causality. It is a *dispositio ultima*.

> Now according to St. Thomas it is the case with a *dispositio ultima* that on the one hand as *causa materialis* it logically precedes the *forma* and yet on the other hand that it depends for its subsistence on the formal causality of the *forma*, so that to affirm its presence is simultaneously to affirm with inner necessity the presence of the formal causality of the *forma* and conversely.[9]

Thus, through quasi-formal causality the beatific vision and the *lumen gloriae* exist in a relation of mutual priority. The beatific vision, as its formal cause, logically precedes the *lumen gloriae,* which as material cause of the beatific vision exists as its necessary presupposition.[10]

In view of the continuum between grace and glory and the ontology of the beatific vision, Rahner now proposes a solution for the relation of created and uncreated grace. The sources of revelation show that we fail to do justice to the essence of uncreated grace if we hold that man has uncreated grace only because he first possesses created grace. This difficulty is overcome by

---

[8] "Zur scholastischen Begrifflichkeit," *Schriften,* 1: 360.

[9] "Zur scholastischen Begrifflichkeit," *Schriften,* 1: 361.

[10] This almost dialectical notion of quasi-formal causality has its roots in Rahner's notion of emanation; see *Geist,* 245, 251, 261–62, 265–66. Carr, *Theological Method of Karl Rahner,* 80, notes this same point. Other commentators criticize the oddity of this quasi-formal causality: Vass, *Mystery of Man,* 87, 109, and C. Ernst, "Some Themes in the Theology of Karl Rahner," *Irish Theological Quarterly* 32 (1965), 256.

saying that "God communicates himself to the man to whom grace has been shown in the mode of *formal* causality, so that this communication is not then merely the consequence of an efficient causation of created grace."[11] Thus, the communication of uncreated grace constitutes a union between God and man by way of formal causality and can be conceived of, under a certain respect, as logically and really prior to created grace. Indeed, it precedes created grace, which, as the ultimate disposition to the union, can exist only when God's formal causality is actually being exercised upon man. Such an explanation does not undermine the teaching of the Council of Trent on the necessity of created grace for Justification, Adoption, and so on, for created grace is seen as the *causa materialis* for the formal causality that God exercises by graciously communicating his own being to the creature. Thus, the teaching of Trent is maintained in that the material and formal causes possess a reciprocal priority. Furthermore, because created grace as *dispositio ultima* can exist only along with the actual formal causality of the form for which it is the *dispositio,* it is correct to say: "If created grace is given, so too necessarily by that very fact uncreated grace, and, hence, the whole grace of justification, is communicated to man."[12] Finally, this ontological union (between God and creature in uncreated grace) by no means indicates a vague unity of nature; on the contrary, as the presupposition of the *visio,* it implies the highest degree of unity in the clearest distinction (although this unity in distinction traditionally is seen as the result of the *visio* itself).

Pursuing these conclusions, Rahner offers an innovative solution to another scholastic problem—namely, the question whether God's indwelling in and conjunction with the justified man is appropriated only to the divine persons or whether through grace there arises a relationship between man and God peculiar to each divine person. In the scholastic view, according to which indwelling is merely a relationship of God to man resting entirely on created grace, this question can be answered only in the sense of mere appropriation. "But if uncreated grace is *not,* ontologically speaking, a pure consequence of created grace as a

[11] "Zur scholastischen Begrifflichkeit," *Schriften,* 1: 362.
[12] "Zur scholastischen Begrifflichkeit," *Schriften,* 1: 370.

qualitative accident, if rather the view proposed here is correct, then the question that has just been put is by no means immediately yet answered."[13] Scripture and the Church Fathers attest that the attribution of determinate relations of the recipient of grace to the three divine persons is not merely a matter of appropriation but is intended to give expression to a proper relationship in each case. Then, defining the "communication of the hypostasis" as a true ontological communication of the hypostasis, Rahner argues:

> If it is true that in the *visio beatifica* that alone can be grasped which really immediately in its very self communicates itself to the knowing mind, in quasi-formal causality after the fashion of a *species impressa,* ontologically prior to knowledge as such, *then* this holds good equally of the three divine persons each in his own personal property. In other words, they are either not beheld immediately as such in the *visio beatifica,* or, in logical priority to the *visio* as a conscious act, they have each, *as* divine, mutually distinct persons, their own proper quasi-formal causality upon the created spirit, a causality which makes it possible for these divine persons to be possessed "consciously" and, what is more, immediately.[14]

Because uncreated grace is given in quasi-formal causality and man's relationship in grace is a nonappropriated relation to the three divine persons, this neither does injury to the principle of the unity of efficient causality in the creative action of the three-fold God *ad extra,* nor does it make the indwelling conjunction of the three divine persons into a hypostatic union.

2. NATURE AND GRACE

Presupposing this understanding of the relationship of uncreated and created grace and of quasi-formal causality, Rahner finally addresses the problem of grace and nature in the strict sense in a number of influential articles written between 1950 and 1960.

---

[13] "Zur scholastischen Begrifflichkeit," *Schriften,* 1: 372. This central Rahnerian assertion is treated in a detailed way in chapter 3.

[14] "Zur Scholastischen Begrifflichkeit," *Schriften,* 1: 373; "Natur und Gnade," *Schriften,* 4: 222–23.

A. Critique of Extrinsicism

In the context of the debate provoked by de Lubac and the so-called *nouvelle theologie* concerning the rediscovered patristic notion of a natural desire for the beatific vision, Rahner repeats much of the criticism leveled at the current "textbook" conception of grace and nature.[15] According to this view, grace often appears as a mere superstructure, imposed on nature by God's free decision in such a way that the relationship between the two is no more intense than noncontradiction, no more than a *potentia oboedientialis* understood purely negatively. Nature acknowledges the end and the means of the supernatural order as, in themselves, its highest goods, but it is not at all clear why it should be much concerned with these goods. "A free being could always reject such a good without thereby having inwardly the experience of losing its end."[16] This is especially the case in the average textbook view, wherein grace remains absolutely beyond consciousness.

Furthermore, according to this textbook view, man can know what *precisely* pure human nature is and how far *precisely* it extends. It is tacitly presupposed that whatever man comes to know, independently of revelation, about himself or in himself belongs to his nature and, therefore, that a sharply circumscribed concept of man's pure nature can be produced out of the anthropology of everyday experience. Man's concrete nature is merely "disturbed" by the purely external decree of God commanding the acceptance of the supernatural.[17] Because original sin and its consequences result in a state of man that ought not to be only because of a divine decree binding from without, man is not even disturbed in the immanent experience of his nature by original sin. "In short, what by himself he experiences of himself here and now he could have in this view also experienced in an order of pure nature."[18]

---

[15] See W. Dych, *Karl Rahner* (London: Geoffrey Chapmann, 1992), 32–48, and S. Duffy, *The Graced Horizon: Nature and Grace in Modern Catholic Thought* (Collegeville, Minn.: Liturgical Press, 1992), 85–114, for the background to this debate on grace and nature. J. Kenny, "Reflections on Human Nature and the Supernatural," *Theological Studies* 14 (1953), 281–84, gives a good summary of the critique leveled against this traditional "textbook" approach.

[16] "Über das Verhältnis von Natur und Gnade," *Schriften,* 1: 324.

[17] "Über das Verhältnis," *Schriften,* 1: 325.

[18] "Über das Verhältnis," *Schriften,* 1: 325–26.

This view, in Rahner's opinion, is indeed open to serious objection. Not only must God's vocation to supernatural communion appear as a disturbance to pure nature, which otherwise acts in its own sphere, but also the theory risks attributing all that man experiences to nature even though all are de facto called to grace and glory. There is no reason to deny that man's ordination to the supernatural can exist even before it is fulfilled in justifying grace. Indeed, what God decrees for man must be *eo ipso* an interior ontological constituent of man's concrete quiddity. For if man's concrete quiddity depends utterly on God, his binding disposition must be *eo ipso* precisely what man *is*, not just a juridical decree of God. Moreover, if God gives man a supernatural end and this end is first *in intentione*, then man *is* always and everywhere inwardly *other* in structure than he would be if he did not have this end.

B. *Critique of the* Nouvelle Theologie

In reaction against this extrinsicism, the circle of theologians identified with the *nouvelle theologie* sought to emphasize the intrinsic desire of man for God and the orientation of nature to grace, for which it was created. According to the anonymous author "D," the inner reference of man to grace is constituent of man's nature in such a way that the latter cannot be conceived without it—that is, as "pure" nature—and that therefore the concept of *"natura pura"* becomes incapable of complete definition.[19]

Rahner disagrees with this view, pointing out that the absolute gratuitousness of grace is and must be the starting point for all Catholic theology. He formulates the issue at stake: "Is it still possible to conceive of grace as gratuitous supposing that the existential, consisting in the inner and unconditional reference to grace and the beatific vision, were a constituent of man's 'nature' in the sense that man as such could not be thought of without it?"[20] This reference to the beatific vision is regarded in the *nou-*

---

[19] "D" was the anonymous author of an article that Rahner takes as representative of the school of the *nouvelle theologie;* see [D.], "Ein Weg zur Bestimmung des Verhältnisses von Natur und Gnade," *Orientierung* 14 (1950), 138–41.

[20] "Über das Verhältnis," *Schriften,* 1: 330. The preservation of the absolute gratuity of grace is one of Rahner's central concerns; see, for example, *Hörer 1,*

velle theologie as such an intrinsic constituent of man's nature that the withholding of the end of this directedness is incompatible with God's wisdom and goodness, and, in this sense, the end is unconditional. On these presuppositions, grace and the beatific vision in fact no longer can be said to be gratuitous. The precise point at issue is: grace is not gratuitous just for an imagined or hypothetical man, but also for man who is *already actually in existence*. This point is significant, for it would appear that the proponents of the *nouvelle theologie*, albeit unwittingly, go no further than the assertion of the gratuity proper to creation, distinguishing grace from other created things only in respect of the greatness of the gift, not in respect of the gratuity itself. For a less than personal entity, they argue, it is surely true that unconditional reference to an end and the gratuity of this end are incompatible assumptions. But is this equally true, they ask, when a personal being is in question? Is it not precisely the essence of a personal being that he is ordained to personal communion with God in love and must receive just this love as free gift? The example, replies Rahner, lacks cogency:

> Can that person, who has *himself created* such an ordination to the personal and intimate communion of love between two persons (in our case man and God), once this has been presupposed, still simultaneously refuse this communion without offending against the meaning of this creation and his very creative act itself? The question, however, is to be answered in the negative. For, if the ordination cannot be detached from the nature, then the fulfillment of the ordination, precisely from God's point of view, is owed. And as all admit, just this is false. [21]

C. The "Supernatural Existential"

Having, then, rejected both the extrinsicism of the scholastic theory of grace and also the unconditional reference of nature to grace proposed in the *nouvelle theologie,* Rahner proposes his own tentative solution to the problem.

100, 103, 112; *Sacramentum Mundi IV,* 1969 ed., s.v. "Trinität," by Karl Rahner, 1014; "Fragen der Kontroverstheologie über die Rechtfertigung," *Schriften,* 4: 250, 264–65; "Natur und Gnade," *Schriften,* 4: 234; "Glaubensakt und Glaubensinhalt," *Schriften,* 15: 157.

[21] "Über das Verhältnis," *Schriften,* 1: 332.

First, man must be *able* to receive this love that is God; he must have a congeniality for it. Thus, he must have a real "potency" for it, and he must have this *always*. As he in fact is, he is created for it; he is called into being so that Love might bestow itself. To this extent, this "potency" is what is inmost and most authentic in him. "The capacity for the God of self-bestowing personal Love is the central and abiding existential of man as he really is."[22]

Second, the real man as God's real partner should be able to receive this love as what it necessarily is: a free gift. The central, abiding existential, consisting in the ordination to the threefold God of grace, must itself be gratuitous; that is, it must be a *supernatural existential*,[23] for the existential for supernatural grace (which consists of a longing for and an ordination to God's love) allows grace to be gratuitous only when it itself is gratuitous. "Were he simply this existential and were this his nature, then it would be unconditional in its essence, i.e. once it had been given, the love which is God would 'have to' be offered by God."[24]

Third, the man who receives the love of God in supernatural grace is able, in the light of revelation, to recognize the very existential for this love as un-owed to him, the real man. It is *this* knowledge, derived from revelation, that allows him to distinguish and delimit what he always is (that is, his concrete indissoluble quiddity) into what is this gratuitous real receptivity, this supernatural existential, and into what is left over as remainder when this innermost center is subtracted from the substance of his concrete quiddity, his nature.

> "Nature" in the theological sense (as opposed to nature as the substantial content of an entity always to be encountered in contingent fact), i.e., as the concept contraposed to the supernatural, is consequently a remainder concept [*Restbegriff*].[25]

But this "pure" nature, in spite of the fact that its possible existence must be affirmed, is not an unambiguously delimitable, de-

---

[22] "Über das Verhältnis," *Schriften,* 1: 338–39.

[23] K. Eberhard, "Karl Rahner and the Supernatural Existential," *Thought* 46 (1971): 537–61, provides an excellent critical study of Rahner's theory of the supernatural existential. See also Vass, *Mystery of Man,* 64–83, for a summary of Rahner's theory and the criticisms made of it.

[24] "Über das Verhältnis," *Schriften,* 1: 340.

[25] "Über das Verhältnis," *Schriften,* 1: 340.

finable quantity.[26] Given that all men in the concrete order of existence live under the influence of the supernatural existential, no clear and absolute distinction can be made between this nature and the supernatural. The philosophical concept of man will not coincide simply with the content of the theological concept of man's pure nature, for the philosophical concept of man will in all probability contain more—that is, some elements of the supernatural, although not recognized as such. This lack of clarity concerning the "pure nature" is only to be expected because man can analyze himself only within the region of God's supernatural loving will. Man can never find his nature in a "chemically" pure state, separated from its supernatural existential.

> Nature in this sense continues to be a remainder concept, but a necessary and objectively justified one, if one wishes to achieve reflexive consciousness of that gratuitousness of grace which goes together with man's inner, unconditional ordination to it. Then in fact this unconditional ordination must itself be grasped as gratuitous and supernatural.[27]

Having defined pure nature as a *Restbegriff* and insisted on its necessity to safeguard the gratuity of grace, Rahner attempts to fill out its definition. The spiritual nature is of its essence an unlimited dynamism, an openness for all being, an openness that must include an openness for the supernatural without thereby of itself demanding fulfillment in the supernatural unconditionally.[28] This openness is not a mere nonrepugnance. It is an inner ordination, provided only that it is not unconditional. As such, it is defined as a *"potentia oboedientialis"* for divine self-communication. To prevent identifying this unlimited dynamism of the *spiritual nature* with that dynamism that we experience in our concrete spiritual existence, in which the supernatural existential may be at work already, Rahner postulates a natural end for man.[29]

---

[26] "Über das Verhältnis," *Schriften*, 1: 341; "Fragen der Kontroverstheologie," *Schriften*, 4: 269–70; "Natur und Gnade," *Schriften*, 4: 231, 235; "Probleme der Christologie von Heute," *Schriften*, 1: 204; "Zur Theologie der Menschwerdung," *Schriften*, 4: 140.

[27] "Über das Verhältnis," *Schriften*, 1: 341–42.

[28] Human nature as dynamism is based, of course, on Rahner's earlier metaphysical understanding of man as spirit in the world; see *Geist*, 263, 265–66, 285; *Hörer 1*, 89, 101.

[29] *Hörer 1*, 24, 100, 224; "Natur und Gnade," *Schriften*, 4: 234; "Die Freiheit in der Kirche," *Schriften*, 2: 100.

There is no reason why it [the natural spiritual dynamism] could not retain its meaning and necessity even without grace if, on the one hand, one can learn to see it as the indispensable transcendental condition of the possibility of a spiritual life at all, and, on the other hand, this spiritual life, although in comparison with the beatific vision it remains eternally *in umbris et imaginibus,* can at any rate be shown to be neither meaningless nor harsh but can always be seen as a positive, though finite good which God could bestow even when he has not called man immediately before his face.[30]

Here the natural end at first appears to be a static natural good that might terminate a natural dynamism. But immediately thereafter Rahner notes that even according to the *nouvelle theologie* the pure philosophy of man's nature is not capable of discerning the possibility of a *visio beatifica.* Even the exponents of this theory "must hold that a spiritual life toward God as an end approached merely asymptotically is not to be dismissed as meaningless from the start."[31] Here it seems that man's natural dynamism has meaning even without attaining fulfillment in an end or in a fulfilling good. So Rahner leaves ambiguous the understanding of a natural end: Is it a good that terminates a natural dynamism, or is the perpetuation of the dynamism itself the finite good? Either choice seems to involve difficulties. Understanding the natural end as a terminating good limits man's intellectual dynamism to something finite, a position contradicting Rahner's understanding of man in *Geist* as unlimited openness or openness for all of being. Yet to understand perpetual progress in approximation to an always outstanding goal condemns nature as such to frustration. To be naturally oriented to an unattainable goal perverts the notion of nature by divorcing nature from its end. Upon such a deluding nature no such consistent metaphysical argument can be constructed. Yet Rahner may be seeking to uphold these tensions by use of his dialectical analogy. Insofar as nature can be conceptualized—that is, grasped in a finite concept—its orientation is toward a finite natural end such as traditional scholasticism postulated. But insofar as man is understood dynamically, he transcends all limitation. By changing perspectives insofar as the dynamic orientation can be

---

[30] "Über das Verhältnis," *Schriften,* 1: 342–43.
[31] "Über das Verhältnis," *Schriften,* 1: 343.

expressed in the concept of being and insofar as concepts can be transposed to a dynamic scheme of interpretation, Rahner can hold that the "remainder concept" allows a finite goal while the dynamism prevents nature from being closed in upon itself. Neither perspective should be absolutized. The proper response to the nature-grace relation consists in the oscillation between both perspectives.

D. Grace and Revelation

In another major article, written in 1960, Rahner returned to the grace-nature problem,[32] repeating much of his earlier thought but also developing a clearer understanding of the operation of the supernatural existential through which man's natural spiritual transcendence receives a new supernatural a priori formal end. All men in the concrete order of existence live and act, he holds, within a supernatural horizon of which they are unthematically conscious even before any thematic act of justifying faith that finds its subsequent expression in the Gospel message. Here Rahner's thought begins to undergo that change of emphasis toward the priority of transcendental grace that will become increasingly marked later on and that will provide the foundations for his theory of the "anonymous Christian."

Having summarized his earlier thought on the relation of un-created and created grace, and having drawn out the trinitarian consequences of this new understanding, Rahner returns to the Thomistic doctrine of the specific object of the act entitatively elevated to the supernatural, an object that cannot be attained formally by any natural act. In such a context, *object* does not mean "something present like other objects, distinguishable from them and placed beside them by reflection." A formal object is rather the a priori horizon given in consciousness, under which, in grasping the individual a posteriori object, everything is known that is grasped as an object strictly speaking. Now the formal end of the man in the theoretical state of pure nature—that is, the a priori horizon under which everything is grasped and known— would be the horizon of all being (or *esse commune* in *Geist*), the

---

[32] "Natur und Gnade," *Schriften*, 4: 209–336.

term of man's natural dynamic transcendence.[33] However, through the supernatural existential, the spirit's natural transcendence to all being becomes supernaturally elevated toward the God of eternal life (*esse absolutum* in *Geist*).[34] Through this supernatural elevation, *esse absolutum*, or God himself, constitutes the "new" a priori horizon under which man's acts receive a "new" formal supernatural end to which he is oriented dynamically.[35] Because in the concrete order all men in fact have been called by God to a supernatural destiny (and man in "pure nature" does not exist, nor ever has existed), they always and originally exist under the influence of this supernatural elevation. This is precisely what Rahner means by human nature's "supernatural existential." It orients man to the reception of "strictly supernatural grace," so man experiences it not as a datum of knowledge or as an abstract and merely consequent summing up of what is common to many individual objects, but as the a priori horizon, given in consciousness, under which everything is grasped as an object.[36] It follows that the communication of grace (the divine *pneuma*) to man is not just a transconscious entitative elevation of the conscious moral acts of man. On the contrary, grace affects man's conscious life, not just his being but his very existence.[37]

---

[33] *Geist*, 190, 208, 210, 215. See chapter 1, notes 72 and 73, for the distinctions Rahner makes concerning the term of human transcendence.

[34] *Geist*, 190.

[35] "Zum theologischen Begriff der Konkupiszenz," *Schriften*, 1: 408; "Natur und Gnade," *Schriften*, 4: 224–25; "Glaube und Sakrament," *Schriften*, 16: 391; "Glaubensakt und Glaubensinhalt," *Schriften*, 15: 157; K. Rahner, *Das Dynamische in der Kirche*, Quaestiones Disputatae no. 5 (Freiburg, Basel, Vienna: Herder, 1958), 108–9 (translations from *The Dynamic Element in the Church*, translated by W. O'Hara [London: Burns and Oates, 1964]); "Das neue Bild der Kirche," *Schriften*, 8: 346–47; "Zur Frage der Dogmenentwicklung," *Schriften*, 1: 62–63; "Einige Bemerkungen zu einer neuen Aufgabe der Fundamentaltheologie," *Schriften*, 1: 209.

[36] "Natur und Gnade," *Schriften*, 1: 224–25.

[37] Man can experience grace consciously: "Natur und Gnade," *Schriften*, 4: 224, 230; "Zum theologischen Begriff der Konkupiszenz," *Schriften*, 1: 408–9; "Über die Erfarung der Gnade," *Schriften*, 3: 108; "Glaube und Sakrament," *Schriften*, 16: 391; "Glaubensakt und Glaubensinhalt," *Schriften*, 15: 155–56; "Über den Begriff des Geheimnisses," *Schriften*, 4: 84; *Das Dynamische in der Kirche*, 108–9; "Kirche, Kirchen, und Religionen," *Schriften*, 8: 359–66; "Zur Frage der Dogmenentwicklung," *Schriften*, 1: 62; "Überlegungen zur Dogmenentwicklung," *Schriften*, 4: 24; "Zum heutigen Verhältnis von Philosophie und Theologie," *Schriften*, 10: 72; "Einige Bemerkungen," *Schriften*, 12: 209; "Theologie und Anthropologie," *Schriften*, 8: 60.

Acts inspired supernaturally by grace consequently are not confined to the justified. In the concrete existential order, the entitative spiritual life of man is lived out in the realm of the salvific will of God, of his prevenient grace, or, in other words, under the influence of the supernatural existential.[38] Man lives always and consciously in the presence of God, even when he does not "know" it thematically and does not consciously believe it. "God is the unexpressed but real 'whither' of the dynamism of all spiritual and moral life in the realm of spiritual existence which is in fact founded, that is supernaturally elevated, by God."[39] It follows, then, that even outside the process of official revelation, the history of human religion is a product not merely of natural reason and sin, but also and more profoundly of the natural spirit and grace. Thus, when an individual is summoned by the message of faith from the visible church, it is not the first time that he comes into spiritual contact with the reality preached by the church: such conceptual knowledge is not primary. "The call only makes him consciously aware of—and of course forces him to make a choice about—the grace which already encompassed him inarticulately but really as an element of his spiritual existence."[40] The

---

[38] That man originally and always lives under grace through the influence of the supernatural existential is another central Rahnerian affirmation; see "Zum theologischen Begriff der Konkupiszenz," *Schriften*, 1: 408; "Über das Verhältnis," *Schriften*, 1: 338–39; "Fragen der Kontroverstheologie," *Schriften*, 4: 250, 270–71; "Natur und Gnade," *Schriften*, 4: 227; "Überlegungen zum personalen Vollzug des Sakramentalen Geschens," *Schriften*, 10: 410, 413–14, 426; "Glaube und Sakrament," *Schriften*, 16: 391; *Sacramentum Mundi III*, 1969 ed., s.v. "Offenbarung," by K. Rahner, 834; K. Rahner and J. Ratzinger, *Offenbarung und Überlieferung*, Quaestiones Disputatae no. 25, (Freiburg, Basel, Vienna: Herder, 1965), 15 (translations from *Revelation and Tradition*, translated by W. O'Hara [London: Burns and Oates, 1966]); "Zur 'Offenbarungsgeschichte' nach dem II. Vaticanum," *Schriften*, 12: 243; "Glaubensakt und Glaubensinhalt," *Schriften*, 15: 156; "Christologie im Rahmen," *Schriften*, 9: 238; K. Rahner and W. Thüsing, *Christologie—Systematisch und Exegetisch*, Quaestiones Disputatae no. 55 (Freiburg, Basel, Vienna: Herder, 1972), 59; "Kirche, Kirchen und Religionen," *Schriften*, 8: 359–60; "Was ist Häresie?" *Schriften*, 5: 528; "Zur Geschichtlichkeit der Theologie," *Schriften*, 8: 100.

[39] "Natur und Gnade," *Schriften*, 4: 228

[40] "Natur und Gnade," *Schriften*, 4: 228–29. It is this element in Rahner's theory of the supernatural existential that has provoked much criticism. See, for example, Carr, *Theological Method of Karl Rahner*, 260–62; Vass, *Mystery of Man*, 75–76; Molnar, "Is God Essentially Different?" 588; J. Ratzinger, "Vom Verstehen des Glaubens: Anmerkungen zu Rahners *Grundkurs des Glaubens*," *Theo-*

preaching expressly awakens what is already present in the depths of man's being, not by nature but by grace. Grace always surrounds man, even the sinner and the unbeliever, as the inescapable setting of his existence.

Here Rahner again insists on the concept of a pure nature that theoretically would exist with its own natural end even if the supernatural existential were removed. The fact that man is conscious of his nature only as already supernaturally elevated by grace does not thereby signify that he is now in the concrete order completely ignorant of what his nature is,[41] for the nature of a spiritual being and the nature of its supernatural elevation are not opposed to each other like two things that lie side by side so that they must be kept either separate or confused. Rather, the real "definition" of man's nature is a *potentia oboedientialis* for divine grace, such that he must look to grace for its *absolute* fulfillment yet must reckon with a *nonfrustrating* absence of such an absolute fulfillment. To be ordained to grace *(Hingeordnetheit auf die Gnade)* and to be so constituted that there is an exigency for grace *(exigitive Ausgerichtetheit),* which would render the whole ordination to grace futile if grace were not actually imparted, are by no means the same thing.[42]

---

logische Revue 74 (1978), 183–84. All of these commentators argue that the supernatural existential theory relativizes the unicity of Christ and the importance of explicit Christianity. For a defense of Rahner's theory against these charges, see K. Weger, "Das 'anonyme' Christentum in der heutigen Theologie," *Stimmen der Zeit* 194 (1976), 328–32.

[41] Some of Rahner's commentators have noted his insistence on the preservation of the grace-nature distinction: Carr, *Theological Method of Karl Rahner,* 200–201, 261; Eberhard, "Karl Rahner and the Supernatural Existential," 538–41; McCool, "The Philosophy of the Human Person," 548–49; Weger, "Das 'anonyme' Christentum," 327. However, it must be noted that when some commentators pay insufficient attention to the dialectical subtlety of Rahner's theology, they are led to interpret him only in terms of the dynamic, unifying side of his thought and therefore also to blur, or even to abolish, the grace-nature distinction: Allik, "Karl Rahner on Materiality," 380–86, esp. 385 n. 31; Buckley, "Within the Holy Mystery," in O'Donovan, ed., *A World of Grace,* 34–39, 45; T. O'Meara, "A History of Grace," in O'Donovan, ed., *A World of Grace,* 82; O. Hentz, "Anticipating Jesus Christ: An Account of Our Hope," in O'Donovan, ed., *A World of Grace,* 111, 115.

[42] "Natur und Gnade," *Schriften,* 4: 234. The grounding for this verbal distinction is, of course, far from transparently clear, but it links up with Rahner's earlier notion of the goal of the created spirit as a "roaming through the finite to greet the infinite from afar" (*Hörer 1,* 100).

This supposition arises from the absolute (not infinite) value and validity of every personal act in itself. If it be granted, it follows that there can be no spirit without a transcendence open to the supernatural; but spirit is meaningful without supernatural grace. Hence, its fulfillment in grace cannot be determined by its essence, though it is open for such grace.[43]

Rahner's continued insistence on the concept of pure nature and its possible natural end, even within his more dynamic and unifying view of nature and the supernatural existential, is significant. It constitutes another example of that oscillating structure of thought that we have observed already and through which he attempts to hold together important dialectical distinctions within an existentially unified worldview. A notable instance of this typically Rahnerian thought process is found in his treatment of the nature-grace problem within the Scotist perspective on the incarnation and grace, a perspective Rahner definitively adopts in the 1950s.[44]

3. THE SCOTIST PERSPECTIVE

Turning his attention to the relation between the incarnation and the order of grace, Rahner calls into question the traditional scholastic presupposition that the connection between the two was merely de facto—that although God *had* in fact decreed that the order of grace should depend on the incarnate Word, things *might* have been quite otherwise. He argues for a readoption of the "Scotist" perspective on the creation and the incarnation. Nothing in the principles of Catholic theology prevents taking the Scotist point of view, which considers the primal act of God as his self-exteriorization in the incarnation, in which everything else is in fact given. Even though the fact of creation (as nature) does not necessarily imply the actual realization of the self-exteriorization of God in the incarnation, the possibility of creation can rest

---

[43] "Natur und Gnade," *Schriften,* 4: 234.

[44] "Probleme der Christologie," *Schriften,* 1: 185; *Sendung und Gnade,* 62–63; "Die Christologie innerhalb einer evolutiven Weltanschauung," *Schriften,* 5: 185.

on the possibility of the incarnation.[45] This perspective allows a deeper understanding of the immanent Trinity and ascribes to grace a much more radically Christological character. The Logos, who has become part of the world, is not merely the de facto mediator of grace by his merit—which became necessary only because Adam had cast this grace away—but is also the person who by his free incarnation creates the whole order of grace and nature as his own presupposition.

Rahner examines the implications of the Scotist perspective in greater detail in the context of a review[46] of Hans Küng's book *Rechtfertigung*.[47] In this book, Küng expounds the thesis that the actual order of creation (of man and the world) is so founded on Christ that the world even in its natural state is in fact everywhere and always a Christian thing, even though it would be possible to some extent theoretically to "prescind" from this view and imagine another world without Christ. Hence, all sin is against Christ, and the conservation of the natural state of man as something capable of salvation is already the grace of Christ. The "nature" of man that is still present and capable of salvation in the sinner is not the *remnant* that survives unharmed in sin, but the beginning of salvation constantly renewed by God's goodness in Christ, which opposes sin and its universally destructive tendency. This new beginning stems from the unrepentant loyalty of God toward his covenant, which has ordained all creation from the start to his absolute "yes" in Christ. This eternal affirmation upholds everything and can sustain eternally even a given temporal event, as when it envisages the temporal and spatial determinations of the eternal Logos in the flesh. It follows, for Küng, that free will, insofar as it survives after sin, is not merely a natural, neutral good (lacking only what it should have, its supernatural elevation), but actually a grace of Christ. It remains only because God's merciful loyalty to his covenant in Christ continues to preserve it.

---

[45] "Natur und Gnade," *Schriften*, 4: 222; "Fragen der Kontroverstheologie," *Schriften*, 4: 266; "Probleme der Christologie," *Schriften*, 1: 185, 205; *Sendung und Gnade*, 55, 63; "Die Christologie innerhalb einer evolutiven Weltanschauung," *Schriften*, 5: 201, 215; *Sacramentum Mundi IV*, s.v. "Selbstmitteilung Gottes," 523–24; "Buch Gottes—Buch der Menschen," *Schriften*, 16: 279.

[46] "Fragen der Kontroverstheologie," *Schriften*, 4: 237–71.

[47] H. Küng, *Rechtfertigung: Die Lehre Karl Barths und eine katholische Besinnung* (Einsiedeln: Benziger, 1957).

Rahner argues that we can say at once that the creation of nature takes place in Christ because "the first primal and comprehensively eternal will of God is his own self-expression, through which the Logos of God comes to exist in the emptiness of the nondivine, and that in *this* act of will, God wills the humanity of Christ and hence creation in general as its setting."[48] Likewise, the de facto creation takes place as the presupposition that God creates simply because he decrees to have a history of love giving itself—a covenant. Hence, in this eternal decree, he wills the natural creation as it actually is; once it exists by virtue of *this* will, it can never be excluded from this covenanting will of God. Finally, sin denounces and destroys the covenant with God, so far as it can, and it contradicts what upholds the natural creation in the existing order of things.

However, this original, eternal will of God, intent on his supernatural self-communication, must bring about a distinction within the structure of the creature that will enable it to receive this divine self-communication for what it is—namely, gratuitous. "God can only impart himself, and will to impart himself, by creating something for whose very existence this communication is pure grace."[49] God owes it to the sheer sovereignty of his love *not* to make the creature itself the presupposition of this act of personal love, except in such a way that even when created and instituted it must receive as free grace that for which it was created. Therefore, the creation could have been created without this communication.

Within this perspective, the very existence of the creature after sin as something that can be saved must itself be a grace owing to God's decree to impart himself, to uphold his covenant, to be incarnate in Christ. In the actual order of things, this is true even with regard to man's continued existence. But "this 'grace,' whereby this nature continues to exist on account of grace, is not simply the same grace as the divine self-communication itself."[50] Before and after sin, there is the same discrepancy between the

---

[48] "Fragen der Kontroverstheologie," *Schriften,* 4: 266. This notion of Logos coming to exist in the "emptiness" of the nondivine interestingly seems to imply a notion of formal causality in which God becomes the form of the void.

[49] "Fragen der Kontroverstheologie," *Schriften,* 4: 267.

[50] "Fragen der Kontroverstheologie," *Schriften,* 4: 268.

two graces as between natural creation and God's self-communication to it, as between nature and supernatural grace, as between
creation and covenant. This is perhaps seen most clearly insofar as
the "grace" of the conservation of the natural man in and in spite
of sin remains ambiguous in itself and for us. We can never know
whether the sparing and the preservation of the sinner is for judgment or for a new salvation, whether we use it aright or pervert
it by sin.

> If this split did not exist within the one concrete human being, if
> even "in Christ" our nature was not still ambivalent—as real grace
> never is—it would be incomprehensible that creation could really
> *not* believe and that unbelief could be more than really appar-
> ent—or ultimately quite harmless.[51]

A subject whose being or nature were grace would be, even as a
subject, the pure affirmation of God and would be able do nothing else but ratify the affirmation of God in Christ: he would
have to believe. Because the subject is real and therefore very
"objective," there would be no difference at all between objective and subjective redemption, no possible contrast between the
two dimensions that would be more than apparent, without this
objective inclination in human nature. "Not only are there grades
of being in Christ, there are also essential graduations in the gratuitousness of grace itself."[52] An example of the first would be the
permanence of free will in the sinner. It can be called a "grace"
in Christ because it is willed and preserved *by reason of* the divine
decree with regard to God's self-communication in Christ and
with regard to the forgiveness of sins that is already predefined in
that decree. Thus, free will in itself, even in the present order of
things, is a "grace" of creation, but not in itself a grace of Christ.
An example of the second case would be the communication of
the Holy Spirit, which is grace in the strictest sense. If the higher
makes the lower its presupposition as the condition of its own
possibility, the lower does not thereby cease to be lower than the
higher. "The grace of the strictly supernatural procures for itself
the grace of creation as its own presupposition on a lower level,

---

[51] "Fragen der Kontroverstheologie," *Schriften,* 4: 268.
[52] "Fragen der Kontroverstheologie," *Schriften,* 4: 268.

maintains and animates it by virtue of the stronger will of God with regard to the higher grace: but it still leaves it as the lower grace."[53]

For this reason, the church, when speaking of justification, does *not* use the word *grace* to designate the human nature that survives in sin. Everything exists in Christ, but there are degrees in this "everything." The lower degree has its existence only in Christ; the higher degree consists essentially of the self-communication of God in Christ. Both imply fundamentally an essential difference from merely "having existence," even though mere "existence" is given in the actual order of things only because originally God decreed to impart himself.

As evidence of gradated grace, Rahner appeals to the scholastic concept of "medicinal" or "healing" grace, which is "entitatively natural" yet modally supernatural *quoad fontem et finem* because God gives it to sinners for the sake of Christ and in view of man's supernatural end. This classic distinction finds its profoundest justification within the Scotist perspective developed by Küng. As Rahner puts it,

> Since everything is created in Christ and for him, and since from the start "nature" is always and irrevocably conceived by God as the presupposed condition of possibility of grace strictly speaking, nature itself cannot be entitatively supernatural grace. But it is *always* and *necessarily* endowed with a supernatural finality in its existence. . . . It is modally supernatural. The unity *and* difference of nature and (entitatively supernatural) grace, precisely from the point of view of gratuitousness, result from the same principle. Hence, nature is not simply and nondialectically nongrace . . . it is not the substructure which could exist even without the superstructure, but the lower, which though the presupposition of the higher still depends on the higher because in the last resort all depends on the highest—who freely willed to be the love that imparts itself.[54]

It is clear that in insisting on the distinction between the "grace of creation" and "strictly supernatural grace," Rahner is preserving the double gratuity of grace and nature even within this Sco-

---

[53] "Fragen der Kontroverstheologie," *Schriften,* 4: 269.
[54] "Fragen der Kontroverstheologie," *Schriften,* 4: 270–71.

tist perspective. In doing so, he is allowing for human freedom and the possibility of the rejection of the offer of "strictly supernatural grace" in a world called and preserved through the "grace of creation." However, it would seem that Rahner's perspective here has changed slightly from his earlier notion of the supernatural existential. The supernatural existential previously was not to be associated with "strictly supernatural grace," whereas in this perspective neither is it to be thought of as given in the "grace of creation." Either perspective seems to create problems. If the supernatural existential were given with the "grace of creation," it would imply that nature itself has an unconditional ordination to the supernatural. If it were "strictly supernatural grace," it would imply that all men always possess uncreated grace as an a priori of their human nature, which would therefore infringe human freedom.

It would seem within this perspective that there exists a threefold structure of graced creation, all given in view of the incarnation. First, man is created as a dynamic natural openness to all being. As such, he is dynamically open to the supernatural and finds in God, and ultimately in Christ, his absolute fulfillment. However, this fulfillment is not owed to him, and he apparently can find fulfillment in a lesser natural good. This is the "grace of creation." Second, man is endowed originally and always with a "supernatural existential" that elevates his natural dynamic transcendence, unconditionally orienting him toward God. This is not a "grace of creation," but neither is it apparently "strictly supernatural grace." Finally, man is offered "strictly supernatural grace," traditionally called "uncreated grace," which is the indwelling of the Holy Spirit, the self-communication of God himself.

4. Conclusion

With this admittedly ingenious theory, Rahner sought to overcome many of the problems that bedeviled preconciliar debate over grace and nature. However, his theory is itself not completely free of tensions.

First, there seems to be within Rahner's thought a double no-

tion of nature.[55] On the one hand, in order to preserve the gratuity of grace against the assertions of the *nouvelle theologie* and in
line with the conceptualizing and distinguishing side of his
thought, he insists on the concept of pure nature, defining it
rather statically as a "remainder concept."[56] Yet he simultaneously
affirms that this "remainder concept" cannot be defined, a strange
affirmation indeed to make about a concept (but nevertheless
consistent with his original oscillating concept of being). On the
other hand, against the extrinsicism of the Scholastics and in line
with the dynamic, unifying side of his thought, Rahner also defines human nature as pure transcendence to all being, as an active
potentia oboedientialis that must look to supernatural grace for its
absolute fulfillment but must reckon with a nonfrustrating absence of such fulfillment. To this end, Rahner insists that to be
ordained to grace *(Hingeordnetheit auf die Gnade)* and to be so constituted that there is an exigency for grace *(exigitive Ausgerichtetheit),* which would render the whole ordination to grace futile if
grace were not actually imparted, are by no means the same
thing.[57] Yet the grounds for this insistence are anything but transparently clear. Furthermore, Rahner seems unable to define the
natural end of this dynamic human nature. What is the goal of
man's natural dynamism? Is it some natural good, something that
man rests in, or is the perpetual asymptotic transcendence toward
the goal itself a goal?

Second, Rahner's innovative notion of the supernatural existential is also somewhat problematic. It does not seem by any
means clear what precisely this supernatural existential is and how
it can be distinguished from nature as such. If, as Rahner argues,
nature is to be defined as natural dynamic transcendence to all
being, then this open transcendence must include, as he admits, a
dynamic openness to the supernatural and to God. And if this is
so, it is difficult to see why such a nature would need a supernatu-

---

[55] Vass, *Mystery of Man,* 32–33, 52, notes this double notion of nature in relation to Rahner's definition of *person.*

[56] This "static" concept of nature, which I have noted already, is seen very
clearly in one of Rahner's early articles considering the nature of concupiscence,
where nature is contrasted with person as that which is impenetrable and unillu-
minated, offering resistance to the person's free and total disposition of himself:
"Zum theologischen Begriff der Konkupiszenz," *Schriften,* 1: 390–400.

[57] "Natur und Gnade," *Schriften,* 4: 234.

ral existential in order to orient it to God.[58] How, indeed, according to Rahner's own definitions, it would be possible to distinguish the dynamic openness of nature and the dynamic orientation of the supernatural existential is far from transparently clear. It is also not immediately clear what the distinction is between the "grace" of the supernatural existential and what Rahner calls "strictly supernatural grace,"[59] for if we apply the conclusions of Rahner's early ontology of grace to his theory of the supernatural existential, we reach some apparently surprising conclusions. According to Rahner, every man in concrete existence lives under the influence of the supernatural existential. This existential, which elevates man's natural transcendence, giving it a new supernatural end, is itself gratuitous; that is, it is the result of grace. Yet in Rahner's ontology of grace, uncreated grace through quasi-formal causality effects created grace in the created spirit. The two types of grace exist in mutual priority to the extent that where one is given, so too necessarily is the other. Therefore, every individual who lives under the influence of the supernatural existential—that is, every individual who exists—by virtue of this supernatural existential possesses, at least as an offer, originally and always (albeit gratuitously) not just created grace but also uncreated grace and hence the whole grace of justification.

Third, if all men originally and always possess this supernatural existential and the uncreated grace that causes it through quasi-formal causality, then it is difficult to see how man remains in any real sense free, especially if it is God who through the offer of grace effects its acceptance.[60] And if man already and always has

---

[58] Vass, *Mystery of Man,* 75, actually asserts that Rahner's dynamic nature is not essentially different from that proposed by the *nouvelle theologie.* I would maintain, of course, that what is involved here is nothing other than a characteristic Rahnerian switching of perspectives consistent with his foundational structure of thought as dialectical analogy.

[59] Both Carr, *Theological Method of Karl Rahner,* 201, and L. Roberts, *The Achievement of Karl Rahner* (New York: Herder, 1967), 137, argue that the supernatural existential must be identified with supernatural grace. Eberhard, "Karl Rahner and the Supernatural Existential," insists that it cannot be so identified.

[60] That grace effects its own acceptance is another major Rahnerian affirmation: "Wort und Eucharistie," *Schriften,* 4: 318, 323; "Fragen der Kontroverstheologie," *Schriften,* 4: 251, 257; "Natur und Gnade," *Schriften,* 4: 226–27; "Gerecht und Sünder zugleich," *Schriften,* 6: 273–74; "Überlegungen zum personalen Vollzug," *Schriften,* 10: 421; *Sacramentum Mundi III,* s.v. "Offenbarung,"

an experience of grace, which involves a conscious experience of God in his innermost threefold reality and therefore is termed revelation, expressed categorically throughout human history, it is difficult to see why he needs the evangelical proclamation of the Gospel by the church, other than as a mere explicitization of what he already and originally is and experiences. To these problems, however, we will have to return in a later chapter.

837, 841; Rahner and Ratzinger, *Offenbarung und Überlieferung,* 19, 23; "Über den Begriff des Geheimnisses," *Schriften,* 4: 54, 65; " 'Ich glaube an Jesus Christus,' " *Schriften,* 8: 215–16; "Christologie im Rahmen," *Schriften,* 9: 204–5; "Zur Frage der Dogmenentwicklung," *Schriften,* 1: 62; *Mysterium Salutis I,* 1965 ed., s.v. "Kerygma und Dogma," by K. Rahner and K. Lehmann, 635; *Sendung und Gnade,* 118; "Der eine Jesus Christus und die Universalität des Heils," *Schriften,* 12: 260. Vass, *Theologian in Search of a Philosophy,* 89–92, and *Mystery of Man,* 155, notes the implications of this theory of grace for human freedom, arguing that despite Rahner's protestations to the contrary, his understanding of man's graced state of existence does not seem to leave room for the absolute contradiction of atheism.

3

The Trinity

As DISCUSSED in the previous chapter on his theology of grace, Rahner asserts that in describing the self-communication of God to the soul, the axiom that all works of the Trinity *ad extra* are common to the three persons of the Trinity need no longer apply to the workings of grace. The soul's knowledge of God possesses a mysterious knowledge of the three persons in relation to itself, for they affect the soul in a manner transcending efficient causality. Thus, appeal can be made to man's experience of grace in order to explain the distinctions of the three divine persons as modes of the one divine mystery. We experience God in history as he really is—Father, Son, and Spirit—and the identity of the economic and immanent Trinity can be affirmed. This affirmation became the foundational axiom for Rahner's trinitarian theology and has become dominant in Catholic trinitarian theology ever since.

In this chapter, we will again observe the dialectical structure of Rahner's thought in his systematic treatment of the Trinity, noting how he tries to emphasize the dynamic unity of the economic and immanent Trinity, without thereby sacrificing the important distinction between them and between God and the world. I first examine the grounds he gives for his foundational trinitarian axiom, then its consequences for the methodology of trinitarian theology, especially for the use of the concept "person," before finally looking at his developed understanding of the Trinity.

1. "THE ECONOMIC TRINITY *Is* THE IMMANENT TRINITY"

In a number of articles dating from the 1960s, Rahner attempts to give a systematic treatment of the Trinity as such. Noting the lack of momentum toward future development regarding this dogma, he suggests that the ground for such apparent lack of interest in the Trinity is that most normal Christians are in praxis almost Unitarians.[1] If the doctrine of the Trinity were to be dropped, very little in the life of the church would change or have to change. The doctrine of the Trinity, in other words, has drifted into a state of isolation with regard to the rest of Christian theology. This isolation is rendered legitimate because the outward divine operations generally are considered as "common" to the three divine persons; hence, the world as creation cannot tell us anything about the inner life of the Trinity. "To put it crassly and not without exaggeration, when the treatise is concluded, its subject is never brought up again."[2]

Now, according to Rahner, this isolation of the treatise on the Trinity quite simply has to be wrong, even if only on the ground that the Trinity is itself a mystery of salvation. We should be able to show that all dogmatic theology must in some way be referred to as the primordial mystery of Christianity. It is Rahner's fundamental contention that the basic thesis that establishes this connection between the treatises and presents the Trinity as a mystery of salvation might be formulated as follows: "the 'economic' Trinity is the 'immanent' Trinity, and the 'immanent' Trinity is the 'economic' Trinity."[3] With this axiom, it is possible to develop systematically a doctrine of the Trinity that (a) does justice to the trinitarian teaching of the magisterium, (b) more adequately explains the biblical evidence concerning the threefold structure of the economy of salvation, and (c) helps us to understand that the Trinity is present in both the act of faith and the life of the believing Christian. If it is possible to propose such a doctrine of

---

[1] "Bemerkungen zum dogmatischen Traktat 'De Trinitate,'" *Schriften*, 4: 104–5; *Sacramentum Mundi IV*, s.v. "Trinitätstheologie," by K. Rahner, 1023; *Mysterium Salutis II*, 1967 ed., s.v. "Der dreifaltige Gott als transzendenter Urgrund der Heilsgeschite," by K. Rahner, 319 (translations from *The Trinity*, translated by J. Donceel [London: Burns and Oates, 1970]). An interesting assertion in light of Rahner's statement elsewhere that most normal Christians suffer from a type of practical tritheism: *Mysterium Salutis II*, s.v. "Der dreifaltige Gott," by K. Rahner, 342.

[2] *Mysterium Salutis II*, s.v. "Der dreifaltige Gott," 322.

[3] Another central affirmation of Rahner's whole theological system: *Mysterium Salutis II*, s.v. "Der dreifaltige Gott," 328, 332, 336–37, 339, 344, 352, 370, 382–84; "Bemerkungen zum dogmatischen Traktat," *Schriften*, 4: 115, 123, 125; *Sacramentum Mundi IV*, s.v. "Trinität," 1011; *Sacramentum Mundi IV*, s.v. "Trinitätstheologie," 1024; "Natur und Gnade," *Schriften*, 4: 221; "Über den Begriff des Geheimnisses," *Schriften*, 4: 95–98; Rahner and Thüsing, *Christologie*, 69; "Theologie und Anthropologie," *Schriften*, 8: 48.

the Trinity, then, says Rahner, he will have justified this foundational axiom.[4]

In one way, of course, this axiom is a defined doctrine of faith,
for the second divine person, God's Logos, became man, and *only*
he became man; hence, there occurred at least *one* mission and
one reality in salvation history that is not merely appropriated to
some divine person, but which is proper to him. This one case,
therefore, shows up as false the statement that there is nothing in
history that cannot be said equally of the Triune God as a whole
and of each person in particular.[5] In this light, "we are sure that
the following statement is also true: that no adequate distinction
can be made between the doctrine of the Trinity and the doctrine
of the economy of salvation."[6]

A. The Order of Grace

That the economic Trinity *is* the immanent Trinity is seen most
clearly in the theology of grace, where each one of the three
divine persons communicates himself to man in gratuitous grace
in his own personal particularity and diversity.[7] This trinitarian
communication is the ontological ground of man's life of grace
and eventually of the direct vision of the divine persons in eternity. It is God's "indwelling," "uncreated grace," understood not

---

[4] P. Molnar has criticized this foundational axiom of Rahner's trinitarian theology comprehensively in the following works: "Is God Essentially Different?"
614; "The Function of the Immanent Trinity in the Theology of Karl Barth:
Implications for Today," *Scottish Journal of Theology* 42 (1989): 383–99; "Can We
Know God Directly? Rahner's Solution from Experience," *Theological Studies* 46
(1985), 230 ff. and 248 ff. It is also interesting to note that although Molnar
asserts that Rahner's axiom is in conflict with Barth's trinitarian theology on
the grounds that it relativizes God's freedom, his article "The Function of the
Immanent Trinity," 367–99, offers a different view. Torrance argues quite to the
contrary that Rahner's and Barth's trinitarian theology are united in this axiom;
see T. Torrance, "Toward an Ecumenical Consensus of the Trinity," *Theologische
Zeitschrift* 31 (1975): 227, 339, 348 n. 29.

[5] "Bemerkungen zum dogmatischen Traktat," *Schriften,* 4: 115–16; *Sacramentum Mundi IV,* s.v. "Trinität," 1012; *Mysterium Salutis II,* s.v. "Der dreifaltige
Gott," 329.

[6] *Mysterium Salutis II,* s.v. "Der dreifaltige Gott," 329.

[7] "Bemerkungen zum dogmatischen Traktat," *Schriften,* 4: 127; *Sacramentum
Mundi IV,* s.v. "Trinität," 1012–13; *Mysterium Salutis II,* s.v. "Der dreifaltige
Gott," 336–39.

only as a communication of the divine nature but primarily as a communication of "persons." This self-communication of the persons occurs according to their personal peculiarity—that is, according to and in virtue of their mutual relations. A divine person's communication of himself otherwise than in and through his relations to the other persons would presuppose that each single divine person would be something absolute and not merely relative. We then would no longer be speaking of the Trinity.

> In other words: these three self-communications are the self-communication of the one God in the three relative ways in which God subsists. The Father gives himself to us too as *Father*, that is, precisely because and insofar as he himself, being essentially with *himself*, utters himself and *in this way* communicates the Son as his own, personal self-manifestation; and because and insofar as the Father and the Son, welcoming each other in love, drawn and returning to each other, communicate themselves *in this way*, as received in mutual love, that is, the Holy Spirit. God relates to us in a threefold manner, and this threefold, free, and gratuitous relation to us is not merely a copy or an analogy of the inner Trinity, but *is* the Trinity itself.[8]

If this communication between God and man is really *self-communication*, then God does not give some share of himself by creating finite realities through *efficient* causality. Rather, in a *quasi-formal* causality, he bestows himself really and in the strictest sense of the word. Scripture testifies that God's self-communication has a threefold aspect.

We must avoid two misunderstandings. On the one hand, this threefold aspect of God's self-communication should not be interpreted as a merely verbal unfolding of a communication that in itself contains no distinctions. The origin of God's self-communication, its existence as it expresses and utters itself, and the welcoming acceptance of that self-communication, brought about by God himself, are not just "the same thing" signified by different words. Rather, the *Father,* the *Word,* and the *Spirit* (however deficient all these words may be) point to a true distinction, to a double mediation within this self-communication. On the other hand, the history of this self-communication has shown

---

[8] *Mysterium Salutis II,* s.v. "Der dreifaltige Gott," 337.

ever more clearly that this double mediation by word and spirit is not a created kind of mediation, in which God would not be communicated as he is in himself. The testimony of faith tells us that the economic self-communication of God is truly and really threefold, for the mediations of God among us are no created intermediaries. Such an affirmation would be basically Arian and would do away with a true *self*-communication of God.

> It follows that this real mediation of a divine kind in the dimension of salvation history must also be a real mediation in the inner life of God. The "threefoldness" of God's relation to us in Christ's order of grace is already the reality of God as it is in itself: a three-personal one.[9]

B. Consequences for the Methodology of Trinitarian Theology

The acceptance of this foundational axiom concerning the identity of the economic and immanent Trinity means that the way in which the mystery of the Trinity has been expounded tradition-ally will change. First, we will look for an access to the doctrine of the Trinity in Jesus and in his Spirit, as we experience them through faith in salvation history,[10] for in these two persons the immanent Trinity itself is already given. The Trinity, then, is not revealed to us primarily in statements; rather, the statements ex-press what we have already experienced. For those who reject this methodology, the Trinity is something that can be told about only in conceptual statements, so the doctrine begins to take on the abstract, impractical character that is customary in the text-book approach. But if it is true that we really can grasp the con-tent of the doctrine of the Trinity only by going back to the history of salvation, there should never be a treatise on the Trinity in which the doctrine of the "missions" is anything but central.

Presupposing this methodology, the treatise should follow the same order as the history of the revelation of this mystery and, following the ancient tradition of the Church Fathers, should look for an implicit revelation of the Trinity in the Old Testa-

---

[9] *Mysterium Salutis II*, s.v. "Der dreifaltige Gott," 339.

[10] For a good summary of Rahner's axiom as the ground of salvation history, see E. Jüngel, "Das Verhältnis von 'ökonomischer' und 'immanenter' Trinität," *Zeitschrift für Theologie und Kirche* 72 (1975): 353–64.

ment. This process in its turn would remove the common impression that in the doctrine of the Trinity certain nonscriptural concepts have been applied to utterances in the New Testament with which, considered in themselves, they had *absolutely nothing* in common.[11] In this way, moreover, we do not have to begin our explanation of the Trinity with the concept of "person," which because of the secular meaning of this word often encourages a practical tritheism among Christians today. We may begin rather from the self-revelation of God (the Father) as given in salvation history, as mediated by the Word in the Spirit. Then we can show that these distinctions in "God-for-us" are in fact the distinctions within "God-in-himself."[12]

This attempt to understand the immanent Trinity from the revelation of the economic Trinity will not diminish in any way the ultimate, irreducible mystery of the Trinity,[13] for the Trinity is always a mystery not so much because of the logical difficulties involved but on account of the fact that it is essentially identical with the mystery of the self-communication of God to us in Christ and in the Spirit. Man understands himself ultimately only when he has realized that he is the one to whom God communicates himself. "Thus we may say that the mystery of the Trinity is the last mystery of our own reality, and that it is experienced precisely in this reality."[14] This statement does not imply that we might from this experience conceptually objectify the mystery by mere individual reflection, but it does provide us with a methodological principle for the whole treatise on the Trinity—namely, that the Trinity is a mystery whose paradoxical character *(paradoxaler Charakter)* is preluded in the paradoxical character of man's existence and that therefore all statements of the Trinity will naturally point to real life. Thus, it is clear that for Rahner the doctrine of the "missions" is from its very nature the starting point for the doctrine of the Trinity, which not only should be presupposed tacitly, but also should be posited as such in the treatise.

---

[11] *Mysterium Salutis II,* s.v. "Der dreifaltige Gott," 342.

[12] *Mysterium Salutis II,* s.v. "Der dreifaltige Gott," 344.

[13] *Sacramentum Mundi IV,* s.v. "Trinität," 1013. *Mysterium Salutis II,* s.v. "Der dreifaltige Gott," 345–47.

[14] *Mysterium Salutis II,* s.v. "Der dreifaltige Gott," 346.

2. Rahner's Systematic Outline of Trinitarian Theology

Presupposing his basic axiom as the foundation of trinitarian theology, Rahner explains more precisely what is properly meant by this economic Trinity, which is the immanent Trinity. Of course, we already have a provisional understanding of the economic Trinity in our experience of salvation history and in its biblical expression, which remains forever the inexhaustibly rich starting point of our deliberations. It is precisely this understanding of the economic Trinity in salvation history that must be conceptualized systematically in such a way as to express theologically the "immanent Trinity."

In speaking of the economic Trinity, we are concerned with the two distinct, yet related, ways of the free, gratuitous, self-communication of God to man that occur in Jesus and the Spirit. When we speak of the self-communication "of God," we presuppose that God is the "Father"—that is, "the simply unoriginate God, who is always known and presupposed, who communicates *himself* precisely when and because his self-communication does not simply coincide with him in lifeless inactivity."[15] In his self-communication, God remains the one who is free, incomprehensible, and unoriginate, and through his self-communication he in no way threatens his absolute integrity. Given this idea of God's self-communication, which transcends the communication proper to creatures, the decisive question emerges: How can the two ways in which this self-communication (economically) occurs—that is, through the Son and the Spirit—be seen as internally related yet distinct moments of the *one* self-communication of God, so that the distinction can be brought under a "concept"?

Catholic theology has not always understood these two ways of divine self-communication as internally related. It too often has accepted the incarnation and the descent of the Holy Spirit as two actualities connected only by an extrinsic bond and has assumed implicitly that each divine person might have become man or that there might have been an incarnation of the Logos, which in principle would not have implied the descent of the Holy Spirit.

---

[15] *Mysterium Salutis II*, s.v. "Der dreifaltige Gott," 371.

The difference between the incarnation and the descent of the Spirit, insofar as both of them are soteriological realities, has not always been clear.

Rahner begins from the opposite assumption. He presupposes that when God freely steps out of himself in self-communication, it is and *must be* the Son who appears historically in the flesh as man. It is and *must be* the Spirit who brings about the world's acceptance in faith, hope, and love of this self-communication.[16] The self-communication is always, in itself, God's free decision, but once this free decision is presupposed, the economic relationship between the Son and the Spirit is necessary because it is based on the inner nature of God himself. There is no doctrinal reason against adopting this position, for it agrees with the ancient pre-Augustinian tradition, and it helps us to reach an integral understanding of the doctrine of grace and of Christology. If we were to assume the alternative position, then salvation history would tell us nothing at all about the Father, the Son, and the Spirit, and the doctrine of the Trinity would become nothing more than a verbal accompaniment of a salvation history, which would be absolutely unchanged if there were no Trinity at all.[17]

A. Formal Exposition of Divine Self-Communication (the Economic Trinity)

If we presuppose the existence of God, then the concept of "divine self-communication" in itself is at least both rationally and theologically unobjectionable. For it cannot be dismissed auto-

---

[16] That only the Logos could become man is a central Rahnerian assertion: *Mysterium Salutis II*, s.v. "Der dreifaltige Gott," 329, 332, 397; *Sacramentum Mundi IV*, s.v. "Trinität," 1011; "Natur und Gnade," *Schriften*, 4: 222–23; "Probleme der Christologie," *Schriften*, 1: 204; "Zur Theologie der Menschwerdung," *Schriften*, 4: 138–39, 149; "Dogmatische Fragen zur Osterfrömmigkeit," *Schriften*, 4: 162; *Sacramentum Mundi II*, s.v. "Jesus Christus," 949; "Zur Theologie des Symbols," *Schriften*, 4: 292–93; "Bemerkungen zum dogmatischen Traktat," *Schriften*, 4: 117–23; "Über den Begriff des Geheimnisses," *Schriften*, 4: 94–96. However, G. Mansini, "Quasi-formal Causality and Change in the Other: A Note on Karl Rahner's Christology," *The Thomist* 52 (1988), 300–303, criticizes this assertion on the grounds that visibility and invisibility or accessibility and inaccessibility do not indicate relations of opposition and therefore do not indicate personal properties.

[17] *Mysterium Salutis II*, s.v. "Der dreifaltige Gott," 373–74.

matically *either* as mythology (given that *any* knowledge of God
at all must give rise to the question about God's relationship *to*
us and to the possibility of his self-communication at least as an
asymptotic limit idea) *or* as an a priori compromise of the essential
mystery of God (because the concept of divine self-communication
includes mystery in itself).

If we presuppose this concept, then as its very condition of possibility "it reveals to us a fourfold group of dual aspects: *(a)* Origin—
Future; *(b)* History—Transcendence; *(c)* Invitation—Acceptance;
(d) Knowledge—Love."[18] These four basic aspects appear first
from our point of view as creatures and as men, but there are two
reasons why this should not arouse any suspicion of modalism.
First, we are speaking of self-*communication*. Hence, the concept
of an "addressee" can never be excluded. Second, creation as it is
must be considered a moment of God's self-communication; it is
the condition of the possibility of constituting an addressee. Hence,
the postulation of the four double aspects of a self-communication
of God first "from below," from our point of view, does not necessarily imply that something is added to this self-communication.
These structures of the world and of the person may be conceived
as the reality that, although distinct from God, comes into being
precisely when and insofar as God presupposes, as a condition of
its possibility, the addressee of his self-communication. "The self-
communication of the free, personal God who gives himself as a
person, presupposes a personal recipient. . . . If God wishes to
step freely outside of himself, he must create man."[19]

Given that the four double aspects become intelligible under
the assumption that the human personal subject is the addressee
demanded by the divine self-communication, which creates him
as the condition of its own possibility, it is necessary to consider
these aspects separately.

In agreement with the nature of the addressee, this communication as communicated (but still going on) has an origin and a
future (the first couple of aspects): beginning *(Anfang)* when the
addressee is created by the communicator, a beginning *(Herkunft)*
that aims at a future.

---

[18] *Mysterium Salutis II,* s.v. "Der dreifaltige Gott," 374. See also *Sacramentum
Mundi IV,* s.v. "Trinität," 1015.

[19] *Mysterium Salutis II,* s.v. "Der dreifaltige Gott," 375.

History and transcendence are the second couple of aspects under which God's self-communication comes because in it God as transcendent origin of man gives himself wholly and immediately to man for his salvation. If there occurs, therefore, a self-communication of God to historical man, who is still becoming, it can occur only in this unifying duality of history and transcendence.

If man is the being with the one duality of origin and future, if he is history in (into) transcendence and thus the free being, then God's self-communication must also mean the difference between offer and acceptance (the third couple of aspects).

The fourth couple of aspects seems at first to be of a quite different nature: knowledge and love, actuation of knowledge and actuation of love. However, "knowledge and love in their duality describe the reality of man. Hence, a self-communication of God to man must present itself to man as a self-communication of absolute truth and absolute love."[20]

Each side of the four aspects form a unity, and thus there are only *two* basic manners of God's self-communication that condition one another. Origin, history, and offer clearly constitute an integral unity. The offer of divine self-communication is the origin of the world and of history, the master plan according to which the world is projected. Furthermore, if God's self-offering is a real offer to historic men, then it has taken place definitively and irrevocably only when it is historically *there* in "the absolute bringer of salvation," only when the proffering of divine self-communication not only constitutes a world as the addressee of its offer, but posits itself irrevocably as historical.[21] In order to understand why truth belongs on this side of the equation, we need to consider the definition of truth. "Truth is not first a correct grasping of a state of affairs. It consists first in letting our own personal essence come to the fore."[22] This true revealing of self to others is what Rahner calls "fidelity." Hence, truth is first the truth that we do, the deed in which we firmly posit ourselves for ourselves and for others, the deed that waits to see how it will be received.

---

[20] *Mysterium Salutis II,* s.v. "Der dreifaltige Gott," 378.
[21] *Mysterium Salutis II,* s.v. "Der dreifaltige Gott," 379.
[22] *Mysterium Salutis II,* s.v. "Der dreifaltige Gott," 379.

Insofar as the process of self-communication constitutes itself as origin, history, and offer, it shows itself as truth. Divine self-communication as a "revelation" of God's nature is truth for us; it occurs as faithful offer, and in this way it posits a beginning and becomes definitely established in the concreteness of history. However, as such, it is not yet *the* promise that has already penetrated into the addressee and been accepted by him, becoming love and begetting love in him.

Of the four opposed aspects, it is relatively easy to establish the unity of future and transcendence; "transcendence arises where God gives himself as the future."[23] Furthermore, if the self-communication is to be understood as *absolutely* willed by God, then it must carry its acceptance with it: "The freedom of the acceptance as a power and as an act must be conceived as posited by God's creative power, without in any way impairing the nature of freedom."[24] Finally, the self-communication that wills itself absolutely and creates both the possibility of its acceptance and this acceptance itself is precisely what is meant by love. It is, in fact, the specifically divine "case" of love because it creates its own acceptance and because this love is the freely offered and accepted self-communication of the person.

If the divine self-communication to man occurs, it possesses and must possess these two basic modalities: self-communication as truth and as love. This self-communication, insofar as it occurs in truth, happens in history, and insofar as it happens in love, it opens this history in transcendence toward the absolute future. This is not evident at once, for history as concrete, in which the irrevocability of the divine self-communication is made apparent, and transcendence toward the absolute future are apparently opposites, and as such they keep the one divine self-communication separated in its modalities. But "this historic manifestation as truth can be perceived only in the horizon of transcendence toward God's absolute future; this absolute future is irrevocably promised as love by the fact that this promise is established in concrete history."[25] Insofar as these two statements are true, the two mo-

---

[23] *Mysterium Salutis II,* s.v. "Der dreifaltige Gott," 380.
[24] *Mysterium Salutis II,* s.v. "Der dreifaltige Gott," 381.
[25] *Mysterium Salutis II,* s.v. "Der dreifaltige Gott," 381.

dalities of divine self-communication are not separated, nor are they tied together simply by divine decree. They constitute the one divine self-communication that assumes the form of truth in history, of origin and offer, and of love in transcendence toward the freely accepted absolute future.

B. Transition from Economic to Immanent Trinity

The differentiation of God's self-communication in history (of truth) and in spirit (of love) must belong to God "in himself"; otherwise, this difference, which undoubtedly exists, would do away with God's *self*-communication.[26] Therefore, by applying to the immanent Trinity what we have deduced about the economic Trinity, we can say that there is real difference in God as he is in himself between one and the same God, insofar as he is (at once and necessarily) the unoriginate who mediates himself to himself (Father), the one who is truth uttered for himself (Son), and the one who is received and accepted in love for himself (Spirit). And, as a result, he is the one who can communicate himself freely.

Moreover, this real differentiation is constituted by a double self-communication of the Father, by which the Father communicates *himself*, while as the one who utters and receives he posits, precisely through this self-communication, his real distinction from the one who is uttered and from the one who is received. That which is communicated rightly may be called divinity, hence the essence of God.

Finally, the bond between the original self-communicator and the one who is uttered and received, a bond that implies a distinction, must be understood as "relative" (or relational). This follows simply from the sameness of the essence.[27]

C. A New Terminology

Finally, Rahner turns his attention to the problems inherent in the use of the concept "person" in his trinitarian theology. He

---

[26] *Sacramentum Mundi IV,* s.v. "Trinität," 1016; *Mysterium Salutis II,* s.v. "Der dreifaltige Gott," 382.

[27] *Mysterium Salutis II,* s.v. "Der dreifaltige Gott," 384; *Sacramentum Mundi IV,* s.v. "Trinität," 1016–17.

sees three interrelated questions that need to be addressed: first, whether the concept "person" is suited to express what is meant in the Trinity; second, what the concept properly means in *this* context; and third, whether with his alternative systematization he has arrived at a statement equal to the statement made by the official doctrine of the church with the use of the concept of "person."

Because the term *person* is used neither in the New Testament nor at the beginning of trinitarian doctrine, we are allowed to adopt a critical stance and to regard its use as unabsolute. We know that faith in the Trinity can exist without reference to this concept. Moreover, in the doctrine of the Trinity, this concept has aspects not found in any other context, for "person" as a concrete concept, in contrast with "personality," means not formally the distinction as such, but those who are distinct. It is clear that in reference to God we may not speak of three persons in the same way that we do elsewhere; when we usually speak of three persons, we directly intend by the term *person* also a "rational nature." In such a context, nature is in fact multiplied, but this is not so in the case of the Trinity. It should be noted, furthermore, that this difficulty occurs for all notional statements about the Trinity whenever numbers are used. "At any rate, if we wish to understand the use of 'three persons' correctly we must always return to the original experience of salvation history. . . . Our generalization (of three persons) is, at least at first, a logical explanation, not some new extra knowledge not included in the original experience."[28]

Addressing the second question, what the concept "person" properly means, Rahner affirms that the central problem with the concept is that today it almost always implies a spiritual center of activity, subjectivity, and liberty, but there are precisely *not* three such centers in God.[29] In God there is only one essence, hence

---

[28] *Mysterium Salutis II,* s.v. "Der dreifaltige Gott," 386. See also *Sacramentum Mundi IV,* s.v. "Trinität," 1018, and "Bemerkungen zum dogmatischen Traktat," *Schriften,* 4: 131–32.

[29] Rahner often makes this assertion that the concept "person" essentially has changed in meaning through its historical development: *Mysterium Salutis II,* s.v. "Der dreifaltige Gott," 344, 353–54, 387–88; *Sacramentum Mundi IV,* s.v. "Trinität," 1007, 1018–19; *Sacramentum Mundi IV,* s.v. "Trinitätstheologie," 1029; "Bemerkungen zum dogmatischen Traktat," *Schriften,* 4: 132–33; "Pro-

one absolute self-presence, and there is only one self-utterance of the Father, namely the Logos, with the Logos being not the one who utters, but the one who is uttered. Therefore, there is no *mutual* love between Father and Son, for this mutuality would presuppose two acts. Rahner even goes so far as to deny that there is within the Trinity a mutual "thou."[30] But there is loving self-acceptance of the Father, and this self-acceptance gives rise to the distinction. Of course, that which we call "three persons" in God exists in God with self-awareness. There is in God a knowledge of these three persons, a knowledge about the Trinity both as "consciousness" and as "object" of knowledge, but there are not three consciousnesses; rather, the one consciousness subsists in a threefold way.[31] This difficulty is not overcome merely by defining the concept of "person" in such a way that, as applied to God, it does not include this distinct "personality." The term *person* should help us to understand what is meant in the present case, and it therefore should not be modified to conform to the thing that is meant. The church has not been able in the past and cannot now control the development of meaning of a particular term within the development of a language. Hence, the church as a whole now has a problem with the intelligibility of the concept of "person." Although it is clearly not the duty of the single theologian to dispense with the use of such an important theological concept, every theologian nevertheless must try to explain the real meaning of *person* using other words and so preserve the doctrine from misunderstanding.[32]

In seeking new ways of expressing the essential truth of the Trin-

---

bleme der Christologie," *Schriften*, 1: 180–81; *Sacramentum Mundi II*, s.v. "Jesus Christus," 928; *Mysterium Salutis I*, s.v. "Kerygma und Dogma," 694; "Lehramt und Theologie," *Schriften*, 13: 84–85. See also Lennan, *The Ecclesiology of Karl Rahner*, 195–96.

[30] *Mysterium Salutis II*, s.v. "Der dreifaltige Gott," 366 n. 29, 387. This lack of an inner-trinitarian "thou" has been much criticized. See, for example, Wong, *Logos-Symbol*, 208–11, 223–24, 266; J. A. Bracken, "The Holy Trinity as a Community of Divine Persons. II. Person and Nature in the Doctrine of God," *Heythrop Journal* 15 (1974), 259; Torrance, "Toward an Ecumenical Consensus," 344.

[31] *Mysterium Salutis II*, s.v. "Der dreifaltige Gott," 387.

[32] *Sacramentum Mundi IV*, s.v. "Trinität," 1019. "Bemerkungen zum dogmatischen Traktat," *Schriften*, 4: 132–33. *Mysterium Salutis II*, s.v. "Der dreifaltige Gott," 388.

ity, we return to our fundamental axiom concerning the identity of the economic and immanent Trinity. We affirm that the one self-communication of the one God occurs in three different "manners of givenness" or "modes of presence" *(drei verschiedenen Gegebenheitsweisen)*, in which the one God is given concretely for us in himself and not vicariously by other realities through their transcendental relation to God. If we translate this idea in terms of the immanent Trinity, we may say: the one God subsists in three distinct manners of subsisting *(drei distinkten Subsistenzweisen)*.[33] "Distinct manners of subsisting" would then be the explanatory concept, not for person, which refers to that which subsists as distinct, but for "personality" *(Personalitas)*, which makes God's concrete reality, as it meets us in different ways, into precisely this one who meets us thus. This "meeting-us-thus" must be conceived always as belonging to God in and for himself. The single "person" in God would then be: God as existing and meeting us in this determined distinct manner of subsisting. This phrase "says simply the same as the definition of 'person' in Thomas: 'that which subsists distinctly (in a rational nature).' "[34]

Rahner recognizes the difficulties inherent in the use of the word *manner* and says that, as with all other concepts used about the Trinity, it is used analogically, yet there are advantages that justify its use. "Three persons" says nothing about the unity of these three persons, whereas of itself *manner* at least suggests the possibility that the same God, as distinct in a threefold manner, is concretely tripersonal. Neither is *manner* something subsequent, for the concrete Godhead is necessarily in these manners of subsisting. Also, compared with the word *personality,* the expression "distinct manners of subsisting" has the advantage of not readily insinuating the multiplication of essence and of subjectivity.[35]

---

[33] *Mysterium Salutis II,* s.v. "Der dreifaltige Gott," 389–91; *Sacramentum Mundi IV,* s.v. "Trinität," 1019–20; *Sacramentum Mundi IV,* s.v. "Trinitätstheologie," 1030; Rahner and Thüsing, *Christologie,* 68. Both Torrance ("Toward an Ecumenical Consensus," 338) and Bracken ("The Holy Trinity," 257–60) note Rahner's verbal distinction and the consequent implication of a distinction between the immanent and the economic Trinity. See also Wong, *Logos-Symbol,* 150–52, 157, 162, 211.

[34] *Mysterium Salutis II,* s.v. "Der dreifaltige Gott," 389–90.

[35] Bracken, "The Holy Trinity," 260, questions whether Rahner's "manners of subsistence" is really an improvement on the traditional person-nature defi-

Applying this phrase to the traditional statements of the dogma, we say that the one God subsists in three distinct manners of subsisting. These manners of subsisting of Father, Son, and Spirit are distinct as relations of opposition; hence, these three are not the same one. Nevertheless, the Father, Son, and Spirit are the one God, each in a different manner of subsisting. In this sense, we may count three in God. God is threefold through his three manners of subsistence. God as subsisting in a determined manner of subsisting (such as Father) is "someone else" than God subsisting in another manner of subsisting, but he is not "something other." The manners of subsisting are distinct through their relative opposition to one another; they are real through their identity with the divine essence. Finally, the one and same divine essence subsists in each of the three distinct manners of subsisting; hence, "he who" subsists in one such manner of subsisting is truly God. The concept of "distinct manners of subsistence" can be used, therefore, not to replace the concept "person," but alongside it to explain it.[36]

3. CONCLUSION

Rahner's understanding of the Trinity has much to recommend it. With it he has worked out many of the implications of his epistemological metaphysics—most notably the fundamental assertion of the convertibility of being and truth. He has also taken his theology of grace to its logical conclusion, for given the fluidity of the grace-nature distinction noted earlier, he can argue that the Trinity no longer is proposed to our belief only on the testimony of an external witness but can be experienced by man in grace. Indeed, revelation as a whole is no longer seen as a series of propositions to which faith assents, but as a personal relationship in which God makes himself known by communicating himself to man in grace as man accepts that divine self-communication. Hence, Rahner can conclude that man in grace can find

nition, and Torrance, "Toward an Ecumenical Consensus," 245–49, criticizes the phrase on the ground that we cannot and should not drop the term *person*.

[36] *Mysterium Salutis II,* s.v. "Der dreifaltige Gott," 392.

the ground for his belief by reading his own subjectivity. In fact, by studying his own structure under grace, man can know the truth of God, even the inner-trinitarian life. In all this, we see the unifying and dynamic tendency of Rahner's thought, together with a continually stronger emphasis on the priority of transcendentally given grace, the beginnings of which were noted in the previous chapter.

However, that is only one side of the structure of dialectical analogy that grounds Rahner's thought. We find him simultaneously making distinctions that, although necessary, do not seem to fit into the dynamic thrust of his thought and that create, therefore, a certain tension in his theology. Thus, despite his continual assertion of the identity of the economic and immanent Trinity, he nevertheless at other times, in line with the more conceptualizing side of his thought, appears to distinguish between the economic Trinity as "three different modes of presence" *(drei verschiedenen Gegebenheitsweisen)* and the immanent Trinity as "three distinct manners of subsistence" *(drei distinkten Subsistenzweisen),* and between the missions of the Trinity and the inner processions, arguing that the latter are the foundation of the former.[37] Furthermore, so strongly is the unity of being, consciousness, and will stressed that in inner-trinitarian relations no mutual "thou" is spoken, and the Son only receives the Father's love without loving the Father in return.[38] However, without an inner trinitarian opposition it is difficult to see how the humanity of Christ can be attributed to the Logos alone, a problem we must return to in the context of Rahner's approach to Christology.

Finally, in line with the whole nature of man as *Schwebe* and the foundational analysis of the *conversio ad phantasma,* Rahner tries hard to ground man's internal experience of the Trinity in history and to bind it to God's definitive and irrevocable revelation in Jesus, the absolute bringer of salvation.[39] However, in the light of his own ontology of grace, which assigns to man a permanent supernatural existential, it is not yet clear why such a histori-

---

[37] *Mysterium Salutis II,* s.v. "Der dreifaltige Gott," 389–91; *Sacramentum Mundi IV,* s.v. "Trinität," 1019–20; *Sacramentum Mundi IV,* s.v. "Trinitätstheologie," 1030.

[38] *Mysterium Salutis II,* s.v. "Der dreifaltige Gott," 366 n. 29, 387.

[39] *Mysterium Salutis II,* s.v. "Der dreifaltige Gott," 379, 381.

cal revelation of the economic Trinity is absolutely necessary. Furthermore, the emphasis of Rahner's economic approach that the starting point for all trinitarian theology is and must be personal experience of salvation history only brings into relief the problem of objectivity. For it would seem that for Rahner there exists no objectivity, neither here nor elsewhere, that is not attained over and through personal subjectivity.[40]

---

[40] "Kirchliche Christologie zwischen Exegese und Dogmatik," *Schriften,* 9: 205. "Theologie und Anthropologie," *Schriften,* 8: 53–54. See also Knasas, "'Esse' as the Target of Judgement," 228–29, and McCool, "Philosophy of the Human Person," 561–62, who note this problem of objectivity within the Rahnerian system.

4

Symbol and Becoming

IN A SEMINAL ARTICLE dating from 1958, Rahner proposed a radically new understanding of the nature of symbol in which he
once again developed the conclusions of his earlier epistemological metaphysics, this time with a view to laying the foundations
for a comprehensive understanding of the relationship of spirit
and matter, in which he proposed that matter should be understood as the symbol of spirit.[1] It was subsequently in trying to
synthesize this understanding of the matter-spirit relationship with
the scientific theory of evolution that Rahner developed his understanding of "becoming" as active self-transcendence. And it
was through this theory of becoming that he eventually sought to
show the compatibility of an evolutionary development of matter
into spirit not only with his own understanding of matter, but
also with traditional magisterial teaching concerning the direct
divine creation of the human soul.

Because of the importance of this Rahnerian symbol theory,
and its recurring relevance in the whole of his theology, it will be
necessary in this chapter to examine carefully not only the theory
but also its origin in Rahner's metaphysics and its development
within the context of his theology in general.[2]

1. SYMBOL

The common understanding of symbol—that two realities, each
of which is already constituted in its essence, are able to "agree"

---

[1] "Zur Theologie des Symbols," *Schriften,* 4: 275–311. For a good and comprehensive summary of Rahner's symbol theory, see Wong, *Logos-Symbol,*
75–82.

[2] Hugo Rahner, "Eucharisticon fraternitatis," in Metz et al., eds., *Gott in Welt,*
897, wrote that Rahner's symbol theory encapsulated the whole of his understanding about God's presence in the world. For an evaluation of the overall
importance of this symbol theory in the structure of Rahner's thought, see also

with one another and on the basis of this "agreement" are able to refer to one another and hence be used by us as a symbol for one another—is only a derivative mode of symbolic being. To begin an analysis of symbol in this way would make it impossible to distinguish really genuine natural symbols *(Realsymbol)* from merely arbitrary signs, signals, and codes *(Vertretungssymbol).* Anything could be a symbol of anything else; the orientation from the symbol to the thing symbolized could run the other way around or be determined merely accidentally by the human observer.

A. Being Is Plural

Prescinding from any historical analysis of the development of the notion of symbol, Rahner sets himself the task of looking for the highest and most primordial manner in which one reality can represent another. "And we call this supreme and primal representation, in which one reality renders another present (primordially 'for itself' and only secondarily 'for others'), a symbol: the representation which allows the other 'to be there.'"[3] Such an original concept of symbol is grounded in the fact that any being, and in fact every being, is in itself plural.[4] This is axiomatically true because every finite being as such bears the stigma of the finite by the very fact that it is not absolutely simple.[5] An intrinsic plurality and distinction need not, however, always be merely the stigma of the finiteness of a being. On the contrary, the mystery of the Trinity reminds us that there is a true and real, even if only

---

G. McCool, "Is St. Thomas' 'Science of God' Still Relevant Today?" *International Philosophical Quarterly* 14 (1974), 450–54; L. Puntel, "Zu den Begriff 'transzendental' und 'kategorial' bei Karl Rahner," in *Wagnis Theologie,* edited by H. Vorgrimler (Freiburg: Herder, 1979), 189–98.

[3] "Zur Theologie des Symbols," *Schriften,* 4: 279. Wong, *Logos-Symbol,* 255–62, interestingly links this Rahnerian notion of symbol with the Pauline concept of *mysterion.*

[4] Although this is a rather startling affirmation when stated so bluntly, it is really only the logical conclusion of Rahner's metaphysical starting point, for, as we have seen, the very term that Rahner uses to describe the foundational unity of being and knowing, *Beisichsein des Seins,* itself seems to imply a duality in unity, a self-presence, rather than an absolute and simple identity at the most basic level of being: *Geist,* 83, 236 ff.; *Hörer 1,* 55–57, 60–61.

[5] "Zur Theologie des Symbols," *Schriften,* 4: 280.

relative, distinction of persons in the supreme simplicity of God and hence a plurality, at least in this sense, in God himself. It is therefore quite thinkable that the pluralism of the finite creature is not merely a consequence of its finiteness but also a consequence of that divine plurality that does not imply imperfection but is the supreme fullness of unity. Thus, we can say "that being is plural in itself, and formulate this as a general principle without restrictions. On this supposition, we do not need to take it as merely part of the ontology of the finite as such."[6] Rather, a being is of itself, independently of any comparison with anything else, plural in its unity.

B. Unity Through Plurality

These plural moments in the unity of a being must have an inner agreement among themselves by virtue of the unity of the being, and this agreement cannot be a simple juxtaposition of the moments that are there originally. Such a unity would be merely the subsequent conjunction of separate elements that once stood on their own, which would betray the profound Thomistic principle *"non enim plura secundum se uniuntur."*[7] Thus,

> A plurality in an original and an originally superior unity can only be understood as follows: the "one" develops, the plural comes from an original "one," in a relationship of origin and consequence; the original unity, which also forms the unity which unites the plural, maintains itself while resolving itself and "dis-closing" itself into a plurality in order to find itself precisely there.[8]

A consideration of the Trinity reveals that the "one" of unity and plurality is an ontological ultimate that may not be reduced to an

---

[6] "Zur Theologie des Symbols," *Schriften,* 4: 281. See also Rahner and Ratzinger, *Episkopat und Primat,* 97, and Rahner's *Sendung und Gnade,* 58–59.

[7] This is, as we have seen, an essential affirmation of Rahner's metaphysics; *Geist,* 217–18; *Hörer 1,* 51–52, 147.

[8] "Zur Theologie des Symbols," *Schriften,* 4: 282. This very dialectical notion of unity in and through plurality of course has its foundations in Rahner's understanding of emanation, which displays the same dialectical structure: *Geist,* 245, 251, 261–62, 265–66. Some commentators noted this similarity: Wong, *Logos-Symbol,* 95; Hurd, "Being Is Being-Present-to-Itself," 71–78; and McCool, "St. Thomas' 'Science of God,'" 450. McCool also noted the Hegelian overtones in Rahner's symbol theory (453), as did Pearl, "Dialectical Panentheism," 126–27.

abstract and merely apparently "higher" unity and simplicity: it cannot be a "hollow and lifeless identity." In order to be one, being as such emerges into a plurality, the paradigm of which process is the Trinity.

C. Plurality Symbolizes Unity

The distinct moments deriving from the "one" that make for the perfection of its unity come essentially from this most primary unity: they have therefore a more primary agreement with it than anything that can be produced by efficient causality. This means that each being, as a unity, possesses a plurality—implying perfection—formed by the specific origin of the plural from the ontological unity: the plural is in agreement with its source in a way that corresponds with its origin and hence is an expression of its origin by an agreement that it owes to its origin. "Since this holds good for being in general, we may say that each being forms, in its own way, more or less perfectly according to its own degree of being, something distinct from itself and yet one with itself, 'for' its own fulfillment."[9] This differentiated being, which is still originally one, is in agreement because derivative; and because it is derivatively in agreement, it is expressive. This line of thought enables Rahner to assert the first principle of his theology of symbol: "Being is of itself symbolic because it necessarily 'expresses' itself."[10]

D. Being Comes to Itself Through Its Symbol

Being expresses itself because it must realize itself through a plurality in unity. Although this plurality is often the indication of finiteness, it also can be something positive, and we see traces of this positiveness even in our finite beings, for the self-constitutive act whereby a being constitutes itself as a plurality is also the condition of possibility for possession of self in knowledge and love.

---

[9] "Zur Theologie des Symbols," *Schriften,* 4: 283.

[10] "Zur Theologie des Symbols," *Schriften,* 4: 284. This principle clearly is only the expression in terms of his symbol theory of the *Schwebe* of unity in duality, which, as we have seen, Rahner postulates at the most basic level of being; see chapter 1, note 28.

The Thomistic principle that *"in tantum est ens cognoscens et cogni-tum, in quantum est ens in actu"* means that the degree of *"reditio completa in seipsum"* is the indication of its degree of being, and therefore "being-present-to-self" is only another way of describing the actuality of being—that is, the intrinsic self-realization of being. Then it follows that a being "comes to itself" in its expression, in the derivative agreement of the differentiated that is preserved in the perfection of the unity.[11] Realization as plurality and as possession of self cannot be disparate elements simply juxtaposed in a being because possession of self is not just an element, but the content of that which we call being (and hence self-realization). And it comes to itself in the measure in which it realizes itself by constituting a plurality, which means that each being, insofar as it is and realizes its being, is itself primarily "symbolic." It expresses itself and possesses itself in doing so:

> It gives itself away from itself into the "other" and there finds itself in knowledge and love because it is by constituting the inward "other" that it comes to (or from) its self-fulfillment, which is the presupposition or the act of being present to itself in knowledge and love.[12]

A being comes to itself by means of an expression, insofar as it comes to itself at all. The expression, or "symbol," is *the* way of knowledge of self, possession of self, in general. [13]

E. Being Is Known Through Its Symbol

Such an understanding of being is, however, the only starting point from which one can arrive at a correct theory of symbol in general, where the symbol is the reality in which another attains knowledge of a being, for knowledge is not a process that takes place only in the knower. On the contrary, the knowability and the actual knowledge of a being (as object of knowledge) depend on the degree of actuality in the thing to be known. If beings are

---

[11] Once again we see the logical consequences of Rahner's foundational thought—here his understanding of the analogy of being—worked out in his theory of symbol. See *Hörer 1,* 64–65.

[12] "Zur Theologie des Symbols," *Schriften,* 4: 285.

[13] J. Buckley critically assesses Rahner's symbol theory in "On Being a Symbol: An Appraisal of Karl Rahner," *Theological Studies* 40 (1979), 453–73.

of themselves symbolic insofar as they realize themselves in plurality and possess themselves in this derivative agreement of the "other" with its primordial origin, the same holds good for the knowledge of these beings by others. A being can be known and is known, insofar as it is itself ontically (that is, "in itself") symbolic because it is ontologically (that is, "for itself") symbolic. Therefore,

> as a being realizes itself in its own intrinsic "otherness" (which is constitutive of its being), retentive of its intrinsic plurality (which is contained in its self-realization) as its derivative and hence congruous expression, it makes itself known. . . . The being is known in this symbol, without which it cannot be known at all: thus it is symbol in the original (transcendental) sense of the word.[14]

Thus, Rahner can assert a second principle in his theory of symbol—namely, that the symbol strictly speaking (that is, a *"Realsymbol"*) is the self-realization of a being in the other, which is constitutive of its essence.[15]

F. Application to Christology

This theology of symbol clearly has implications for the whole of theology. If, for example, the Logos, as reality of the immanent divine life, is generated by the Father as his image and expression, then this process is necessarily given with the divine act of self-knowledge; without it, the absolute act of divine self-possession in knowledge cannot exist. Then we must say:

> The Father is himself, by the very fact that he opposes to himself the image which is of the same essence as himself, as the person who is other than himself, and so he possesses himself. But this means that the Logos is the "symbol" of the Father, in the very sense which we have given the word: the inward symbol which remains distinct from what is symbolized, which is constituted by

---

[14] "Zur Theologie des Symbols," *Schriften,* 4: 286.

[15] Having established, therefore, a symbolic plurality within being itself, which reflects the original unity in diversity of being and knowing, we now see in this second principle a reflection of Rahner's analysis of sensibility, whereby, as we saw in the first chapter, the unity in diversity of being is developed to include matter: *Geist,* 87, 89, 92, 389, 405; *Hörer 1,* 151–54.

what is symbolized, where what is symbolized expresses itself and possesses itself.[16]

In a theology of symbol, therefore, Christology will form the central chapter, for if the humanity that the Logos assumes is considered only as that well-known reality that we know in ourselves, and if this humanity subsists in only a static, ontic sense—that is, as borne or taken on by the Logos—then the humanity has no doubt the function of a signal or a uniform with regard to the Logos, but not in full truth the function of a symbol as we have defined it. The Logos would make himself perceptible through a reality that was alien to him and might have been chosen from a whole series of such realities. Such an understanding would make Jesus the revelation of the Father through his doctrine but not through what he *is* in his human nature. Applying Rahner's notion of symbol to Christology, however, we can say that

> the incarnate word is the absolute symbol of God in the world, filled as nothing else can be with what is symbolized. He is not merely the presence and revelation of what God is in himself. He is the expressive presence of what, or rather who, God wished to be, in free grace, to the world, in such a way that this divine attitude, once so expressed, can never be reversed, but is and remains final and unsurpassable.[17]

The Thomistic presupposition that the act of existence of Christ's humanity is the act of existence of the Logos supports this argument, for "the being of the Logos . . . must be thought of as exteriorizing itself, so that without detriment to its immutability in itself and of itself, it becomes *itself* the existence of a created reality, which must in all truth be predicated of the being of the Logos."[18] The humanity of Christ is the real-symbol of the Logos in the most radical sense.

G. *Application to All of Theology*

With this understanding, we are still only at the beginning of a comprehensive theology of symbol, for clearly this understanding

---

[16] "Zur Theologie des Symbols," *Schriften,* 4: 292. In "Dialectical Panentheism," 128–80, Pearl notes the Hegelian or dialectical character of Rahner's symbol Christology.

[17] "Zur Theologie des Symbols," *Schriften,* 4: 293–94.

[18] "Zur Theologie des Symbols," *Schriften,* 4: 295.

of symbol is intrinsic to the understanding of almost all the major theological tracts. In natural theology, for instance, because of the humanity of Christ, the symbolic reality of all things now receives an infinite extension:

> If the individual reality, by making the all present, also speaks of God, ultimately by its transcendental reference to him as the efficient, exemplary, and final cause, this transcendence is made radical, even though only in a way accessible to faith, by the fact that in Christ this reality no longer refers to God merely as its cause: it points to God as to him to whom this reality belongs as his substantial determination or as his own proper environment.[19]

In ecclesiology, when we say that the church is the persisting presence of the Word in space and time, we imply at once that it continues this symbolic function of the Logos in the world. And the sacraments are obviously par excellence symbols according to this definition, which is validated in the basic axiom of traditional sacramental theology, *"Sacramenta efficiunt quod significant et significant quod efficiunt."* Such an understanding also provides an answer to the much-debated question concerning sacramental causality. As soon as one sees the sacraments as the actions of God on man, the question no longer arises as to how the sacramental sign "works on" God; it is no longer possible to ask whether the sign produces grace by "physical" or "moral" causality. At no stage can the sign be seen apart from what is signified; it is understood a priori as a symbolic reality, which the signified itself brings about in order really to be present itself. But we can, on the other hand, see that the sacrament is precisely the "cause" of grace, *insofar as* it is its sign, and that the grace—seen as coming from God—is the cause of the sign, bringing it about and so alone making itself present.[20] Finally, eschatology will not indicate the final disappearance of the sign and symbol in favor of a naked immediacy of God and creature face to face. The true and proper symbol, being an intrinsic moment of the thing itself, has a function of mediation that is not opposed in reality to the immediacy of what

---

[19] "Zur Theologie des Symbols," *Schriften,* 4: 296–97.

[20] For a critique of Rahner's notion of symbolic causality, see D. Tappeiner, "Sacramental Causality in Aquinas and Rahner," *Scottish Journal of Theology* 28 (1975), 252–57.

is meant by it, but is a mediation to immediacy. "In the end, of course, many signs and symbols will cease to be. . . . But the humanity of Christ will have eternal significance for the immediacy of the *visio beata*. The incarnation of the Logos may well be considered as the indispensable presupposition for strictly supernatural grace and glory."[21]

To Rahner's understanding of the church, the sacraments, and the significance of Christ we shall return later. However, on the nature of symbol, he concludes with two more principles:

> The principle that the concept of symbol—in the sense above defined—is an essential key concept in all theological treatises, without which it is impossible to have a correct understanding of the subject matter of the various treatises in themselves and in relation to other treatises. The principle that God's salvific action on man, from its first foundation to its completion, always takes place in such a way that God himself is the reality of salvation because it is given to man and grasped by him in the symbol, which does not represent an absent and merely promised reality but exhibits this reality as something present, by means of the symbol formed by it.[22]

H. The Body as Symbol of the Soul

That the body can and may be considered as the symbol of man follows from the Thomistic doctrine that the soul is the substantial form of the body.[23] Man is not composed, strictly speaking, of a soul and body, but of a soul and *materia prima*.[24] This matter is

---

[21] "Zur Theologie des Symbols," *Schriften*, 4: 302. That the humanity of Christ constitutes a *permanent* gateway for the creature to God is an important Rahnerian affirmation: "Die ewige Bedeutung der Meschheit Jesu für unser Gottesverhältnis," *Schriften*, 3: 56–57, 60; "Zur Theologie der Menschwerdung," *Schriften*, 4: 151; "Dogmatische Fragen zur Osterfrömmigkeit," *Schriften*, 4: 161, 170. See also Wong, *Logos-Symbol*, 61–62.

[22] "Zur Theologie des Symbols," *Schriften*, 4: 303. This symbol theory, which is so central to Rahner's whole view of reality, has not been accepted universally. For interesting critiques of the notion, see De h-Ide, "Rahner and Lonergan," 65; Tappeiner, "Sacramental Causality," 253–54; Buckley, "On Being a Symbol," 453–73.

[23] *Geist*, 254, 325; *Hörer 1*, 154–55, 161.

[24] *Geist*, 326; "Zur Theologie des Symbols," *Schriften*, 4: 305; "Der Leib in der Heilsordnung," *Schriften*, 12: 421.

of itself the strictly potential substratum of the substantial self-realization of the anima, which by imparting itself gives its reality to the passive potentiality of *materia prima* so that the soul is precisely the act in this potentiality. "It follows at once that what we call body is nothing else than the actuality of the soul itself in the 'other' of *materia prima,* the otherness produced by the soul itself, and hence its expression and symbol in the very sense which we have given to the term *symbolic reality.*"[25] Furthermore, precisely as the outgoing of the spirit into the emptiness of *materia prima,* the body is the condition that makes spiritual and personal self-discovery possible, not an obstacle in its way. There clearly can be no coming to self except by way of exit into the bodily reality, into which the spirit first reaches out in order to find itself, going out of itself to form itself in order to return to self.[26] This understanding of the body as the symbol of the soul obviously is not easily reconciled with an evolutionary worldview where matter apparently evolves into self-consciousness. However, before seeing how Rahner reconciles these two perspectives, we need to look further at the exact relationship of matter and spirit.

2. RELATION OF SPIRIT AND MATTER

Rahner frequently asserts his acceptance of magisterial teaching on the distinction of matter and spirit.[27] However, he maintains simultaneously that the magisterium never has defined adequately the concepts "spirit" and "matter"; therefore, if these magisterial teachings are to be understood, it is necessary to know what spirit and matter really signify.[28]

---

[25] "Zur Theologie des Symbols," *Schriften,* 4: 305. See also *Geist,* 326, 379.

[26] "Der Leib in der Heilsordnung," *Schriften,* 12: 423. Based clearly on Rahner's foundational understanding that presence-to-self is originally and always possible only in and through presence-to-the-other: *Geist,* 235, 242, 244, 250, 256–57, 287, 313, 344–45, 382–83, 387; *Hörer 1,* 147–48, 151, 156, 176, 202, 208.

[27] "Die Einheit von Geist und Materie," *Schriften,* 6: 196, 201, 209; K. Rahner and P. Overhage, *Das Problem der Hominisation,* Quaestiones Disputatae nos. 12–13 (Freiburg, Basel, Vienna: Herder, 1961), 16, 21, 23, 44; "Der Leib in der Heilsordnung," *Schriften,* 12: 418.

[28] "Die Einheit von Geist und Materie," *Schriften,* 6: 196–97; Rahner and Overhage, *Das Problem der Hominisation,* 44.

To this end, Rahner asserts that what is meant by *spirit* is an a priori datum of human knowledge from which alone we are able to determine metaphysically what is meant by *material* and *matter*.[29] It would be an unmetaphysical and materialistic prejudice to think that man is occupied first of all with matter and must then discover spirit subsequently, laboriously, and most problematically.

On the contrary, it follows from the origin of human knowledge that spirit is a proper, original reality that cannot be derived from anything else. From this alone can it be said what matter in itself really is. The distinction of spirit and matter, therefore, cannot be conceived as an absolute metaphysical separation of the two realities,[30] both because they can be apprehended only by being brought together and because apprehension is not merely the ideal cognizance taken by a knower of an object, but rather occurs when the object communicates itself in a real ontological process and builds itself really and ontologically into knowledge. If this process is possible, there must be an inner relationship between the knower and the known, even though the known is something "material." "Sense perception is to be considered merely as the condition for the possibility of spiritual knowledge which the latter creates for itself by distinguishing it from itself and thus asserts once more the 'relationship' between spirit and matter."[31]

In the Christian conception, matter is retraced in its whole being to the creative act of God, who is called spirit. Although matter cannot be interpreted simply as a part of the reality of God, the origin and what develops out of it, even something created, cannot be simply and completely separate and dissimilar.[32]

---

[29] *Hörer 1*, 154–55; Rahner and Overhage, *Das Problem der Hominisation,* 44, 48–49 (translations from *Hominisation,* translated by W. O'Hara [London: Burns and Oates, 1965]); "Die Einheit von Geist und Materie," *Schriften,* 6: 197, 200–201; "Die Christologie innerhalb einer evolutiven Weltanschauung," *Schriften,* 5: 189.

[30] "Die Einheit von Geist und Materie," *Schriften,* 6: 198; "Der Leib in der Heilsordnung," *Schriften,* 12: 419–20.

[31] "Die Einheit von Geist und Materie," *Schriften,* 6: 202; *Geist,* 287, 291, 296; *Hörer 1*, 177, 181; Rahner and Overhage, *Das Problem der Hominisation,* 50.

[32] The *unity* in diversity of matter and spirit is another central Rahnerian affirmation: Rahner and Overhage, *Das Problem der Hominisation,* 22–23, 49–50; "Die Einheit von Geist und Materie," *Schriften,* 6: 187, 190, 206, 214; "Der

What we call material has always been seen, at least in Thomistic philosophy, as a limited and in a sense "frozen" spirit, as limited being, whose being as such, i.e., prescinding from the real negativity and limitation of this being . . . is exactly the same being which outside such a limitation means being-conscious-of-itself, knowledge, freedom and transcendence toward God. This limitation in material being, of course (its not being-conscious-of-itself in transcendence toward absolute being), is of a metaphysical kind that is constitutive of the essence.[33]

It must not be imagined that this inner real negativity belonging to the nature of a particular material being can be overcome by this being of its own power and that it thus can change itself into spirit by a mere intramundane process of becoming. This unlimiting of the limited (called material), however, does happen in the spirit, above all where the spirit itself enters so closely into materiality that it differentiates materiality from itself and keeps that materiality as a factor of its own becoming as a spirit, of its becoming-conscious-of-itself, that is, in man. What thus is lifted out of its negativity in and by the spirit is precisely the "spiritual reality" and positivity of the material, not just anything that would be known in its objectivity as alien to the spiritual; it is a moment of the spirit and of the fullness of being itself. Only in this way can Christian philosophy explain the Christian dogma that the soul is the form of the body;[34] for Thomistic philosophy, every reality in man, including every positive material reality, is the reality and the expression of his spirit.[35] "Thus the bodily nature of man is necessarily a factor in man's spiritual becoming; it is not something alien to the spirit, but a limited moment in

---

Leib in der Heilsordnung," *Schriften,* 12: 415, 423; "Die Christologie innerhalb einer evolutiven Weltanschauung," *Schriften,* 5: 187–88, 190; "Vom Geheimnis des Lebens," *Schriften,* 6: 182; *Sacramentum Mundi II,* s.v. "Jesus Christus," 942; "Christologie im Rahmen," *Schriften,* 9: 229–30; "Philosophie und Philosophieren in der Theologie," *Schriften,* 8: 87.

[33] "Die Einheit von Geist und Materie," *Schriften,* 6: 203; Rahner and Overhage, *Das Problem der Hominisation,* 51–52; see also *Geist,* 257, 267–68. Pearl, "Dialectical Panentheism," 131, notes the Hegelian influence in this description of matter as "frozen spirit."

[34] *Geist,* 254, 325; *Hörer 1,* 154–55, 161.

[35] See *Geist,* 326–27, 329, 351, 382.

the achievement of the spirit itself."[36] This is true also of the rest of the material world, particularly because the material world must be conceived from the start as the environment and as the broadened corporeality of the spirit.[37] It is ontologically quite indifferent to this process whether the realities of matter and spirit present themselves as existing simultaneously or as following one another in time, especially because it by no means is established clearly that God could have created the material world without the inner necessity of simultaneity and unity with those spiritual beings whom we call "angels."[38]

> Matter is, therefore, the bringing-itself-to-appearance of the personal spirit in the finite world and hence is from its very origin related to the spirit, is a moment in the spirit, and indeed a moment of the eternal Logos as he freely but in fact exists, and this for all eternity.[39]

3. EVOLUTION AND THE PROBLEM OF BECOMING

Presupposing this understanding of spirit and matter, Rahner is in a position to examine whether his understanding of matter-spirit is compatible, first, with an evolutionary worldview and, second, with the Christian dogma of the direct divine creation of the soul.

Both science and metaphysics can, each from its own angle,

---

[36] "Die Einheit von Geist und Materie," *Schriften,* 6: 204; Rahner and Overhage, *Das Problem der Hominisation,* 52–53. Grounded in *Geist,* 379, 382–83, 405, and in *Hörer 1,* 178.

[37] "Die Einheit von Geist und Materie," *Schriften,* 6: 204; "Der Leib in der Heilsordnung," *Schriften,* 12: 426–27; "Die Christologie innerhalb einer evolutiven Weltanschauung," *Schriften,* 5: 190; "Kirche und Parousie Christi," *Schriften,* 6: 366.

[38] That angels are linked to the material world: "Die Einheit von Geist und Materie," *Schriften,* 6: 204; see also 191–92, 200, 208. "Buch Gottes—Buch der Menschen," *Schriften,* 16: 280; Rahner and Overhage, *Das Problem der Hominisation,* 47–48; "Vom Geheimnis des Lebens," *Schriften,* 6: 182; *Sacramentum Mundi II,* s.v. "Jesus Christus," 943; "Christologie im Rahmen," *Schriften,* 9: 230.

[39] "Die Einheit von Geist und Materie," *Schriften,* 6: 205. This assertion is important in the context of Christology, to which we will return later. See also *Schriften,* 6: 203, 206; Rahner and Overhage, *Das Problem der Hominisation,* 52–54; "Der Leib in der Heilsordnung," *Schriften,* 12: 422; "Die Christologie innerhalb einer evolutiven Weltanschauung," *Schriften,* 5: 192–95.

quite well think of God as the transcendent ground of all reality, but precisely for that reason cannot think of him as a partial factor and component in the reality with which we are confronted or as a member of its causal series. "For unaided metaphysics, therefore, God cannot be met with among other things as one of them. His activity is not an item in our experience, but is present as the ground, implicitly and simultaneously affirmed, of every reality met with and affirmed."[40] This fundamental conception has even become a methodological principle of the natural sciences, insofar as a phenomenon encountered is explained by being referred back to another phenomenon as its cause. Recourse to God as an explanation of a phenomenon experienced is not an explanatory option in the natural sciences.

Accepting the direct creation of the soul by God as a predicamental intervention within creation seems to postulate an event in which secondary causes within the closed causal series are suddenly replaced by God himself. Can we not instead say that God is the cause of the soul because by definition he is the cause of everything, but that he is cause in the way in which it is proper to him, and to him alone, to be a cause?

> The concept of God's operation as an enduring, active support of cosmic reality must be elaborated in such a way that this divine operation itself is envisaged as actively enabling finite beings themselves by their own activity to transcend themselves, and this in such a way that if the concept holds good in general, it will also hold good for the "creation of the spiritual soul."[41]

A. Becoming in the Cognitive Process

In order to establish this theory, we require two presuppositions. First, a genuine ontological concept can be proved by a transcendental deduction; its validity is made plain by showing that it is

---

[40] Rahner and Overhage, *Das Problem der Hominisation*, 58. See also *Geist*, 232, 387–92; *Hörer 1*, 15, 87, 110, 187; "Über den Begriff des Geheimnisses," *Schriften*, 4: 74, 78.

[41] Rahner and Overhage, *Das Problem der Hominisation*, 61. For a good analysis of Rahner's theory of becoming, see H. Falk, "Can Spirit Come from Matter?" *International Philosophical Quarterly* 7 (1967): 549–55.

implicitly affirmed as valid even when it is merely inquired into or even when its validity is expressly contested or doubted. Second, for human beings, the ontologically first and fundamental case or paradigm of a being and of its fundamental properties is found in the being himself who knows and acts. The mental event as such is the individually occurring real and actual event.[42] The physical must be regarded as a deficient mode of that being that is immanently present to itself and precisely thereby brings its own ontological nature as an objective datum before itself. "From that too it follows that if a genuine concept of becoming is to be attained, it must be attained in the operation of cognition itself."[43]

Looking at the ontological process of cognition, we find there the paradigm for inner-worldly becoming. Man is the finite knowing being whose transcendence to all being is the condition of possibility of his presence to self and his knowledge of the other. This horizon of being is not an object but rather the condition of possibility of all objects, that which is essential in all intellectual knowledge. It is, in its own way as term, an immanent component of transcendence as a reality belonging to spirit. To say that it is immanent means that the spiritual dynamism is not oriented toward it merely as a matter of fact, as if it could arbitrarily fix on another goal; in such a case, its dynamic nature would be independent of the transcendent term. Rather, the dynamism exists and can exist only because it tends precisely toward that term and therefore is sustained by it. The orienting term of transcendence is immanent in the dynamic tendency in such a way that it can enjoy that immanence only in virtue of being above the tendency and superior to it, "untouched" by it.

> The dialectical formula, asserting that it is by being above it that the orienting term is in the dynamic tendency as one of the factors that constitute it, is a formula that is both complex and single and cannot be resolved without detriment to the phenomenon in question.[44]

---

[42] Rahner and Overhage, *Das Problem der Hominisation,* 70–71. This assertion is, of course, only another consequence of Rahner's starting point that being *is* knowing: *Geist,* 82–83 passim.

[43] Rahner and Overhage, *Das Problem der Hominisation,* 71.

[44] Rahner and Overhage, *Das Problem der Hominisation,* 73.

The orienting term of transcendence moves the movement of the mind; it is the originating cause, the fundamental ground and reason of the mind's transcendental dynamism.[45]

B. Becoming As Self-Transcendence

Turning now to inner-worldly becoming, we can say that this becoming is the becoming of something really new that has an intramundane origin and yet is not simply the same as that from which it originates. Becoming is always and of its essence a self-transcendence of the cause, effected by the lower itself in an active surpassing of self. Thus, real becoming is not just duplication but a surpassing of self in which what becomes really becomes more than it was, and yet this more is not simply something added to it from outside.[46]

Hence, the agent's rising beyond and above itself in action and becoming takes place because the Absolute Being is the cause and ground of this self-movement in such a way that the latter has this fundamental ground immanent within it as a factor intrinsically related to the movement. It is true self-transcendence, not merely a passive being lifted beyond self. Yet it is not on that account a movement within Absolute Being because the latter, though a factor immanent in the self-movement of the subject of change that is advancing beyond itself, at the same time remains free and unaffected above it, unmoved but giving movement, an unmoved mover.[47] Precisely for that reason it follows that the movement

---

[45] Though not clearly elaborated in Rahner's earlier works, this notion of the term of transcendence moving the mind is grounded in his notion of the *Vorgriff* as the dynamic desire for the horizon of its transcendence: *Geist*, 263, 265–66, 285, 315; *Hörer 1*, 101.

[46] "Die Einheit von Geist und Materie," *Schriften*, 6: 210; Rahner and Overhage, *Das Problem der Hominisation*, 74–75.

[47] This idea of becoming as active self-transcendence is central to Rahner's thought: Rahner and Overhage, *Das Problem der Hominisation*, 74–78; "Die Einheit von Geist und Materie," *Schriften*, 6: 210–14; Rahner and Ratzinger, *Offenbarung und Überlieferung*, 13; *Sacramentum Mundi III*, s.v. "Offenbarung," 332; "Die Christologie innerhalb einer evolutiven Weltanschauung," *Schriften*, 5: 191, 199, 205; "Vom Geheimnis des Lebens," *Schriften*, 6: 172, 180; *Sacramentum Mundi II*, s.v. "Jesus Christus," 942; "Christologie im Rahmen," *Schriften*, 9: 230, 235–37; "Kirche und Parousie Christi," *Schriften*, 6: 356; "Kirchliche Christologie," *Schriften*, 9: 213; K. Rahner and W. Thüsing, *A New Christology*, translated by D. Smith and V. Green (London: Burns and Oates, 1980), 24;

does not cease to be self-movement when it becomes self-transcendence but attains its own proper nature thereby.[48]

> All finite causality is truly such in virtue of being that is operative both as immanent within it and as raised transcendent above it. This is so always and essentially, but that is precisely what gives finite causality its identity. And for the same reason, causality can in this perspective of movement from within by being as such be attributed to finite beings in regard to what is more than themselves.[49]

C. Nature and Self-Transcendence

From this notion of active self-transcendence, it follows that the nature or essence of each particular being "does not determine the limits of what can be produced in the advance beyond itself";[50] otherwise, there would be no real *self*-transcendence at all. Nevertheless, the essence of a being can be an indication that "although the agent transcends itself, the starting point of the movement always remains also the limiting law of what can directly come out of it."[51] Rahner claims support for his understanding from Thomistic metaphysics, where the various essences are only different grades of limitation of being. An essence low in the scale as regards what is positive in it is therefore not purely unlike and in contradiction to a higher essence. It is a lower nature in comparison with a higher because it contracts or limits being more narrowly than the latter.[52] If in its becoming it were

---

Rahner and Thüsing, *Christologie,* 13. See also Tremblay, *Finitude et devenir,* 22–23, 293, for an interesting analysis of Rahner's notion of becoming.

[48] A number of commentators have noted the Hegelian influence in this Rahnerian notion of becoming: Wong, *Logos-Symbol,* 126–27; K. Fischer, *Der Mensch als Geheimnis* (Freiburg, Basel, Vienna: Herder, 1974), 346; Pearl, "Dialectical Panentheism," 119–37; Carr, *Theological Method of Karl Rahner,* 86; Ernst, "Some Themes in the Theology of Karl Rahner," 256; Tremblay, *Finitude et devenir,* 39, 47 n. 1, 48 nn. 2 and 6, 87.

[49] Rahner and Overhage, *Das Problem der Hominisation,* 75–76. "Die Einheit von Geist und Materie," *Schriften,* 6: 211.

[50] Rahner and Overhage, *Das Problem der Hominisation,* 76.

[51] Rahner and Overhage, *Das Problem der Hominisation,* 76–77; "Die Einheit von Geist und Materie," *Schriften,* 6: 211–12.

[52] This understanding is grounded, as we have seen, in Rahner's metaphysics: *Geist,* 159, 161, 170–72, 180.

to move beyond itself, even in the sense of transcending its own essence, such transcendence would not involve the positing of a purely disparate being absolutely alien to its nature. In a similar way, absolute dynamic, transcendent orientation toward being in general does not of itself make it possible for everything to be known at any moment by a finite knowing subject. The particular subject matter of knowledge is supplied by experience in each case and is the norm and limit of cognition. Becoming as self-transcendence in virtue of absolute being, therefore, does not exclude the question of the more precise sequence of stages of becoming, which opens out limitlessly. In such a causal sequence, just what and in what way something can follow something else directly can be determined only from actual experience. "If what has been said is correct . . . it is possible quietly to affirm that these principles can also be applied to the evolutionary development of material things toward spirit."[53]

D. Divine Creation of the Soul and Active Self-Transcendence

On the specific issue of the body–soul relation, the church holds that the spiritual soul of man is created directly by God. This one instance seems to involve viewing God's creative act as different from everywhere else where God acts as the transcendent ground of all reality. Divine causality that can be localized historically at certain points in space and time appears to be what characterizes the supernatural operation of God in sacred history, in contrast to the natural relation of God to his world, where God effects everything through secondary causes. But this apparent problem is solved if God's creation of the soul is seen as an example of Rahner's notion of "becoming."

> But if the operation of a creature is in principle to be regarded as a self-transcendence in such a way that the effect is not derivable from the essence of the creature acting and yet must be considered as effected by this agent, it is possible to say, without anxiety, if such a general concept of becoming and operation is presupposed, that the parents are the cause of the entire human being and so also

---

[53] Rahner and Overhage, *Das Problem der Hominisation*, 78. "Die Einheit von Geist und Materie," *Schriften*, 6: 213. See Tremblay, *Finitude et devenir*, 289 ff. Vass maintains that this idea of matter transcending itself into spirit is an unscientific and empty theory that cannot be proved: *Mystery of Man*, 47–49.

of its soul because that not only does not exclude but positively includes the fact that the parents can only be the cause of the human being in virtue of the power of God, which renders possible their self-transcendence and which is immanent in their causality without belonging to the constitutive factors of their essence.[54]

4. Conclusion

Rahner's theory of symbol is both innovative and brilliant. Because all being is in itself plural and because the plural moments in the unity of a being must have an inner agreement, being as such develops or emerges into a plurality. This plurality, which is still originally one, is in agreement because derivative; and because derivatively in agreement, it is expressive or symbolic. Thus, being is symbolic insofar as it necessarily expresses itself, and because this expression is the way in which it communicates itself to itself, a being comes to itself by means of its expression insofar as it comes to itself at all.

The prime analogue of this process is to be found in the Trinity, in the relationship of the Father with the Logos. But it is also clear that a similar relationship exists between the soul and the body of man, thus indicating that being can express itself in the other of matter in order to come to itself. This serves as the basis of Rahner's explanation of the relationship between matter and spirit. For Rahner has already argued, in his analysis of human knowing, that the intellect enters into the other of matter by allowing sensibility to emanate from it and so comes to itself. Now he elaborates on this theory of emanation, arguing that the body of man is the symbol of his spirit, distinct from the spirit, yet constituted by the spirit, where the spirit expresses itself and possesses itself. Such an understanding can hold only if the relationship of spirit and matter is such that a metaphysical separation of the two realities would be unthinkable, which is possible only if we define matter as "frozen" spirit. Matter is not alien to the spirit, but a limited moment in the achievement of the spirit itself and, indeed, in the light of the incarnation of the Logos, a moment of the eternal Logos itself.

---

[54] Rahner and Overhage, *Das Problem der Hominisation,* 82. Pearl, "Dialectical Panentheism," 134, notes that Rahner's argument here is dangerously close to panentheism.

Furthermore, this relationship can be shown to be compatible with an evolutionary worldview providing only *(a)* that matter is seen as existing solely in view of spirit and *(b)* that God, as the ground of all inner-worldly becoming, is immanent within the process precisely by being transcendent of it. That such dialectical conditions of possibility can be grounded rationally is established through an analysis of the process of human knowing, where, as we have seen, the substantial unity of spirit and material sensibility is established and where the term of the human dynamism is immanent within the dynamism precisely by transcending it. Thus, the evolutionary development of matter toward spirit is both possible and fully compatible with traditional Christian affirmations concerning the distinction of matter and spirit and the direct divine creation of the soul.

Rahner's understanding of both symbol and becoming is highly dialectical and is clearly grounded in that flexible structure of dialectical analogy that is basic to his metaphysical foundation and that enables him to hold together traditional polarities throughout his theology. In line with the dynamic unifying side of his thought, he asserts that being is plural in its unity and that it symbolizes itself to be itself; that matter and spirit are unified to the extent of defining matter as "frozen spirit"; and that in the process of inner-worldly becoming God is immanent in the process of self-transcendence. Yet simultaneously, in line with the conceptualizing and distinguishing side of his thought, he asserts the real distinction between the symbol and the symbolized and between spirit and matter, and that God is transcendent of the process of becoming precisely by being immanent. Applying this symbol theory to the Trinity, he argues that the Logos is the symbol of the Father and uses this connection as the theological justification of his whole theory. However, when he also says that the humanity of Christ is the symbol of the Logos, he seems to make no distinction between the symbolic nature of the eternal Logos and the symbolic nature of the finite humanity of Christ; in doing so, he appears to incorporate matter into the eternal life of the Trinity. To this problem as well as to Rahner's problematic definition of matter as "frozen spirit" we shall return later, for although this formulation clearly manifests his dialectical structure of thought in which matter and spirit are both one and yet distinct, it nevertheless seems to bring him very close to philosophical monism.

5

History and Revelation

RAHNER unifies his whole theory of revelation under the one analogous concept of "word of God." From the inner "word" of grace, through the categorical "word" of revelation strictly speaking, to the church and ultimately the sacraments, the whole work of God's self-communication to man can be described as various degrees of the one "word" spoken by God to his spiritual-physical creation. Through this unified approach to revelation in which, true to the basic structure of man *(Schwebe),* the inner word of grace and the outer word of official revelation are linked intrinsically in a relationship of unity in diversity, Rahner seeks to avoid both the immanentism of modernism and a merely extrinsic concept of revelation.[1]

In this chapter, I analyze the development of Rahner's theory of revelation. I note how the dialectical structure of his thought enables him to keep a balance between the two perspectives of the relationship between inner and outer words and how this same structure is apparent in his similarly two-fold understanding of the Catholic Church and the sacraments. Finally, I again note, this time in the context of his theology of revelation, the development that occurs in his thought in the mid-1960s and becomes increasingly prevalent in his later work.

1. The "Word of God"

A. Grace as the "Inner Word of God"

Catholic understanding of human salvation has never been considered as a type of extrinsic divine imputation of the justice of Christ to man, and therefore the church has always insisted that

---

[1] Carr, *Theological Method of Karl Rahner,* 106, notes this emphasis in Rahner's early works.

man's act of faith is necessary for his salvation. However, lest such human faith be regarded in a Pelagian fashion as self-justification, the church also insists that this human act of faith must itself be determined by grace. In view of the reality of sin, grace is always the condition of possibility of any salutary act on the part of man and is therefore at least logically prior to any such act. Hence, the acceptance of the gift of divine revelation is itself part of the gift insofar as this grace works as *efficacious grace* to bring about the act of acceptance and works as *elevating grace* to bring it about in its quality. This prevenient grace of God, which constitutes man's act in its reality and bestows on that act its quality, is to be qualified as enlightenment and inspiration, and, hence, "it is, by definition, 'word,' that is, spiritual self-communication of God to the creature, especially as this grace is not this or that created reality, but the real self-communication of God in 'uncreated' grace."[2]

B. The Relationship of Inner and Outer "Word of God"

Given the nature of man as *Schwebe,* the inward self-communication of God in grace, "verbal" though it is in itself, alone cannot be adequate for the normal and fully developed act of its acceptance. Of itself it would remain to a certain extent merely a transcendental, unobjectified knowledge of this gracious act of God on man, which could not be brought into the region of reflective consciousness.[3] If the verbal communication of God were already complete in the inner word of grace, man would accomplish his salvation only in the nonreflective transcendence of his being, while the dimension of worldly categories remain outside the scope of salutary acts.[4] However, if man is essentially and primor-

---

[2] "Wort und Eucharistie," *Schriften,* 4: 319; "Über den Begriff des Geheimnisses," *Schriften,* 4: 54–55.

[3] This idea follows of course from Rahner's foundational understanding of man as that being who must go out of himself in order to be present-to-self: *Geist,* 235, 242, 244, 250, 256–57, 287, 313, 382–83, 387; *Hörer 1,* 147–48, 151, 156, 176, 202, 208. See also Vass, *Mystery of Man,* 37; Allik, "Karl Rahner on Materiality," 371–72; Girotto, "Il problema dell'essere," 572–73.

[4] Wong, *Logos-Symbol,* 233–35; Vass, *Theologian in Search of a Philosophy,* 16, 121–23; Carr, *Theological Method of Karl Rahner,* 189–91, 203, 206, 262–64. All three commentators fail to see the double emphasis here and consequently interpret only the outer categorical word in terms of the unifying dynamic side of Rahner's thought as a posterior expression of grace.

dially a being in community, even in his salutary decision, then
knowledge of his grace cannot be given adequately by his inner
experience of grace alone. It must come to him also from without, though not exclusively, from the world, from the community, from the history of salvation, which is a social event
historically transmitted.

> But this means that the proclamation of the word of God, that is,
> the word insofar as it is conveyed by the *historical,* external salvific
> act of God as an intrinsic moment of this act and by the community
> of believers, belongs necessarily to the inner moments of God's
> salvific *action* on man.[5]

To understand this statement we must recall the essential connection that (in view of the nature of man and of symbol) always
must exist between the inner word of grace and the external,
historical, social, and ecclesiastical word of revelation.[6] On the
one hand (in line with the dynamic, unifying side of Rahner's
thought), the inner word comes to categorical expression in the
outer word. On the other hand and simultaneously (in line with
the conceptualizing, distinguishing side of his thought), the outer
word is still necessary, for inner and outer words exist in a relationship of mutual priority. The external, historical word expounds the inner one, brings it to the light of consciousness in
the categories of human understanding, compels man definitely
to make a decision with regard to the inner word, transposes the
inner grace of man into the dimension of the community, and
renders it present there. It makes possible the insertion of grace
into the external historical field of human life. Nonetheless, only
the inner grace makes it possible for man to hear the external,
historical word of God strictly as the word of God. "In a word,

---

[5] "Wort und Eucharistie," *Schriften,* 4: 320; *Sacramentum Mundi IV,* s.v.
"Selbstmitteilung Gottes," 524–25. See also *Hörer 1,* 20, 111, 197, 227.

[6] This relationship of mutual priority between the transcendental and the categorical is central to Rahner's thought and has been well noted: Vass, *Theologian
in Search of a Philosophy,* 24, 47, 121, and *Mystery of Man,* 55–56, 95–96, 123,
132, 154, 378; Carr, *Theological Method of Karl Rahner,* 59, 87–88, 206, 262;
Moloney, "Seeing and Knowing," 412; J. Cawte, "Karl Rahner's Conception
of God's Self-Communication to Man," *Heythrop Journal* 25 (1984), 269–70;
Girotto, "Il problema dell'essere," 577–78; Honner, "Unity-in-Difference,"
485; Lennan, *Ecclesiology of Karl Rahner,* 53–54.

for the full normal accomplishment of the personal self-disclosure of God to the personally actualized man, the inner word of grace and the external historical word come together as the mutually complimentary moments of the one word of God to man."[7] Assertions about God's salvific action on man are, therefore, of their nature assertions about the word of God—understood as two-fold in the unity of the inner and outer word. This understanding of mutual priority allows Rahner to conclude that in the

> efficacious preaching of the word of God, that which is preached takes on the character of an event. It means that the grace of God is not merely spoken of, but takes place as an event in this utterance. The word of grace and grace itself must then always be distinguished as moments of a total process because they do not simply coincide, any more than the efficacious sacramental sign is simply identical with the grace which it signifies and produces. But this does not change the fact that the word and reality in contrast to ordinary human speech are essentially related to one another and form a unity.[8]

The word of God in its full, original sense is not to be taken as a set of doctrinal propositions "about something."[9] It is not just the intellectual description of something that exists and is available completely independently of this doctrinal instruction. It is rather a revelatory, actualizing word, in which and under which the thing designated is present in a reciprocal relationship of such a kind that the word is formed by the thing that thus comes, and the thing comes by making itself thus audible.

C. The Analogous Nature of the "Word of God"

This word, which occurs in the form of an event, takes place in the church in essentially varying degrees of concentration and intensity. It is analogous; that is, it is capable of and subject to inner changes.[10] There are degrees, which are, in fact, degrees of how the word of God makes the reality present. The reality in

---

[7] "Wort und Eucharistie," *Schriften*, 4: 321.
[8] "Wort und Eucharistie," *Schriften*, 4: 325.
[9] Lennan, *Ecclesiology of Karl Rahner*, 48–49, 82, 140.
[10] "Was ist ein Sakrament?" *Schriften*, 10: 381–82.

question always strives for a single all-embracing goal, which is
that God should bestow himself totally on man in man's total
acceptance. But this single and absolute goal of grace is reached
only by stages in finite man, who is involved in history. There is,
therefore, an inner variability of the one essence of the word of
God, from the prophetic word through the doctrinal word to
the sacramental word, which is its supreme and most intensive
realization, where what is spoken and what is symbolized are truly
one.[11]

D. The Sacrament as "Word of God"

When speaking of the sacraments, we are accustomed to distinguish between the word and the element, or, in hylomorphic
terms, between form and matter. But this distinction, correct
though it may be, ought not to obscure that both elements participate in the symbolic character of the sacrament and hence in its
quality of being *word*. The sacramental action, too, has the character of a word. Thus, it is perfectly legitimate to subsume the
whole sacrament under the concept of "efficacious word." In
some sacraments, this efficacious word must be pronounced in a
form that includes the element of the ritual action. This is due to
the positive decree of him who institutes the efficacious word.
"For sign and words . . . are of exactly the same nature";[12] thus,
the whole sign of grace, no matter what form it takes, must par-
take of the character of the word. Concerning matter and form,
we must remember that it cannot be true that the material element of the sacrament (water and so on) is decisive for the constitution of the sacrament. A purely material thing in the nature of
an object can never function as a sign in such a way that the
supernatural reality can be attained through it alone.[13]

If all that has been said so far is true, the only question that
remains is whether the sacraments can be distinguished clearly and
sufficiently from other forms of God's efficacious word.

---

[11] "Wort und Eucharistie," *Schriften,* 4: 327.

[12] "Wort und Eucharistie," *Schriften,* 4: 330.

[13] "Wort und Eucharistie," *Schriften,* 4: 331; "Was ist ein Sakrament?" *Schriften,* 10: 380.

E. *The Distinction Between the Sacramental and the Nonsacramental "Word of God"*

In the classic definition of the sacraments, the generic concept "sign" is specified by the addition of the phrase *"(signum) efficax gratiae—ex opere operato."* The same formal process of logic also must be applied to the concept "word," and the sacrament can be defined as "the word of Christ on the lips of the church, which confers grace *ex opere operato.*"[14] According to Rahner's own argument, every word of God efficaciously bestows grace, and the concept of *opus operatum* is, therefore, not particularly clear. A new definition of *opus operatum* is necessary if we are to hold on to the old definition of sacrament. Two features, when taken together, constitute the objective content of this definition: "the word as the fullest actualization of the church in its absolute commitment, and the word spoken in the decisive situations of human salvation."[15] To understand why these two features cover the concept of *opus operatum* and determine it more exactly than is usual, we must reflect on the nature of the church as "primary sacrament."[16]

The church, in its concrete reality, is the permanent sign that God not merely offers the grace of his self-communication, but in the triumphant efficaciousness of his grace also powerfully brings about the acceptance of this offer. It is not just that the world can be saved if it wills; it in fact is saved as a whole because God brings it about in Christ that the world does will to be saved. The history of salvation is not yet closed for the individual, but as a whole the history of salvation is already decided positively.[17]

---

[14] "Wort und Eucharistie," *Schriften,* 4: 336.

[15] "Wort und Eucharistie," *Schriften,* 4: 337; "Fragen der Sakramententheologie," *Schriften,* 16: 401.

[16] "Überlegungen zum personalen Vollzug," *Schriften,* 10: 424–26; "Was ist ein Sakrament?" *Schriften,* 10: 384–86.

[17] That in Christ the whole of history already is decided positively: "Wort und Eucharistie," *Schriften,* 4: 338; "Überlegungen zum personalen Vollzug," *Schriften,* 10: 415; *Sacramentum Mundi III,* s.v. "Offenbarung," 834–35; Rahner and Ratzinger, *Offenbarung und Überlieferung,* 15–16; "Buch Gottes—Buch der Menschen," *Schriften,* 16: 282, 290; "Die Christologie innerhalb einer evolutiven Weltanschauung," *Schriften,* 5: 203; Rahner and Thüsing, *A New Christology,* 25; "Zur Frage der Dogmenentwicklung," *Schriften,* 1: 60; *Sendung und Gnade,* 68; "Der eine Jesus Christus," *Schriften,* 12: 269.

"And of this eschatological situation . . . the church, as historically visible, is the sign, the historical audible word which proclaims this victory and in which this victory constitutes itself present in the world."[18] This means that the reality of the church has the character of a sign, finally and forever. The pre-Christian and other non-Christian manifestations of God's salvific dealings with men in the realities of accessible history can be rendered ineffective by men's disbelief—as is still possible today with regard to individual words of God to individual men. But the church is of itself the final, irrevocable, eschatologically permanent word of salvation to the world. Hence, the church is the primary sacrament.

Within this perspective, the concept of *opus operatum* may be envisaged in its real meaning. This concept cannot be defined simply by saying, in the formal juridical terms of decretal theology, that such a process is efficacious of itself and without merit on the part of the subject of the process, for there are other processes (for example, prayer offered in the name of Jesus) of which the same may be said. Rather, the *opus operatum* is to be taken as the supreme degree of the church's actuality, as the act of its self-realization, and as such is much more proper to its nature than if it were something static and substancelike, less dependent on an act being done.

> It follows at once that such an act participates in the nature of the church, as described when we said that it was the final, inviolable, and intrinsically definitive sign of God's absolute self-bestowal on the world in this triumphant grace. And precisely the same may be said of the basic acts of the church. Where it actualizes itself in an ultimate commitment of its being toward an individual . . . no longer provisional and conditional in a dialectical dialogue: this is precisely what we should describe as an *opus operatum*.[19]

The *opus operatum* is the eschatologically efficacious word of God as the absolute self-realization of the church according to its essence as the primary sacrament.

---

[18] "Wort und Eucharistie," *Schriften*, 4: 338; "Fragen der Sakramententheologie," *Schriften*, 16: 400–401; "Was ist ein Sakrament?" *Schriften*, 10: 386.

[19] "Wort und Eucharistie," *Schriften*, 4: 340; "Einleitende Bemerkungen zur allgemeinen Sakramentenlehre bei Thomas von Aquin," *Schriften*, 10: 397–98; "Was ist ein Sakrament?" *Schriften*, 10: 387.

F. All Other Words Ordained to the Sacramental "Word of God"

Every word of God on the lips of the church—which precedes, accompanies, and follows the sacramental word of the church—always and everywhere must be considered as ordained to the sacramental word.

> For God does not say all sorts of things to men, and his words are not a miscellany of disconnected subjects. In the last resort, he utters only one thing, which is himself as eternal salvation. . . . And hence the diverse words have all an intrinsic connection and derive their sense and value from this one concentration of meaning, which comes to a climax in the sacramental word.[20]

There exists between the sacramental word of God in the church and other words of the church's preaching the same relationship as between the sacramental process of justification and the nonsacramental. There is one sacramental process of justification, and it is necessary for salvation. "But the church and the theologians have never maintained . . . that there could be no nonsacramental justification because otherwise the value and necessity of sacramental justification would disappear."[21] We must not start by taking the two things as independent realities: they are phases and moments of the same process. The salvation of the one, complete, efficacious word of God has its history and its phases; each phase shares the being of the whole, while the whole reality is truly present and effective in each phase. This does not make the succeeding phase superfluous. On the contrary, the full and effective presence of the whole reality in each phase is what really demands the succeeding phase because only in the fully formal, historical, and tangible whole—that is, in the sacrament—does the essentially envisaged whole reach its full manifestation—a manifestation that is of the essence of the thing in an incarnational structure of salvation. "They are phases of the self-realization and historical self-presentation of the one and the same essence of the one efficacious word of God, which, where (and only where) it attains under God and Christ its unambiguous, historical and ecclesio-

---

[20] "Wort und Eucharistie," *Schriften,* 4: 345.
[21] "Wort und Eucharistie," *Schriften,* 4: 346.

logical presence, its embodiment and eschatological absoluteness, is called sacrament."[22]

G. The Eucharist as "Word of God" par Excellence

All that has been said hitherto comes in the Eucharist to an unsurpassable climax. The Eucharist is "word" because here the incarnate Logos of God is himself present in his substance.

> The Eucharist is not only the supreme case of those acts of self-realization of the church which are called sacraments; it is the real origin of all other sacraments—which in their turn are so much the self-realization of the church that all other words and actions of the church have essentially the function of serving these acts of self-realization and are only really justified and intelligible in the light of the sacraments. And then we may say that the Eucharist is simply the word of God in the church, which supports and conveys all other words, which forms the center whence all the reality of the church derives its meaning. The Eucharist is the word of the church absolutely.[23]

Notions concerning the Protestant Church as the church of the Word and the Catholic Church as the church of the sacrament, and concerning two tables in the church, one of word and one of sacrament, are based simply on misinterpretations and stunted versions of Catholic doctrine. The Eucharist is in all truth the sacrament of the word absolutely. To understand this properly we must bear in mind that, according to the Council of Trent, Christ is present by virtue of the *panis vinique benedictio,* the consecration. The Council emphasized expressly that the body and blood of Christ are present *vi verborum.* Therefore, if we say that Christ is present under the species, we also can say that Christ is present only through the permanent validity of the anamnesis, that is, the words of consecration. The explanatory words of Christ are not merely the efficient cause of this sign, but an intrinsic constitutive element of it. Thus, the words of consecration remain as an element of the sacramental sign even after the actual moment of consecration.

---

[22] "Wort und Eucharistie," *Schriften,* 4: 347.
[23] "Wort und Eucharistie," *Schriften,* 4: 349.

The Eucharist is and remains the presence of the Lord through and under the efficacious word, which has two components: the purely material one, the indeterminate in itself and needing to be determined, of the physical species of bread and wine, and the more spiritual one, formal, determinative, clear, and declaratory, that of the explanatory words of the Lord. And both are needed—both having the character of sign and hence of a word—to form the one sign in this sacrament, through which he that is signified is present.[24]

2. GRACE AS HISTORICAL REVELATION

We now have seen how Rahner's early theory of revelation holds together; however, as I have indicated, in a number of important later articles Rahner's perspective changes decisively in one important respect.[25] Although continuing to insist that the inner word of God must be expressed in the outer categorical word, he seems to move away from a mutual priority between the inner word of grace and official, historical revelation, toward an understanding of grace itself as revelation, which, because it occurs in history and is mediated historically, itself constitutes historical revelation, without, he insists, thereby relativizing the meaning of official historical revelation as such. At this later stage presupposing the priority of grace (in line with the unifying side of his thought), Rahner argues that grace, the inner word of divine revelation offered to all people, comes to categorical expression (true to the fundamental nature of man as *Schwebe*) in *any* historical or categorical factor that mediates this grace to itself and brings it to consciousness.[26] This transcendentally grace-given revelation can

---

[24] "Wort und Eucharistie," *Schriften,* 4: 352–53; "Einleitende Bemerkungen," *Schriften,* 10: 397–98.

[25] Carr, *Theological Method of Karl Rahner,* 27, notices this change, as does Ratzinger, "Vom Verstehen des Glaubens," 182, who is critical of such an assertion.

[26] "Einleitende Bemerkungen," *Schriften,* 10: 402; "Überlegungen zum personalen Vollzug," *Schriften,* 10: 413, 416, 418–419, 427. Rahner's commentators often stress this emphasis to the exclusion of the other side of his thought: for example, J. Carmody, "The Realism of Christian Life," in O'Donovan, ed., *A World of Grace,* 143–44; A. Callahan, "Karl Rahner's Theology of Symbol: Basis for His Theology of the Church and the Sacraments," *Irish Theological Quarterly* 49 (1982), 200–201; Molnar, "Is God Essentially Different?" 615.

be termed *historical revelation* and can be valid as mediating grace to itself even if categorically false. However, true to the foundational structure of his thought and lest the whole process of revelation threaten to dissolve into some form of modernistic relativism, Rahner insists (in line with the distinguishing, conceptualizing side of his thought) that what is termed *official historical revelation* is nevertheless a necessary part of the whole process as the fullest and truest expression to which all grace dynamically tends and that therefore symbolically causes all previously given grace, through the notion of mutual priority.[27] It is only in the light of divinely guaranteed official revelation that we are able to distinguish between true and false categorical mediations of transcendental revelation.

A. Grace as Historical Revelation

In two articles dating from the mid- and late 1960s, Rahner poses the question of how revelation, despite its directly divine origin, can constitute the very core of human history. How, in other words, "can revelation be present everywhere and at all times for the salvation of all men in all ages, without ceasing to be a free act of God which we, in our view of history, cannot count on?"[28] The fundamental principle required to answer this question is found in the standard Christian doctrines of grace, the salvific will of God, and the necessity of faith for salvation. If these doctrines are taken seriously and applied to the doctrine of revelation, then it is possible, without falling into modernism, to recognize that the history of revelation is the historical self-unfolding of the transcendental relation between man and God, which is constituted by God's self-communication. "This communication of grace is supernatural but is made to every mind inescapably and always, and can itself rightly be called revelation."[29] However, transcen-

---

[27] "Personale und sakramentale Frömmigkeit," *Schriften*, 2: 128. Rahner's commentators often miss this point: Vass, *Mystery of Man*, 137–38, 140, 142–43, 150; Ratzinger, "Vom Verstehen des Glaubens," 178–86; Carr, *Theological Method of Karl Rahner*, 189–91.

[28] *Sacramentum Mundi III*, s.v. "Offenbarung," 832; Rahner and Ratzinger, *Offenbarung und Überlieferung*, 13.

[29] That grace can be interpreted as revelation: *Sacramentum Mundi III*, s.v. "Offenbarung," 833; "Zur 'Offenbarungsgeschichte,'" *Schriften*, 12: 243–44. This

dence actually operates only in history and in fact always is mediated historically. "Consequently this absolute transcendence directed toward the absolute presence of the ineffable mystery giving himself to men has a history, and this history is what we call the history of revelation."[30] Active revelation always presents two aspects. On the one hand, it constitutes man's supernaturally elevated transcendence as his permanent (grace-given) existential. As such, it is the transcendental experience of the absolute closeness of God. On the other hand, the active revelation event is also a historical mediation and conceptual objectification of this supernaturally transcendental experience. The latter takes place in history and, taken in its totality, constitutes the whole of history.

B. World History Is the History of Revelation

This perspective is the basis for Rahner's well-known affirmation that the history of revelation, both transcendental and predicamental, is coextensive with the spiritual history of mankind as such,[31] for the history of supernatural salvation is operative everywhere in history because God wants all to be saved. Now, if salvation is impossible without faith and faith is impossible without revelation strictly speaking, then we must assume that every human being is elevated by grace in his transcendental intellectuality in a nonexplicit manner and that this supernatural existential itself constitutes for every human being a revelation of God through his self-communication in grace. This grace-given fun-

---

assertion has been criticized as a relativization of both human and divine freedom: Eicher, *Die Anthropologische Wende,* 368; Molnar, "Is God Essentially Different?" 575–77, 593, 602; Simons, *Philosophie der Offenbarung,* 43.

[30] *Sacramentum Mundi III,* s.v. "Offenbarung," 834; Rahner and Ratzinger, *Offenbarung und Überlieferung,* 14.

[31] That salvation history is coextensive with world history: *Sacramentum Mundi III,* s.v. "Offenbarung," 834–35; Rahner and Ratzinger, *Offenbarung und Überlieferung,* 15–16; "Kirchliche Christologie," *Schriften,* 9: 213; "Kirche, Kirchen, und Religionen," *Schriften,* 8: 361, 363–64, 370; "Zur 'Offenbarungsgeschichte,'" *Schriften,* 12: 249–50; "Überlegungen zum personalen Vollzug," *Schriften,* 10: 413–15; "Glaube und Sakrament," *Schriften,* 16: 394; "Buch Gottes—Buch der Menschen," *Schriften,* 16: 290; "Zum heutigen Verhältnis von Philosophie und Theologie," *Schriften,* 10: 70; "Zum Verhältnis zwischen Theologie und heutigen Wissenschaften," *Schriften,* 10: 108. See also Lennan, *Ecclesiology of Karl Rahner,* 114–16, and Tremblay, *Finitude et devenir,* 289.

damental subjective disposition can be regarded as a word of revelation, provided that it is remembered that such transcendental
revelation always is mediated historically and that man's historical
reality can never be without language. That reality never consists
in dead facts because the interpretation of the facts is itself a constitutive factor of any historical event. "No revelation . . . is given
solely by this transcendentally experienced openness of man to
the triune God. What is given is something more, and this forms
the basis of all the articles of faith and is the condition of their
very possibility."[32]

C. Official Revelation within General Historical Revelation

The graced transcendental a priori openness of man to God is
necessarily accomplished in the history of the action and thought
of mankind in a more or a less explicit way. There consequently
can never be a history of transcendental revelation in isolation,
and all historical mediation, whether Christian or not, can be perceived as valid in bringing about and authenticating the absolute
experience of God. Although grace validly can be mediated to
itself and expressed through all of human history, it has an inner
dynamic toward its categorically truest and fullest mediation and
expression.[33]

> It is what is called the history of revelation, in the usual sense,
> when it really is the history of the true self-interpretation of this
> supernaturally transcendental experience, and not its misinterpreta-
> tion, and when . . . in accordance with his [God's] supernatural
> saving providence it is explicitly known as such.[34]

The unique and final culmination of this history of revelation
in fact has occurred already and has revealed the absolute and
irrevocable unity of God's transcendental self-communication to

---

[32] *Sacramentum Mundi III*, s.v. "Offenbarung," 836; Rahner and Ratzinger,
Offenbarung und Überlieferung, 18.

[33] That grace tends toward its fullest categorical expression: *Sacramentum Mundi
IV*, s.v. "Selbstmitteilung Gottes," 524–25; "Zum Verhältnis zwischen Theo-
logie und heutigen Wissenschaften," *Schriften*, 10: 108; "Glaubensakt und
Glaubensinhalt," *Schriften*, 15: 158.

[34] *Sacramentum Mundi III*, s.v. "Offenbarung," 834; Rahner and Ratzinger,
Offenbarung und Überlieferung, 15.

mankind and of its historical mediation in the one God-man Jesus Christ, who is at once God himself as communicated, the human acceptance of this communication, and the final historical manifestation of this offer and acceptance. It is toward this ultimate and complete divine revelation, in which transcendental grace and its categorical manifestation are united perfectly, that grace in its own dynamic essence tends, and, as Rahner will argue in line with the distinguishing side of his thought, it is in view of this complete revelation that all grace is originally bestowed.[35]

All history in the concrete is the history of God's transcendental revelation, but such concrete history is never revelation pure and simple, for revelation in ordinary history is always mingled with error, misinterpretation, guilt, and abuses. It is a history of salvation and of sin. This history in no way excludes but on the contrary actually implies a genuine history of official guaranteed revelation, toward which all transcendental grace-given revelation tends; it only indicates that in the concrete historical order, truth and error always will be found together. Furthermore, if the history of religion is that part of general history where the theological nature of man becomes the focus of explicit attention, it will be the most explicit part of the history of revelation, where the transcendental experience will be both interpreted and misinterpreted most explicitly.[36]

3. Conclusion

Rahner's theory of revelation is fascinating and important, for in his progressive elaboration of the theme a definite change of perspective is clearly apparent, which is vital for the future development of his thought and which has been seized on and misinterpreted by many of his commentators.

Having united the whole of revelation under the one analogous concept of "word of God," Rahner analyzes the nature of God's

---

[35] "Die Christologie innerhalb einer evolutiven Weltanschauung," *Schriften*, 5: 203; "Der eine Mittler und die Vielfalt der Vermittlungen," *Schriften*, 8: 230–31; *Sendung und Gnade,* 61; "Der eine Jesus Christus," *Schriften*, 12: 269.

[36] *Sacramentum Mundi III,* s.v. "Offenbarung," 837; Rahner and Ratzinger, *Offenbarung und Überlieferung,* 18–19.

self-communication to man. In his early phase (pre-1965), he continues the process begun in his work on grace and on symbol; namely, he elaborates a theory of revelation very much in accordance with the foundational structure of his thought. On the one hand, in line with the dynamic unifying side of his thought, he argues that the inner word of grace must according to the nature of man as *Schwebe* come to categorical expression in the outer historical word of "official revelation," in the church, and ultimately in the sacraments. In this way, he proposes a novel interpretation of *ex opere operato,* guaranteeing the effective operation of the church and the sacraments. On the other hand and simultaneously in line with the conceptualizing, distinguishing side of his thought, he stresses that the inner and outer words stand in a relationship of mutual priority to one another and that the outer word is therefore intrinsically necessary and causative of the inner word. Thus, he also can guarantee real human freedom before the categorical word of revelation.

Rahner's dialectical analogy is particularly clear here, and the tension within this structure of thought is equally clear. If all men really are free to accept or reject God's revealing word of grace, the logical possibility must be admitted that all men through mortal sin can reject it. Then the question would inevitably arise: How can the outer word of revelation, the church or the sacraments, continue to be the expression of grace in the world if all men really are without grace?

Furthermore, a question must be raised concerning the causality exercised by the outer word on the inner word. Exactly what type of causality is being evoked here? Certainly, causality such as Rahner has described it cannot fall under the category of efficient causality because the outer word never occurs apart from a graced subject. In a temporal sense, the received grace is actually prior to its categorical expression. The causality of the outer word, therefore, must be characterized as final causality: God's intention in originally bestowing his grace is to bring it to categorical expression. But upon whom does this final causality work? Here yet again we see Rahner's double emphasis. In one sense, of course, this final causality works on man in that the grace that comes to categorical expression is the grace primordially bestowed on him. In another sense, it must also have an effect on God in that it is

God who from the beginning intends the sacramental expression. This effect is problematic but is ultimately also the ground upon which Rahner will insist later that God's will becomes irrevocable in Christ and in the sacraments. And to this notion of causality we must return in due course.

By 1965, perhaps influenced by the Second Vatican Council and the changing atmosphere in the Catholic Church, Rahner's perspective is clearly changing. From the mid-1960s onward (although this tendency is apparent even in the revised edition of *Hörer* in 1963), the dynamic unifying side of his thought becomes ever more prominent. Abandoning the mutual priority of inner word of grace and outer categorical word of revelation, Rahner argues that all men who live under the supernatural existential in fact are involved originally and always in a grace-given self-transcendence toward God, which can be interpreted correctly as revelation. To define grace as revelation is a real novelty in Catholic theology and a radical step within Rahner's own system. Because of the nature of man as *Schwebe,* this grace-given transcendence (revelation) obviously occurs only within history and is necessarily brought to categorical expression in history. But now, instead of a unity in distinction between grace and historical revelation, between inner and outer Words of God, Rahner argues that this inner grace-given revelation can come to expression in any categorical word of history at all. This is obviously the basis for his often repeated assertion that all history is revelation history, and it later will also be the basis for his controversial theory of anonymous Christianity. However, even here in this later very dynamic and unifying approach, Rahner maintains his balance and remains true to the fundamental structure of dialectical analogy. For in spite of holding that the inner word of grace comes to expression in any categorical word, he insists simultaneously, in line with the distinguishing, conceptualizing side of his thought, on the necessity of "official" categorical revelation in the Old and New Testaments, in the church, and in the sacraments as the end to which all transcendentally given grace tends, its final cause and the hermeneutical key by which categorically correct and incorrect historical mediations of transcendental grace can be distinguished.

Rahner clearly is following through and working out the consequences of his foundational epistemological metaphysics. Whether the conclusions he reaches with this admittedly ingenious theory of revelation are either completely internally consistent or truly compatible with a Christian view of history and revelation remains open to question.

6
Christology

CHRISTOLOGY WAS, for Rahner, both the center of all mysteries, because all mysteries are revealed in Christ,[1] and the focal point of two of the major themes of his theological enterprise: the relations of infinite to finite and of grace to nature. As early as 1954, Rahner had noted the difficulties besetting traditional Christology and sketched the outlines of his own solutions to these problems.[2] But it was not until the late 1950s and early 1960s that he turned his full attention to Christology. In some of his initial writings about Christ, he treated the theological basis for devotion to the Sacred Heart, and it was in this context that he developed his seminal and important notion of the "real-symbol."[3] From this notion of "real-symbol" flow his Christology from above and his Trinitarian theology.[4] Then, in the late 1960s and 1970s, as scriptural exegesis won more independence from dogmatic theology and St. John's Gospel became heavily discounted as a historical source, Rahner turned his attention to the problems arising from studies about the historical Jesus in an attempt to show that even the meager results of historical criticism permitted a Christology from below that accorded with the traditional affirmations about Jesus.[5] In this chapter, I examine both of Rahner's Christologies, from above and from below, noting how the dialectical structure of his thought allows him in both approaches to emphasize, on the one hand, the real unity of God and man in Christ (in line

---

[1] "Zur Theologie der Menschwerdung," *Schriften*, 4: 137; "Theologie und Anthropologie," *Schriften*, 8: 43 f. Carr, *Theological Method of Karl Rahner*, 126, sees the Christology as the key to Rahner's whole theological project.

[2] "Probleme der Christologie," *Schriften*, 1: 169–222.

[3] "Zur Theologie des Symbols," *Schriften*, 4: 275–311.

[4] See chapter 3, note 3.

[5] McDermott, "Christologies of Karl Rahner," 87–123, 297–327, has noted and criticized comprehensively the structure and relationship of Rahner's Christology from above and from below. A less-detailed assessment of Rahner's Christology can be found in B. Marshall, *Christology in Conflict: The Identity of a Saviour in Rahner and Barth* (Oxford: Blackwell, 1987), 15–114.

with the dynamic, unifying side of his thought) and, on the other hand, the real humanity of Jesus in relation to God (in line with the conceptualizing, distinguishing side of his thought). I also note some of the tensions that exist within each approach and between both, ultimately raising the question of whether these two Christologies are joined coherently.

1. CHRISTOLOGY FROM ABOVE

It was in searching for a theological justification for the Catholic practice of adoration of the Sacred Heart of Jesus that Rahner first developed his symbol Christology. Through this symbol theory, he initially was concerned to stress the unity of Christ's human nature with the Logos so that the whole body of Jesus, right down to its individual members (especially his heart) and all his actions, might be interpreted as real expressions of God in the world and thus be worthy of adoration. This symbol theory is very nuanced. In describing the relationship between the symbol and the symbolized, a familiar twofold structure emerges that enables the two poles of unity and diversity to be held together in an oscillation that is grounded in Rahner's foundational thought and that, he argues, is necessary to maintain the almost dialectical assertions of traditional Christology.

A. Symbol and the Trinity

Using the Trinity to show that a plurality in a being is not necessarily an imperfection, Rahner constructed (see chapter 4) a general ontology based on the insight that each being forms something distinct from itself and yet one with itself for its own fulfillment. This differentiated being, which is still originally one, is in agreement because derivative, and because derivatively in agreement it is expressive or symbolic.

B. The Logos as the Symbol of the Father

From such an understanding, the theology of the Logos becomes the supreme form of the theology of symbol. The Logos is the

"Word" of the Father, his perfect image, his self-expression. Thus, we can and must conclude that the Father *is* himself by the very fact that he opposes to himself the image, which is of the same essence as himself, as the person who is other than himself, and so he possesses himself. "This means that the Logos is the 'symbol' of the Father, in the very sense that we have given the word."[6]

This notion of the Logos as symbol of the Father, together with the assertion that the economic Trinity and immanent Trinity are identical,[7] forms the basis for the rejection of the traditional proposition that *each* of the divine persons can enter into his own hypostatic relationship to a given reality in the world and so can "appear,"[8] for the Father is by definition the unoriginate and invisible, and the Son is by definition the symbol or word of the Father. A revelation of the Father without the Logos and his incarnation, therefore, would "be like speaking without words."[9] Otherwise, the Logos as the inner-trinitarian image of the Father would not possess any special character of symbol for the world. The economic Trinity would not be the same as the immanent Trinity. The Father might reveal himself without reference to the Son, and the statement "the Word of God became man" would mean little more than "one of the Trinity became man." On the contrary, it is precisely because God "must" express himself inwardly that he also can utter himself outwardly.[10] "And when this God utters himself as himself into the *void,* this expression speaks *out* this immanent word and not something which could be true of another divine person."[11]

C. *The Humanity of Christ as the Symbol of the Logos*

When Rahner considers the incarnation and the relationship of the humanity of Christ with the Logos, the key concept is not

---

[6] "Zur Theologie des Symbols," *Schriften,* 4: 292.

[7] See chapter 3, note 3.

[8] See chapter 3, note 16.

[9] *Mysterium Salutis II,* s.v. "Der dreifaltige Gott," 333.

[10] "Zur Theologie des Symbols," *Schriften,* 4: 293. "Zur Theologie der Menschwerdung," *Schriften,* 4: 149.

[11] "Zur Theologie der Menschwerdung," *Schriften,* 4: 149. Although this assertion is central to Rahner's Christology, it is difficult, in the light of his equally

that of an "assumption," which presupposes what is to be assumed as something obvious, but rather that of "symbol" as applied to the humanity of Christ. If the humanity that is "assumed" in the incarnation were considered only as that reality that we know in ourselves and that is only very generally the image and likeness of God, and if this humanity is supposed to subsist only in a static, ontic sense—that is, as "borne" and "taken on" by the Logos—then the Logos would have made himself perceptible through a reality that was of itself alien to him and that might have been chosen at random from a whole series of such realities. Such a theology, as we have already noted, would make Jesus the revelation of the Father only through his doctrine but not through what he *is* in his human nature.

The correct way to understand the humanity of Christ is as the symbol of the Logos in the preeminent sense of the term *symbol*. If we apply Rahner's symbol theory to Christology, the same double emphasis that we have already observed reemerges. On the one hand (in line with the dynamic, unifying side of Rahner's thought), when the Word becomes man, his humanity is not prior to its assumption. It is something that comes to be in essence and existence when the Logos empties and expresses himself. As evidence for this interpretation of the incarnation is the Thomistic doctrine that the humanity of Christ exists by the existence of the Logos.[12] According to this doctrine, the being of the Logos, considered as that which is received by procession from the Father, must be thought of as so exteriorizing itself that, without detriment to its immutability, it *itself* becomes the existence of a created reality, which must then in all truth be predicated of the being of the Logos. The humanity is the self-disclosure of the Logos himself. When God, expressing himself, exteriorizes himself, that very thing appears that we call the humanity of the Logos.[13]

> The Absolute, or, more correctly, he who is the absolute, has, in the pure freedom of his infinite and abiding unrelatedness, the pos-

---

strong assertion that there is no inner-trinitarian "thou" (see chapter 3, note 30), to see how it can be grounded on or consistent with his understanding of the Trinity.

[12] "Zur Theologie des Symbols," *Schriften*, 4: 295.

[13] *Sacramentum Mundi II*, s.v. "Jesus Christus," 952.

sibility of himself becoming that other thing, the finite; God, in and by the fact that he empties *himself,* gives *himself* away, *effects* the other as his own reality.[14]

Lest the humanity of Christ be interpreted in a Monophysite way, Rahner also asserts (in line with the conceptualizing and distinguishing side of his thought) that the humanity of Jesus is most independent—that is, truly human—by the very fact of its total dependence on the Logos. In Jesus Christ is verified in the most radical way[15] the general thesis (central to Rahner's Christology) that in the relationship between God and creature dependence and independence exist and grow not in inverse proportion but in direct proportion.[16] Christ is most radically man, and his humanity is most independent precisely because of its being taken up, by its being constituted as the self-utterance or symbol of God.

This juncture of dependence and independence, unity and diversity, in the symbol allows Rahner to face the dialectical problem of the immutability of God and the mutability implied by the incarnation. On the one hand, because the symbol and the symbolized are really one (dynamic view), God really can *become* something: "he who is unchangeable in himself can *himself* become subject to change in *something else.*"[17] On the other hand, he can do this only because the symbol and the symbolized are also truly distinct (conceptual view), and therefore, despite his real becoming, God always remains God, *actus purus.* "Indeed, his

---

[14] "Zur Theologie der Menschwerdung," *Schriften,* 4: 148.

[15] "Probleme der Christologie," *Schriften,* 1: 184–85; "Die ewige Bedeutung," *Schriften,* 3: 56; "Die Christologie innerhalb einer evolutiven Weltanschauung," *Schriften,* 5: 205; *Sacramentum Mundi II,* s.v. "Jesus Christus," 939; "Kirchliche Christologie," *Schriften,* 9: 212–13.

[16] That in the relationship of God and the world dependence and independence grow in direct and not inverse proportion is another central Rahnerian proposition: "Zur Theologie der Menschwerdung," *Schriften,* 4: 151; "Probleme der Christologie," *Schriften,* 1: 182–83, 185, 202–3, 212; "Die ewige Bedeutung," *Schriften,* 3: 53, 56; *Sacramentum Mundi II,* s.v. "Jesus Christus," 948, 951; "Kirchliche Christologie," *Schriften,* 9: 211; *Kleines Theologisches Wörterbuch,* 1961 ed., s.v. "Hypostatische Union," by K. Rahner and H. Vorgrimler, 177; *Sendung und Gnade,* 92; "Überlegungen zur Dogmenentwicklung," *Schriften,* 4: 92.

[17] "Zur Theologie der Menschwerdung," *Schriften,* 4: 147; "Über den Begriff des Geheimnisses," *Schriften,* 4: 95; "Probleme der Christologie," *Schriften,* 1: 196, 202, esp. n. 2.

power of subjecting himself to history is primary among God's free possibilities precisely because he is God. . . . For this reason Scripture defines him as love, whose prodigal freedom is the indefinable itself."[18]

D. The Chalcedonian Definition

This symbol Christology enables Rahner to interpret the almost dialectical affirmations of the Chalcedonian definition.

(i) The Undivided Diversity of Natures in Christ

It was implied in the formula of the Chalcedonian definition and explicitly maintained by the Scholastics that the human nature of the Logos possessed a real human self-consciousness that faced the eternal Logos in a genuinely human attitude of adoration.[19] However, precisely this human self-consciousness seems threatened when the Chalcedonian definition of "one person in two natures" is interpreted in the light of the modern concept of "person." It is consequently the primary task of a modern Christology so to formulate the Christological dogma that the Lord is clearly recognized as that true man who, standing before God on our side in free human obedience, is mediator not only in virtue of the ontological union of two natures but also through his activity, which is directed to God (as obedience to the will of the Father). More precisely stated, the task of modern Christology is to explain "how freedom can belong to someone with whom it is not identical, whose intrinsic core it does not constitute; why this freedom is neither subjugated to the 'person' distinct from it nor in a position to rebel against it."[20]

As we have seen, only a divine person, through his freely constituted symbol, can possess as his own a freedom really distinct from himself in such a way that this freedom does not cease to be

---

[18] "Zur Theologie der Menschwerdung," Schriften, 4: 148.

[19] "Probleme der Christologie," Schriften, 1: 178; " 'Ich glaube an Jesus Christus,' " Schriften, 8: 215; Sacramentum Mundi II, s.v. "Jesus Christus," 948; "Kirchliche Christologie," Schriften, 9: 210; Rahner and Thüsing, Christologie, 53.

[20] "Probleme der Christologie," Schriften, 1: 182.

truly free even with regard to the divine person possessing it, as the ontological subject whom it qualifies.[21] The relation between the Logos-person and his human nature should be conceived so that here both independence and radical proximity equally reach a unique and qualitatively incommensurable perfection, which remains once and for all the perfection of a relation between Creator and creature. Therefore, the metaphysical formulation of the truth, that "this human history is the pure and absolute revelation of God himself," can be supplemented by another formulation: that "this human history, by the very fact of being God's own pure and radical revelation, is the most living of all, the most free before God from the world toward God, and thus mediatorial, because it is the history of God himself *and* because it is supremely creaturely and free."[22]

(ii) The Unconfused Unity of Natures in Christ

Within this perspective, the "unconfused unity" of natures proposed by the Chalcedonian definition also is to be conceived. In the traditional scholastic doctrine that the Logos in no way "changes" when he assumes human nature, it is difficult to see how Jesus could have been a man in the way that we are men. Furthermore, if in scholastic doctrine not only is this humanity of the Logos created by the one God (not the Logos alone), but every influence on it is also the object of the operation of the whole Trinity as a single efficient cause *ad extra,* then all that this humanity possesses is what can be given to any man—that is, grace, knowledge, virtue, and the *visio beatifica.*

We arrive at an apparent conundrum: "we need someone who is not as we are, so that we may be redeemed. But as soon as we say it, the door beyond which we who thirst for redemption sit seems finally to shut."[23] Or, with the Chalcedonian definition as the starting point, the problem can be posed formally: What remains of the "indissolubly one" when the "unconfused" is taken seriously in all its consequences? How are we then to interpret the "inseparably"?[24]

---

[21] "Probleme der Christologie," *Schriften,* 1: 182.
[22] "Probleme der Christologie," *Schriften,* 1: 184.
[23] "Probleme der Christologie," *Schriften,* 1: 199.
[24] "Probleme der Christologie," *Schriften,* 1: 200.

The answers to these questions require again a concept of unity based on Rahner's theory of symbol. The only way in which Christ's concrete humanity may be conceived of in itself as diverse from the Logos is by thinking of it *insofar as* it is united to the Logos. The unity with the Logos must constitute it in its diversity from him—that is, precisely as a human nature; the unity must itself be the ground of the diversity.

> In this way, the diverse term as such is the united [*geeinte*] reality of him who as prior unity (which can thus only be God) is the ground of the diverse term and therefore, while remaining "immutable" in himself, truly comes to be *in* what he constitutes as something united with him *and* diverse from him [*mit ihm Geeinte und von ihm Verschiedene*].[25]

If what makes the human nature existent as something diverse from God and what unites this nature with the Logos are *strictly* the same, then we have a unity that *(a)* as uniting unity *(einende Einheit)* cannot be confused with the united unity *(geeinte Einheit)*; that *(b)* unites precisely by making existent and in this way is grasped in a fullness of content without any relapse into the empty assertion of the united unity; and, finally, that *(c)* does not make the "unconfused" of the Chalcedonian definition look like an external counterbalance to the unity, always threatening to dissolve it again.

(iii) The Hypostatic Union

The principle of unity in Christ traditionally was seen to lie in the divine person of the Logos, to whom belong the two diverse natures in a substantial, indissoluble, and hypostatic unity. It is interesting, therefore, that Rahner does not really develop a notion of "person" in his consideration of the unity in diversity of natures in Christ. In fact, it seems that in referring the unity of natures to the unique climax of the Creator-creature relationship, where radical dependence and independence reach their irreversible high point, his reflections remain entirely at the level of nature (as *Schwebe*). Within this perspective, which is clearly

---

[25] "Probleme der Christologie," *Schriften,* 1: 202.

consistent with the whole structure of his thought as dialectical analogy, the notion of Hypostatic Union seems to be almost a formal principle signifying only this oscillating unity. Thus, Rahner asserts that "God's self-utterance (as content) [that is, conceptually] is the man Jesus, the self-utterance (as event) [that is, dynamically] is the Hypostatic Union."[26]

E. The Death and Resurrection of Jesus

In giving himself fully to man, God posits the other as his own reality and accepts the other in the very positing of it and thus becomes an other, man. In the Logos's unity with man is created the perfect human response to the divine self-communication. Jesus Christ freely gives his humanity into the divine mystery so as to receive everything from it, and therefore man, the *potentia oboedientialis*, is absolutely fulfilled in him,[27] for the free creature has so given himself to God that God can exist in that man.[28] Now, this total acceptance of the divine assumption by the free creature necessarily must involve death in the infralapsarian order of things (where death is the birth of life set free).[29] Within the life of Jesus, the Cross must be seen as the ultimate moment of the free, human, total self-giving of Christ to the Father.[30]

---

[26] *Sacramentum Mundi II,* s.v. "Jesus Christus," 952–53. See also *Lexikon für Theologie und Kirche,* 1986 ed., s.v. "Jesus Christus," by K. Rahner, 956 ff.; "Probleme der Christologie," *Schriften,* 1: 200–203; "Zur Theologie der Menschwerdung," *Schriften,* 4: 150.

[27] That man is the obediential potency for the Hypostatic Union: "Zur Theologie der Menschwerdung," *Schriften,* 4: 142–44, 148–49; "Probleme der Christologie," *Schriften,* 1: 191 n. 1, 204; *Sacramentum Mundi II,* s.v. "Jesus Christus," 930; *Lexikon für Theologie und Kirche,* s.v. "Jesus Christus," 956; "Dogmatische Erwägungen," *Schriften,* 5: 234; " 'Ich glaube an Jesus Christus,' " *Schriften,* 8: 216. This rather strange assertion that the Hypostatic Union is the absolute fulfillment of human nature would seem to imply that all men have an obediential potency to become Jesus, an assertion that we will return to later in the context of Rahner's discussion of the *visio beatifica*.

[28] "Zur Theologie der Menschwerdung," *Schriften,* 4: 142.

[29] "Dogmatische Fragen zur Osterfrömmigkeit," *Schriften,* 4: 167.

[30] On the other hand, it must be noted that Rahner also asserts that the very "assumption" of human nature in the incarnation constitutes in the terms of his symbol theory the total human acceptance of the divine self-communication, and therefore the perfect human response would seem to occur at the annunciation and not only in the death of Christ. Perhaps here we see also Rahner's characteristic double emphasis: in the dynamic event of divine self-communica-

The death of Christ cannot be regarded merely as a happy ending to his sufferings. Such an understanding of death is inadequate and highlights the need for a new theology of death.[31] Death is not merely the separation of body and soul. It is also the supreme act of man in which his whole previous life is gathered up in the final decision of his freedom and mastered. The human death of Christ is, therefore, of its nature the totality of the life of Christ in act, the definitive act of his freedom, the complete integration of his time on earth with his human eternity.[32]

The resurrection of Christ is not just another event *after* his passion and death. Rather, the resurrection is the manifestation of what happened in the death of Christ—that is, the handing over of the whole bodily man to the mystery of the merciful loving God by the concentrated freedom of Christ as he disposed of his whole life and existence. The soteriological significance of the resurrection lies in the fact that

> a piece of this world, real to the core but occupied by the pure and sovereign power of the dispassionate freedom of Christ, is surrendered in the total self-mastery, which can be achieved by fallen man only in the act of death, to the disposition of God, in complete obedience and love. This is Easter and the redemption of the world.[33]

The resurrection of Christ is essentially the event in which God irrevocably adopts the creature as his own reality by his own divine primordial act, as he has done "already" in the incarnation of the Logos.[34]

---

tion we find the perfect human response; yet in categorical terms this event occurs only at death insofar as the distance between the human and divine persists until the human finds its perfect expression on Golgotha.

[31] "Probleme der Christologie," *Schriften,* 1: 215–16; Rahner and Thüsing, *A New Christology,* 38–39; "Dogmatische Fragen zur Osterfrömmigkeit," *Schriften,* 4: 160, 164.

[32] "Dogmatische Fragen zur Osterfrömmigkeit," *Schriften,* 1: 165. K. Rahner, *On the Theology of Death,* translated by C. Henkey (New York: Herder, 1961), 39, 43–46, 65 f., 70–75. Ratzinger, "Vom Verstehen des Glaubens," 185, criticizes what he calls the inadequacy of Rahner's theology of the Cross.

[33] "Dogmatische Fragen zur Osterfrömmigkeit," *Schriften,* 4: 166.

[34] *Sacramentum Mundi II,* s.v. "Jesus Christus," 922; Rahner and Thüsing, *Christologie,* 45. Once again, if God already and irrevocably has adopted man in the incarnation, it is not completely clear why this adoption is said to occur only in the resurrection.

F. Salvation

The meaning of the death and resurrection of Jesus introduces the question of man's salvation. Seeing the incarnation as essential to God's unique plan for man's divinization even apart from sin,[35] Rahner always insisted on Jesus' humanity as the essential, per-during mediator of man's relation with God,[36] and after sin he argued that we participate in Christ's mediating reconciliation.[37] This mediation continues even in the *visio beatifica*. There, God's immediacy to the spirit is mediated through Christ's humanity, for just as the *visio beatifica* does not destroy but in fact demands the created *lumen gloriae* as its mediation, so also Christ's humanity remains as a finite mediator of the infinite God.[38] Rahner admits that this mediation is difficult to demonstrate,[39] for it is difficult to see exactly how Jesus' humanity actually does mediate salvation to all men. But because Jesus Christ is the ultimate ground and the cause of God's relation to the world, the Hypostatic Union must be considered as the cause of all grace.[40] In the incarnation, all of reality is seen to enter into the very constitution of the Logos as his environment. Thereby reality attains in its relation to God a radicality more profound than what is given in its transcendental openness to God as the exemplary, efficient, and final cause of this world. In the resurrection, the process of reality's glorification and divinization begins irreversibly. As a real, physical part of the world and its history, Jesus necessarily affects it ontologically in its physical, spiritual, and moral unity.[41] Rahner unfortu-

---

[35] "Probleme der Christologie," *Schriften*, 1: 185; "Die Christologie innerhalb einer evolutiven Weltanschauung," *Schriften*, 5: 205–6; *Sendung und Gnade*, 62–63.

[36] "Dogmatische Fragen zur Osterfrömmigkeit," *Schriften*, 4: 170; *Lexikon für Theologie und Kirche*, s.v. "Jesus Christus," 955 f., 957.

[37] "Einige Thesen zur Theologie der Herz-Jesu-Verehrung," *Schriften*, 3: 409.

[38] That the humanity of Christ is the permanent mediator of God to man: "Zur Theologie des Symbols," *Schriften*, 4: 302 f.; "Dogmatische Fragen zur Osterfrömmigkeit," *Schriften*, 4: 161, 170; "Die ewige Bedeutung," *Schriften*, 3: 57–59, 60; "Zur Theologie der Menschwerdung," *Schriften*, 4: 151. Wong, *Logos-Symbol*, 61–62, interestingly links this notion of the eternal mediation of the humanity of Christ with Rahner's understanding of ecstasy.

[39] "Die ewige Bedeutung," *Schriften*, 3: 58.

[40] "Die ewige Bedeutung," *Schriften*, 3: 56; "Probleme der Christologie," *Schriften*, 1: 185f.; *Lexikon für Theologie und Kirche*, s.v. "Jesus Christus," 957 f.

[41] That all of history is so interrelated that what happens to one individual has

nately does not explain how this influence of one part on others in the web of history, however preeminent, justifies Christ's unique mediatorship as cause of salvation for all others.

2. CHRISTOLOGY FROM BELOW

In the next period of his Christological thought, extending from the early 1960s to its culmination in the Christology lectures delivered in Münster with the exegete Wilhelm Thüsing, Rahner does not deny what he wrote previously. He still maintains that Christ was intended as the fulfillment of creation even apart from sin and that the world was created as the precondition of God's self-expression. One still finds statements from him that God radically accepted humanity in the incarnation, that Jesus' humanity is the perfect expression of God or of the Logos *ad extra,* which lets God be present in the world, and that the preexistent God, immutable in himself, has taken on the fate of another.[42] But by this point Rahner has grown wary of the traditional descent Christology with its mythological overtones, which he believes modern people find difficult to accept;[43] although maintaining the truth of the traditional "ontic" descent Christology, he tries to develop a new ontological Christology. Such an attempt is both necessary, in order to make Christology more intelligible, and justifiable on the grounds that a translation of either Christology into the terms of the other is both possible and legitimate.[44] Very

---

an effect on all other people is a central Rahnerian affirmation: "Dogmatische Fragen zur Osterfrömmigkeit," *Schriften,* 4: 166 f.; "Probleme der Christologie," *Schriften,* 1: 185, 188; Rahner and Thüsing, *A New Christology,* 37; Rahner and Thüsing, *Christologie,* 49; "Zur Frage der Dogmenentwicklung," *Schriften,* 1: 53; *Sendung und Gnade,* 60; "Der eine Jesus Christus," *Schriften,* 12: 257, 265; "Der Leib in der Heilsordnung," *Schriften,* 12: 409, 413; "Der eine Mittler," *Schriften,* 8: 223, 226, 231; *Sacramentum Mundi II,* s.v. "Jesus Christus," 943.

[42] "Die Christologie innerhalb einer evolutiven Weltanschauung," *Schriften,* 5: 213–16; "Christologie im Rahmen," *Schriften,* 9: 213, 236, 239; "Der eine Mittler," *Schriften,* 8: 230, 232; "Kirchliche Christologie," *Schriften,* 9: 213; "Vom Geheimnis des Lebens," *Schriften,* 6: 178 f.; Rahner and Thüsing, *Christologie,* 68 f.; *Sacramentum Mundi II,* s.v. "Jesus Christus," 933, 951–53.

[43] Rahner and Thüsing, *Christologie,* 58; *Sacramentum Mundi II,* s.v. "Jesus Christus," 927–29.

[44] Rahner and Thüsing, *Christologie,* 46, 54; *Sacramentum Mundi II,* s.v. "Jesus Christus," 930, 934–36, 947; "Zur Theologie der Menschwerdung," *Schriften,* 4: 189–92, 194.

concerned to preserve the human experience of Christ, he warns against a Monophysite interpretation of the phrase "Jesus is God,"[45] and, relying on the real diversity of natures in Christ, he studies the human in Jesus as far as possible. Nevertheless, he aims at a reconciliation with the traditional descent Christology along two paths: by showing Christ as the culmination of mankind's evolutionary history and by analyzing the historical evidence about Jesus' consciousness of his person and mission that grounds the later faith of the Catholic Church.

2.1. Evolutionary Christology (from Below)

In the consideration of matter and spirit, I noted how Rahner's notion of matter as "frozen spirit" and an evolutionary worldview can be reconciled only on the double precondition that matter exists only for and in view of spirit and that God, as the ground of all inner-worldly becoming, is immanent within the process precisely by being transcendent of it. In this way, both the unity of matter and spirit and of God and the world can be maintained within the dynamism of the evolutionary process along with the simultaneous distinction of each from the other. In his evolutionary Christology, Rahner takes this line of thought a stage further, arguing that God's self-communication in grace and ultimately in the incarnation is logically the final stage and inner rational of the whole unified evolutionary process. Within this perspective, he defines the "savior" both as the unique climax of the evolutionary process, the point where God's self-communication is radically and irreversibly accepted by man, and as the definitive self-communication of God, where the Logos in creating and accepting his corporeality expresses himself and lets himself be present in the world. The Hypostatic Union is the highest possible event within the process of God's self-communication to man and as such, within a historical evolutionary process that lives from its end, is the final cause of all grace given to man and the irrevocable expression of God's salvific will. In this event, given the reality of sin, redemption also occurs.

---

[45] Rahner and Thüsing, *Christologie,* 55–57; *Sacramentum Mundi II,* s.v. "Jesus Christus," 927, 928 f.

A. Evolution Toward Man

Presupposing the fundamental unity of matter and spirit, Rahner argues that their condition of mutual relatedness cannot be conceived of as a simply static condition. It itself has a history. Man comes to himself as someone who has existed already in time, both in himself and in his surroundings, for matter has developed out of its inner being in the direction of spirit, and this can have occurred only through a process of self-transcendence.[46] Hence, if man is the self-transcendence of living matter, then the history of nature and spirit forms an inner, graded unity in which natural history develops toward man, continues in him as *his* history, is conserved and surpassed in him, and thus reaches its proper goal with and in the history of the human spirit.

B. Grace as the Consummation of the Evolutionary Process

Every man in his corporeality is an element of the cosmos. This self-presence of the cosmos in the spirit of the individual man is still in the process of becoming and is in its very initial stage of a continuing history. If in the final analysis evolution proceeds in a single direction and ordination, this process by which the cosmos gradually becomes conscious of itself in man must also have a final result. According to Christian faith, this final result is the immortality of the soul. In fact, this self-transcendence of the cosmos in man reaches its final consummation only when the cosmos in the spiritual creature is not merely something set apart from its foundation, but something that receives the ultimate self-communication of its ultimate ground in that moment when the direct self-communication of God is given to the spiritual creature in grace and glory.[47] In other words, when God does not merely create something other than himself, when he also gives himself

---

[46] "Die Christologie innerhalb einer evolutiven Weltanschauung," *Schriften*, 5: 191; "Vom Geheimnis des Lebens," *Schriften*, 6: 172, 180, 182–83; "Christologie im Rahmen," *Schriften*, 9: 230; *Sacramentum Mundi II*, s.v. "Jesus Christus," 942. See chapter 4, note 47.

[47] That grace is the highest stage of the evolutionary process: "Vom Geheimnis des Lebens," *Schriften*, 6: 180, 184; *Sacramentum Mundi II*, s.v. "Jesus Christus," 942; "Christologie im Rahmen," *Schriften*, 9: 238.

to this other to such an extent that he himself becomes its inner-most life, evolution attains itself.[48]

The goal of the world consists in God's communicating himself to it. Because the spiritual subjectivities in the cosmos (human beings) are free, the history of the self-consciousness of the cosmos is also a history of the intercommunication of these spiritual subjects. God's self-communication is, therefore, communication of freedom and intercommunication among many cosmic subjectivities. As an event that takes place historically in a specifically spatiotemporal manner, it calls on the freedom of men; when it is accepted freely, it beatifies.[49]

C. Evolution Toward the Savior

The "savior" is that historical person who realizes the principle of God's absolute communication of himself and inaugurates this self-communication for all men as something happening irrevocably.[50] This does not imply that God's self-communication begins in time only with this person, but that in this person it reaches its climax. The moment in which the irreversible character of this historical self-communication of God becomes manifest refers equally to the communication itself and to its acceptance.[51] And insofar as a historical movement already exists in virtue of its end, it is absolutely legitimate and indeed necessary to think of the whole movement of God's communication of himself to the human race as something based on this event. "The whole move-

[48] "Die Christologie innerhalb einer evolutiven Weltanschauung," *Schriften*, 5: 199; "Vom Geheimnis des Lebens," *Schriften*, 6: 180, 183–84.

[49] "Die Christologie innerhalb einer evolutiven Weltanschauung," *Schriften*, 5: 202; "Christologie im Rahmen," *Schriften*, 9: 239.

[50] "Die Christologie innerhalb einer evolutiven Weltanschauung," *Schriften*, 5: 202–3; "Vom Geheimnis des Lebens," *Schriften*, 6: 178; *Sacramentum Mundi II*, s.v. "Jesus Christus," 933–34.

[51] That the savior is the one in whom God's self-communication is irrevocably both offered and accepted: "Die Christologie innerhalb einer evolutiven Welt-anschauung," *Schriften*, 5: 204, 212; "Der eine Mittler," *Schriften*, 8: 229–30; " 'Ich glaube an Jesus Christus,' " *Schriften*, 8: 216; *Sacramentum Mundi II*, s.v. "Jesus Christus," 944; "Kirchliche Christologie," *Schriften*, 9: 213; "Christologie im Rahmen," *Schriften*, 9: 238–39; Rahner and Thüsing, *A New Christology*, 37; "Der eine Jesus Christus," *Schriften*, 12: 266.

ment of this history lives only for the moment of arrival at its goal and climax."[52]

We now can see the meaning of "Logos" and of "Hypostatic Union" within an evolutionary worldview.[53] On the one hand, the savior is himself a historical moment in God's saving action exercised on the world, a part of this history of the cosmos itself. This is what is meant in the Christian dogma that Jesus is true man. "Jesus is the one who, by what we call his obedience, his prayer, and the freely accepted destiny of his death, has achieved also the acceptance of his divinely given grace and direct presence to God that he possesses as man."[54] On the other hand, the divine Logos both creates and accepts his corporeality, a part of the world, as his own reality. He brings it into existence as something other than himself in such a way that this very materiality expresses him, the Logos himself, and lets him be present in his world. His taking hold of this part of the one material-spiritual world reality then quite legitimately may be thought of as the climax of that dynamism in which the Word, who supports everything, supports the self-transcendence of the world as a whole.

> If we presuppose this, however, as the "normal" consummation of the history of the cosmos and of the spirit, without implying that this development must *necessarily* go on this far or has already done so, then we must say that this limit notion of the savior implies that notion of the hypostatic union of God and man which constitutes the real content of the Christian dogma of the incarnation.[55]

D. The Relationship of Christ with All Men (the Hypostatic Union as the Condition of the Bestowal of Grace)

Now the crux of the problem concerning the incarnation emerges. The final and absolute self-transcendence of the spirit

---

[52] "Die Christologie innerhalb einer evolutiven Weltanschauung," *Schriften*, 5: 203.

[53] Pearl, "Dialectical Panentheism," 136, criticizes this understanding of the Hypostatic Union within an evolutionary worldview for seeming to distinguish Christ from all other men only in degree and not in essence.

[54] "Die Christologie innerhalb einer evolutiven Weltanschauung," *Schriften*, 5: 204.

[55] "Die Christologie innerhalb einer evolutiven Weltanschauung," *Schriften*, 5: 206.

into God must be conceived as something that happens in all spiritual subjects. How then does the doctrine of the Hypostatic Union of a determined single human nature with God's Logos fit into this basic conception?

Rahner's thesis is that even though the Hypostatic Union is in its proper nature a unique event and (when seen in itself) is certainly the highest conceivable event, it is an intrinsic factor of the whole process of the bestowal of grace on the spiritual creature in general. If this total event of the divinizing sanctification of humanity attains its consummation, this consummation must of its nature be a tangible phenomenon in history and hence occurs in such a way as to spread out spatiotemporally from one point. It must be an irrevocable reality in which God's self-communication proves itself not merely as a temporary offer but as an absolute offer accepted by man, and in accordance with the nature of the spirit it must become conscious of itself.

Apart from the beatific vision, every self-manifestation of God takes place through a finite reality (through a word or event). As long as this finite mediation (endliche Vermittlung) is not in the strictest sense a divine reality itself, it is transitory and surpassable.[56] Hence, if the reality in which God's absolute self-communication is pledged and accepted for the whole of humanity is to be the final and irrevocable divine self-communication, then it not only must be posited by God but must be God himself. If this is so, then it must be a human reality that belongs absolutely to God—in other words, exactly what we call the Hypostatic Union. Hence, "whenever God, by his absolute self-communication, brings about man's self-transcendence into God in such a way that both these factors form the irrevocable promise made to all men, which has already reached its consummation in this man, there we have a Hypostatic Union."[57] In thinking of a "hypostatic union," we must not cling to a simple model of unity. The Hypostatic Union is an "assumption" and a "unification" that has the nature of a self-communication; there is "assumption" so that God's reality may be communicated to what is assumed—that is,

---

[56] "Die Christologie innerhalb einer evolutiven Weltanschauung," Schriften, 5: 211; Rahner and Thüsing, A New Christology, 35–36.

[57] "Die Christologie innerhalb einer evolutiven Weltanschauung," Schriften, 5: 210.

the human nature. But the very communication intended by this "assumption" is the communication of grace and glory, which are intended for all. In us, this communication is possible and effected precisely by the union and acceptance that occurs in the Hypostatic Union. There is theologically nothing against the hypothesis that grace and the Hypostatic Union can be thought of only together and that as a unity they signify one and the same free decision of God to institute the supernatural order of salvation.[58] The Hypostatic Union takes effect interiorly for the human nature of the Logos precisely and only in what traditional theology prescribes for all men as their goal and consummation—that is, the direct vision of God enjoyed by the created human soul.[59] Rahner even says explicitly that the nature of man is an obediential potency for a hypostatic union.[60] It does not differ from our grace by what is pledged in it, for this is grace in both cases.

> Yet it differs from our grace by the fact that Jesus is our pledge, and we ourselves are not the pledge but the recipients of God's pledge to us. But the unity of the pledge and the inseparability of this pledge from the one who pledges . . . must be conceived in accordance with the peculiar nature of the pledge. If the real pledge made to us is precisely the very human reality itself which has been given grace and in which and through which God pledges himself to us in his grace, then the unity of the one who pledges and the pledge cannot be considered as a merely moral one . . . but must be conceived as an *irrevocable* unity between this human reality and God.[61]

The Hypostatic Union means that in the human reality of Jesus, God's absolute self-communication is simply and irrevocably present; it is both declaration and acceptance, both something

---

[58] That the Hypostatic Union is the condition of possibility for the general bestowal of grace: "Die Christologie innerhalb einer evolutiven Weltanschauung," *Schriften*, 5: 208, 210–11; "Der eine Mittler," *Schriften*, 8: 230, 232, 235.

[59] That the *visio beatifica* is the intrinsic constitutive element of the Hypostatic Union: "Die Christologie innerhalb einer evolutiven Weltanschauung," *Schriften*, 5: 209; "Probleme der Christologie," *Schriften*, 1: 190–91; "Dogmatische Erwägungen," *Schriften*, 5: 234; *Sacramentum Mundi II*, s.v. "Jesus Christus," 950.

[60] *Sacramentum Mundi II*, s.v. "Jesus Christus," 930.

[61] "Die Christologie innerhalb einer evolutiven Weltanschauung," *Schriften*, 5: 212.

effected by God himself and a reality of God himself, unmixed and yet inseparable and hence irrevocable. Such is likewise the pledge of grace to us.

E. Redemption

Within this evolutionary perspective, where the cosmos is seen to evolve toward spirit, the history of the cosmos receives its structures and its interpretation from spirit and freedom, not from matter. Wherever there is freedom, there also can be guilt insofar as freedom closes itself against God. Such an evolutionary worldview does not exclude, therefore, the possibility of sin. Hence, if we see God's self-communication as reaching a climax in the incarnation, we expect redemption to occur also at this climax.[62] The world and its history are from the outset based on the absolute will of God to communicate himself radically to the world. In this self-communication and in its climax (the incarnation), the world becomes the history of God himself.[63] Hence, insofar as sin is found in the world, it is from the outset embraced by the offer of divine self-communication and the will to forgive. Although on account of Christ this offer is not conditioned by sin, it becomes necessarily an offer of forgiveness and of victory over guilt. Thus, redemption cannot be regarded as a merely moral or legal transaction:

> It is the communication of divine grace and takes place in the ontological reality of God's self-communication. It is, therefore, in any case the continuation and accomplishment of that existential process which consisted from the very beginning in the supernatural pardoning and divinization of humanity.[64]

2.2. Consciousness Christology (from Below)

During the same period that Rahner was elaborating this evolutionary Christology, he also was attempting elsewhere, in the face

---

[62] "Die Christologie innerhalb einer evolutiven Weltanschauung," *Schriften*, 5: 215.

[63] "Die Christologie innerhalb einer evolutiven Weltanschauung," *Schriften*, 5: 215; *Sacramentum Mundi II*, s.v. "Jesus Christus," 946, 951.

[64] "Die Christologie innerhalb einer evolutiven Weltanschauung," *Schriften*, 5: 216.

of growing skepticism regarding the historical accuracy of the Gospels, to justify the traditional Christology of the church using the sketchy remnant of historical data allowed by the historical critical methods of exegesis.

Taking the event of the incarnation as that point at which God accepts the world irrevocably and the world definitively accepts God's offering of himself, Rahner defines the "savior" as the *absolute* bringer or mediator of salvation. Given his foundational assertion that being is presence-to-self, it would be inconceivable that such an absolute savior not be conscious of his identity. Examining Scripture for evidence about Jesus of Nazareth's understanding of himself, we find that even before Easter he saw himself as the absolute bringer of salvation,[65] and this self-consciousness is enough to ground the later Christological definitions of the church.

Given the total unity between the Logos and his assumed human nature that makes itself felt in his human self-consciousness, it is not at all mythological to assert that Jesus possessed the *visio beatifica*. However, in order to make room for Jesus' growth in knowledge as well as for his feelings of agony and forsakenness (also witnessed to by the Scriptures),[66] it is necessary to reinterpret the *visio beatifica* as a *visio immediata,* which Christ possesses without a beatific effect on his human nature. The operation of this *visio immediata* on Jesus' human self-consciousness is to be considered as similar to the operation of the preapprehension of the horizon of all being in all human consciousness—that is, as an all-pervading, unthematized, subjective condition that is only gradually conceptually objectified in the course of a man's historical development.[67]

---

[65] *Mysterium Salutis II,* s.v. "Der dreifaltige Gott," 357; *Sacramentum Mundi II,* s.v. "Jesus Christus," 933, 945; "Kirchliche Christologie," *Schriften,* 9: 214–15, 218; Rahner and Thüsing, *A New Christology,* 9–10; Rahner and Thüsing, *Christologie,* 66.

[66] That Christ in his human consciousness questioned, "erred," and so on: Rahner and Thüsing, *Christologie,* 28 f.; "Kirchliche Christologie," *Schriften,* 9: 206, 210 f.; "Probleme der Christologie," *Schriften,* 1: 194; *Sacramentum Mundi II,* s.v. "Jesus Christus," 951; Rahner and Thüsing, *A New Christology,* 23; "Altes Testament und christliche Dogmatik," *Schriften,* 12: 238.

[67] See R. Moloney, "The Mind of Christ in Transcendental Theology: Rahner, Lonergan, and Crowe," *Heythrop Journal* 25 (1984): 288–300, for an interesting comparison of Rahner's and Lonergan's consciousness Christologies.

A. The Historical Jesus and the Christ of Faith

Because salvation takes place precisely within history as the history of God's action on man, the "word" must be a constitutive element in the saving event itself, so much so that without it an event cannot really belong to saving history at all. Catholic theology must maintain, therefore, that there was a Jesus of Nazareth, who in his own understanding of himself even before Easter had something to do with what Christian faith believes and proclaims of Jesus Christ the risen Lord. Otherwise, the life of Jesus and his death would not have constituted a saving event.[68] It is a question of critical importance, therefore, whether the findings of contemporary exegesis about the pre-Easter Jesus' awareness of himself, his task, and his person are still a sufficient point of departure for the New Testament Christologies found in Paul and John and for the church's dogmatic teaching about Jesus Christ.[69]

B. The "Is" of the Christological Definitions

Before we address the question of Jesus' pre-Easter self-consciousness, we need a correct understanding of the church's Christology, avoiding the Monophysite tendency implicitly present in much contemporary catechesis and piety.[70] According to the definition of the Council of Chalcedon, without prejudice to the truth of the Hypostatic Union, Jesus *really is* a man. Thus, when we say that "Jesus is God," the word *is,* as employed in this formula, suggests a further *is,* a further synthesis between the subject and the material content of the predicate than what occurs, for instance, when we say "Fritz is a man." This latter assertion affirms not merely that this humanity is one with the subject Fritz, but that there is a real identity between the two. In the case of Jesus, however, his humanity is precisely not identical with God

---

Moloney argues that whereas Rahner sees Christ's immediate vision of God as occurring in Jesus' self-consciousness, Lonergan sees it as occurring in Christ's knowledge.

[68] "Kirchliche Christologie," *Schriften,* 9: 198–99; Rahner and Thüsing, *Christologie,* 25, 30f.; "Bemerkungen zur Bedeutung der Geschichte Jesu für die katholische Dogmatik," *Schriften,* 10: 212–17.

[69] "Kirchliche Christologie," *Schriften,* 9: 200–201.

[70] "Kirchliche Christologie," *Schriften,* 9: 209–10.

in this way.[71] Because of a general failure to appreciate this distinction, the average Christian may have difficulty accepting that Jesus trembled, adored God, and faced a fate that was dark even to him. Yet we must accept these things if we are to be true to Christian faith,[72] for the Jesus of the Chalcedonian definition has a subjective center of action that is human and creaturely in kind. Therefore, in his freedom, Jesus was confronted with God, the inconceivable, and underwent all those experiences that we have, but in a more radical form. In fact, if the principle of a direct and not inverse relationship of dependence and independence in the God-creature relationship is applied here,[73] Jesus' human experiences happened not in spite of but rather *because* of the Hypostatic Union.

C. Jesus as the Absolute Bringer of Salvation

The absolute savior, as a metaphysical and substantial reality, has no further content beyond what can be expressed in the affirmation: he is the eschatological (that is, the unsurpassable and abiding) mediator of our relationship with God.[74] This being the case, Rahner asserts that even the findings of contemporary exegesis allow us to say that the pre-Easter Jesus understood himself precisely in this way, as the eschatological event of salvation. When exegesis emphasizes that the pre-Easter Jesus spoke in the first instance not so much of his own person but of the advent of the Kingdom of God, this emphasis should not be a problem for us. If this Kingdom of God has come definitively, victoriously, and unsurpassably in Jesus' person and message, and if Jesus declares exactly this to be the case, then ipso facto he has spoken about his person. "We understand his true nature only when we see it as absolutely one with his function in saving history."[75]

This conclusion brings us to the central assertion of Rahner's

---

[71] "Kirchliche Christologie," *Schriften*, 9: 210; *Sacramentum Mundi II*, s.v. "Jesus Christus," 927–28; Rahner and Thüsing, *Christologie*, 56.

[72] "Kirchliche Christologie," *Schriften*, 9: 210–11; "Dogmatische Erwägungen," *Schriften*, 5: 236; *Sacramentum Mundi II*, s.v. "Jesus Christus," 950–51.

[73] See note 16 in this chapter.

[74] "'Ich glaube an Jesus Christus,'" *Schriften*, 8: 217.

[75] "Kirchliche Christologie," *Schriften*, 9: 216.

consciousness Christology—that everyone who is genuinely a Christian will concede that the message Jesus addresses to him is unsurpassable. The implications contained in this statement are immense. Every prophet must allow for the fact that saving history remains open to further unforeseeable and sometimes revolutionary developments beyond any to which he can point. The message Jesus utters through his person and through his words can be the unsurpassable and abiding word of God only if the reality it constitutes is God's own reality in the manner that we seek to express by the term *Hypostatic Union*. Even taken alone, this statement contains in itself the whole Christology of the church.[76] It does not deny but actually implies that, in the dimension of Jesus' own conscious reflection upon himself, his self-understanding had a history of its own. This history attained its definitive fullness only in his resurrection. Only in that event did it also become credible in a definitive sense for us.

D. The Visio Immediata of Jesus

Theology traditionally has attributed to Jesus as a man a knowledge that embraces and exhausts all past, present, and future realities, at least to the extent that these realities are related in some way to his soteriological task. Such a theological proposition sounds almost mythological to modern ears and certainly seems to threaten any real human self-consciousness in Jesus. Before we try to understand the real meaning of these traditional statements, however, we must cover a number of preliminary observations. First of all, knowledge has a multilayered structure, and "it is absolutely possible that in relation to the different dimensions of consciousness and knowledge, something may be known and not known at the same time."[77] Second, there is among these forms of knowledge an a priori unobjectified knowledge about oneself. Reflection can never quite lay hold of this basic condition.[78] Finally, against the Greek philosophical ideal of man, it can be shown with comparative ease that a certain kind of ignorance is a

---

[76] "Kirchliche Christologie," *Schriften*, 9: 217–8.
[77] "Dogmatische Erwägungen," *Schriften*, 5: 227–28.
[78] "Dogmatische Erwägungen," *Schriften*, 5: 229.

necessary factor in the very nature of the self-realization of the person in the historical decision of freedom.[79]

Recognizing these presuppositions, we are in a position to approach the question of Jesus' self-consciousness and to ask for what reasons one must ascribe to Jesus, even during his lifetime on earth, the kind of direct vision of God enjoyed by the blessed in heaven. In this context, we should not speak of the beatific vision, but of a *visio immediata,* involving absolute nearness and immediacy to the infinite God, but not automatically implying a beatific effect. Indeed, in view of Christ's death agony and his feeling of forsakenness, the question still remains: What evidence is there to suggest that Christ during his earthly life enjoyed a *visio immediata?*

There are two basic theological answers to this question. The first attributes this direct vision to Jesus because even on earth he must have had all those perfections that are not absolutely incompatible with his earthly mission. The *visio immediata* is really an additional perfection and gift granted to Jesus, a perfection that is not ontologically bound up with the Hypostatic Union but is connected with it by a certain moral necessity, just as for similar reasons Christ is credited with infused knowledge. Such argumentation is not absolutely persuasive, for it relies on the presuppositions of Greek philosophy that perfection consists in perfectly clear conceptual knowledge and has not been defined by the magisterium. Thus, this first answer, which Rahner calls the *extrinsicist theory,* has not a great deal to recommend it.[80]

The second answer regards the *visio immediata* as an intrinsic constitutive element of the Hypostatic Union simply given with it. Rahner accepts this position and elaborates it within the context of Thomas's epistemological ontology and its key axiom: insofar as being is self-conscious and analogous, the more being an existent has, the more conscious it is of itself.[81] Now, if the Hypostatic Union implies the self-communication of the Logos of God to the human nature of Christ, the Hypostatic Union must be the highest conceivable actualization of the reality of a crea-

---

[79] "Dogmatische Erwägungen," *Schriften,* 5: 230, 243 f.

[80] "Dogmatische Erwägungen," *Schriften,* 5: 232–33.

[81] "Dogmatische Erwägungen," *Schriften,* 5: 234; "Probleme der Christologie," *Schriften,* 1: 189; see chapter 1, note 18.

ture; a higher actualization would be absolutely impossible. Therefore, according to the fundamental relation between being and self-consciousness, this highest ontological determination of the created reality of Christ must of necessity be conscious of itself.[82]

> Given that this self-consciousness is a property of the human reality, then this ontological self-communication of God is also (and indeed specially and primarily) a factor in the self-consciousness of the human subjectivity of Christ. In other words, a purely ontic Hypostatic Union is metaphysically impossible to conceive. The *visio immediata* is an intrinsic element of the Hypostatic Union itself.[83]

E. Jesus' Human Self-Consciousness

Deriving Christology in this way indicates how we are to conceive the union of Christ's human consciousness with God. The direct presence to God, considered as a basic condition of Christ's soul, is the plain self-awareness and necessary self-realization of this substantial union with the person of the Logos himself. It is nothing more than the original unobjectified consciousness of divine sonship, which is present by the mere fact that there is a Hypostatic Union.[84] This consciousness of sonship and of direct presence to God is situated at the subjective pole of Christ's consciousness. The best way to understand it is to compare its characteristic nature with the intellectually subjective, basic condition of human spirituality in general. "It rests on a simple self-awareness which does not 'reflect' or objectify itself, but which is always already present to itself by way of this apparently colorless, basic condition of the spiritual being and by way of the horizon within which all traffic with the things and notions of daily life takes place."[85]

To this innermost primitive and basic condition on which rests all other knowledge and activity there belongs in Jesus that direct

---

[82] "Probleme der Christologie," *Schriften,* 1: 190.
[83] "Dogmatische Erwägungen," *Schriften,* 5: 235; *Sacramentum Mundi II,* s.v. "Jesus Christus," 950–51; "Probleme der Christologie," *Schriften,* 1: 190.
[84] "Dogmatische Erwägungen," *Schriften,* 5: 237.
[85] "Dogmatische Erwägungen," *Schriften,* 5: 237.

presence to God as the intrinsic subjective element of the hypostatic "assumption" of the human spiritual nature of Jesus by the Logos. Hence, the basic condition of direct presence to God not only is reconcilable with but moreover demands a genuinely human spiritual history and development of the man Jesus.[86] Only in the course of long experience could he learn to express to himself what he is and what he always already saw in his basic self-consciousness. In other words, just as there occurs in human beings the reflexive process of becoming conscious of what always already has been understood consciously in an unobjectified manner, so Christ's consciousness becomes more aware of divine Sonship and his basic condition of direct presence to God.

> Hence, it is absolutely meaningful . . . to attribute to Jesus at the same time an absolute basic state of being directly present to God from the very beginning and a development of this original self-consciousness of the created spiritual nature being handed over to the Logos.[87]

These two natures are not merely not mutually contradictory; they demand each other.

In conclusion, we can and indeed must accept that there was nescience *(Nichtwissen)* in Christ at various stages of his human development. The magisterium has not condemned this proposition, and if Christ was truly human, it must be true.[88] It is perfectly legitimate, therefore, for exegetes to try to trace the development of Jesus' self-consciousness: not only did his teaching develop, but also his self-awareness.

3. Conclusion

Rahner's Christology is complex and brilliant. Throughout it, the operation of his dialectical analogy is particularly clear. In his

---

[86] That Christ's human consciousness of his divine identity gradually develops: "Kirchliche Christologie," *Schriften,* 9: 206–7, 211, 218; "Dogmatische Erwägungen," *Schriften,* 5: 239–40; Rahner and Thüsing, *Christologie,* 28; *Sacramentum Mundi II,* s.v. "Jesus Christus," 950.

[87] "Dogmatische Erwägungen," *Schriften,* 5: 240.

[88] B. Lonergan, *De Verbo Incarnato* (Rome: Gregoriana, 1964), 400, rejects the idea that nescience is necessary for freedom.

Christology from above, he asserts that Christ's humanity is truly united to the Logos as its symbolic reality (dynamic view) and yet also really diverse from the Logos and therefore genuinely human and free (conceptual view); God really becomes in the "other" (dynamic view) and yet remains truly God *actus purus* distinct from the world (conceptual view); God therefore really is affected by history, and his salvific will becomes irrevocable in the historical Christ event (dynamic view), yet he always remains immutable in himself (conceptual view). In Rahner's Christology from below, this structure is no less apparent. Matter and spirit are really one yet truly distinct; God is immanent within the evolutionary process precisely by being transcendent of it; Christ is the inner rational and final cause of the whole evolutionary process yet the unique and unpredictable climax thereof; Christ enjoyed an immediate vision of God in virtue of his being hypostatically united with the Logos, yet this immediate vision is objectified only gradually, thus allowing for a genuine and free human self-consciousness in Jesus.

The tensions within this characteristically dialectical approach are also particularly apparent in Rahner's Christology. In his Christology from above, if the Logos really expresses himself in Jesus' human nature to the extent that even parts of Jesus' body, such as his heart, are symbols of the Logos, it is not clear how any opposition to the Logos could ever arise in Jesus' human self-consciousness. How, therefore, could Jesus experience dread, trembling, or forsakenness if all his human expressions are those of the Logos? Similarly, because of the nature of symbol as Rahner defined it, he has to assert that the reality of Jesus is God himself, despite all his warnings about Monophysitism and about saying "Jesus is God."[89] He certainly states that the humanity of Christ is not identical with the Logos (conceptual view),[90] but his equally strong assertions stressing Jesus' divinity (dynamic view) nevertheless do seem to threaten this humanity, and his Christology from above then seems to tend precisely toward Monophysitism, where the human reality of Jesus is seen to be activated totally by the Logos as its expression.

---

[89] "Zur Theologie des Symbols," *Schriften,* 4: 293–95.
[90] See, for example, Rahner and Thüsing, *Christologie,* 22 f.

Despite this tendency in his Christology from above, in his later Christological work Rahner emphasized the human reality of Jesus and constructed a Christology from below, based on the human experience of Jesus. Whether this emphasis on Christ's humanity really encompasses the traditional Christology of the church, as he claimed it did,[91] is open to question. If, for instance, Jesus' self-consciousness consists in openness to transcendence (through an unthematized *visio immediata*) and simultaneous orientation to the historical/categorical, then his consciousness does not seem to be different from any other human being's, limited by ignorance and susceptible to error. Furthermore, if the Hypostatic Union essentially is constituted by the *visio immediata,* cannot any human being surpass Jesus, whose vision was only immediate and not beatific? Similarly, with regard to the will, because it is theoretically possible for any human being to realize total dedication to God (something that the church actually affirms as having occurred in the Blessed Virgin Mary), it does not seem clear how Jesus' total acceptance of the will of the Father can be equivalent to the Hypostatic Union with its unique claim for Jesus as God incarnate. Indeed, when Rahner does assert that Jesus accomplishes what we cannot, he never gives any reason for our incapacity.[92] This Arian tendency, in which Christ is interpreted as the greatest of creatures in a special relationship with God, is reinforced further by the lack of an explanation of how the Logos can be a real "subject." This is a real dilemma insofar as the divine principle of activity is common to all three "ways of subsistence," and in the immanent Trinity neither the Son nor the Holy Spirit can stand in a certain opposition to the Father in order to address him as "thou." Rahner restricted the Johannine words of Christ to the Father, "As you are in me and I am in you" (John 17:21), to the economy of salvation (see chapter 3).[93] Without an innertrinitarian "opposition," it is difficult to attribute the humanity to

---

[91] "Kleine Anmerkungen zur systematischen Christologie Heute," *Schriften,* 15: 228.

[92] *Sacramentum Mundi II,* s.v. "Jesus Christus," 936; "Das christliche Verständnis der Erlösung," *Schriften,* 15: 236–38; "Zur Theologie der Menschwerdung," *Schriften,* 4: 150.

[93] *Mysterium Salutis II,* s.v. "Der dreifaltige Gott," 366 n. 29. Wong, *Logos-Symbol,* 204–5, also notes this problem but argues that the Father *is* Jesus' "thou."

the Logos alone, and despite his assertion that only the Logos could become incarnate, Rahner affirms that Jesus' humanity is the highest expression of God almost as often as he asserts that it is the expression of the Logos. Thus, the divine nature alone might be considered as exercising its influence on Jesus' human nature and communicating itself quasi-formally to make Jesus the greatest of creatures.

Concerning the unity of humanity and divinity in Jesus, one might ask how, if other finite subjects and the environment (conceptual view) influence human subjectivity,[94] the immutable Logos can be said to be one with Jesus' human subject (dynamic view). But if the Logos cannot be influenced, what does the incarnation mean to him? To speak of "becoming in another" (dynamic view) while remaining changeless in oneself (conceptual view) appears the height of paradox, for as long as God is considered *actus purus,* mutable realities cannot be identified with God or influence him in any way. It is clear that Rahner wanted to join Jesus' humanity and through him the whole world to the God of salvation, so that Jesus is *now* and in eternity "the perduring openness of our finitude to the living God."[95] This juncture of Jesus' humanity with God's eternity seemingly implies, however, the divinization of the humanity. Otherwise, if diverse from God, it cannot demand the absolute adherence traditionally claimed in Christian faith for the historical Jesus.

What we are dealing with here is nothing other than the traditional problem of how to understand the unity of God and man, infinite and finite, transcendental and categorical, which, according to Christian belief, occurs in Jesus Christ. In the established Christology of the Catholic Church, it is the notion of "person" that traditionally has grounded this union in diversity of God and man in Christ, but, as previously noted, throughout his Christological writings Rahner failed to develop a fully coherent notion of "person" upon which to ground such a dialectical union.[96]

---

[94] "Christologie im Rahmen," *Schriften,* 9: 238; Rahner and Thüsing, *Christologie,* 20 f.

[95] "Die ewige Bedeutung," *Schriften,* 3: 57.

[96] McDermott, "Christologies of Karl Rahner," 308–26, has criticized comprehensively this lack of a coherent notion of "person" as a central weakness in Rahner's Christology. See also H. Vogels, "Erreicht Karl Rahners Theologie den kirchlichen Glauben? Kritik der Christologie und Trinitätslehre Karl Rahn-

Because of this lack of a notion of "person," he had to rely instead on the spiritual dynamism that is man (as *Schwebe*) in order to join man to God. Although within such a perspective the two poles might be recognized as somehow diverse, their dynamic relation, each reflecting and somehow encompassing the mysterious reality of the other, renders it impossible for Rahner to distinguish clearly between the two natures.

The key question remaining unresolved in Rahner's Christology is how the redemptive act achieved in Jesus was simultaneously an act of the Logos as the ontological free subject and also a free, human act. Rahner answered the question, as we have seen, by referring it to the unique climax of the Creator-creature relationship, where radical dependence and independence reach their irreversible high point.[97] Here, the role ascribed to the *visio immediata* in Jesus' human consciousness also can be understood, for that is also the peak of the God-man relationship, and accordingly Rahner considered it an inner constitutive moment of the Hypostatic Union. But again the central difficulty concerning the lack of a coherent notion of "person" as opposed to "nature" reappears. The immediate vision of God generally is viewed as the highest perfection of human *nature,* and when Rahner understands the Hypostatic Union as the climax of the Creator-creature relationship, his considerations seem to remain entirely on the level of *nature.* The *Aktzentrum* of Jesus seems to be nothing more than Jesus' free, conscious human subjectivity on which the Logos exercises an influence no different in essence from that exercised on any other finite subject. Yet the Logos is said also to be "a subject expressing himself in Jesus Christ."[98] There seem to be two free, conscious subjects in Jesus. This notion appears to be dangerously close to Nestorianism, and Rahner seems to have been aware of this danger, for in a number of other writings he attempted to address the problem by asserting that God's self-utterance *as content* constitutes the nature, or man Jesus, whereas the self-utterance *as event* constitutes the person, or Hypostatic

---

ers," *Wissenschaft und Weisheit* 52 (1989), 21–62, esp. 53, for a strong criticism of Rahner's confusion of person and nature.

[97] *Sacramentum Mundi II,* s.v. "Jesus Christus," 948.

[98] *Sacramentum Mundi II,* s.v. "Jesus Christus," 948.

Union.[99] Although such statements are problematical and, when considered in themselves, even paradoxical, in them Rahner is only being true to the fundamental structure of his thought as dialectical analogy. Through this structure, he is attempting to maintain that genuine balance necessary for any Christology. Nonetheless, it is clear that reliance on this structure alone, together with the lack of a fully coherent notion of "person," seems to threaten that very balance and to introduce tensions into his Christology that stretch it to the limits of coherence.

---

[99] *Sacramentum Mundi II,* s.v. "Jesus Christus," 952. See also K. Rahner, *Karl Rahner in Dialogue: Conversations and Interviews, 1965–1982,* edited and translated by H. Egan (New York: Crossroad, 1986), 127, where Rahner in an interview stated his preference for an "orthodox Nestorianism" in Christology.

7
Ecclesiology

WITH THE EXCEPTION of a few articles dating from the early 1950s, it was not really until the beginning of the 1960s that Rahner turned his attention to ecclesiology. During the time of the Second Vatican Council and especially in the period following it, Rahner devoted numerous articles and lectures to various aspects of ecclesiology, bringing his fundamental idea of the church as *Ursakrament* to bear on many of the problematic issues that arose in the postconciliar church.

In this chapter, I first examine Rahner's understanding of the church and how its nature is fulfilled in the "events" of the sacraments. I then review his notion of *ius divinum,* his understanding of the constitution of the church, and his explanation of how the church's nature is manifested both in its social structure and in its teaching office. Finally, I study his understanding of the relationship between the Catholic Church and the other Christian churches and his theory of "anonymous Christianity," by which he seeks to elucidate the relation of non-Christians to the one church of Christ.

1. THE NATURE OF THE CHURCH As *Ursakrament*

The eternal Logos has become of one race and family with us. This one human race is not merely the logical sum of individual human beings, but an actually real unity by the will of God.[1] Because Jesus is man, a human nature has been divinized, and because this man Jesus is a member of the one human race, this whole human race is called to a supernatural destiny in and through him. By the gracious coming of the Logos in the flesh in

---

[1] "Die Gliedschaft in der Kirche nach der Lehre der Enzyklika Pius XII 'Mystici Corporis Christi,'" *Schriften,* 2: 84–86; "Das neue Bild der Kirche," *Schriften,* 8: 340, 348.

the unity of the race, in the one history of humanity, mankind as a whole has become a consecrated humanity—that is, the "people of God."[2] Precisely because humanity is already the "people of God" and not just what it has yet to become, it receives in the church as a juridical organization its institutional structure according to Christ's will at its foundation. The structure of the visible church, therefore, is the constitution of a reality that exists before it receives such a constitution. Just as a state exists because logically, if not necessarily in time, the nation is prior to it with its unity of territory, history, civilization, and so on, so also a similar relation holds between the church as a juridically organized society and the reality of the "people of God."[3]

There is an official public history and private, individual history.[4] The history of a nation is not simply the sum total of the individual private lives of the human beings who compose that people. There is also the history of the nation as a nation, as a whole. The same is proportionately true of the sacred history of salvation and eternal loss. In this sacred history, there is the private history of the individual's grace and sin, as well as the public, official, "political" history of humanity and the nations in eternal welfare and ruin. To this latter type of history Christ belongs, in a unique way. "Christ is the primal sacramental word of God, uttered in the one history of mankind, in which God made known his irrevocable mercy that cannot be annulled by God or man and did this by effecting it in Christ, and he effected it by making it known."[5]

Now, the church is the continuance of that real, eschatologically triumphant presence in the world, in Christ, of God's salvific will, effecting what is uttered by uttering it in sign. Therefore, the church is the living fundamental sacrament *(Ursakrament)*.[6] From

---

[2] K. Rahner, *Kirche und Sakramente,* Questiones Disputatae no. 10 (Freiburg, Basel, Vienna: Herder, 1960), 13 (translations from *The Church and the Sacraments,* translated by W. O'Hara [London: Burns and Oates, 1974]); "Die Gliedschaft in der Kirche," *Schriften,* 2: 87–89, 91.

[3] *Kirche und Sakramente,* 12; "Die Gliedschaft in der Kirche," *Schriften,* 2: 90.

[4] *Kirche und Sakramente,* 16–17.

[5] *Kirche und Sakramente,* 17.

[6] The notion of the church as *Ursakrament* became popular through the work of O. Semmelroth, *Die Kirche als Ursakrament* (Frankfurt: Knecht, 1953). For a good account of the development of this notion, see L. Boff, *Die Kirche als*

Christ, it has a fundamentally sacramental structure as both the grace-filled "people of God" and the categorical manifestation of this reality.[7] Historically visible in space and time through its social constitution and teaching office, on the one hand, and through its sacramental life, on the other, the church is the body and bride of Christ, who abides in the church as the presence in the world of God's historical and eschatological promise of himself.[8]

> As an historical and social entity, the church is always and un-changeably the sign which brings with it always and inseparably what it signifies. As with Christ the distinction between his God-head and his humanity remains without confusion, though they are inseparable; so also, sign and reality, manifest historical form and Holy Spirit are not the same in the church but as in Christ are not separable any more either.[9]

2. THE CHURCH AS CHURCH OF THE SACRAMENTS

If the church is the fundamental sacrament, salvation is offered and promised to the individual by his entering into positive rela-tionship with the church.[10] This relationship can have various de-grees of intensity, but if the individual is to attain salvation such a relationship never can be entirely lacking. In the distinction be-

---

Sakrament (Paderborn: Bonifacius Druckerei, 1972), who discusses Rahner's contribution on 314–22. A. Dulles, *Models of the Church* (New York: Doubleday, 1974), 78, has criticized the notion for introducing a "narcissistic aestheticism" into ecclesiology that glorifies the church as the earthly home of the Spirit.

[7] "Die Gliedschaft in der Kirche," *Schriften*, 2: 93; *Kirche und Sakramente*, 17, 20; "Dogmatische Randbemerkungen zur Kirchenfrömmigkeit," *Schriften*, 5: 383; "Über den Episkopat," *Schriften*, 6: 376; "'Ich glaube die Kirche,'" *Schriften*, 7: 110.

[8] "Die Gliedschaft in der Kirche," *Schriften*, 2: 93; *Kirche und Sakramente*, 17, 20; "Dogmatische Randbemerkungen," *Schriften*, 5: 383; "Über den Episko-pat," *Schriften*, 6: 376; "'Ich glaube die Kirche,'" *Schriften*, 7: 110.

[9] *Kirche und Sakramente*, 18. Rahner's ecclesiology has been criticized for its lack of scriptural basis: U. Schnell, *Das Verhältnis von Amt und Gemeinde im neueren Katholizismus* (Berlin: W. de Gruyter, 1977), 210–13; M. Kehl, *Die Kirche als Institution: Zur theologischen Begründung des institutionellen Charakters der Kirche in der neuen deutschsprachigen katholischen Ekklesiologie* (Frankfurt: Knecht, 1976), 221. Rahner is defended against this criticism, though, in R. Kress, *The Church: Communion, Sacrament, Communication* (New York: Paulist Press, 1985), 170–71, and in Lennan, *Ecclesiology of Karl Rahner*, 77.

[10] Lennan, *Ecclesiology of Karl Rahner*, 37, 43.

tween the two aspects, grace-filled people of God and the juridical constitution of that people, an objective means of discerning
the degrees of intensity of membership in the church is given.[11]

If the church as means of grace has a sacramental structure—
that is, is based on the unity in diversity of the grace-filled
"people of God" and its historically manifest concrete embodiment—this sacramental structure must be true also of access to
the means of grace, of entry into the church, and of the individual's further acceptance of grace from it. This does not mean that
any and every conferral and acceptance of grace present in the
church as *Ursakrament* has the nature of a sacrament in the strictest
sense.

> Where the church in its official organized, public capacity precisely
> as the source of redemptive grace meets the individual in the ulti-
> mate accomplishment of its nature, there we have sacraments in the
> proper sense, and they can be seen then to be the essential functions
> that bring into activity the very essence of the church itself.[12]

In the sacraments, the church attains the highest actualization of
what it always is. The individual's obtaining of grace cannot consist simply in his approval and consent to the mere presence of
this redemptive grace. "Only by its own act does a community
with an organized structure acquire reality and validity for the
individual who at first is outside it."[13] A society must "enroll"
him if he is to enter it. Only in that way is it manifest that God's
redemptive grace in Christ is a free grace, his own operation in
us and not a factual reality always of necessity present. This act of
the church in regard to man will necessarily bear within it the
structure of the church's own nature. It will be sacramental.

From the notion of the church as *the* fundamental or primal
sacrament *(Ursakrament)* emerges the idea of an individual sacrament as an instance of the fullest actualization of the church's
essence and the saving presence of Christ's grace for the individual. Such an approach achieves a more adequate understanding

---

[11] *Kirche und Sakramente,* 20; "Thesen über das Gebet," *Schriften,* 5: 477–78,
482; "Das neue Bild der Kirche," *Schriften,* 8: 340; "Kirche, Kirchen, und Religionen," *Schriften,* 8: 373.

[12] *Kirche und Sakramente,* 21, 22, 37, 85.

[13] *Kirche und Sakramente,* 21.

of the sacraments in general than is possible with the traditional approach to sacramental theology. This viewpoint permits, for instance, a deeper understanding of the notion of *opus operatum* (see chapter 5). When applied to one of the sacraments—those acts of the church for an individual in which the church's nature is accomplished—*opus operatum* simply says what has already been said about the church in general: the sacrament is the definitive sign of God's grace in the world, which cannot be deprived of meaning and which is rendered present by being manifested in the church.

This approach also explains what the tradition holds about the "reviviscence" of the sacraments. It is not a question of coming to life again, but of a sacramental sign becoming effective; the sign still persists with its signification, an irrevocable word of God addressed to the individual, because the human being actually does accept it within the span of time in which, from the nature of the sign, the proffer of grace still subsists. This span of time varies with each sacramental sign because of the different meaning of each. The reviviscence of the sacraments is, therefore, simply a property that accompanies their character as an *opus operatum*. This approach also easily explains the efficacy of the sacraments in terms of symbolic causality.[14] The church in its visible historical form is an expression of the eschatologically triumphant grace of God; in that spatiotemporal form, this grace is made present. Because the sacraments are the actual fulfillment of the church's very nature, in regard to individual human beings these sacramental signs are efficacious. Their efficacy is that of the intrinsic symbol.[15] "This visible form is itself an effect of the coming of grace, it is there because God is gracious to men: and in this self-embodiment of grace, grace itself occurs."[16] The sacramental sign is the cause of grace inasmuch as grace is conferred by being signified. And this presence of grace in the sacraments is simply the actuality of the church itself as the visible manifestation of grace.

The principle that the church is the *Ursakrament* also indicates that the existence of the sacraments need not be always based on

---

[14] *Kirche und Sakramente,* 31–37. See chapter 4 for a fuller treatment of sacramental symbolic causality.

[15] "Die Gliedschaft in der Kirche," *Schriften,* 2: 78.

[16] *Kirche und Sakramente,* 36.

a definite statement in which the historical Jesus explicitly instituted a certain definite sacrament, for a fundamental act of the
church in an individual's regard, in situations that are decisive for
him, is ipso facto a sacrament. This would be the case even if only
later in the history of the church reflection were directed explicitly to the sacramental character of the act. The institution of a
sacrament can follow, therefore, simply from the fact that Christ
founded the church with its sacramental nature. Finally, it becomes clear also that the treatise *De sacramentis in genere* should
not consist (as in the theology of the Scholastics) in an abstract
formulation of the nature of the individual sacraments but properly should be seen as a part of the treatise *De ecclesia*. The latter
rightly precedes doctrine about the individual sacraments, for
only on the basis of this doctrine about the church, the fundamental sacrament, can we recognize the sacramentality of several
sacraments.

3. THE CONSTITUTION OF THE CHURCH

As the fundamental sacrament of God's salvific will in Christ, the
church fulfills its nature not just in those actions manifesting its
nature in regard to an individual, which we call sacraments. It also
manifests itself in history through its juridical and social organization and in its teaching office. Both its constitution and its magisterium participate in its sacramental nature. They express in
history the church's nature, as grace-filled "people of God," effecting what they symbolize precisely by making it manifest. Before turning our attention to the constitution of the church,
however, we should examine Rahner's notion of the *ius divinum,*
which is crucial for his understanding of this constitution and
which has important implications for his understanding of the development of doctrine.[17]

At many points, the constitutional law of the church and sacramental law declare a certain norm to be of divine positive law.

---

[17] For an account of the historical development of the notion of *ius divinum* in
Catholic theology, see A. Dulles, *A Church to Believe In: Discipleship and the Dy-
namics of Freedom* (New York: Crossroad, 1982), 82–87. For a brief summary of
Rahner's treatment, see Lennan, *Ecclesiology of Karl Rahner,* 64–68.

Such a norm, it is maintained, can be traced back to Christ and cannot be changed even by the church itself. The traditional difficulty with this theory lies in bringing the historical proof that certain particular norms are *de iure divino*. Protestant theologians in many cases have disputed that Christ instituted a particular norm or institution and have refused to accept the proofs brought forward by Catholic dogmatic theology and canon law on the grounds that they are inconclusive.

The Catholic dogmatic theologian and canonist knows that not *everything* relative to the concrete historical form in which such a regulation appeared in another age is already *iuris divini,* for the reality divinely instituted is actually real and properly effective only in a particular temporally determined form.[18] Historical criticism compares one form with another and legitimately indicates the historical conditioning of the form. This conditioning can be conceded by anyone who says that this "divine law" has existed in the church from the very beginning, for he need maintain only that the divinely instituted reality existed in a form different from its present-day form. Historical criticism should not maintain, at least not in principle, that such an institution either must have existed even in earlier times in its present form or did not exist at all. "This tacit presupposition is the basis of many historical proofs of the nonexistence of a currently claimed divine law: according to this presupposition, nature and form are simply identical. Yet there can be identity of nature under different forms."[19] The phenomena of the church can be explained adequately only if one is able to conceive of the identity of nature throughout the historical variation of its form and the difference of form in spite of the same nature of divine law.[20]

This statement merely throws the problem into clearer relief rather than solving it, for the question arises of how a change of form actually took place while leaving the nature untouched.

---

[18] "Über den Begriff des 'Jus divinum' im katholischen Verständnis," *Schriften,* 5: 251.

[19] "Über den Begriff des 'Jus divinum,'" *Schriften,* 5: 252. "Es gibt nun aber einmal Wesensidentitaet in Gestaltwandel." This is a strange use of the word *form*. Rahner presumably intends to signify the historical categorical form as expression of the nature of the *ius divinum*.

[20] "Über den Begriff des 'Jus divinum,'" *Schriften,* 5: 252: "Gestaltverschiedenheit trotz desselben Wesens götlichen Rechtes."

Although the nature and its historical concrete form cannot be found separately, it is the task of theology to distinguish what is essential to a particular form and what is not. The solution cannot be simply an affirmation that anything that was recognized in the past as being *iuris divini* is essential to the nature. As in the similar and analogous problem of the development of dogma, the problem occurs precisely in those cases where the revealed nature of a particular norm or proposition was not recognized clearly until later.

> How, then, can one recognize the revealed character of the earlier statement if in the past it did not carry—at least in a clearly recognizable manner—the mark of revelation, and if this recognition as revealed must not be the consequence of the present definition but rather the pre-supposition of the lawfulness of this definition, at least for the church's magisterium itself?[21]

In the context of the present discussion, how can one argue that a law is *iuris divini* if it is not historically clear that it came from Christ and that it was held to be *iuris divini* in the early church? Rahner proposes his own solution to the problem in a series of points.

First, there are one-way *(einbahnige)* historical processes that are no longer reversible *(umkehrbar)*, even if these processes are not necessary.[22] Thus, even if a reality is not present from the very beginning of a historical process, this does not necessarily mean that it is nonessential and reversible.[23]

Second, there are processes within an historically existing reality that can be recognized as legitimate in view of its nature, even though they spring from a free decision. This is true even if these processes and decisions can be proved to be neither obligatory nor the only possible ones available for the nature of the historically

---

[21] "Über den Begriff des 'Jus divinum,'" *Schriften,* 5: 255.

[22] "Über den Begriff des 'Jus divinum,'" *Schriften,* 5: 257, 262, 267–68, 271; "Über den Episkopat," *Schriften,* 6: 377–78; "Was ist ein Sakrament?" *Schriften,* 10: 390; Rahner and Thüsing, *A New Christology,* 28–29; *Kirche und Sakramente,* 52; "Der theologische Ansatzpunkt für die Bestimmung des Wessens des Amtspriestertums," *Schriften,* 9: 369; "Grundsätzliche Bemerkungen zum Thema: Wandelbares und Unwandelbares in der Kirche," *Schriften,* 10: 255. See also Lennan, *Ecclesiology of Karl Rahner,* 117.

[23] "Über den Begriff des 'Jus divinum,'" *Schriften,* 5: 259.

evolving reality. A society, a state, or a church also can be the subject of such decisions.

Third, it is possible to conceive of such a historical decision—a decision in conformity with nature even though not necessary by nature—that is of a juridical nature and itself both creative of law and irreversible. Therefore, if and where a law is irreversibly established, it must be understood to be in conformity with nature. Furthermore, it is possible to conceive that such an irreversible juridical decision and establishment also can be of the necessity of nature. For it is unhistorical to think that what is necessary by nature in an existent therefore also must have been present from the very start and hence that the mere fact of something appearing at a later point in time by being (explicitly or implicitly) established as a law already proves that it was not of the necessity of nature. "If this is basically correct, then it must be said absolutely that something which appears later on can still be something necessarily belonging to the nature."[24]

An irreversible, law-establishing decision of the church that is in conformity with its nature can be regarded as *iuris divini* when it took place at the time of the primitive church.[25] Furthermore, the period of history traditionally designated as lasting to the death of the last apostle really refers to the era of the primitive church in an inclusive sense, for it was not the apostles alone who were the vessels of the process of revelation still going on in the primitive church.[26]

This conclusion implies a way of understanding revelation as it occurs in human experience, as "decision."[27] It is not just a purely passive hearing of a proposition communicated word for word. The fact, for instance, that a gospel is inspired depends also on the

---

[24] "Über den Begriff des 'Jus divinum,'" *Schriften*, 5: 262. It is precisely this notion of bringing to categorical expression only later in history something that is nevertheless essential to the nature of the church that Rahner will use to justify the development of doctrine in the Catholic Church.

[25] "Über den Begriff des 'Jus divinum,'" *Schriften*, 5: 262, 268, 271; *Kirche und Sakramente,* 52; "Über den Episkopat," *Schriften*, 6: 377–78; "Der theologische Ansatzpunkt," *Schriften*, 9: 369; "Grundsätzliche Bemerkungen," *Schriften*, 10: 255; "Heilige Schrift und Tradition," *Schriften*, 6: 125; "Buch Gottes—Buch der Menschen," *Schriften*, 16: 283.

[26] "Über den Begriff des 'Jus divinum,'" *Schriften*, 5: 264; "Über den Episkopat," *Schriften*, 6: 378. See also Lennan, *Ecclesiology of Karl Rahner,* 61–62.

[27] "Über den Begriff des 'Jus divinum,'" *Schriften*, 5: 265.

real decision to write it, a decision belonging to the particular evangelist who no doubt experienced the writing as his own spontaneous decision. "Why should we not, on the one hand, regard the election of Matthias and his co-option into the apostolic college . . . as revealed and, on the other hand, regard it as brought about by the decision to choose him and indeed revealed *in* this very decision?"[28] Free events certainly can have the character of revelation in the primitive church.

Such a law–establishing decision quite easily can take the form of a choice among *several* possibilities. The other possibilities neglected in favor of the chosen one may be not only physically but also ethically and juridically possible. In other words, the establishment of the law may be truly a decision.[29] If and insofar as such a decision can be regarded as a process of revelation, what exactly has been revealed by this decision? First of all, the legitimacy of this decision—that is, its conformity to the church's nature—is revealed. It is also possible to assert that the irreversibility of this decision and hence its permanently binding character for all later generations of the church are also revealed. In other words, at least at the beginning, structures and laws *de iure divino* came into existence in the primitive church because a decision, made in conformity with its nature but not a priori recognized as intrinsically necessary, occurred that selected one of many possibilities for shaping the constitution of the church and its law. "Even the divine law of the church is a divine human law."[30]

This notion of the *ius divinum* follows logically from Rahner's foundational metaphysics, where nature is always seen as dynamic or developmental and extending into the supernatural because of the natural desire for the supernatural.[31] Furthermore, Rahner's understanding of freedom is an "Augustinian" freedom: it primarily is engaged freedom or liberated freedom that is most itself when choosing what it should choose—that is, it is most free in

---

[28] "Über den Begriff des 'Jus divinum,'" *Schriften*, 5: 266.

[29] "Über den Begriff des 'Jus divinum,'" *Schriften*, 5: 268; "Über den Episkopat," *Schriften*, 6: 378; "Grundsätzliche Bemerkungen," *Schriften*, 10: 255.

[30] "Über den Episkopat," *Schriften*, 6: 272.

[31] Rahner's notion of *ius divinum* is reviewed critically by W. Altmann, *Der Begriff der Tradition bei Karl Rahner* (Berne: Lang, 1974), 196–202, and by Dulles, *A Church to Believe In*, 91–92.

the beatific vision. The oppositions, therefore, between "nature" and "history," as those between "natural necessity" and "freedom," which were so obvious in the conceptualist theology, are apparent only for Rahner.[32]

Finally, it is not a priori impossible to ask whether there might be a law or structure *de iure divino* that is or has been decided on by the postapostolic church through an irreversible decision in conformity with its nature. Indeed, it is not superfluous to ask whether one might expect a development of constitution and of law in the early church that took place *after* the time of the primitive church but that nevertheless still can be called of divine law.[33]

4. The Teaching Authority of the Church

Just as the church's fundamental nature is manifested categorically through its social and juridical constitution, so also its nature is historically manifested in its solemn teaching office. Just as through the gradual thematization of its self-consciousness the church's deepening understanding of itself can lead to developments in the concrete forms of its social constitution that thereby do not contradict the *iuris divini* nature of that same constitution, so also through the same process of gradual thematization the teaching office of the church can come to a deeper understanding of itself as expressed in the dogmatic formulations of its magisterium. Although these dogmas may appear to be novel, they are in fact only the thematizations and categorical expressions of a consciousness that the church has always had of itself unthematically. They are infallible not because of some sort of episodic intervention in history on the part of the Holy Spirit but precisely because they are the historical expressions (or symbols) of the church, whose essence is the presence in history of the self-revelation of the God of truth.

---

[32] For the background to Rahner's notion of freedom, see J. Bonsor, *Rahner, Heidegger, and Truth: Karl Rahner's Notion of Christian Truth—The Influence of Martin Heidegger* (Lanham, Md.: University Press of America, 1987), 89–116.

[33] "Über den Episkopat," *Schriften,* 6: 274–75. See also Lennan, *Ecclesiology of Karl Rahner,* 67.

A. The Basis and Extent of the Church's Teaching Authority

In considering the traditional conceptual model of what is meant by the teaching authority of the church, one is struck by the absence of any reference to the church as such. The church as hearing and believing is merely that which is addressed, that to which authority is directed. Rahner believes that although Vatican II attempted to surpass this perspective, it did not really go far enough in the right direction.[34]

The apostles could have been the bearers of a teaching authority only to the extent that they themselves were believers and hearers, for they always preached as members of a community of believers, and the exercise of such authority necessarily claims the allegiance of faith. Their preaching was not merely addressed to the believing community but also proceeded from it. It bore witness to a faith brought into being by God alone in Jesus Christ, and it was only on this basis that it also justified its own formal authority.

The teaching authority does not constitute the church as such. "On the contrary, for authority of this sort to be able to exist at all a believing church has already to be in existence as its necessary prior condition."[35] The basic principles of this position are to be found in traditional ecclesiology. For instance, in the First Vatican Council the standards of the teaching authority actually exercised in general in the church determined the nature and extent of the pope's authority to teach. In other words, the pope's teaching authority derives from that of the church as a whole.[36] Even when Vatican II says that the pope's and bishops' teaching authority derives directly from Christ and not from the church and in this way is not subject to agreement from the church, the council also says that in any ex cathedra definition the pope is not acting as a private individual but as the supreme teacher of the universal church. His charism is the charism of the church's infallibility. *Dei Verbum* 8 further states that the deposit of faith to which the

---

[34] "Das kirchliche Lehramt in der heutigen Autoritätskrise," *Schriften*, 9: 341.

[35] "Das kirchliche Lehramt," *Schriften*, 9: 343; "Zum Begriff der Unfehlbarkeit in der katholischen Theologie," *Schriften*, 10: 316–17.

[36] See Lennan, *Ecclesiology of Karl Rahner*, 192–93.

teaching office is bound includes all that it itself is and all that it believes. This statement constitutes a further indication that the teaching office not only is oriented actively toward the church with a content of faith that it initially possesses of its own account, but also at the same time is derived from the believing church itself.[37]

The derivation of the authority of the teaching office from the whole church is significant because God does not intervene frequently in history to preserve us from error. The real effectiveness of the authority vested in the church's official teachers consists in the belief that through God's self-revelation in grace to the world and its absolute appearance in Jesus Christ the church is constituted as *the* experience in faith of this self-revelation of God, which can never again sink under error.

> Because the irreversibly victorious experience of the self-revelation of God, which is called the church, has, as a community and as a society, an institutional nature and therefore an office in which it realizes the fullness of its nature, this office as teaching office participates in the victorious permanence of the truth of God in the world, which is the innermost *entelecheia* of the history of the world and the coming-to-self of the world in its relationship to God.[38]

This means that the church's teaching office must show itself as it really is according to its own understanding of its nature. Those in authority are obliged morally to study and to consult before exercising their authority.[39] They must be conscious of the living awareness of the faith in the church, for they derive their ideas from this awareness. The church's own absolute assent of faith, however unreflective, must precede any definitional decision of the teaching office, "so that in a case of this kind the specific charism of the teaching office consists, strictly speaking, in its 'infallible' confirmation of this absolute assent of faith on the part of the church as a whole, which has already been arrived at."[40]

---

[37] "Das kirchliche Lehramt," *Schriften,* 9: 344.
[38] "Das kirchliche Lehramt," *Schriften,* 9: 345.
[39] "Das kirchliche Lehramt," *Schriften,* 9: 347; "Vom Dialog in der Kirche," *Schriften,* 8: 443–44; "Lehramt und Theologie," *Schriften,* 13: 81.
[40] "Das kirchliche Lehramt," *Schriften,* 9: 347.

B. Practical Consequences

In this context, the question of democracy with regard to the teaching office of the church naturally arises. Because democracy is neither a scriptural nor a traditional concept, we must be cautious about trying to introduce it into ecclesiology. It is, however, necessary to reject straight away any reactionary prejudice that any democratic system of voting is from the outset incompatible with the nature of the church's teaching office. From the council of the apostles right down to Vatican II, votes have been taken in matters of doctrine. It conversely would be impossible for the pope to make an ex cathedra decision in opposition to the clear majority of the bishops of the church, though the term *impossible,* as applied here, does not signify any limitation of his formal and juridical authority, but rather recognizes a limitation that is inherent in the reality itself and in the moral norms that have to be observed when the pope arrives at any such decision.

> Given that the pope proposed to define a doctrine which was contrary to the conviction of the great majority of the church's members, and that too as expressed by the undoubted representatives of these, and given that . . . the pope himself does not receive any fresh revelations, how could he ever know that the doctrine that he proposed to define was in fact contained in divine revelation?[41]

According to the Second Vatican Council, no such situation is in fact possible. The pope's teaching, as formulated in ex cathedra decisions, is derived from the faith of the universal church, and this derivation is ensured by the taking of a "vote," though this vote can take place in the most varied of ways. If, therefore, we decide to regard any vote as a democratic element, then the teaching office of the church has something to do with democracy.[42]

The next question concerns the participants in such a vote. According to a Catholic understanding, the universal episcopate has *iure divino* a right to participate in any such "vote" with and

---

[41] "Das kirchliche Lehramt," *Schriften,* 9: 350. How the victory of orthodoxy in the context of the Arian crisis can be explained within this perspective is not transparently clear.

[42] "Das kirchliche Lehramt," *Schriften,* 9: 351; *Das Dynamische in der Kirche,* 63–64.

under the pope. This right does not necessarily deny others a right to participate according to human law, even if they are not acting in episcopal or quasi-episcopal roles. Another valid ground for participation would be special competence in a particular field. It is at least *possible* for the church to extend such a right to nonepiscopal members, even though it would be acting *de iure humano*. Indeed, the nature of the case may demand morally that it so extend the right to vote. However, if such cases were to arise, the difference between divine and human law in the church would be a very relative one because, on the one hand, the divine law of the church's constitution always and inevitably must exhibit a concrete form that is subject to the conditions of particular epochs and because, on the other hand, every *ius humanum* entailing a moral duty to act in such and such a way in a specific situation conceals within itself a basic core of necessity that derives from God. "From this it follows that the *ius divinum* attributed to the universal episcopate ultimately signifies merely that the united bishops . . . represent the abiding assurance and the abiding visible manifestation of the *continuity* of the right of the teaching office in the church to be heard and obeyed."[43]

Finally, we must clarify the precise relation existing between the formal authority of the teaching office and the *fides quae* that is intended to mediate the formal authority of the church to the *fides qua* of the individual believer. First, the formal authority of the teaching office is not the primary and most fundamental datum in the content of faith such that all other elements in that faith are based on this one as their necessary foundation. To this extent, Augustine's famous saying that he would not believe the Gospel if it were not for the authority of the church is wrong.[44] "Precisely in order to be Catholic in our belief, we must turn Augustine's axiom 'the other way around,' by saying 'I would not believe in the authority of the church if I were not moved to do so by the gospel.'"[45] This is not to deny that there is also a *mutual*

---

[43] "Das kirchliche Lehramt," *Schriften,* 9: 353.

[44] "Das kirchliche Lehramt," *Schriften,* 9: 359; "Bietet die Kirche letzte Gewissheiten," *Schriften,* 10: 290. See Lennan, *Ecclesiology of Karl Rahner,* 36.

[45] "Das kirchliche Lehramt," *Schriften,* 9: 360. In one sense, it would seem that Augustine's axiom was correct, for the church, of course, existed before the Gospels. But perhaps Rahner is looking at the "gospel" not as a book but rather as a preaching event.

relationship of interdependence between the church, its institutional structures, and its officialdom, on the one hand, and the
true substance of the faith, on the other, as recognized in the
conscience of the individual believer. But within this mutually
conditioning unity there is still an objective order, and in this
order belief in the church's teaching office is sustained both objectively and subjectively by a reality of the faith prior to this
teaching office and to faith in it.

5. The Church, the Churches, and Anonymous Christians

If all grace even before Christ is ordered toward him and therefore also toward the church, then the question naturally arises
concerning the status of those who, for whatever reason, remain
inculpably outside of the visible church throughout their lives.

A. Foundational Principle

Rahner proposes a fundamental principle upon which this traditionally difficult problem can be answered and upon which his
whole theory of "anonymous Christians" is based.[46] This fundamental principle is that God truly and sincerely wills *all* men to be
saved, and in virtue of this will he offers every man, in whatever
circumstances, a genuine possibility of attaining to salvation.[47]
The possibility of attaining this salvation, therefore, is such that it
can remain unrealized only if it is frustrated by the real, grave,
and personal guilt of the subject to whom it is offered.[48]

Salvation in this sense is not a *created* gift of God, but in the
deepest sense is God himself. This self-bestowal of God is both

---

[46] The most detailed study of the development and significance of Rahner's
anonymous Christianity theory is N. Schwerdtfeger, *Gnade und Welt: Zum
Grundgefüge von Karl Rahners Theorie der "anonymen Christen"* (Freiburg: Herder,
1982). Kehl, *Die Kirche als Institution*, 189–90, gives a critical assessment of
Rahner's theory.

[47] "Die anonymen Christen," *Schriften*, 6: 546; "Bemerkungen zum Problem
des 'anonymen Christen,'" *Schriften*, 10: 535; "Der eine Jesus Christus," *Schriften*, 12: 252–53, 257.

[48] "Die anonymen Christen," *Schriften*, 6: 550; "Bemerkungen zum Problem
des 'anonymen Christen,'" *Schriften*, 10: 538; "Anonymes Christentum und
Missionsauftrag der Kirche," *Schriften*, 9: 503.

the divine offer imparted to man as a gift and the possibility for a creature endowed with spiritual faculties to receive what is offered. "God himself *is* the salvation and at the same time the power to receive the salvation."[49] This implies two things. First, the divine self-bestowal penetrates to the ultimate roots of man's being, radically reorienting the natural transcendence of his nature toward the immediate presence of God.[50] It is a "supernatural existential" that can be recognized in itself as "revelation" and, hence, if accepted by the individual, albeit unthematically, is also faith.[51] This does not mean that man must always have a conscious awareness of this supernatural existential in his life.[52] Second, this transcendentality of man as spiritual does not remain a separate department of human life *over and above* the historical context in which he is involved. The supernatural existential is achieved, according to the nature of man (as *Schwebe*) in and through his existence as engaged in human living. It is made manifest, although this manifestation does not have to be explicitly and thematically religious. The presence of this abiding supernatural existential in man has the effect of making salvation or "saving" history coextensive with human history.[53]

> To this extent we can and must say that either saving history or its opposite, the history of perdition, is taking place wherever man of his own free decision either voluntarily undertakes his own mode of existence or alternatively protests against it.[54]

"Revelation history" is always and everywhere taking place. When we explicate this notion in conscious thought and make it

---

[49] "Kirche, Kirchen, und Religionen," *Schriften*, 8: 359.

[50] "Die anonymen Christen," *Schriften*, 6: 547; "Bemerkungen zum Problem des 'anonymen Christen,'" *Schriften*, 10: 539. See chapter 2, note 38.

[51] "Dogmatische Randbemerkungen," *Schriften*, 5: 405; "Das neue Bild der Kirche," *Schriften*, 8: 346–47; "Die Gliedschaft in der Kirche," *Schriften*, 2: 91; "Die anonymen Christen," *Schriften*, 6: 549; "Bemerkungen zum Problem des 'anonymen Christen,'" *Schriften*, 10: 542. See chapter 5, note 29.

[52] "Natur und Gnade," *Schriften*, 4: 224–25; "Kirche, Kirchen, und Religionen," *Schriften*, 8: 360; "Über die Erfarung," *Schriften*, 3: 105–9; *Das Dynamische in der Kirche*, 108–9.

[53] "Kirche, Kirchen, und Religionen," *Schriften*, 8: 361, 363–64, 370; "Bemerkungen zum Problem des 'anonymen Christen,'" *Schriften*, 10: 541. See chapter 5, note 31.

[54] "Kirche, Kirchen, und Religionen," *Schriften*, 8: 361.

a theme for religious investigation, the result is the history of religion and religious ideas. And this process of making the salvation and revelation history of the supernatural existential an explicit object and theme for man's religious thought can be guided positively or even demanded by God as part of his plan to save man. Within this broader context of salvation and perdition history, however, something more is attained, something that we can call the *explicit* and *official* history of salvation, which is apprehensible to Christians in the Old and New Testaments.[55]

This official, explicit salvation history, unalloyed by human error and attested by God himself, is brought to its climax and goal in Jesus Christ.[56] In him as the God-man in person,[57] there takes place God's absolute and irrevocable self-bestowal upon man and at the same time man's total and perfect acceptance of this divine self-bestowal, which issues also in the most sublime effects. The supernatural existential present in all humanity tends dynamically toward its irrevocable climax in Jesus Christ.[58] To the extent that this is true and to the extent that every movement toward a goal derives its direction and force from the goal itself, it can be said that the whole of salvation and revelation history, *both* as universally present in all men *and* in its explicit and official form, is dependent on Jesus Christ and derives its direction and forward movement from him.[59]

B. The Absolute Character of Christianity

In attributing an absolute character to Christianity, we do not intend that the salvation and revelation history of God is identical with that particular area in the religious history of mankind confined to the Old and New Testaments. We say something quite different—namely, that the whole of salvation history is coexistent with the history of mankind. As such, the whole of it is

---

[55] See chapter 5, note 33.
[56] See chapter 6, note 51.
[57] "Kirche, Kirchen, und Religionen," *Schriften,* 8: 362: "in Jesus Christus, in dem sich als der Person des Gottmenschen," and so on.
[58] "Die anonymen Christen," *Schriften,* 6: 548–49.
[59] "Die anonymen Christen," *Schriften,* 6: 549; "Anonymes Christentum," *Schriften,* 9: 508–9; "Jesus Christus in den nichtchristlichen Religionen," *Schriften,* 12: 378. See chapter 6, note 58.

sustained by the grace that finds its supreme and irreversible historical manifestation in the God-man Jesus Christ. The God-man is the supreme and climactic point in God's bestowing of himself on mankind.

> Right from its very inception God's plan and God's execution of this plan in the implementation of his will to save all men proceeded from the God-man as its starting point and proceeds toward him as its goal. And because of this the whole of salvation and revelation history is Christian right from its inception even before there has been any conscious recognition of this in it.[60]

This explanation in no way denies the absolute character of Christ himself or of the church as the visible expression of the abiding presence of Christ, for this history is being impelled toward Christ, even though only in a hidden manner, by this forward, historical unfolding of the grace that is offered to all ages.

C. Non-Catholic Christians

The Catholic Church cannot think of itself as one among many historical manifestations in which one and the same God-man Jesus Christ is made present, as if God offered these manifestations for man to choose whichever he likes. On the contrary, the church must necessarily think of itself as the one, total presence in history of the one God-man in his truth and grace. As such, the church has a fundamental relationship to all people. However, on that account, the other Christian churches and communities need not be regarded simply as entities that should not be there at all. All Christians have a will to be one and to belong to the one true church of Christ. To will this unity is a God-given grace absolutely basic to salvation and, as such, is undoubtedly more fundamental and more absolute than the will that causes non-Catholic Christians and their churches to remain separated from the Catholic Church. This underlying will reveals that an ultimate unity, effective at the invisible and spiritual level, already exists among all Christians, a unity that is already greater than the unity of the church considered merely as a society.[61] Furthermore, all

---

[60] "Kirche, Kirchen, und Religionen," *Schriften,* 8: 363.
[61] "Kirche, Kirchen, und Religionen," *Schriften,* 8: 366.

those Christians outside the Catholic Church who have not committed any serious fault against the claims of their own religious and moral consciences do in fact possess the Holy Spirit of justification and grace. All these Christians are in possession of that to which everything in the church is ordered. "All Christians both within and without the Catholic church, therefore, simply in virtue of being faithful to their own consciences, are united among themselves in the Spirit of the church."[62]

D. Non-Christian Religions

We certainly can recognize the possibility that non-Christian religions before the coming of Christ were "in themselves" and in principle positively willed by God as legitimate ways of salvation. Because the Old Testament and the official means of salvation were not available to all men, and in the light of God's will to save all men, we must presume that every individual must have had some positive grace-given means of salvation available to him. Given the nature of man as a historical and social being (as *Schwebe*), we know that man would not work out his salvation simply by acts of religion that are purely interior. He could do so, therefore, only through the sort of religion that must of its very nature find concrete expression in the social and institutional life of the community.[63] Religions that de facto do exist outside of Christianity and the Old Testament are not merely the outcome of human speculation, human wickedness, or a self-willed decision on man's part to devise a religion for himself instead of accepting it from God. "Instead of this the supernatural existential, the dynamic impulse present in man by the power of grace and impelling him toward the triune God, is at work in all these religions and plays a decisive part in determining the forms in which these religions are objectively expressed."[64] These religions thereby are not rendered "pure" or unadulterated as objective expressions and manifestations of this transcendental self-bestowal of God. They continue to be a mixture of disparate elements, but

---

[62] "Kirche, Kirchen, und Religionen," *Schriften*, 8: 367.

[63] "Jesus Christus in den nichtchristlichen Religionen," *Schriften*, 12: 380–81.

[64] "Kirche, Kirchen, und Religionen," *Schriften*, 8: 370; "Bietet die Kirche letzte Gewissheiten," *Schriften*, 10: 290–94.

through them all the grace of God is constantly at work, and even in the most primitive, corrupt, or grotesque forms this grace still offers to man the ultimate possibility of activating in some way or other that orientation toward the mystery of God that is implanted in him by grace.

The Catholic Christian of today should experience and see the church as the vanguard, as the sacramental sign, the historical tangibility of a saving grace that goes beyond the sociologically tangible and "visible" church—that is, the grace of an *"anonymous Christianity,"* which "outside" the church has not come to itself yet but which "within" the church is present to itself.[65] He will regard non-Christians as anonymous Christians who do not yet know explicitly what they really are by grace.[66] The church will be for him, as it were, the uniformed part of God's soldiers; it is for him that point at which the inner being of the human-divine existence appears also historically and sociologically. Hence, he will look calmly and fearlessly into the world, a world of a thousand opinions and views, without having anxiously to consult statistics to see whether the church is the greatest world organization. He will look into the world with missionary zeal; "he will wish to share his grace with others, for he possesses a grace which these others lack . . . *still* lack."[67] He will go out boldly and full of hope to meet as brothers even those who by their worldview do not wish to be his brother, for he sees in those who have not yet seen clearly what presumably they accomplish already in the deepest dimension of their existence. The Christian sees anonymous Christianity at work in the world and in his fellow human beings in a thousand different and unexpected ways.

---

[65] "Dogmatische Randbemerkungen," *Schriften,* 5: 401; "Das neue Bild der Kirche," *Schriften,* 8: 341. See also Lennan, *Ecclesiology of Karl Rahner,* 147, 149.

[66] "Das neue Bild der Kirche," *Schriften,* 8: 342, 344, 345; "Dogmatische Randbemerkungen," *Schriften,* 5: 401; *Sendung und Gnade,* 103, 104, 106; "Die anonymen Christen," *Schriften,* 6: 549.

[67] "Dogmatische Randbemerkungen," *Schriften,* 5: 403. It is admittedly difficult to see, within this Rahnerian perspective, what *grace* the anonymous Christian actually still lacks. According to Rahner's doctrine of grace, uncreated grace—that is, the indwelling of the Holy Spirit—precedes and affects created grace through quasi-formal causality. Every individual who exists, therefore, by virtue of the supernatural existential possesses, at least as an offer, the whole grace of justification together with a nonappropriated relation to the three divine persons. The categorical expression of that grace is certainly still lacking, but it is not at all clear that the justified pagan really lacks any grace as such.

In his preaching of Christianity to the "non-Christian," the Christian will not proceed from the idea of wanting to convert someone into something that he has not been at all; rather, he will try to make the non-Christian more conscious of what he is.[68] The church is for the Christian like a promise—not merely the promise of the growing conversion of this world into the church, but the promise of a possibility for the world to be saved by the church even where it is not already that church that can be experienced historically.

E. Vatican II and Inculpable Atheism

In the years following Rahner's initial exposition of "anonymous Christianity" his theory provoked a lively theological debate and was subjected to severe criticism by, among others, Henri de Lubac and Hans Urs von Balthasar.[69] In the light of this criticism and of the teaching of the recently concluded Second Vatican Council, Rahner returned to this theme in a number of articles dating from the late 1960s and early 1970s. Although conceding the validity of de Lubac's criticism over the inappropriateness of the term *anonymous Christianity*,[70] Rahner insisted on the validity of his theory in general and on the necessity of the term *anonymous Christian* unless a more suitable alternative, expressing its essential meaning, could be found.[71] He defended his theory by highlighting and attempting to demonstrate the two essential points involved in it. First, there are individuals who stand outside the social unity of the church or of the Christian churches but who nevertheless stand in a positive and salvific relationship to God; in other words, they are justified. Even those who at the

---

[68] "Das neue Bild der Kirche," *Schriften,* 8: 347; "Dogmatische Randbemerkungen," *Schriften,* 5: 405; *Sendung und Gnade,* 103; "Atheismus und implizites Christentum," *Schriften,* 8: 204–5; "Anonymes Christentum," *Schriften,* 9: 508.

[69] H. U. von Balthasar, *Cordula oder Ernstfall* (Einsiedeln: Johannes, 1966); H. de Lubac, *Paradoxe et mystere de l'église* (Paris: Aubier-Montaigne, 1967), 153–56. See also H. Küng, "Anonyme Christen—Wozu?" *Orientierung* 39 (1975), 214–16. For a good defense of Rahner's theory of anonymous Christianity, see Weger, "Das 'anonyme' Christentum," 321–24.

[70] "Bemerkungen zum Problem des 'anonymen Christen,'" *Schriften,* 10: 532.

[71] "Bemerkungen zum Problem des 'anonymen Christen,'" *Schriften,* 10: 532; "Anonymes Christentum," *Schriften,* 9: 499–501.

level of their conscious thought interpret themselves as atheist may be numbered among such individuals. Second, these individuals, although they are non-Christians, are justified through the grace of Christ and through a faith, hope, and love for God, even when this faith, hope, and love is something of which they are not aware objectively. The anonymous Christian, therefore, is "the pagan after the beginning of the Christian mission who lives in the state of Christ's grace through faith, hope and love, yet who has no explicit knowledge that his life is oriented in grace-given salvation to Jesus Christ."[72]

As far as this first point is concerned, there should be no room for doubt among Catholic theologians or Christians.[73] Whatever may have been the course of this development, whatever theological grounds there may be for justifying it, we certainly can say in the light of the teaching of the Second Vatican Council that the Catholic Church regards it as established that it is possible for pagans and even self-professed atheists of goodwill to be justified and to attain to supernatural salvation even though at the level of their concrete worldly circumstances they are not Christians at all.[74] The only necessary condition the council recognized is the necessity of faithfulness and obedience to the individual's own personal conscience. Rahner's second point is that this salvation of the non-Christian is achieved through an act of faith in the true sense. Rahner's doctrine of the anonymous Christian does not involve the belief that anyone can attain to justification and final salvation even without faith in a strictly theological sense merely because he does not act against his own moral conscience.[75] Both Pius XII's declaration against the rigorism of

---

[72] "Bemerkungen zum Problem des 'anonymen Christen,'" *Schriften*, 10: 534.

[73] Rahner briefly traces the development of the church's consciousness in this regard, "Bemerkungen zum Problem des 'anonymen Christen,'" *Schriften*, 10: 534–35; "Anonymes Christentum," *Schriften*, 9: 503–4.

[74] The Second Vatican Council texts that Rahner uses to demonstrate this point are: *Gaudium et Spes*, nos. 19–21 and the fifth paragraph of no. 22; *Lumen Gentium*, no. 16; and *Ad Gentes*, no. 7. For his detailed exegesis of these texts, see "Atheismus und implizites Christentum," *Schriften*, 8: 190–93, and "Die anonymen Christen," *Schriften*, 6: 553–54. See also Lennan, *Ecclesiology of Karl Rahner*, 146–47.

[75] "Was ist Häresie?" *Schriften*, 5: 532; "Der eine Jesus Christus," *Schriften*, 12: 255, 273–74.

Feeney[76] and the doctrine of Vatican II clearly assume that even in these cases of a justified pagan a *fides supernaturalis* is necessary.[77] What is not stated in these official doctrinal declarations—in other words, what the doctrine of the anonymous Christian therefore is concerned with—is *how* it is possible apart from the preaching of the gospel for a true and supernatural faith to be present in the pagan of this kind.

Presuming the distinction between objective "this-worldly" knowledge, on the one hand, and nonobjective, nonthematic consciousness, on the other hand,[78] the theory of the possibility of personal faith in a "pagan" makes two assumptions. First, the supernatural grace of faith God offers to men need not be conceived of as an isolated intervention on God's part at a particular point in a profane world. On the contrary, on the basis of God's universal will to save, it can be interpreted as a grace that, as offered, is a constantly present existential both of the spiritual creature and of the world in general. Second, this grace constantly imparted to the nature of the creature is something of which man is aware *(bewusst)* but not necessarily in a way that implies an objective, thematic knowledge *(gegenständliche Gewusstheit)*. It is present therefore as a new a priori formal end to man's spiritual transcendence. Whether man explicitly recognizes it or not *(reflex weiss)*, he is, in virtue of the grace offered him and implanted in him, oriented toward the immediacy of God as his final end.[79]

> And when man of his freedom accepts himself together with this a priori awareness which is already revelation, then that is present which can in the true and proper sense be called faith, even though this faith has not yet been objectively explicitated or conceptualized as the absolute openness of man to the immediacy of God in his act of self-imparting. Yet this a priori awareness of man (called revelation) is always accepted in faith wherever and whenever an individual in unreserved faithfulness to his own moral conscience accepts

[76] See *Enchiridion Symbolorum Definitionum et Declarationum de Rebus Fidei et Morum,* edited by H. Denzinger and Adolf Schönmetzer (Freiburg: Herder, 1965), 3866.

[77] "Der eine Jesus Christus," *Schriften,* 12: 254–55, 272–73.

[78] Rahner explains this distinction clearly and concisely in the context of the discussion of anonymous Christians in "Atheismus und implizites Christentum," *Schriften,* 8: 197–200. See also "Der eine Jesus Christus," *Schriften,* 12: 275–76.

[79] "Anonymer und expliziter Glaube," *Schriften,* 12: 81–82.

himself in freedom as he is, and so too in the yet unrecognizable implications of the dynamism underlying the movement of his own spirit.[80]

It is perfectly possible to envisage a man who is in possession of that self-imparting of God called grace as the innermost heart of his existence, one who has accepted it in the unreserved faithfulness of his own conscience and who is thereby constituted a believer in a form that, although not objectified in words, is nevertheless real. He would be, in other words, a man who even as a pagan possesses the blessing of salvation, that blessing that is the sole point of concern for Christianity and for its gospel and all its historical institutions. If this is true, concludes Rahner,

> then I cannot see why we should not call such a man an anonymous Christian, seeing that as Catholic theologians we may not doubt that such men both can and actually do exist. For after all he does possess, even though in a way hidden to himself and to others, that which constitutes the essence of what it is to be Christian: the grace of God which is laid hold of in faith.[81]

6. CONCLUSION

Rahner's ecclesiology follows logically from his understanding of man as spirit in the world, his doctrine of grace, and his Christology. The structure of mutual priority between transcendence and the categorical is the fundamental structure of human nature (as *Schwebe*) and is intrinsic to Rahner's understanding of reality. It is to this human nature that God imparts himself in grace in view

---

[80] That "acceptance of self" is equivalent to faith is a central affirmation of Rahner's theory: "Bemerkungen zum Problem des 'anonymen Christen,'" *Schriften,* 10: 541–42; "Anonymer und expliziter Glaube," *Schriften,* 12: 83–84; "Jesus Christus in den nichtchristlichen Religionen," *Schriften,* 12: 371; "Die Gliedschaft in der Kirche," *Schriften,* 2: 91; "Das neue Bild der Kirche," *Schriften,* 8: 346–47; "Überlegungen zum personalen Vollzug," *Schriften,* 10: 413; "Was ist ein Sakrament?" *Schriften,* 10: 385–86; *Sacramentum Mundi II,* s.v. "Jesus Christus," 923, 954; Rahner and Thüsing, *A New Christology,* 16–17; Rahner and Thüsing, *Christologie,* 71; "Bietet die Kirche letzte Gewissheiten," *Schriften,* 10: 290–94; "Kirche, Kirchen, und Religionen," *Schriften,* 8: 357; *Sendung und Gnade,* 82, 118.

[81] "Bemerkungen zum Problem des 'anonymen Christen,'" *Schriften,* 10: 544.

of his universal salvific will. Grace penetrates to the ultimate roots of man's being, radically reorienting the natural transcendence of his nature toward the immediate presence of God. It is a supernatural existential or mode of being that is indeed grace but is nevertheless inserted into man's nature. It imparts, in Thomistic terms, a new formal end to man's transcendence of which he is a priori conscious even if not thematically aware. However, God's inward self-communication in grace cannot alone be adequate for the nature of man. It must, according to the fundamental structure of his nature (as *Schwebe*), be expressed and mediated to itself conceptually. Thus, there exists a mutual priority and unity between the inner word of God's self-communication in grace and the outer word as its manifestation and mediation in history. The relationship between the inner and outer words of God's revelation is twofold. On the one hand (dynamic view), the outer word is seen as but an expression of the previously existing inner word, whereas, on the other hand (conceptual view), a relationship of mutual priority is said to exist between the inner word of grace and the objectively given outer word of categorical revelation. In Rahner's later works, as previously noted, he stresses progressively more the dynamic side of his thought and the priority of grace and argues that this grace can express itself not just in the outer word of official revelation but in any historical word. This historical manifestation of inner grace, therefore, does not have to be explicitly religious. The supernatural existential has the effect of making all history a mediation of God's existentially imparted grace, such that all history becomes salvation history in a broad sense. This broad salvation history, however, is open to error, not in such a way that the grace of the individual that is manifested and mediated through that history is invalidated, but insofar as the categorical expression of this grace has not yet reached its fullest expression. Within this broad salvation history, therefore, man attains to something more. Thus, even in this heavily dynamic perspective, Rahner's balance is not lost in that he continues to insist (in line with the conceptual, distinguishing side of his thought) that grace tends toward a true and full conceptual expression of itself. This expression is found in the explicit and official revelation history of the Old Testament and in its sublime and most absolute form in Jesus Christ, the God–man. The supernatural existential present in all humanity tends dynamically toward its inevitable climax in Jesus Christ. Moreover, because every movement toward a goal derives its direction and force from the goal itself, the whole of salvation history, both explicit and implicit, is dependent on and is caused by Jesus Christ, the real-symbol and final cause of this one grace-filled dynamism. The church in its twofold structure—as grace-filled community of the "people of God" in its historical manifestation as social structure and teaching office, on the one hand, and as sacramental action, on the other—is the real-symbol of Jesus Christ present forever in history. When the individual encounters the visible church and is incorporated into its social constitution through reception of its sacraments, then the grace always present as an offer in the supernatural existential of his nature finds its truest and fullest categorical expression. This does not deny the necessity of Jesus Christ or the causality of the sacraments, for according to Rahner's notion of symbolic causality (and in line with the conceptual, distinguishing side of his thought) this supernatural existential is originally present only because it is manifested in history in its real-symbol, the manifestation causing what it manifests precisely by manifesting it.[82] This manifestation, although temporally subsequent, is metaphysically prior to what it manifests.

In this context, Rahner makes an important distinction between official public history and individual private history. Whereas in public world history grace tends toward and must find its true categorical expression in Jesus Christ, an individual, in his own private history, can be saved through grace, through acceptance of his supernaturally elevated nature, even when this grace fails to reach its full categorical expression. For grace is the self-revelation of God and acceptance of revelation is supernatural faith. To say that in Jesus Christ something definitive and irrevocable has happened means that in world history grace has come to its truest and fullest categorical expression. As such, Jesus Christ is the real-symbol of all grace and therefore its cause in both pri-

---

[82] Interesting as this theory of symbolic causality is, it is not entirely clear how Rahner can avoid implying that the causality of the symbol is exercised on God himself, thus making God subject to inner-worldly causality. This idea is obviously problematical (see chapter 4), yet it is in agreement with the whole notion of God becoming in the other and with the basic unity of God and the world.

vate and public salvation history. Even where the symbol is lacking or deficient in personal history, grace is present and effective only because the symbol is manifested in public world history. After Jesus Christ, grace in its fullest and absolute form is definitively and irreversibly present in the world.

The church as real-symbol of Christ shares in the definitive nature of the Christ event, and the sacraments as real-symbols of the church are this definitive event as applied to the life of the individual. This is the meaning of the phrase *ex opere operato* as applied to the sacraments. They are the definitive categorical expressions of the grace already at work within the individual and within history, the grace that in Jesus Christ has reached its fullest and therefore causative manifestation. Standing before Jesus Christ and before the church and the sacraments, the individual in his own personal history remains free (conceptualizing view). Just as outside Christianity he can refuse to accept himself and his grace-given orientation toward God, so also he can refuse to accept Jesus Christ without thereby invalidating the truth that what he is rejecting is the fullest expression and symbolic cause of the grace that existentially codefines his own nature. So also with the sacraments: an individual can refuse to accept the grace signified and caused by a sacrament without thereby invalidating the truth that this sacrament is in reality the expressive cause of the grace offered to him in the supernatural existential of his nature. Thus, the sacrament can be valid and yet unfruitful. To reject this grace-causing symbol is to contradict one's very "supernaturalized" nature (dynamic view) and, if done culpably, leads to damnation. The refusal is possible, yet it does not contradict the truth of the real-symbol as cause and manifestation of the grace already active in the individual himself.

The difference between the sacraments and any other type of categorical expression of grace consists in this: any "natural" expression of grace, whether explicitly religious or not, is fragile in two directions. Not only can it fail to mediate grace because the individual rejects his supernatural orientation and its categorical expression, but also the symbol itself can be categorically impure or erroneous. The sacrament, on the contrary, as an offered expression of the church, shares in the church's definitive nature as real-symbol of the grace really present in Christ, who represents the fullest categorical form of grace in the world. Hence, the sacrament cannot be deprived of its symbolic meaning. The individual can refuse on a personal level the grace signified and caused without thereby invalidating its truth as a real-symbol on the level of world history. On this point, Rahner changes his perspective significantly. On the one hand, he views the sacraments as posterior expressions of grace already given to the individual; on the other hand, in order to guarantee the validity of the sacramental sign *ex opere operato*, he views the sacraments as infallible causes of grace whose validity is carried by the plural subject of the church even when the individual is not himself in a state of grace. This change of emphasis remains problematical insofar as no reason is given why all men cannot fall into mortal sin, thus invalidating the sacraments and their *ex opere operato* causality.

The church as the real-symbol of Christ in history has a sacramental structure as a supernatural reality and its historical manifestation. Because both its social constitution and its magisterium express its nature, they share in the definitiveness of the Christ event. The church, however, also is always involved in the historical process of categorically thematizing its transcendental self-consciousness, which means that notwithstanding the definitiveness and permanence of the church's nature, the categorical manifestations of this nature can vary during history. There can be, in other words, real development in the concrete constitution of the church and in its dogmatic teaching without contradicting the definitiveness of its nature. This understanding of the relationship between the transcendental nature of the church and its historical manifestations reflects Rahner's foundational analysis of being and knowing, and achieves a remarkable and attractive flexibility in his understanding of the *ius divinum,* the constitution of the church, and the magisterium. Rahner will later use this flexibility between transcendental being and its categorical form to explain the development of doctrine.

8

The Development of Dogma

RAHNER'S FIRST ATTEMPT to address the difficult problem of the development of dogma was an essay published in 1954 prompted by the papal definition of the bodily assumption of Mary. In this essay and in two other early essays devoted to the subject, Rahner approaches the issue of dogmatic development from the perspective of his early understanding of grace and revelation. Within this perspective, he sees divine revelation as coming to man from without in the objectively given categorical word of revelation. Yet man is only able to recognize this categorical word for what it is, the word of God, because his human subjectivity has been elevated first by grace. In this early perspective, then, Rahner sees the outer objective word of revelation as existing in a relationship of mutual priority with the inner operation of grace. This relationship reflects the dynamic *Schwebe* or oscillation revealed in Rahner's original analysis of human being and knowing. Yet, as we have observed throughout his theology, this dynamic *Schwebe* constitutes only one part of his understanding of reality, for, according to the structure of dialectical analogy, there is within the *Schwebe* always and simultaneously a static moment of conceptualization. Within his early theory of revelation, therefore, lest the essential content of revelation threaten to dissolve within an unconceptualizable oscillation, Rahner insists that man necessarily must express the revelation that he has received in a secondary categorical word. Although revelation is already a word from God, man must first accept it and understand it for what it is: it is thematic from the beginning, but the thematization does not fully exhaust it because the Word who became flesh is still the infinite Word. This lack of full thematization allows man to thematize it otherwise in a secondary categorical word. Because of the structure of reality and the nature of man, this secondary word is absolutely necessary.

Thus, for the apostles, the words of Christ constituted the objectively given outer word of revelation. It was, however, only the operation of grace that enabled the apostles to recognize these words as the definitive self-communication of God. The words of Christ existed, therefore, in a objective relationship of mutual priority with the Word speaking them, and this whole objective given of revelation existed in a second relationship of mutual priority with inner grace, which enabled the apostles to perceive a global experience of Christ. True to the structure of dialectical analogy, however, this dynamic experience can be expressed again in their own categorical words. Like the words of Christ, these words do not exhaust the original experience, but in neither case can the revelation be communicated without words. They are in a real sense the theology of the apostles, but are (because of their necessity) an intrinsic part of the revelation received in Christ through divinely authorized witnesses. For this reason, they are *quoad nos* revelation, and at least in their case we can speak of a legitimate development of doctrine.

For subsequent generations, an analogous process occurs. The words of the apostles, the Gospels, constitute not a list of propositions but rather a word/*res* unity. They are revealing words that mediate the whole experience of Christ to which they refer. Grace enables subsequent generations to recognize these words for what they are, revealing words of God. True to the structure of man, this dynamic *Schwebe* between the words of the Gospel and the revelatory event that they mediate can be reexpressed in the secondary categorical words of doctrinal propositions. These secondary propositions, or dogmas, in their turn do not exhaust the original word/*res* of revelation, but they are legitimate ways of interpreting and passing on the event of revelation. This is the basis for Rahner's justification of an ongoing development of dogma.

In Rahner's later works, there is a change of emphasis in his theory of development, which serves as the key to a correct interpretation of his later theology.[1] In a series of articles provoked by Hans Küng's *Unfehlbar? Eine Anfrage* in the early 1970s, Rahner

---

[1] This change of emphasis in Rahner's theory of development has been noted: Hines, *Transformation of Dogma,* 2, 18, 67, 100–101, 145–46, 147, 154–55; A. Nichols, *From Newman to Congar: The Idea of Doctrinal Development from the Victorians to the Second Vatican Council* (Edinburgh: T&T Clark, 1990), 266–69.

identifies grace as revelation and emphasizes both the intrinsic priority of the inner word of grace over its categorical expression and the notion that grace comes to expression in other historical words, which, even if categorically false, nevertheless can validly mediate grace to the individual.[2] Here, as in his theology of grace and revelation, he continues to insist on the necessity and validity of dogma as the fullest and truest expression of this grace.[3] Nonetheless, his equally strong insistence on the limitedness of all human propositions, always relative to the original experience of grace that they express, and on the consequent openness of all dogma to future reinterpretation allows him a wide and attractive flexibility in his understanding of the meaning of particular dogmas. This flexibility enables Rahner to argue against Küng that absolute contradiction of a defined dogma not only is a priori impossible but is also actually unnecessary. On the basis of this flexibility, he argues also for the existence of a legitimate theological pluralism within the church itself.

1. EARLY THEORY OF DEVELOPMENT

In his early work on the development of dogma, Rahner concentrated on the process of development itself. Breaking away from

---

[2] This later emphasis is the basis of the claim some of Rahner's critics have made that in his later work he abandons the notion of dogma in favor of religious pluralism: Carr, *Theological Method of Karl Rahner*, 233, 244–54, 267; Hines, *Transformation of Dogma*, 18, 74, 84, 87, 102, 103, 147, 155; Nichols, *From Newman to Congar*, 234.

[3] That Rahner even in his later work never abandoned the notion of dogma: K. Rahner, "Kritik an Hans Küng," *Stimmen der Zeit* 186 (1970), 369, 371, 373–75; K. Rahner, "Replik," *Stimmen der Zeit* 187 (1971), 158, 160; "Häresien in der Kirche heute?" *Schriften*, 9: 472; "Zum Begriff der Unfehlbarkeit," *Schriften*, 10: 320; "Grundsätzliche Bemerkungen," *Schriften*, 10: 244–46; "Der Glaube des Christen," *Schriften*, 10: 262–63; "Bietet die Kirche letzte Gewissheiten," *Schriften*, 10: 296, 300–301; "Lehramt und Theologie," *Schriften*, 13: 75, 82, 85; "Die Theologie und das Römische Lehramt," *Schriften*, 16: 233, 237, 239. Although Carr and Hines interpret the development in Rahner's thought as a progressive abandonment of dogma, both also note that Rahner simultaneously never denies dogma (Carr, *Theological Method of Karl Rahner*, 237; Hines, *Transformation of Dogma*, 102, 109, 114–15, 119–20, 139), and both attribute this seemingly dialectical double affirmation to a fundamental ambiguity in Rahner's thought (Carr, *Theological Method of Karl Rahner*, 254; Hines, *Transformation of Dogma*, 103, 105, 153, 156). I maintain, of course, that this strange double em-

the traditional scholastic notion of logical deduction from revealed propositions, he seeks a different model that can defend
such developments as the dogma of the Assumption. Before pro-
posing this model, however, he first delineates the essential features
of dogmatic development necessary for a correct understanding
of the process.

A. The Uniqueness of the Process of Development

A reflection on the meaning of the development of dogma is
difficult because the general meaning, possibility, and limits of
the development of dogma cannot be deduced with necessary
exactness from general theological considerations alone but must
be arrived at inductively from the actual facts of such a development. This process is not remarkable, for we discover the possible
from the real. We discover the laws of development of a living
thing from its actual development. "But in our case this has special difficulties, for the living spirit with which we are concerned
here appears in its authentic form in a solitary instance. . . . We
have here a homogeneous process of which there is just one instance."[4] The perfected law of dogmatic development may be laid
down only when the whole unique process has reached its term.

This recognition does not leave the way open to the proliferation of pseudotheological speculation.[5] Such proliferation will not
be realized for three reasons. In the first place, there are certain
laws of dogmatic development that, because they are known a
priori, may be applied to developments in an obvious way in
order to determine whether they are genuine developments. Second, just as with all living things, every advance achieved always

---

phasis is not owing to an ambiguity but rather is grounded in Rahner's foundational structure of thought as dialectical analogy. See also Lennan, *Ecclesiology of
Karl Rahner*, 179, 183, 189–93, 206, 254–55, who also notes Rahner's insistence
on dogma but seems to miss entirely the dialectical nature of this insistence in
the light of Rahner's simultaneous relativization of all propositional statements.

[4] "Zur Frage der Dogmenentwicklung," *Schriften*, 1: 51; "Überlegungen zur
Dogmenentwicklung," *Schriften*, 4: 16–17; *Mysterium Salutis I*, s.v. "Geschichtlichkeit der Vermittlung," 766–67.

[5] "Zur Frage der Dogmenentwicklung," *Schriften*, 1: 52–53; *Mysterium Salutis
I*, s.v. "Geschichtlichkeit der Vermittlung," 762, 766, 777; "Überlegungen zur
Dogmenentwicklung," *Schriften*, 4: 20.

has something final about it and inevitably marks a restriction of future possibilities. "Looked at from this point of view, progress in the development of dogmas must in a certain respect become progressively slower."[6] Third and most decisive, the human factor remains a danger, and no precautionary measures can exclude it unambiguously at the very start; the promise of the Spirit and that alone prevents the actual realization of this danger.

B. The Truth and Openness of Human Propositions

Although it is obvious that a revealed truth remains what it is, remains precisely "true,"[7] all human statements, even those in which faith expresses God's saving truths, are finite. They never declare the *whole* of a reality, for in the last resort every reality, even the most limited, is connected with and related to every other reality.

> The most wretched little physical process . . . can only be described adequately if the investigator possesses the one comprehensive and exhaustive formula for the whole cosmos. But he does not possess such a formula; he could have it if, and only if, he could place himself in his own physical reality at a point which lay absolutely outside the cosmos—which is impossible. This is even more true of spiritual and divine realities.[8]

Statements about spiritual realities can never express these realities adequately, but they are not for this reason false. Because they are true, an infinite qualitative difference separates them from false propositions. But precisely because our statements about the infinite divine realities are finite, every formula in which the faith is expressed can, in principle, be surpassed while retaining its truth.[9]

---

[6] "Zur Frage der Dogmenentwicklung," *Schriften*, 1: 52; *Mysterium Salutis I*, s.v. "Geschichtlichkeit der Vermittlung," 766.

[7] "Zur Frage der Dogmenentwicklung," *Schriften*, 1: 53; *Mysterium Salutis I*, s.v. "Kerygma und Dogma," 686, 688. See also G. Baum, "Truth in the Church: Küng, Rahner, and Beyond," *The Ecumenist* 9 (1971), 40.

[8] "Zur Frage der Dogmenentwicklung," *Schriften*, 1: 53.

[9] That every proposition of faith, being limited, in principle can be surpassed is an affirmation that Rahner holds throughout his theological career: "Zur Frage der Dogmenentwicklung," *Schriften*, 1: 54; *Mysterium Salutis I,* s.v. "Geschichtlichkeit der Vermittlung," 731–32, 771; *Mysterium Salutis I,* s.v.

C. Propositional Development Necessary for Human Understanding

The finiteness of statements about spiritual realities means neither that propositions of faith are meaningless nor that the evolution of these propositions is merely the play of empty curiosity. Such an evolution can have an essential significance for man and for his salvation. The human mind is not like a photographic plate that simply registers anything that falls upon it at a particular isolated moment. Rather, a human being must react, take a stand, and bring any new experience into connection with what he already knows, the whole historical sum of his experience. Addressed by God in revelation, an individual simply cannot understand this word of God without understanding his historical situation.[10] "For it is not just his unchangeable metaphysical 'entity' [*Wesen*] which he has to insert into the economy of God's message, but his concrete, historical, 'contingent' reality, his existence with all it includes."[11] If a human being does all this, no change takes place in the divine reality, nor can the previously true propositions concerning this reality become false, but there can be a certain change in the perspective in which he sees the reality through these propositions.[12]

"Kerygma und Dogma," 653–54, 656, 686–87, 689–90, 693, 697–98; "Zur Geschichtlicheit der Theologie," *Schriften,* 8: 93, 97; "Vom Dialog in der Kirche," *Schriften,* 8: 441; "Das kirchliche Lehramt," *Schriften,* 9: 357; "Bemerkungen über das Charismatische in der Kirche," *Schriften,* 9: 426–27; "Über das Ja zur konkreten Kirche," *Schriften,* 9: 465, 467, 492; "Grundsätzliche Bemerkungen," *Schriften,* 10: 246–51, 258; "Der Glaube des Christen und die Lehre der Kirche," *Schriften,* 10: 279–80; "Bietet die Kirche letzte Gewissheiten," *Schriften,* 10: 302–4; "Zum Begriff der Unfehlbarkeit," *Schriften,* 10: 306, 321; "Lehramt und Theologie," *Schriften,* 13: 75, 78, 83; "Was ist Häresie?" *Schriften,* 5: 570; "Die Theologie und das Römische Lehramt," *Schriften,* 16: 240; *Sendung und Gnade,* 60; "Kirche und Parousie Christi," *Schriften,* 6: 363. See also Carr, *Theological Method of Karl Rahner,* 158–59, 170–71, 178, 220, 267–68; Baum, "Truth in the Church," 38; Hines, *Transformation of Dogma,* 82; Nichols, *From Newman to Congar,* 219; Lennan, *Ecclesiology of Karl Rahner,* 138–40.

[10] *Mysterium Salutis I,* s.v. "Kerygma und Dogma," 692.

[11] "Zur Frage der Dogmenentwicklung," *Schriften,* 1: 55; "Überlegungen zur Dogmenentwicklung," *Schriften,* 4: 17; "Was ist Häresie ?" *Schriften,* 5: 571; "Zum heutigen Verhältnis von Philosophie und Theologie," *Schriften,* 10: 86.

[12] "Überlegungen zur Dogmenentwicklung," *Schriften,* 4: 20; *Mysterium Salutis I,* s.v. "Geschichtlichkeit der Vermittlung," 762, 767; *Mysterium Salutis I,* s.v. "Kerygma und Dogma," 686, 688.

D. Development of Revelation/Dogma, Not Just of Theology

This concept of change within a single abiding truth, moreover, is not concerned only with theology as opposed to revealed faith. De facto there exists not only a development of theology but also a development of dogma, not only a history of theology but also a history of faith.[13] This can be demonstrated a posteriori in two steps. First, the church understands its doctrinal decisions not just as theology but as word of faith—not, indeed, as newly revealed but as the word that utters revelation itself truly and with binding force. Second, this doctrinal word is not always a merely verbal modification of the original revealed propositions; it is very often *not* possible to say that the new doctrinal utterance is simply the old one just differently expressed.[14] For example, the declarations of Nicaea and Florence on the mystery of the Blessed Trinity, which are intended to be propositions of faith and not merely theological explanations, have a fixed meaning. This meaning is proposed as an object of faith even if the individual Christian cannot demonstrate that these declarations say "just the same only in other words" as what he has been able to extract from Scripture and early tradition. Thus, we can conclude that there occurred at least *quoad nos* a development within revelation, not just of theology, in the actual practice of the church when it proclaims a doctrine.

> If these translating propositions are just theology and nothing more . . . if there were no guarantee that the proposition heard has been correctly understood: then on the one hand the proclamation of faith itself could only be a monotonous repetition, with purely material accuracy, of the same propositions of Scripture . . . and on the other hand what we have understood of it, in the situation which is precisely ours, would be subjective theology.[15]

E. The Closure of Revelation

Such a notion does not contradict the traditional teaching of the church that with the death of the last apostle revelation defini-

---

[13] *Mysterium Salutis I,* s.v. "Geschichtlichkeit der Vermittlung," 732.

[14] *Mysterium Salutis I,* s.v. "Geschichtlichkeit der Vermittlung," 728.

[15] "Zur Frage der Dogmenentwicklung," *Schriften,* 1: 58; "Überlegungen zur Dogmenentwicklung," *Schriften,* 4: 11; *Mysterium Salutis I,* s.v. "Geschichtlichkeit der Vermittlung," 729, 757.

tively closed, for it would be false to interpret this proposition as meaning that when the last apostle died, there was left a summary of strictly drafted propositions that was going to be expounded forever.[16] Revelation is not the communication of a definite number of propositions, but a historical dialogue between God and man in which something happens.[17] "Revelation is a saving *happening,* and only then and in relation to this a communication of 'truths.' This continuous Happening of saving history has now reached its never to be surpassed climax in Jesus Christ."[18] Before Christ, even God's enterprise in revealing himself to the world was "open." But now the definitive reality is established; now there is nothing more to come except the unveiling of what is already here. That revelation is closed, therefore, is a positive and not a negative statement, a conclusion as fulfilled presence of an all-embracing plenitude.[19]

F. A New Starting Point in the Word/Res of Revelation

In order to be "closed" in this sense of being definitively present, revelation must have been heard and accepted, which means that the believing church is in possession of the revealed reality itself. Nevertheless, true to man's basic structure as *Schwebe,* a sure knowledge of this reality of divine salvation can be gained only through the faith that comes from hearing and speaks in human concepts and human propositions.[20] Any attempt to transcend this divine message—in some "religious experience" eliminating the faith that hears—so as to grasp this reality in an instant and without reference to the message is delusive and impossible; it must

---

[16] "Überlegungen zur Dogmenentwicklung," *Schriften,* 4: 11.

[17] "Zur Frage der Dogmenentwicklung," *Schriften,* 1: 59; *Mysterium Salutis I,* s.v. "Geschichtlichkeit der Vermittlung," 757, 758, 770; "Zur Geschichtlicheit der Theologie," *Schriften,* 8: 91, 93.

[18] "Zur Frage der Dogmenentwicklung," *Schriften,* 1: 59. This affirmation reflects the basic structure of dialectical analogy: revelation as dynamic event, which when conceptualized gives rise to propositions of faith.

[19] "Überlegungen zur Dogmenentwicklung," *Schriften,* 4: 18; "Zur Frage der Dogmenentwicklung," *Schriften,* 1: 59–60, 67; *Mysterium Salutis I,* s.v. "Geschichtlichkeit der Vermittlung," 732, 738.

[20] *Mysterium Salutis I,* s.v. "Geschichtlichkeit der Vermittlung," 767.

lead inevitably to a modernistic rationalization of Christianity.[21] Christianity is inseparably dependent on the announcing word.[22]

> The believing church possesses what it believes: Christ and his Spirit. . . . It cannot leave the word behind in order to grasp this reality. But no more does it possess a word about the thing instead of the thing itself. Consequently its hearing of the word and its reflection upon the word heard are not *merely* a logical activity, an attempt gradually to squeeze out all the logical virtualities and consequences of the word heard as though it were a numerical sum of propositions. They are a reflection on the propositions heard in living contact with the thing itself.[23]

The starting point of dogmatic development is not, therefore, a list of propositions but rather the word/*res* of revelation itself.

G. The Light of the Spirit as an A Priori of the Process of Development

The Holy Spirit guides the reflection of the church on this word/ *res* of revelation.[24] But the light of faith and the assistance of the Spirit do not mean a sort of supervision like that of a teacher who intervenes only to prevent error.[25] It is much more in the actual result that the light of the Spirit and of faith exert their influence.

---

[21] "Zur Frage der Dogmenentwicklung," *Schriften*, 1: 60, 61; "Überlegungen zur Dogmenentwicklung," *Schriften*, 4: 24; *Mysterium Salutis I*, s.v. "Geschichtlichkeit der Vermittlung," 769; *Mysterium Salutis I*, s.v. "Kerygma und Dogma," 698, 701, 702.

[22] That the "word" is intrinsic to the process of revelation is, of course, central to Rahner's thought: "Überlegungen zur Dogmenentwicklung," *Schriften*, 4: 22–23; *Mysterium Salutis I*, s.v. "Geschichtlichkeit der Vermittlung," 767, 770; *Mysterium Salutis I*, s.v. "Kerygma und Dogma," 690–91, 697, 698, 701–2; "Zur Frage der Dogmenentwicklung," *Schriften*, 1: 60, 61, 77, 78; "Zur Geschichtlichkeit der Theologie," *Schriften*, 8: 93, 97; "Zum heutigen Verhältnis von Philosophie und Theologie," *Schriften*, 10: 86.

[23] "Zur Frage der Dogmenentwicklung," *Schriften*, 1: 61, 64, 67; *Mysterium Salutis I*, s.v. "Geschichtlichkeit der Vermittlung," 757, 760, 772; *Mysterium Salutis I*, s.v. "Kerygma und Dogma," 690–91, 697, 698, 701–2; "Überlegungen zur Dogmenentwicklung," *Schriften*, 4: 19–20, 22–23.

[24] *Mysterium Salutis I*, s.v. "Geschichtlichkeit der Vermittlung," 757, 768–69, 772; "Überlegungen zur Dogmenentwicklung," *Schriften*, 4: 21–22, 24, 29, 37; *Mysterium Salutis I*, s.v. "Kerygma und Dogma," 635; "Zur Frage der Dogmenentwicklung," *Schriften*, 1: 61–63.

[25] "Überlegungen zur Dogmenentwicklung," *Schriften*, 4: 24, 37; "Zur Frage der Dogmenentwicklung," *Schriften*, 1: 63; *Mysterium Salutis I*, s.v. "Geschichtlichkeit der Vermittlung," 769. See also Lennan, *Ecclesiology of Karl Rahner*, 87.

Just as man in his direct apprehension of the objects of everyday life has no reflexive or theoretical awareness of the nature of his intellectual powers or of formal logic, although he nevertheless makes use of both, so also the light of faith and the impulse of the Spirit do not permit of being isolated for inspection. They are the brightness that illuminates the object of faith, the horizon within which it is contained.[26] Knowledge in faith takes place in the power of the Spirit of God, while at the same time that Spirit is the concrete reality believed. It follows that the object of faith is not something merely passive but simultaneously the principle by which it is itself grasped as object.[27] This statement acquires its full significance on the assumption that the actual support given to faith by grace is not just an ontological modality of the act of faith beyond conscious apprehension but also has a specific effect in consciousness (which does not necessarily say that it is reflexively distinguishable).[28] "This effect makes it possible to apprehend the objects of faith given through the hearing of the external announcement, under a 'light,' a subjective a priori under grace (the formal object), which is not available to someone without faith."[29]

If the light of faith, brought by the Spirit and ultimately identical with him, is the horizon within which the individual objects of revelation are grasped, we are to expect a priori a twofold movement within the process of development.[30]

---

[26] "Zur Frage der Dogmenentwicklung," *Schriften,* 1: 62. Just as in Rahner's ontological epistemology, the sensible singular is illuminated by and understood only within the preapprehended horizon of all being, not consciously known but present nonthematically within every act of human knowing: *Geist,* 155–56, 190–91, 216–17, 389 n. 9, 390; *Hörer 1,* 77, 82–83, 100, 183.

[27] "Zur Frage der Dogmenentwicklung," *Schriften,* 1: 61–63; *Mysterium Salutis I,* s.v. "Geschichtlichkeit der Vermittlung," 757, 768, 769, 772. Rahner sees the Spirit as object of faith present within the process of faith in the same way as the goal of man's transcendence is present within the process of transcendence itself, being immanent precisely through its transcendence and vice versa. See chapter 4, note 47.

[28] See Hines, *Transformation of Dogma,* 11; see also chapter 2, note 37.

[29] "Zur Frage der Dogmenentwicklung," *Schriften,* 1: 62–63; "Überlegungen zur Dogmenentwicklung," *Schriften,* 4: 21–22. This notion of the apprehension of objects of faith under the light of a subjective a priori of grace is clearly consistent with Rahner's early notion of grace as elevating human subjectivity to receive the objectively given external word of revelation.

[30] "Überlegungen zur Dogmenentwicklung," *Schriften,* 4: 38; *Mysterium Sa-*

On the one hand, the infinite breadth and intensity of the supernatural a priori must necessarily lead to a constantly increasing articulateness in the unfolding of the objects comprised within its horizon, for each a posteriori object of faith is grasped as a moment of the movement toward the one self-communication of God. As such, each truth of the faith can function only when it is open to more than it contains, and it is open only if it unfolds itself in a greater fullness of assertions. Thus, the dynamism of dogmatic development aims at an ever fuller expression of the individual dogma. It is expansive.

On the other hand, by virtue of the same origin, a countering dynamism must be expected,[31] for the formal a priori of faith is in fact the intensive fullness of what is meant in each individual object of faith, which is none other than the Triune God in his real self-communication. In the act of faith, therefore, in the utterance and hearing of revelation, a synthesis takes place between this a priori and each individual object of faith. But then such a synthesis must also launch the dynamism in the direction of a constantly progressive concentration of the variety of the contents of revelation upon this a priori unity, which is intended in all this variety. "Dogmatic development must also contain a dynamism of compression and simplification, tending toward the blessed darkness of the one mystery of God."[32] It is not at all as if dogmatic devel-

---

lutis, s.v. "Geschtlichkeit der Vermittlung," 772–73. This clearly mirrors Rahner's notion of the role of the concept in the process of human knowing.

[31] *Mysterium Salutis I*, s.v. "Kerygma und Dogma," 696–97. Here again we see the operation of Rahner's dialectical analogy: dogmatic development in its twofold movement reflects the *Schwebe* between dynamism toward the horizon of being and simultaneously the moment of conceptualization.

[32] "Überlegungen zur Dogmenentwicklung," *Schriften,* 4: 39. Hines, *Transformation of Dogma,* 18, 74–75, 84, 88, 101, 123, 147–48, 154–58, makes much play of this second dynamism into mystery, arguing that for Rahner, especially in his later life, it is the essential element of the process of development that fundamentally relativizes the other expansive movement into conceptualization (see also Nichols, *From Newman to Congar,* 234). It must be noted, however, that despite Rahner's late emphasis on this second dynamism, he goes out of his way to make clear that the two dynamisms, which of course mirror the two movements in his foundational epistemology of transcendence to the horizon and sensibility or conceptualization, are inseparably linked as two moments of one process in a relationship of mutual priority: *Mysterium Salutis I*, s.v. "Geschichtlichkeit der Vermittlung," 773; "Überlegungen zur Dogmenentwicklung," *Schriften,* 4: 38–39; "Zur Frage der Dogmenentwicklung," *Schriften,* 1: 77, 78.

opment always must move in the direction of multiplying individual assertions. Just as important is the development in the line of simplification toward an ever clearer view of the single mystery.

H. A New Model

In order to illustrate the process of dogmatic development, Rahner proposes a human analogy, for there exists in the natural order a kind of knowledge that, although itself not articulated in "propositions," is the starting point of an intellectual process that develops into propositions.[33] If we take the example of a young man who has a genuine and vital experience of great love, it is clear that his love may have presuppositions that are simply unknown to him. His love itself is his experience, and he "knows" much more about it than he can "state." If he is intelligent, perhaps he can make the attempt to state what he knows about his love, what he is already aware of in the consciousness of simply possessing the reality. In such a case, it is not merely a matter of the logical development and inference of new propositions from earlier ones, but of the formulation for the first time of propositions about a knowledge already possessed, in an infinite search that approaches its goal only asymptotically.[34] This process is an explication. There is a connection *in re* between an earlier knowledge and later explicit propositions. But the starting point and the procedure are not those of logical explication of propositions.[35]

This case also can be examined from a different angle. The lover knows of his love, and this knowledge forms an essential element in the very love itself. The knowledge is infinitely richer, simpler, and denser than any body of propositions about the love can be.[36] Yet this knowledge never lacks a certain degree of reflexive articulateness: the lover confesses his love at least to himself. And so it is not a matter of indifference to the love itself

---

[33] *Mysterium Salutis I*, s.v. "Geschichtlichkeit der Vermittlung," 761.

[34] "Zur Frage der Dogmenentwicklung," *Schriften*, 1: 75–76.

[35] "Überlegungen zur Dogmenentwicklung," *Schriften*, 4: 34; "Zur Frage der Dogmenentwicklung," *Schriften*, 1: 65.

[36] *Mysterium Salutis I*, s.v. "Geschichtlichkeit der Vermittlung," 771; "Was ist Häresie?" *Schriften*, 5: 568.

whether or not the lover continues to reflect on it; this self-reflection is not the subsequent description of a reality that remains in no way altered by the description.

> Original, nonpropositional, unreflexive, yet conscious possession of a reality on the one hand, and reflexive (propositional), articulated consciousness of this original possession on the other—these are not competing opposites but reciprocally interacting factors of a single experience necessarily unfolding in historical succession. Root and shoot are not the same thing, but each lives by the *other*.[37]

Just such an interrelationship of types of consciousness is found within the process of the development of doctrine. In the first place, it may be supposed that the apostles themselves had a global experience of this kind, lying behind propositions and forming an inexhaustible source for the articulation and explication of the faith in propositions. Christ is the objective content of an experience that is more elemental and concentrated, simpler and yet richer than the individual propositions coined in an attempt to express this experience. Nevertheless, this experience depends for its realization on its actually stating what it knows. The initial degree of self-realization in the experience may be slight, but it cannot be lacking entirely.[38] "Every explication which has been successfully established in propositional form illuminates the original experience, allows it to grow to its proper stature, and becomes an intrinsic factor in the abiding life of this experience itself."[39]

Quoad nos, the apostles' "theology," is original revelation because it is guaranteed by the infallibility of prophetic mission and apostolic inspiration as the new word God intended for us. Yet in a certain sense it is also the apostles' "theology" in relation to a

---

[37] "Zur Frage der Dogmenentwicklung," *Schriften,* 1: 77, 78, 89; "Was ist Häresie?" *Schriften,* 5: 568; *Mysterium Salutis I,* s.v. "Geschichtlichkeit der Vermittlung," 761. On the necessity of the categorical word within the process of development, see R. Richard, "Rahner's Theory of Doctrinal Development," *Proceedings of the Catholic Theological Society of America* 18 (1963), 170; Hines, *Transformation of Dogma,* 4, 17, 24, 26, 91, 155; Nichols, *From Newman to Congar,* 226.

[38] *Mysterium Salutis I,* s.v. "Kerygma und Dogma," 698, 699.

[39] "Zur Frage der Dogmenentwicklung," *Schriften,* 1: 78.

more primitive communication made to them.[40] In their case, we have the right to speak of a development of dogma.[41] The objective connection between the new proposition and the old knowledge is not merely a link between something logically explicit and something logically implicit in two propositions; it is rather a connection between what partially becomes explicit in a proposition and the unreflexive, total spiritual possession of the entire *res.* The explicit proposition is at the same time more and less than its implicit source: more, because as reflexively formulated it elucidates the original simple possession of the reality and in this way enriches it; less, because it never does more than express reflexively and remotely a part of what previously was possessed spiritually.

It can be argued that in the apostles we have an exceptional case because the apostles could pass on only their completed reflexive explication in propositional form and not their original living experience; hence, in every age after them only a logical connection between what is implicit and explicit in propositions can support the possibility of further development of dogma. But the apostles bequeathed not just propositions about their experience. What they bequeathed in Scripture is the word/*res* of revelation, in fact the very reality of what they experienced in Christ.[42] Their own experience is preserved and present together with their word. "Spirit and word together form the permanent active potentiality of an experience which is in principle the same as that of the apostles. . . . This *successio apostolica,* in a full and comprehensive sense, hands on to the postapostolic church . . . not simply a body of propositions but a living experience: the Holy Spirit."[43] To this

---

[40] *Mysterium Salutis I,* s.v. "Kerygma und Dogma," 662–65, 677, 679, 682, 699. This dialectical affirmation that theology is both revelation and more than revelation is really understandable only in the light of Rahner's dialectical analogy in which revelation both is a dynamic event and yet also and simultaneously gives rise to propositions of faith when conceptualized.

[41] "Überlegungen zur Dogmenentwicklung," *Schriften,* 4: 14–15; "Zur Frage der Dogmenentwicklung," *Schriften,* 1: 79; *Mysterium Salutis I,* s.v. "Geschichtlichkeit der Vermittlung," 739–41. See also Hines, *Transformation of Dogma,* 40–42.

[42] *Mysterium Salutis I,* s.v. "Geschichtlichkeit der Vermittlung," 752, 770–71; "Zur Frage der Dogmenentwicklung," *Schriften,* 1: 80–81.

[43] "Zur Frage der Dogmenentwicklung," *Schriften,* 1: 80.

extent, there exists in the postapostolic development of dogma the connection between what is implicit as a living possession of the whole truth in an unreflexive but conscious way and what is always only partially explicit in propositions.

To appreciate the full significance of this alternative model of development we must examine our understanding of propositions. An ordinary statement of everyday life is represented normally, albeit tacitly, under the schema of propositions belonging to mathematics, geometry, or formal logic, which have a fixed content. This is precisely not the case with a normal human proposition. It does indeed have a determinate sense, but any attempt to declare reflexively its content comes up against the intrinsic and irreducible indistinctness of this content.[44] It is easy to establish unambiguously the minimum but not the maximum of what may be in fact its intelligible content. "The proposition is always a kind of window through which a view may be gained of the thing itself."[45] Take, for example, the statement "N.N. is my mother." The minimum content of this statement is clear, but there can be and almost must be an abundance of other things intended at the same time in a statement like this, all of which, in excess of the given minimum of propositional content, the hearer of the proposition can hear concomitantly. The hearer, just like the speaker, looks in and through the proposition at the thing itself.

This sort of communication applies analogously to the sphere of revelation.[46] Revelation also works with human concepts and propositions, but we cannot ignore the irreducible distinction between what is stated explicitly and what is copresent in mind and communicated.

> When for example someone says, "Christ 'died' for us," everyone understands what is meant by dying or death in this statement. But what is meant by "death" in this statement is not . . . just a physiological exit. The whole human experience of death can be really

---

[44] Here again we see the notion of an oscillating concept, clearly grounded in Rahner's original oscillating concept of being.

[45] "Zur Frage der Dogmenentwicklung," *Schriften,* 1: 82. See also Rahner, "Kritik an Hans Küng," 370.

[46] *Mysterium Salutis I,* s.v. "Geschichtlichkeit der Vermittlung," 764–65; *Mysterium Salutis I,* s.v. "Kerygma und Dogma," 677–88.

stated . . . and heard . . . in this word, an experience which neither speaker nor hearer has ever translated adequately and objectively into propositions.[47]

If the hearer should ever arrive at a reflexive, propositional analysis of what the word *death* has always meant to him, it is perfectly possible that what has been analyzed and brought into propositional form may be conceived of still as what the speaker originally communicated. If we believe a speaker when he says something, it is still this very speaker whom we believe when what he says has been explicated in further propositions. Rahner concludes, therefore:

> The immediately intelligible, express statements of revelation in its manifold reality (propositional series A) are heard and questioned with a view to discovering what is copresent to mind and communicated by them, that is, their background and the principle which comprehends the whole of this variety and gives it unity. The basic idea copresent to mind and cosignified [*mit-gesagte*] is extracted by making use of the individual propositions to give a view of the *res* on which they are based; in this way the basic idea is formulated expressly in propositions (propositional series B). It is only from this intermediate propositional series B that the desired terminal proposition is deduced, i.e., recognized as cosignified. If what has been said is correct, it immediately becomes clear that the procedure described does not . . . move outside the sphere of what is, properly speaking, revealed.[48]

The God who speaks surveys in himself from the very beginning all the virtualities of his speech and by his own Spirit in the church inspires, guides, and watches over their very actualization.

With this alternative model of dogmatic development, Rahner has once again worked out the consequences of his foundational metaphysics. The apostles' living encounter with Christ constituted an original graced experience that, true to the structure of reality as dialectical analogy, is necessarily expressed in secondary, historically conditioned words. These words of the apostles, the Gospels, do not exhaust their original experience, but neither can they be lacking. They exist in a relationship of mutual priority

---

[47] "Zur Frage der Dogmenentwicklung," *Schriften,* 1: 85.
[48] "Zur Frage der Dogmenentwicklung," *Schriften,* 1: 85–86.

with the original experience of Christ and his words, which they mediate, and they constitute, therefore, the starting point for dogmatic development. *Quoad nos* they are the word/*res* of revelation and therefore must be expressed necessarily in the historically conditioned words of dogmatic propositions. These dogmatic propositions, again, do not exhaust the original word/*res* of revelation, nor are they completely relativized by it. In this way, Rahner is able to ground the necessity of dogmatic propositions in the structure of dialectical analogy and at the same time establish the possibility of the emergence of new formulations of faith (such as the Assumption) neither formally nor virtually implied in previously defined propositions.

2. LATER DEVELOPMENTS

The publication in 1970 of Hans Küng's controversial book *Unfehlbar? Eine Anfrage* provoked Rahner to consider again the whole question of the nature of dogma.[49] In a lengthy response to Küng's thesis that although the church remains indefectibly in the truth of Christ, no human proposition, even if "infallibly" defined, in principle can be free from possible error, Rahner demonstrates from first principles both the necessity of the teaching authority of the church and the possibility of dogmatic teachings. In this essay, he takes a different starting point from the one he used in his earlier works.[50] Instead of starting his reflections from the nature of revelation and from the relation of the word/*res* to later dogmatic statements, he begins from the individual's grace-given experience of a basic trust in the meaningfulness of existence, arguing that this basic attitude must be expressed in categorical propositions in order to be itself. Even from this changed perspective, the fundamental structure of Rahner's thought as *Schwebe* is clear—that is, transcendentally given grace expressing

---

[49] See also the interesting, and in our context revealing, debate between Rahner and Küng published in *Stimmen der Zeit* 186–87 (1970–71). For a summary of this debate, see J. Hughes, "Infallible? An Inquiry Considered," *Theological Studies* 32 (1971): 183–207; see also Lennan, *Ecclesiology of Karl Rahner*, 203–7.

[50] See Hines, *Transformation of Dogma*, 88, 91.

itself categorically in order to be itself. But here in this later approach to dogmatic development, a clear shift is apparent, a shift mirroring that which we have noted already in Rahner's theology of grace and revelation. Developing the dynamic and unifying side of his thought, he emphasizes more than previously the priority of transcendentally given grace, which he now explicitly identifies as revelation. He also emphasizes more than previously the limitation of all propositional statements and their intrinsic relativity to the original experience of grace.

Posing the question whether there are in the church any ultimate certainties for the believer, Rahner first distinguishes between that attitude of an ultimate calm and assured trust in existence that leads to the hope of salvation and the specific individual propositions taught by the church and intended to offer ultimate certainties. The answer is complicated because the two realities mutually condition one another. Nevertheless, this radical attitude of ultimate trust in the meaning of existence is both logically and psychologically prior to belief in the authority of the church; it is what sustains this belief in the church. Indeed, all certainties in the church's life are based on this fundamental attitude. It is the surest factor of human life, yet involving the greatest exercise of freedom; it is subject to man's responsibility and is threatened most constantly. One should not expect the church, therefore, to free people from the burden of self-responsibility by handing them "prepacked" certainties.[51]

The attitude of trust is achieved in the depth of our freedom, where the primordial light of truth burns. At the same time, this basic freedom stands in relation to an objectified knowledge expressed in propositional form. Such propositions need not be specifically religious propositions for an individual to commit himself categorically in a fundamental attitude of trust.[52] The proposition,

---

[51] That the church should not relieve us of responsibility with regard to the faith: "Was ist Häresie?" *Schriften,* 5: 573, 575; *Das Dynamische in der Kirche,* 25–26, 35–36; "Die Freiheit in der Kirche," *Schriften,* 2: 110–13; "Kirche und Parousia Christi," *Schriften,* 6: 364; "Grundsätzliche Bemerkungen," *Schriften,* 10: 254; "Bietet die Kirche letzte Gewissheiten," *Schriften,* 10: 289; "Disput um das Kirchliche Lehramt," *Schriften,* 10: 355. See also Lennan, *The Ecclesiology of Karl Rahner,* 97–98.

[52] Carr, *Theological Method of Karl Rahner,* 221, criticizes Rahner for relativizing the importance of categorical propositions of faith by arguing that any formula, even if false, can lead the individual to God.

for instance, that "we should give absolute respect to our fellow men" expresses this fundamental attitude in objectified terms. Such statements draw their life from this ultimate trust in the meaningfulness of existence, but simultaneously the free acceptance of this basic attitude of trust draws its life from these statements that give expression to it,[53] for one who assents to such statements will find it easier to achieve the basic attitude of trust from which the statements truly draw their living force.

These expressive-causative propositions may have as their content elements of concrete human history. Thus, the statements "this man is absolutely reliable," "this life cannot be swallowed up into nothingness," and similar affirmations "have a content which is subject to the contingency of history, yet at the same time draw their living force from that ultimate attitude of basic trust and so share in the certainty and sureness belonging to it and throw light upon this attitude of basic trust itself as constituting its concrete objectification."[54] Affirmations about Jesus Christ, the crucified and risen Lord, are to be numbered among such statements. Their message enables the believer to grasp that absolute and irrevocable self-utterance of God to which he assents with an ultimate trust sustained by grace. In this experience, there is a mutual conditioning.

> That ultimate attitude of basic trust, sustained by grace and breaking in upon the freedom of God which we call the grace of faith, constitutes the enabling condition for recognizing Christ with real faith as the ultimate bringer of salvation. . . . Conversely the experience of Jesus for the believer as Christian constitutes a living experience within his own personal history in which he finds the courage to accept in freedom this ultimate basic trust through the grace that is offered to him.[55]

In response to the question whether the church itself can offer any ultimate certainties, the Christian recognizes that faith in Jesus as the ultimate bringer of salvation can never disappear. Faith in

---

[53] Rahner, "Kritik an Hans Küng," 370–71, 373, 376; Rahner, "Replik," 159.

[54] "Bietet die Kirche letzte Gewissheiten," *Schriften,* 10: 292.

[55] "Bietet die Kirche letzte Gewissheiten," *Schriften,* 10: 292–93. See also Hines, *Transformation of Dogma,* 34, 107, 109, 114.

Christ as the manifestation of the grace of God imposing itself victoriously involves faith in the indestructibility of faith in the world. Faith in Jesus Christ consequently implies faith in the survival of a community of faith gathered about Jesus Christ. The belief that the community will always exist belongs to the central content of Christian faith and shares in the certainty, even though derived and fragile, of the fundamental and basic attitude of trust.

Faith in the indestructibility of the church's faith implies also that there are propositions in which this faith of the church is articulated, propositions that share in the indestructibility of faith. It is impossible (given the nature of man as *Schwebe*) for this faith to exist without expression in propositions.[56] It is also impossible for the church to be totally incapable of recognizing its own propositions in individual cases.[57] The church is certainly convinced that it knows of such propositions, which in ecclesiastical language it calls infallible. To the extent that the church believes in such propositions, it extends to its members ultimate certainties. But two points have to be noticed here: first, this certainty can be applied only to one who has accepted the church in faith already; second, the formal authority belonging to a specific proposition taught by the church does not simply replace that interior certainty that an individual Christian has about the proposition once he realizes for himself the intrinsic connection between it and his fundamental attitude of trust.[58]

> If an individual Christian in the concrete given case does not succeed in arriving at this intrinsic connection, then he will generally be permitted to leave an individual derived proposition of this kind respectfully alone or to some extent to regard it as a remote goal to be attained in the development of his own personal history of faith, which is still in process of achievement. At the same time, however, he must obviously not on this account ipso facto deny or reject the proposition concerned on the grounds that he himself cannot or cannot as yet arrive at it or recognize how it is derived from the original wellsprings of faith to which he has attained.[59]

---

[56] "Bietet die Kirche letzte Gewissheiten," *Schriften,* 10: 296; Rahner, "Kritik an Hans Küng," 369–75; Rahner, "Replik," 158, 160.

[57] This conclusion follows, of course, from Rahner's foundational assertion of the unity of being and knowing: see chapter 1, note 17.

[58] Rahner, "Kritik an Hans Küng," 373. See also Hines, *Transformation of Dogma,* 100–101, 112.

[59] "Bietet die Kirche letzte Gewissheiten," *Schriften,* 10: 298.

The church is not exclusively the sum total of those who, by their faith in Jesus Christ, are de facto gathered about him. Insofar as the church has to bear witness actively to this faith, it is a social entity capable of acting positively. Belonging to the essence of faith, therefore, is the notion that the church constitutes a socially structured unity and as such remains abidingly in the truth of Christ.[60] Furthermore, it remains in that truth as expressed in propositional form. In other words, through its socially structured constitution or, more concretely, through its established officials, it achieves its state of abiding in the truth and also standing by true propositions. That social constitution that is inevitable for any community is related as an element in the church to its true and proper nature, to its faith as such. In the church, there consequently exists a genuine teaching authority concretized in the pope and the college of bishops in a unity; under certain circumstances, this officialdom actually can teach a specific proposition as infallible, as dogma to be held and maintained by the church with the absolute commitment of faith. When such a dogma is defined, the individual Christian has the duty to give his assent of faith. In this sense, the church also can offer ultimate certainties in virtue of its teaching authority, even though such certainties are not primary but derived.

Even infallibly defined propositions, though ultimately binding and valid, are expressed in historically conditioned terms and therefore are subject to change.[61] They are analogous in character; that is, they never give full or adequate expression to the reality signified.[62] It is far from easy for the individual Christian to recognize clearly the line between a true proposition, which is subject to these special limitations and historical conditions, and an erroneous proposition, for the infallibility of a proposition promulgated by the teaching authority of the church does not imply that this proposition may not be replaced by another and better

---

[60] *Kirche und Sakramente,* 12; "Die Gliedschaft in der Kirche," *Schriften,* 2: 90.

[61] See note 9 in this chapter; Rahner, "Kritik an Hans Küng," 371; Rahner, "Replik," 146–47, 150.

[62] "Grundsätzliche Bemerkungen," *Schriften,* 10: 247–49; "Was ist Häresie?" *Schriften,* 5: 570; Rahner, "Kritik an Hans Küng," 373. See also Baum, "Truth in the Church," 46.

formulation at some point in the future within the total development of the church's awareness of its faith.[63]

In light of these considerations, Rahner argues that the difference is little more than verbal between someone who maintains
that, with the reservations and due distinctions made above, a
dogmatic proposition is certainly true and incapable of retrospec-
tive revision and another who regards such a proposition as possi-
bly erroneous although still acknowledging that the church itself
abides in the truth.[64] Why then are certain theologians who accept the basic substance of Christianity nevertheless determined
to run counter to the teaching of the church and maintain that it
is possible for dogmatic propositions of the church to be erroner-
ous? What they are seeking to assert amounts to no more than
what the church's own theology already says. Neither are those
who maintain such a position to be regarded as being simply more
honest or open

> when they feel that they must disavow as erroneous propositions
> which are genuinely dogmatic. . . . is this not a way of avoiding
> the necessity of having to interpret earlier dogmatic formulations,
> constantly having to translate them into fresh terms, rather than
> being allowed totally to disregard any continuity in the process of
> expressing the faith in propositional form, as though the substance
> of Christianity in its concrete historical mode was something totally
> outside the statements contained in the New Testament and in the
> official proclamations of the church?[65]

With this assumption, Rahner can achieve in real terms all that
concerns Küng without adopting Küng's thesis of the possibility
of error in each and every statement of Scripture, of the councils,
or of the ordinary and extraordinary magisterium of the bishops
and the pope.[66]

In this later approach to dogma and its development, Rahner

---

[63] "Bietet die Kirche letzte Gewissheiten," *Schriften,* 10: 303; "Zum Begriff
der Unfehlbarkeit," *Schriften,* 10: 310; "Die Theologie und das Römische Lehramt," *Schriften,* 16: 241.

[64] "Bietet die Kirche letzte Gewissheiten," *Schriften,* 10: 304.

[65] "Bietet die Kirche letzte Gewissheiten," *Schriften,* 10: 304.

[66] Baum, "Truth in the Church," 39, criticizes Rahner on the grounds that
both Rahner's and Küng's arguments have the same practical consequences.

remains true to much of what he had written previously and to the fundamental structure of his thought. From his different existential starting point in the grace-given attitude of basic trust (which anticipates the approach he will take in *Grundkurs;* see chapter 9), he continues to insist on the validity of dogmatic propositions as the necessary expressions of this basic attitude, which mediate it to itself and which never can be entirely lacking. However, here, as elsewhere, the change of perspective that began in Rahner's theology of grace in the early 1960s is apparent. Now clearly identifying grace as revelation, Rahner emphasizes the priority of the original experience of grace (the attitude of basic trust), which seems only to come to subsequent expression not only in revealed or dogmatic propositions but also in nonreligious propositions. He also stresses more than previously the intrinsic limitedness or ambiguity of human statements, which are always open to development and change and which need not be contradicted, therefore, even by those who cannot accept them. This later approach then, although intended as a defense of the possibility and necessity of dogma and of the magisterium, marks a change in Rahner's understanding of dogma and leads him to reconsider the doctrine of infallibility and the attitude of both theologians and individual Christians to dogmatically defined propositions. This he does in a series of articles dating from the 1970s.

3. CONSEQUENCES OF THIS LATER UNDERSTANDING OF DOGMA

A. *The Dogma of Infallibility*

Rahner's insistence on the openness of dogma to a future history of interpretation flows logically both from his insistence on the limitation of all human propositions and from his understanding of dogma as the reflection on the original global experience of revelation in grace. It is not, however, transparently clear how such an understanding can be reconciled with the dogmatic definition of papal infallibility of 1870. Rahner argues that the two positions are not ipso facto irreconcilable because the doctrine of infallibility is itself involved in a process of development, within which process it has now reached a stage where it no longer means what it did at the time of the definition.

(i) The Historicity of the Dogma

The declaration of infallibility is itself a proposition that has had a history and will have a further one.[67] As applied to the *pope* as an explicit proposition of faith, the dogma is a datum of relatively late date, even if the infallibility of the church as a whole was a conviction of the church right from the first. In earlier times, infallibility referred primarily to the possession of the reality of salvation in the church as handed down, as something already given and abiding in it. When the ancient councils arrived at certain decisions and formulated fresh propositions, they did so with the awareness of merely formulating the ancient content of faith in different terms. "So clearly was this taken for granted as a self-evident fact that almost down to the *present* day the officially authorized theology denied that there was any *objective* development in the history of dogma."[68] Such an official attitude demonstrates clearly that when the definition of infallibility was achieved, it did not entail any awareness that this definition involved an acknowledgment of the historicity of truth, that the only way we can recognize the possibility of an infallible new decision about the ancient truth is by ascribing a historical dimension to this ancient truth itself. The history of the doctrine of infallibility, therefore, is not merely a history inasmuch as the explicit declaration on infallibility has not always existed with the character of a *juridical* obligation of faith. It is also a history of the actual *meaningful content* of this proposition itself.[69]

(ii) The Dogma Today

The historical development of the dogma of infallibility has arrived at a stage at which any new definition of dogma is incon-

---

[67] Baum, "Truth in the Church," 37, 39–40, 48, notes Rahner's interpretation of the historical limitations of the doctrine of infallibility.

[68] "Zum Begriff der Unfehlbarkeit," *Schriften,* 10: 308–9.

[69] "Zum Begriff der Unfehlbarkeit," *Schriften,* 10: 310.

ceivable.[70] The pluralism of modern society is such that it is no longer imaginable "that any specific and at the same time genuinely *new* proposition can be so expressed that it can be felt throughout to be an expression of the conscious faith of the whole church and so be capable of definition."[71] Furthermore, every new definition requires for its formulation a theology accepted by the whole church. This uniformity in theology no longer exists and will never be restored fully. This does not mean that the dogma hitherto defined will dissolve retrospectively or that the infallible teaching office will no longer have any function of its own. Past dogma does not disappear retrospectively because "it no longer has the *same* history in the future as it has had in the past."[72] To understand this idea we must bear two points in mind: first, man is the supreme historical being who by memory emerges from his past; second, the Christian memory is very simple, consisting in the belief that God, the absolute mystery, has addressed himself to us in Christ and has become our absolute future.[73] Because all previous Christian dogma merely expresses this belief, it will abide, even though it no longer develops in its former manner. It will not become frozen or petrified because the reduction of traditional dogma, which remains valid to the true and indissoluble reality of Jesus, is something that has to be achieved ever anew. The function of the infallible teaching office does not cease because the solemn delimitation of the ancient body of dogma is an abiding task needed to protect it against interpretations that would eliminate it.

(iii) The Development of the Dogma

To grasp the significance of the development of the dogma of infallibility we must examine how the understanding of the

---

[70] That no new dogmas will be defined: "Zum Begriff der Unfehlbarkeit," *Schriften*, 10: 310, 311–13; "Die Theologie und das Römische Lehramt," *Schriften*, 16: 239; "Das kirchliche Lehramt," *Schriften*, 9: 365; "Grundsätzliche Bemerkungen," *Schriften*, 10: 256; "Lehramt und Theologie," *Schriften*, 13: 90. See also Carr, *Theological Method of Karl Rahner*, 253; Hines, *Transformation of Dogma*, 89, 155; Nichols, *From Newman to Congar*, 267–68; Lennan, *Ecclesiology of Karl Rahner*, 194, 196, 206.

[71] "Zum Begriff der Unfehlbarkeit," *Schriften*, 10: 312.

[72] "Zum Begriff der Unfehlbarkeit," *Schriften*, 10: 313.

[73] "Der Glaube des Christen," *Schriften*, 10: 284; "Über den Begriff des Geheimnisses," *Schriften*, 4: 87–89, 98–99.

dogma has changed over the last hundred years under three aspects.

α. The Dogma Within the Totality of Truths of the Faith

The declaration of infallibility is logically very strange. It is a proposition that renders other dogmatic propositions infallibly sure. However, it in itself cannot be sure in *the same* manner as those propositions that it guarantees to be infallibly true. The dogma of infallibility is one individual proposition immanent within a system, not the foundation of the system itself. The declaration of infallibility can be accepted only if the system is itself grasped and accepted without any logical appeal, properly so called, to the declaration of infallibility as such. "It means further that the sureness entailed in the expectation that the pope or a council will not produce any false definitions cannot be any greater . . . than the sureness with which the dogma of infallibility, without being based on itself, has come to be recognized."[74]

β. The Authorized Language of the Teaching Authority

The very nature of religious truth means that it is *incapable* of being expressed otherwise than in inadequate and analogous concepts. Analogous concepts differ from univocal ones in that substitute concepts are always available that also can be used without violating the meaning of the given proposition. Concepts such as person, nature, sin, and infallibility itself are analogous; they are not necessarily determined fully as concepts. A proposition in the opposite sense is not, therefore, necessarily false:

> The proposition, for instance, that there is such a thing as original sin and the proposition that there is not any such thing as original sin cannot of course both be true at the same time so long as the one is taken merely as a denial of the other. But it can be the case that each is understood as having a positive content of its own through which one expresses that which the other leaves open . . . yet itself fails to express because of the analogous nature of the

---

[74] "Zum Begriff der Unfehlbarkeit," *Schriften,* 10: 316.

concepts used in it. And if this is the situation, then both propositions can be correct.[75]

In this case, as in all others in which concepts are used analogously, the reality signified is expressed in such a way that one
aspect is brought into the forefront, while the other, which would
have explicated the merely "analogous" aspects of the concept,
remains in the background. That the reality is expressed in this
way emphasizes what is purely the outcome of conditions: a particular authorized language. Hence, an essential element of the
infallible teaching authority of the church is the right to prefer
one mode of parlance over another. This does not mean that the
question of truth is ipso facto unequivocally effected.[76] "In the
last few decades a clearer historical awareness of this fact has been
achieved . . . and this in itself has the force of ushering a new
epoch in the history of the dogma of infallibility since the First
Vatican Council."[77]

γ. New Dogmatic Formulae

It follows from the newly recognized analogous nature of all concepts that we now have arrived at a situation in history "in which
a new definition can no longer be false because in any such definition the *legitimate* range of interpretation is so wide that it no
longer leaves any room for error outside it."[78] This does not mean
that such a definition therefore would necessarily be devoid of
content or tautological. For a "new" dogma remains or would
remain related through the "old" dogmas, which it is interpreting, to those basic facts of the Christian faith that constitute the
content and the verifiability of such theologically formulated
propositions of faith.

> In this abiding reference to the basic facts of the faith, they [older
> dogmas] have a content which is capable of being clarified by a
> "fresh" dogma of this kind and which perhaps needs to be clarified
> in the specific situation even though the range of possible interpre-

---

[75] "Zum Begriff der Unfehlbarkeit," *Schriften*, 10: 318; "Grundsätzliche Bemerkungen," *Schriften*, 10: 250–51.

[76] "Häresien in der Kirche heute?" *Schriften*, 9: 468.

[77] "Zum Begriff der Unfehlbarkeit," *Schriften*, 10: 319.

[78] "Zum Begriff der Unfehlbarkeit," *Schriften*, 10: 319–20.

tations to be placed on it is in itself so great that it is no longer possible for any proposition to be formulated which can be put forward with the claim of being correct, *and at the same time* such that it necessarily eliminates the "new" dogmatic formulae absolutely (abstracting from the issue of an authorized mode of parlance).[79]

This awareness that a process of interpretation is in principle incapable of conclusion, that all metaphysical and theological statements are limited, is, at least as far as a sociologically effective awareness of faith in the church is concerned, an event that has manifested itself only within the last hundred years. This awareness makes any possible "new" ecclesiastical definition ipso facto "old" from the outset. "In other words even as it is formulated, it is confronted with such a number of possible or conceivable interpretations that it does not signify any real 'advance' in clarification as compared with former statements of faith."[80]

To those who argue that we must slowly forget about the doctrine of the First Vatican Council, Rahner replies that we neither will nor should forget it, but we must accept that this council's teaching on infallibility has been developing throughout the past hundred years and will continue to develop in the future.

> And why not? Identity survives through change. The reality that exists in personal life and in the church is as mysterious as this. We can in fact not even express the dogma of the incarnation of the eternal Logos without doing justice to this paradox if we want to avoid distorting one or other aspect of this Christological dogma.[81]

B. *The Individual and the Magisterium*

(i) Irresolvable Pluralism of Modern Society

Notwithstanding the analogous and intrinsically limited nature of all human propositions and the openness of dogmatic formula-

---

[79] "Zum Begriff der Unfehlbarkeit," *Schriften,* 10: 320. In the sentence "In dieser bleibenden Bezogenheit haben sie eine Inhaltlichkeit, die verdeutlicht werden kann durch ein solches 'neues' Dogma," it is not absolutely clear what the subject of the sentence is. I am presuming that the sentence is referring back to "theologische, formulierte Glaubenssätze" which themselves must presumably be the "alte Dogmen, die selber wieder Interpretations-norm der 'neuen' sind."

[80] "Zum Begriff der Unfehlbarkeit," *Schriften,* 10: 321.

[81] "Zum Begriff der Unfehlbarkeit," *Schriften,* 10: 323.

tions to an unpredictable future of interpretation, Rahner continues to affirm the existence and the validity of dogma.[82] He holds,
however, that in this present age dogma must assume a different
form from that of past ages. In the present, we have a de facto
irresolvable pluralism in human thought.[83] This unavoidable pluralism makes it impossible to achieve a completely *positive* synthesis between what one believes as a committed Catholic Christian
and the other items of knowledge by which one lives in modern
society.[84] Faith has ceased to be a system of ideas, a *Weltanschauung*. It is one particular element in the world of ideas to which the
man of today belongs.[85] Modern man hopes for the eschatological
reconciliation of all truths, while simultaneously maintaining his
protest against any type of worldly ideological totalitarianism.

(ii) Personal Truth and Official Teaching

As a result of this irresolvable pluralism, the modern Catholic has
to recognize and endure the difference that exists between his
own personal truth and the official teaching of the church.

> In view of the pluralism which necessarily exists it is obvious that
> the individual Christian in his awareness neither is nor can be sim-

---

[82] See note 3 in this chapter.

[83] That there is an irresolvable pluralism in contemporary society is a central
tenet of Rahner's later works: "Was ist Häresie?" *Schriften*, 5: 555–59, 562;
"Philosophie und Philosophieren," *Schriften*, 8: 73–76; "Vom Dialog in der Kirche," *Schriften*, 8: 429–30, 440; "Über das Ja zur konketen Kirche," *Schriften*, 9:
481, 487; "Zum heutigen Verhältnis von Philosophie und Theologie," *Schriften*,
10: 79–81; "Die Theologie im interdisziplinären Gespräch der Wissenschaften,"
Schriften, 10: 90; "Zum Verhältnis zwischen Theologie und heutigen Wissenschaften," *Schriften*, 10: 104; "Einige Bemerkungen," *Schriften*, 12: 199–200,
202; "Dogmatische Randbemerkungen," *Schriften*, 5: 395, 400; "Häresien in
der Kirche heute?" *Schriften*, 9: 456–57; "Der Glaube des Christen," *Schriften*,
10: 268–70; "Zum Begriff der Unfehlbarkeit," *Schriften*, 10: 311; "Lehramt und
Theologie," *Schriften*, 13: 89. See also Hines, *Transformation of Dogma*, 83, 89;
Nichols, *From Newman to Congar*, 226. Lennan makes much of the impact of this
idea on Rahner's later thought: *Ecclesiology of Karl Rahner*, 118–20, 128, 133,
148, 165, 182–83, 189, 192, 194, 197.

[84] It is interesting to note in this context that—notwithstanding Rahner's insistence that in light of this irresolvable pluralism no synthetic approach to Christianity is now possible—less than twenty years subsequently the *Catechism of the
Catholic Church* not only has been published but also has been received in the
church.

[85] "Der Glaube des Christen," *Schriften*, 10: 270; "Die Theologie im interdisziplinären Gespräch," *Schriften*, 10: 99; "Theologie heute," *Schriften*, 15: 69–73.

ply the mirror image, the reflection, the echo, the reproduction of the official teaching of the church. He is far too much under the influence of historical conditions for this to be the case, far too much a concrete individual. He can recognize this difference, and he must bear with it.[86]

He will seek to overcome this difference, but only slowly, step by step, and he must be aware that the attempt has never succeeded and never will while we are in our present state of existence.[87]

(iii) The Hierarchy of Truths

The most important thing for a contemporary Christian is to learn how to pray. "If he could do this, and perhaps in doing so still notice that this orientation to God has something to do with Jesus Christ and his cross, then in certain circumstances he may remain in complete ignorance as to the exact number of the sacraments and still be a better Christian than if he had an exact knowledge of this or if he can repeat every catechism answer by heart."[88] Knowledge of the faith must not be equated with faith itself. For instance, that there is such a thing as indulgence is a defined truth, but this does not mean that the individual must be aware of this truth to be a good Christian. When Paul VI says that there is a Christian freedom to avail oneself of indulgences or not to do so, then the individual Catholic can apply this freedom confidently to the question of knowing about indulgences also.[89]

> While objectively speaking there may be no legitimate way of getting rid of a burdensome teaching by personal and resolute denial of one of the church's dogmas, still there is manifestly, at least in the personal life of the individual Christian, a way of "getting rid of it" by failing to notice it, by "postponing" a problematic question to a later date, just as this happens, and must necessarily happen, in other departments of life.[90]

---

[86] "Der Glaube des Christen," *Schriften,* 10: 273.

[87] "Philosophie und Philosophieren," *Schriften,* 8: 78; "Zum heutigen Verhältnis von Philosophie und Theologie," *Schriften,* 10: 78; "Zum Verhältnis zwischen Theologie und heutigen Wissenschaften," *Schriften,* 10: 105.

[88] "Der Glaube des Christen," *Schriften,* 10: 276.

[89] "Der Glaube des Christen," *Schriften,* 10: 276–77; "Hierarchie der Wahrheiten," *Schriften,* 15: 164–65.

[90] "Der Glaube des Christen," *Schriften,* 10: 277. See also Hines, *Transformation of Dogma,* 97, 101–2, 112–13, 116–17; Lennan, *Ecclesiology of Karl Rahner,* 184, 245.

When Vatican II speaks of a "hierarchy of truths," clearly the real *essence* of this total structure of truth is of greater importance than those truths that belong to the periphery. But the total hierarchy is so constituted that the individual may be unaware of the more peripheral truths without this unawareness being any ground for criticizing him. Thus, over and above the objective hierarchy of truths is a subjective hierarchy of truths that is perfectly justified.[91] The act of faith is not directed at will to various objects of faith. Rather, these objects of faith are grasped in an act that in every particular instance is directed toward the single, total reality of faith sustaining faith as an act. *Fides quae* and *fides qua* are identical in their origins because the fundamental reality that is believed in, namely the Holy Spirit, is also the principle of faith itself, its sustaining force and its active movement. In the unfolding development of faith in the individual, this act of faith gradually assimilates the various "objects of faith" and assigns them their place in the single, total movement of the spirit as it yields itself up to God in his self-disclosure.[92]

This process of assimilation necessary to faith is a historical process that develops at both a collective and an individual level. And because the individual is clearly less advanced in this process than the collective faith of the church, the individual cannot in principle deny that his own personal history of faith has still further to go. In his primary and basic act of faith, the individual believer does not need to have assimilated and articulated positively to himself everything that is included objectively in the faith of the church.[93] Even without this articulation, he still possesses the faith of the church because this faith, despite all its incalculably complex articulations, lives, no less than does the faith of the individual, by this single basic act in which an individual surrenders himself in hope and love to the self-revealing God.

(iv) The Ultimate Basis of Faith

The Christian faith, however complicated its formulation becomes, is fundamentally very simple: there is an impenetrable

---

[91] "Hierarchie der Wahrheiten," *Schriften,* 15: 165–67.
[92] "Der Glaube des Christen," *Schriften,* 10: 278.
[93] "Der Glaube des Christen," *Schriften,* 10: 279.

mystery in our lives, namely God, and this God is near to us in Jesus.[94] There is consequently no official doctrine of the church against which one finds himself compelled to assert an absolute negation. "For all the individual statements in the whole doctrinal structure of Catholic Christianity are capable of being read and interpreted as so many concretizations and variations of that quite simple truth that we have just pointed to as the true substance of the Christian revelation."[95] Whoever posits a contradiction to this essential Christian message must reject the whole of Christianity. But those who accept this essential content and have problems only with a more peripheral dogmatic teaching must live by the truth that is prior to all verbal expression. In doing so, they still will not have achieved any overall synthesis. However, provided they accept the possibility of an existential unity of this kind, then they can endure in hope this inevitable and irreducible pluralism in their personal lives.[96]

C. Magisterium and Theology

In order to understand the complex nature of the relationship that should exist between the magisterium and the theologians, we need to remember that dogma is formulated inevitably with the aid of theology, which itself is not dogma,[97] for the actual history of the activity of the magisterium has scarcely been under its own control. "In practice in its defining or authentic doctrinal statements, the magisterium sanctions a development of the church's sense of faith which has been stimulated and sustained by unofficial theology *before* this sanctioning."[98] Furthermore, because theology always follows a proclamation of the magisterium as a subsequent reflection, it cannot be regarded as unimportant for the proclamation of the magisterium itself.

---

[94] "Die Forderung nach einer 'Kurzformel' des Christlichen Glaubens," *Schriften*, 8: 158–64; "Reflexionen zur Problematik einer Kurzformel des Glaubens," *Schriften*, 9: 248–56.

[95] "Der Glaube des Christen," *Schriften*, 10: 284; "Zum Begriff der Unfehlbarkeit," *Schriften*, 10: 313.

[96] "Der Glaube des Christen," *Schriften*, 10: 285.

[97] An interesting affirmation much in line with Rahner's later theology but markedly different from his earlier view of theology as revelation.

[98] "Lehramt und Theologie," *Schriften*, 13: 76.

The task of theology subsequent to the church's teaching consists in examining again and again the synthesis between what really is accepted consciously in faith and its historically conditioned means of expression. It asks whether the teaching can still be assimilated adequately in faith or whether it needs to be expressed in ways more easily accessible today. The statements of the magisterium, therefore, do not simply represent an endpoint but are involved continually in an unfinished process that the magisterium neither inaugurated nor completely controls. "The magisterium and its statements are therefore a normative authority for theology, but conversely theology is an indispensable condition of existence and effective survival for the magisterium."[99]

Certain practical conclusions can be drawn from these considerations concerning the concrete form of the relationship between theology and magisterium. First, on the part of both theologians and the magisterium there must be a genuine will for dialogue.[100] The partners in this dialogue do not have the same function, but the magisterium must discuss and consult.[101]

Second, the declarations of the magisterium in the present day will have to give more evidence for its decisions than it has been accustomed to do.[102] It must demonstrate that its decisions are the result of a preceding dialogue with representatives of the whole theological world.[103] It also would be helpful if the magisterium were to declare explicitly the degree to which its teaching in a particular document is binding.[104] That the magisterium does not do this normally has led in the past to the impression that all Roman documents are basically irreformable. This impression leads to conflicts of conscience, which are objectively superfluous (for instance, the problems surrounding the reception of *Humanae*

---

[99] "Lehramt und Theologie," *Schriften*, 13: 79.

[100] "Vom Dialog in der Kirche," *Schriften*, 8: 443–44; "Das kirchliche Lehramt," *Schriften*, 9: 347; "Lehramt und Theologie," *Schriften*, 13: 81. See also Lennan, *Ecclesiology of Karl Rahner*, 198–99, 223.

[101] "Lehramt und Theologie," *Schriften*, 13: 81.

[102] See Hines, *Transformation of Dogma*, 57.

[103] "Vom Dialog in der Kirche," *Schriften*, 8: 433–36, 443; "Das kirchliche Lehramt," *Schriften*, 9: 347.

[104] "Lehramt und Theologie," *Schriften*, 13: 82, 88; "Die Theologie und das Römische Lehramt," *Schriften*, 16: 233–34; Rahner, "Kritik an Hans Küng," 368. Lennan, *Ecclesiology of Karl Rahner*, 200.

Vitae[105]). "Even when it is a question of teaching that is absolutely binding, of a dogma, dialogue is not closed but can and must always be carried forward; but it is particularly appropriate when it is a question of merely authentic statements of the magisterium."[106]

Third, in this dialogue, the magisterium and theologians must admit that they can take up positions with regard to one another that are absolutely correct, even binding in faith, and expressly presented as such, but that nevertheless are amalgamated with ideas, terms, horizons of understanding that are not binding in faith and perhaps can and must be eliminated in the course of history. These sorts of amalgamations should be the central object of dialogue between the magisterium and theologians. In a dialogue of this kind, real decisions of the magisterium can and sometimes must be made in virtue of its formal authority, and theologians must respect these decisions to the extent required by their particular binding force.

> But neither does the fact of such a decision and the duty of theologians to respect it mean that after these declarations of the magisterium all dialogue is at an end and the theologians have nothing more to do but to hand on and defend the decision. . . . For such a decision does not leave everything quite clear, since respect for it still leaves open the question of what it does and does not contain and whether it also implicitly transmits amalgams which are not purely and simply binding.[107]

Finally, the task of the magisterium changes with the changing mental climate in which it has to operate. Faced by the insuperable pluralism of our modern society, which extends into the church as an insuperable pluralism of theologies,[108] the task of the

---

[105] Rahner, "Kritik an Hans Küng," 366–68; Rahner, "Replik," 153–55; "Die Theologie und das Römische Lehramt," *Schriften,* 16: 245. See Lennan, *Ecclesiology of Karl Rahner,* 201–3.

[106] "Lehramt und Theologie," *Schriften,* 13: 82–83; "Die Theologie und das Römische Lehramt," *Schriften,* 16: 241.

[107] "Lehramt und Theologie," *Schriften,* 13: 87; "Die Theologie und das Römische Lehramt," *Schriften,* 16: 241.

[108] The existence of an insuperable pluralism in modern theology: "Philosophie und Philosophieren," *Schriften,* 8: 77–80; "Zum heutigen Verhältnis von Philosophie und Theologie," *Schriften,* 10: 79, 81; "Die Theologie und das Römische Lehramt," *Schriften,* 16: 240; "Häresien in der Kirche heute?" *Schriften,* 9:

magisterium is not now nor will it be in the future so much the supervision of the detailed work of theologians as the defense and vivid, up-to-date expression of the basic substance of Christian faith. At a time of worldwide atheism and skepticism, threatening the basic substance of Christianity even while giving a fresh shape to its themes, the magisterium will have to find a way, with all the resources of the Spirit, of constantly conveying both completely and vividly that basic substance to all humanity, particularly outside Europe.[109]

4. Conclusion

Between his earlier and his later works on dogmatic development, Rahner's own thought on the topic was itself subject to an evolution or a change of emphasis. This change has been noted elsewhere, especially by Mary Hines in her book *The Transformation of Dogma,* which attributes it to "an ambiguity at the heart of Rahner's writings."[110] She explains this change of emphasis by reference to Rahner's deepening personal mysticism[111] and argues that, according to Rahner, the future history of dogma in consequence will be transformed into a history where plural and inculturated formulations of faith will play an increasingly secondary role to concrete action on behalf of one's neighbor and contemplation of the silent mystery.[112]

It is my contention that such an analysis of the change in Rahner's theory of the development of dogma fails to take sufficient note of the subtlety and complexity of his thought. I maintain that this change of emphasis is clearly consistent with the rest of Rahner's theology and can be interpreted correctly only in the light of the foundational structure of his thought as dialectical analogy. In his earlier works (more in line with the conceptualiz-

---

467–68. See also Hines, *Transformation of Dogma,* 90, 115, 119, and Nichols, *From Newman to Congar,* 267–68.

[109] "Lehramt und Theologie," *Schriften,* 13: 91.

[110] Hines, *Transformation of Dogma,* 103.

[111] Hines, *Transformation of Dogma,* 101, 119–24, 148.

[112] Hines, *Transformation of Dogma,* 18, 115, 132, 155–58. See also Carr, *Theological Method of Karl Rahner,* 253.

ing, distinguishing side of his thought), Rahner argues that the process of development begins not in a series of propositional statements of faith but in a global experience of the word/*res* of revelation. Revelation is seen, therefore, as a dynamic event (a *Schwebe* between the words of Christ and the Gospels and the original experience to which they refer) that, when conceptualized, results in propositions of faith. These propositions themselves display a dialectical structure, being in one sense "less" and in another sense "more" than the original experience of revelation. This dialectical structure accounts for the twofold direction of dogmatic development, simultaneously toward greater explication and toward greater simplification. The development of dogma is not the logical deduction of what is formally or virtually implied in a set of revealed propositions, but the gradual categorical thematization of this original word/*res* possessed by the church in the grace of the Spirit. These propositional thematizations (dogmas) are intrinsically necessary according to the fundamental nature of man but exist in a twofold dialectical relationship with the word/*res* of revelation: they are both relative and changeable, yet, when conceptualized, they are definitive and permanent.

In his later works, Rahner is less concerned with the specific process of the development of dogma than with the nature and meaning of dogma as such. Presupposing the priority of grace, which he identifies as supernatural revelation and which results in an attitude of fundamental trust in the meaningfulness of existence, Rahner argues (true to the structure of man as *Schwebe*) that this grace must be mediated by an outer historical word, but he emphasizes much more than earlier (in line with the more dynamic, unifying side of his thought) this historical word as an expression of previously given grace. This historical word does not have to be specifically Christian in order to mediate saving grace to the individual, and it is always and essentially relative to the inner experience of grace that it categorically expresses. Nevertheless, the balance of Rahner's earlier perspective is not lost. He continues to insist (in line with the conceptualizing side of his thought) that grace tends dynamically to its truest and fullest expression in Jesus Christ, the church, and its dogmas; thus, even in his later works and notwithstanding his assertions about the intrinsic limitations of all human propositions, he continues to propose and defend both the necessity and validity of the categorical word of revelation and of dogma. This insistence on the necessity of the categorical word—which reflects his insistence on the static, conceptualizing moment within the dynamism of the knowing process—is fundamental to his understanding of revelation and of the development of dogma. It serves as the basis of his trenchant, often repeated rejection of modernism, which sees the conceptualized dogma as entirely derivative from a primordial experience that cannot be thematized.[113] Any suggestion that in his later works Rahner somehow moves away from the necessity of the categorical word toward a "dogma-free" retreat into mystery is a misunderstanding not only of his theory of the development of dogma but also of the whole structure of his thought and understanding of reality.

The real problem with Rahner's understanding of dogma and its development seems to be not that he abandons the necessity of categorical, propositional words within the process of development but rather that the essential content of such propositions seems to be incapable of clear definition, despite his repeated insistence on their existence and validity.[114] This incapacity is grounded in Rahner's own foundational epistemology, where, as we have seen, the concept is also relativized, despite his affirmation of its existence; it is incapable of essential definition owing to the inadequacy of his understanding of the passive intellect.[115] Rahner's insistence on the necessity of categorical propositions within revelation grounds the existence and validity of dogma and of an infallible magisterium. But his equally dogged insistence on the limitedness of all human concepts, even when infallibly defined, seeks flexibility in the interpretation of dogma and openness to a possible future development, which can include new, different, and even contradictory formulations of a particular dogma without thereby denying the infallibility of earlier propositions. In light of this flexibility of interpretation and of the irresolvable pluralism of modern society, Rahner asserts the existence

---

[113] Both Hines (*Transformation of Dogma*, 7, 9, 16, 46) and Nichols (*From Newman to Congar*, 222) note Rahner's rejection of modernism.

[114] An attribute of the concept as a whole and grounded in Rahner's oscillating concept of being.

[115] See chapter 1, note 84.

of a new and legitimate theological pluralism within the church. This pluralism would have been inconceivable before the Second Vatican Council because it makes the absolute contradiction of a given dogma by a believing Christian both unnecessary and meaningless. Instead of contradicting a dogmatic teaching that he finds difficult, a Christian simply can ignore it while waiting for a new and better formulation. The question remains open whether, in the light of the relativization of all human propositions, dogmatic or otherwise, Rahner's notion of infallible dogma is anything other than the verbal affirmation of a reality that does not in fact exist in an essentially meaningful way.

9

Final Synthesis and Conclusions

IN HIS FINAL AND MONUMENTAL WORK *Grundkurs des Glaubens,* published in 1976, Rahner attempted to draw together and synthesize his whole theological project. *Grundkurs* provides us not only with a summary of Rahner's system but also with a fascinating vantage point from which we can review the development of his ideas, observing both the changes and the continuity in his methodology and in the structure of his thought.

In this last great work, the later development that we have noted throughout Rahner's theology is brought to its clearest expression. Throughout *Grundkurs,* therefore, we find a heavy stress on the unifying and dynamic side of his thought. The unity of matter and spirit, the existential unity of grace and nature, man's natural desire for the beatific vision, and the priority of grace are all emphasized. Rahner drops the notions of quasi-formal causality, of nature as a *Restbegriff,* and of revelation as "indoctrination." In Christology, he emphasizes, perhaps more than ever, the real humanity of Jesus, the development of his human self-consciousness, the irreversibility of the universal salvific will of God, and the resurrection of Jesus into the faith of the apostles. However, even in this final synthetic work, with all its dynamic and unifying emphasis, Rahner remains true to the balance of his foundational structure of thought. Thus, in *Grundkurs* he continues to maintain all the distinctions necessary for orthodox Catholic theology: the distinction of matter and spirit, the gratuity of grace, and the validity and necessity of the objective categorical word of God within the dynamism of revelation and the development of dogma. Rahner ends *Grundkurs* most significantly with three brief creedal statements that, although somewhat strange and impractical, nevertheless in themselves indicate that even at the end of his theological career he never abandoned the necessity of the dogmatic word within the process of God's dynamic self-communication to man.

In *Grundkurs,* in the light of his changed perspective, Rahner's methodology is slightly different from that of his earlier works. Rather than taking the dogmas of the church as his starting point and attempting to justify them by showing their congruence with the transcendental structure of man, in *Grundkurs* he begins with transcendental experience and tries to expound from this experience the essentials of Christian dogma. In this chapter, therefore, I attempt to summarize my conclusions about the Rahnerian synthesis. Then, using *Grundkurs* as the clearest summary of his later theology, I show how despite the developments in both his methodology and perspective there is a fundamental continuity in the structure of his thought as dialectical analogy. This continuity means that even at the end of his theological development, and despite the complex and subtle flexibility achieved in his synthesis, the same tensions are still present in his later work as were apparent in his original epistemological metaphysics.

In this chapter, therefore, I summarize the conclusions of the previous chapters and compare these conclusions with the final synthetic positions taken in *Grundkurs* before drawing conclusions at the end of each section.[1]

1. PHILOSOPHICAL BASIS

A. Early Thought

(i) Man as *Schwebe*

It was Rahner's metaphysical starting point in *Geist* and *Hörer* in the ultimate and irreducible nature of the original question that originally led him to posit the notion of man as *Schwebe*. For a question implies simultaneously both knowledge and ignorance and therefore the necessity of man's question about being reveals that he is simultaneously present to all of being and yet not present

---

[1] In previous chapters, I have referred sometimes to essays Rahner wrote after the completion of *Grundkurs*. I did this in order to make a complete presentation of Rahner's final position on various issues outside of *Grundkurs,* which remains nevertheless the overall synthesis of his later thought.

to being. Man is himself, then, an oscillation or *Schwebe;* he stands at his goal, which is also his beginning, being, and yet he is not there. As we have seen, this notion of *Schwebe* dominated Rahner's view of reality and formed the basis for the future development of his thought.

(ii) Being as Presence-to-Self

From this understanding of man as *Schwebe,* Rahner was able to deduce two fundamental metaphysical principles concerning being and matter. First, he was able to deduce the primordial unity of being and knowing. Because being can be questioned, it must be knowable. The necessity of man's question can be grounded, therefore, only if knowing is not something extrinsically added to being but rather is itself the presence-to-self of being *(Beisichsein des Seins)*. Second, the *Schwebe* of man reveals the existence of (prime) matter, for if being is presence-to-self, then a question can ever arise only if the being of the questioner involves a certain nonbeing, which hinders its complete self-reflection or self-mastery. On the one hand, then, matter is that which prevents self-consciousness, yet, on the other hand, insofar as matter enters the composition of a being that is self-reflective, matter can become the knowing being's proper object. Being and matter constitute, therefore, a diversity in unity, and man is revealed as that being whose presence-to-self is in itself a presence-to-the-other. Man is, in other words, a *schwebende Mitte* between the total presence-to-self of independent being and the actual abandonment to matter.

(iii) Knowing

This metaphysical structure of man as dynamic *Schwebe* is reflected in Rahner's analysis of the process of human knowing. Given Rahner's starting point, this similarity between the structure of man and the structure of knowing is not surprising, for being is presence-to-self. Thus, for Rahner, human knowing consists fundamentally in a dynamic *Schwebe* between the sensible singular and the horizon of all being. Because being is knowing, knowledge of another is possible only if the being of the knower himself is the being of the other—in other words, only if the knower in sensibility already and always has entered into otherness. But knowledge of the other as "other" is possible only if the knower is not "lost" in the other but rather can place himself over against the other, can return to himself. This ability to place oneself over the other and so return to self occurs, according to Rahner, in a preapprehension or *Vorgriff* of all being, which itself reveals that the essence of the spirit is potency for and dynamic orientation toward being as such. Therefore, Rahner concludes, in its desire for being as such the spirit lets sensibility emanate, which emanation constitutes the spirit's decisive *conversio ad phantasma*.

(iv) The Concept

Lest human knowing dissolve into an unconceptualizable *Schwebe* between the categorical singular possessed already and always in sensibility, and the preapprehended horizon of being, Rahner insists that within the dynamism of knowing there is always and simultaneously a moment of conceptualization. This moment of conceptualization, which for Rahner consists not in the literal liberation of a form from a material supposite but rather in the recognition of the limitation and therefore of the potential repeatability of a sensibly intuited object, is possible only because in the *Vorgriff* the spirit already has transcended what is sensibly intuited in its dynamic desire for being as such. Thus, insofar as the spirit lets sensibility emanate in its desire for the preapprehended horizon of all being (which emanation constitutes the fundamental *conversio*), wherever anything is known in sensibility it is already abstracted, and both sensibility and abstraction are revealed as moments within the one dynamism of human knowing, the *conversio ad phantasma*. Within this perspective, the concept is never a "pure form" but rather always remains related to a "this" *(Diesda)* and stands in relation to the judgment as a possible to an actually realized synthesis. What was traditionally referred to as the passive intellect is reduced to a mere name *(Titel)*, indicating that the spirit for itself effects and then possesses the receptive faculty of sensibility.

Within this dynamic process of human knowing, the concept, which implies a moment of abstract distance, seems to be endangered. But Rahner always insisted on both its necessity and validity, for there can be no "that" without a "what," and every judgment contains some conceptual element. Moreover, he also affirmed the existence of an oscillating concept of being which, in its analogous unity, stretches from matter's nonbeing to God's infinity. Because this concept refers to the same reality as the judgment, all of reality can be conceptualized. Rahner held on to the necessity of the concept so strongly because this distinguished his position from modernism, which saw the concept as merely something secondary to man's perception of God and reality and therefore capable of being surpassed. Thus, though from one point of view the concept apparently is relativized as being only a part of the judgment that is transcended in the movement beyond abstraction, from another perspective it provides an absolute stability because it contains in itself the whole movement of the judgment.

(v) Dialectical Analogy

There is, then, an analogy in knowing, and it is this analogy that grounds all of what we call univocal knowledge and not vice versa. This analogy consists in a *Schwebe* or an oscillation between the dynamic movement of the judgment, on the one hand, and the static moment of conceptualization, on the other. These two factors within the knowing process exist in a relationship of mutual priority, and Rahner himself seems to alternate between the two in his explanation of the unity in diversity of human knowing. This double emphasis or *Schwebe* between unifying dynamism and conceptual distinction constitutes in fact, as we have seen, a remarkably flexible structure of thought, which when applied to theology allows Rahner both to unite dialectically and to hold in distinction the traditional antinomies of Christian thought. It is, therefore, this structure of dialectical analogy that enables him to maintain the unity of God and the world, spirit and matter, grace and nature, while simultaneously maintaining the distinctions between them. This continual switching of perspective, so characteristic of Rahner's thought, is not simply contradiction or ambiguity but is based on the analogous structure of man himself, who is precisely the constant oscillation between these perspectives. Man is the *schwebende Mitte* between spirit and matter, God and the world, the transcendental and the categorical, judgment and concept: all the distinctions must be preserved, but they are properly preserved only in the constant *Schwebe* that is true dialectical analogy.

B. Grundkurs

In the short but highly significant epistemological introduction to *Grundkurs,* Rahner returns to the analysis of human knowing that had been his theme in *Geist* and *Hörer.* He approaches the problem this time not from the inalienable necessity of the question and the structure of the judgment but rather from the unity in diversity of the subjective transcendental experience.

(i) Being as Presence-to-Self

Thus, in *Grundkurs,* Rahner asserts that there is in man an "inescapable *unity in difference between one's original self-possession and reflection,*"[2] for there is not just the purely objective "in itself" *(Ansich)* of a reality, on the one hand, and the clear and distinct idea of it, on the other. Rather, there is a more original unity of reality and its "self-presence," which is more and is more original than the unity of this reality and the concept that objectifies it. When I love, am tormented, am sad, and so on, this reality is an original unity of reality and its own self-presence, a unity that is not totally mediated by the concept that objectifies it. This unity of reality and the original self-presence of this reality in the person is already present in man's free self-realization.[3] This is one side of the question.

A moment of reflection and consequently of universality and spiritual communicability belongs even to this original knowledge

---

[2] *Grundkurs des Glaubens: Einführung in den Begriff des Christentums,* 6th ed. (Freiburg, Basel, Vienna: Herder, 1984), 26; translations from *Foundations of Christian Faith: An Introduction to the Idea of Christianity,* translated by W. Dych (New York: Crossroad, 1978).

[3] *Grundkurs,* 27. Although differently formulated, this assertion reflects Rahner's foundational metaphysical thesis that "Sein ist Bei-sich-Sein": *Geist,* 40 n. 8, 49 n. 1, 82–83, 87, 88 n. 15; *Hörer 1,* 50, 52, 57, 86, 88, 91. See chapter 1, note 17.

itself. This original unity between reality and its knowledge of itself always exists in man only with and in and through what we can call language, and thus also with and in and through reflection and communicability.[4]

The tension between original knowledge and its concept is not something static. It has a history in two directions. There is a tendency toward greater conceptualization.[5] But there is also a movement in the opposite direction. Reflection, conceptualization, and language have a necessary orientation to that original experience in which what is meant and the experience of what is meant are still one.[6] Insofar as religious knowledge also manifests this tension, there is within theology this dual movement in its irreducible unity in difference.[7] This tension is a fluid relationship and not simply something static.[8]

(ii) Knowledge of the Other

Because we imagine the essential nature of human knowledge after the model of a tablet on which an object from outside is inscribed, we end up with the problem of how an "in-itself" of something can "get into" knowledge.[9] In reality, knowledge has a much more complex structure, for the spiritual knowledge of a personal subject is a knowledge in which the knowing subject possesses in knowledge both itself and its knowledge. In knowl-

---

[4] *Grundkurs*, 27. Here we see that Rahner continues to insist on the moment of conceptualization within the dynamism of human knowing, as he had done earlier: *Geist*, 114, 132, 134, 147, 181; *Hörer 1*, 160. Yet here, as earlier, the concept displays a dialectical nature both less than the original experience and yet necessary to it.

[5] *Grundkurs*, 27. This tendency is the basis of Rahner's notion of the expanding, conceptualizing movement in the development of dogma: "Zur Frage der Dogmenentwicklung," *Schriften*, 1: 76–77, 78, 89; "Was ist Häresie?" *Schriften*, 5: 568; *Mysterium Salutis I*, s.v. "Geschichtlichkeit der Vermittlung," 761.

[6] *Grundkurs*, 28; *Geist*, 40 n. 8.This is the basis of Rahner's other notion of the simplifying movement in the development of dogma: "Was ist Häresie?" *Schriften*, 5: 568; *Mysterium Salutis I*, s.v. "Geschichtlichkeit der Vermittlung," 771. This dialectical double movement is, as I have pointed out, meaningful only in the light of Rahner's oscillating notion of the concept.

[7] *Grundkurs*, 27–28.

[8] *Grundkurs*, 28.

[9] *Grundkurs*, 28; *Geist*, 88, 141–42.

edge, not only is something known, but the subject's knowing is always coknown.

In the simple and original act of knowledge, whose attention is focused on some object that encounters it, the knowing that is coknown and the knowing subject that is coknown are not the objects of the knowledge. Rather, the consciousness of the act of knowing something and the subject's consciousness of itself—that is, the subject's presence to itself—are situated at the subjective pole of the single relationship between the knowing subject and the known object. Moreover, this coknown, unthematic self-presence of the subject and its self-knowledge is not merely an accompanying phenomenon in every act of knowledge that grasps an object so that the knowledge of this object is completely independent of the structure of the subjective self-presence. Rather, the structure of the subject itself is an a priori; that is, it forms an antecedent law governing what and how something can become manifest to the knowing subject.[10] This in no way implies that the realities that present themselves cannot manifest themselves as they really are. A keyhole, for example, forms an a priori law governing what key fits in, but it thereby discloses something about the key itself.[11]

> The a priori structure of a faculty of knowledge is disclosed most simply by the fact that it is constant in every individual act of knowledge of an object that is given to it, and indeed even when the object of this act is, or rather would be, the denial or the impugning of these a priori structures.[12]

(iii) The Transcendental Experience

The a priori structure of this self-possession is, without prejudice to the mediation of this self-possession by the experience of sense

---

[10] *Grundkurs,* 30. The structure of the agent intellect as the a priori of human knowing: *Geist,* 155–56, 190–91, 216–17, 389 n. 9, 390; *Hörer 1,* 77, 82–83, 100, 183.

[11] In the language of *Geist,* "the a priori structure of the spirit becomes the form of the sensibly given" (294, 297, 315, 321, 325).

[12] *Grundkurs,* 30.

objects in time and space, pure openness for absolutely everything, for being as such *(Sein überhaupt).*[13] This is shown by the
fact that man experiences himself as conditioned and limited by
sense experience. In this experience of limitation, however, he
necessarily has transcended this sense experience already. He has
posited himself as the subject of a preapprehension *(Vorgriff),*
which has no intrinsic limit because even the suspicion of such an
intrinsic limitation of the subject posits this preapprehension itself
as going beyond the suspicion.[14]

Rahner calls the subjective, unthematic, and necessary consciousness of the knowing subject the *transcendental experience.* It is
an experience because this knowledge, unthematic but ever present, is a moment within and a condition of possibility for every
concrete experience of any and every object.[15] It is transcendental
because it belongs to the necessary and inalienable structures of
the knowing subject. "Transcendental experience is the experience of *transcendence,* in which experience the structure of the
subject and therefore also the ultimate structure of every conceivable object of knowledge are present together and in identity."[16]
This transcendental experience, of course, is not merely an experience of pure knowledge, but also of will and freedom, for the
same character of transcendentality belongs also to them.[17]

---

[13] *Grundkurs,* 31. This a priori structure of self-possession is equivalent to the
Vorgriff of the horizon of all being, as described in *Geist,* and is the basis of
Rahner's notion of man as dynamism: *Geist,* 282, 287, 296, 394, 405. See also
Ratzinger, "Vom Verstehen des Glaubens," 179.

[14] *Grundkurs,* 31. Thus, the basic structure of Rahner's earlier epistemology is
affirmed here again: *Geist,* 208, 210, 215, 218, 232, 282, 287; *Hörer 1,* 77, 98,
190.

[15] *Grundkurs,* 31. In the language of *Geist ,* "the preapprehension of all being
is the a priori condition of possibility of all knowledge" (115, 155, 165, 190–91).
Hörer 1, 77, 81, 84–86, 94, 99, 129, 179–80; "Probleme der Christologie,"
Schriften, 1: 169–70; "Zur Theologie der Menschwerdung," *Schriften,* 4: 138;
"Über den Begriff des Geheimnisses," *Schriften,* 4: 59. See chapter 1, note 53.
See also Ratzinger, "Vom Verstehen des Glaubens," 180, who criticizes Rahn-
er's understanding of the transcendental experience for confusing transcenden-
tality with transcendence.

[16] *Grundkurs,* 31–32. That the structure of the knowing subject is ultimately
identical with the structure of the object known: *Geist,* 226–8, 230, 270, 282,
296–97; *Hörer 1,* 68, 85, 86, 88, 91, 99.

[17] See also *Hörer 1,* 128, where Rahner made a similar affirmation.

(iv) The Term of Man's Transcendence

There is present in this transcendental experience, moreover, an unthematic and anonymous knowledge of God.[18] Hence, the original knowledge of God is not the kind of knowledge in which one grasps an object that happens to present itself directly or indirectly from outside.[19] It rather has the character of a transcendental experience.[20] Furthermore, if man is a being of transcendence toward the holy and absolutely real mystery of God, and if the term and source of the transcendence, in and through which man as such exists and which constitutes his original essence as subject and as person, is this absolute and holy mystery, "then strangely enough we can and must say: mystery in its incomprehensibility is what is *self-evident* in human life."[21] What is intelligible, therefore, is grounded in mystery, and mystery is something with which we are always familiar, something that we love, even when we are terrified by it or perhaps even annoyed and angered and want to be done with it.

(v) Man as *Schwebe*

What is meant by man's subjectivity is made clear when we say that man is a transcendent being—that is, a being who is always present to himself in his entirety. In his openness to everything and anything, whatever can come to expression can be at least a question for him,[22] and in the fact that he affirms the possibility of a merely finite horizon of questioning, this possibility is surpassed already, and man shows himself to be a being with an infinite horizon. Man is the spirit, therefore, who experiences himself as

---

[18] *Grundkurs,* 32. This affirmation was also central in Rahner's earlier work: *Geist,* 189–90, 191, 232, 390; *Hörer 1,* 81–82, 84, 87, 97.

[19] *Geist,* 232, 287–92; *Hörer 1,* 15; "Über den Begriff des Geheimnisses," *Schriften,* 4: 74.

[20] Here again the dialectical structure of Rahner's thought is apparent in that the original transcendental experience of God occurs in silence and yet must necessarily be conceptualized.

[21] *Grundkurs,* 32–33. Ratzinger, "Vom Verstehen des Glaubens," 179, argues that Rahner, notwithstanding his sweeping condemnation of Platonism, is influenced heavily here by a Platonic-Augustinian interpretation of Thomas.

[22] *Grundkurs,* 42; *Geist,* 71–72; *Hörer 1,* 46–48.

spirit in that he does not experience himself as pure spirit.[23] Man is not the unquestioned and unquestioning infinity of reality; he is rather the question that can never be settled or adequately answered by him. "Insofar as man is a transcendent being, he is confronted by himself, is responsible for himself, and hence is person and subject."[24]

Man's responsibility and freedom are not a particular, empirical datum in human reality alongside other data.[25] Rather, like subjectivity and personhood, so too responsibility and freedom are realities of transcendental experience; that is, they are experienced when a subject as such experiences himself and, hence, precisely not when he is objectified in a subsequent scientific reflection. Freedom is, then, not the power to be able to do this or that, but the power to decide about oneself and to actualize oneself.[26]

But man as a being of transcendence and of freedom is also essentially and at the same time a being in the world, in time, and in history.[27] The question of salvation, therefore, cannot be answered by bypassing man's historicity and his social nature, for time, world, and history mediate man to himself. "Transcendentality and freedom are realized in history."[28] If, moreover, man's historicity and therefore his concrete history is an intrinsic and

---

[23] In the language of Geist, man is the schwebende Mitte between God and the world.

[24] Grundkurs, 45.

[25] Grundkurs, 46–50. This notion of freedom is found also in the earlier works: Geist, 298–99, 302, 311, 371, 372; Hörer 1, 174, 207–8.

[26] Ratzinger, "Vom Verstehen des Glaubens," 184, criticizes this idea of liberated freedom, which is recurrent in Grundkurs and is a development from his earlier works.

[27] In the language of Geist, "the starting point of any attempt to understand ourselves is necessarily where we are: in the world" (47, 53, 75–76, 79, 89, 127, 129, 232, 244, 404–5); see also Hörer 1, 202–3.

[28] Grundkurs, 51. This central affirmation that according to the nature of man as Schwebe the transcendental always is and must be mediated by and through the categorical—an affirmation grounded in Geist (404–6) and in Hörer 1 (82–83, 174, 176, 178, 181, 183–85, 189, 202–3, 208)—is constantly reaffirmed throughout Grundkurs (61, 67, 145, 155, 174, 175, 207, 235, 264–65, 268, 270, 273, 276, 306, 333, 337, 376) and of course reflects one of the central affirmations of Rahner's theological project: Sendung und Gnade, 61, 93. See "Theologie und Anthropologie," Schriften, 8: 45; Rahner and Thüsing, Christologie, 11, 39; Mysterium Salutis II, s.v. "Der dreifaltige Gott," 377, 381–82; Sacramentum Mundi III, s.v. "Offenbarung," 833–34, 838, 840; "Glaubensakt und Glaubensinhalt," Schriften, 15: 157.

constitutive element of a spiritual and free subject, then it is precisely in history that the subject must work out his salvation by finding it there as offered to him and accepting it. If historicity is an existential of the subject himself, then "salvation history and history as such must be ultimately coexistent."[29]

In spite of his free subjectivity, man experiences himself as being at the disposal of other things. First of all, he is in the presence of being as mystery. But man also experiences himself as one to whom a historical situation has been given without his having chosen it, which places him in the quite specific situation that characterizes his nature: insofar as he experiences his historical conditioning, he is already beyond it in a certain sense, but nevertheless he cannot leave it behind. "Being situated in this way between the finite and the infinite is what constitutes man and is shown by the fact that it is in his infinite transcendence and in his freedom that man experiences himself as dependent and historically conditioned."[30]

(vi) Mystery and Analogy

In *Grundkurs,* Rahner stresses perhaps more than ever, and with less reservations, the dynamic orientation of existential man to God.[31] Man knows explicitly what is meant by "God" only insofar as he allows his own transcendence to enter into his consciousness, accepts it, and objectifies in reflection what is already present in his transcendentality. This transcendental knowledge of God is both an a posteriori knowledge insofar as man's transcendental experience of his free subjectivity takes place only in his encounter with the world and simultaneously an a priori knowledge in that man's basic orientation to absolute mystery, which constitutes

---

[29] *Grundkurs,* 52, 150, 194, 305, 397–98. That history as such *is* salvation history is also, as we have seen, a recurrent notion in Rahner's thought. See chapter 5, note 31.

[30] *Grundkurs,* 53. See also *Geist,* 67–68, 93–94, 406: man as the *schwebende Mitte* between God and the world, the infinite and the finite.

[31] As we have seen, after *Geist* Rahner no longer saw man as oriented to a horizon of being distinct from God, but even in *Hörer* he stressed man's existential orientation to God: *Hörer 1,* 82, 85, 89, 110, 126, 130, 136–37, 196–97, 206; "Über den Begriff des Geheimnisses," *Schriften,* 4: 69; "Dogmatische Erwägungen," *Schriften,* 5: 238. See chapter 1, notes 72 and 73.

his fundamental experience of God, is a permanent existential of man as a spiritual subject. This means that man's explicit, conceptual knowledge of God is always a reflection upon his transcendental orientation toward mystery. Some degree of reflection is always necessary.[32] The term of our experience of transcendence is always present as nameless and indefinable, as something not at our disposal.[33] Every name defines, and the infinite horizon, which is the term of transcendence, cannot itself be given a name, for that would be to objectify it, to understand it as one object among others, and to define it conceptually. But all the conceptualizing that we have to do remains true only to the extent that in this act of defining and expressing objectively the term of transcendence as the act's condition of possibility, once again an act of transcendence toward the infinite term of this transcendence takes place. By its very nature, the condition that makes possible distinguishing and naming cannot itself have a name.[34]

The term of transcendence is indefinable because the horizon itself cannot be present within the horizon. This nameless and indefinable term of transcendence, which is distinguished from everything else only from its own side and hence differentiates everything else from itself, is absolutely beyond our disposal. And for this reason the term of this transcendence is mystery.[35]

We can speak about transcendental experience, therefore, only

---

[32] *Grundkurs,* 61–62; "Zur Frage der Dogmenentwicklung," *Schriften,* 1: 76–77, 78, 89; "Was ist Häresie?" *Schriften,* 5: 568; *Mysterium Salutis I,* s.v. "Geschichtlichkeit der Vermittlung," 761. See chapter 8, note 22.

[33] This central affirmation of *Grundkurs* that God is indefinable and nameless stands in a certain tension with Rahner's simultaneous affirmation that there is a *Gottesbegriff* without which man would not be man; see his "Meditation über das Wort 'Gott,'" *Grundkurs,* 54–61. Not only is this double emphasis clearly grounded in Rahner's dialectical analogy, but the word *God* also displays the dialectical structure that I have noted is common both to Rahner's original concept of being and to the historical words of revelation and dogma in that it is part of man (56–57) but also contains the whole (59).

[34] *Grundkurs,* 70–71. Rahner again seems to oscillate between the dynamic unity of God and the world as "das Erste und das Letzte" (*Grundkurs,* 67) and the distinction between God and the world with his affirmation of God as the ground of reality and therefore different from all else (*Grundkurs,* 70). Here the emphasis is clearly on the former aspect of unity, yet never to the total exclusion of the distinction.

[35] *Grundkurs,* 72–73. Yet Rahner simultaneously affirms that this unnamable mystery is called God and that it is this mystery that Jesus calls "Father" (69).

by means of what is secondary to it, and for this reason we have to speak about it always in language of "on the one hand . . . on the other hand" and "not only . . . but also." Hence, a statement about this mystery is always an original statement caught in an irresolvable tension or oscillation between the categorical origin of our reflexive statement and its attaining that toward which the statement is really pointing—namely, the term of transcendence. We do not produce this tension at a logically subsequent midpoint between a univocal "yes" and an equivocal "no." "It is rather a tension [*Schwebe*] which we ourselves as spiritual subjects originally *are* in our self-realization, and which we can designate by the original term 'analogy' if we understand what this word means in its original sense."[36]

C. Conclusion

Although Rahner's approach in *Grundkurs* is different from the approach he took in his earlier works, beginning not with an analysis of man's knowledge of the world but rather in the pure subjectivity of the human knower, a clear continuity in his thought can be observed. Just as in *Geist* and *Hörer* his foundational metaphysical assertion is the luminosity of being, so also in *Grundkurs* his fundamental starting point is the irreducible unity in diversity of reality and its self-presence. Just as in *Geist* and *Hörer* the decisive moment in the knowing process is the preapprehension of all being, or the *Vorgriff*, which allows the recognition of the limitation of the sensibly known object and therefore the formation of the concept, so also in *Grundkurs* the decisive element is the a priori structure of being, which involves an openness to absolutely everything and which Rahner now calls the "transcendental experience." Just as in *Geist* and *Hörer* Rahner insists on the necessity of the concept (albeit a rather strange, oscillating concept) as a moment within the knowing process, so also in *Grundkurs* he maintains that a moment of universality and reflection is intrinsic to the original knowledge of man—arguing that because this con-

---

[36] *Grundkurs*, 80; *Geist*, 67–68, 93–94, 406. Here again we see the fundamental structure of Rahner's thought: the dynamism or *Schwebe* of man constitutes the foundational analogy, within which dynamism there is a conceptual moment that allows distinction and differentiation.

cept is both "less" than the original experience and yet also necessary to it, there is a tension between this original knowledge and its concept that has a history in two directions. In both his earlier works and here in *Grundkurs*, Rahner argues that within the pre-apprehension of all being or the transcendental experience there is an unthematic or anonymous knowledge of God that forms the horizon of all understanding and that makes metaphysics possible as the elaboration of the ground of all human knowledge. And just as in *Geist* and *Hörer* Rahner argues that, in view of the *excessus*, the analogous grounds the univocal and not vice versa, so also in *Grundkurs* he argues, in line with the whole dialectical structure of his thought, that all "clear" conceptual knowledge is grounded in mystery. Finally, in both *Geist* and *Hörer* and also in *Grundkurs* a crucial tension becomes apparent concerning the validity of the concept. For just as in *Geist* and *Hörer*, despite Rahner's repeated assertions about the existence and necessity of the concept, the concept is relativized owing to the inadequacy of his understanding of the passive intellect, so also in *Grundkurs* and again despite his insistence to the contrary, the concept seems to be threatened and incapable of essential definition. The problem is not that Rahner denies the necessity of the concept; quite the contrary, the problem is that despite his insistence on its necessity and validity he seems incapable of completely grounding this assertion within the dynamic *Schwebe* that is human being and knowing. This weakness of the concept in his foundational philosophy has consequences that become apparent throughout the development of his theology and account for the progressively stronger emphasis on the dynamic, unifying side of his thought.

One essential development that does occur between Rahner's foundational works and his later thought is that in his later works and very clearly in *Grundkurs* Rahner drops all mention of *esse commune* as the point of reference of man's intellectual dynamism, referring it instead directly to God. This development obviously effects his understanding of the grace-nature relationship, to which we now turn.

2. NATURE AND GRACE

A. Early Thought

In his earliest works on nature and grace, we saw how Rahner proposed a realignment of the scholastic approach to created and uncreated grace. Having rejected the traditional notion of uncreated grace being given as a consequence of created grace, and having established a continuum between the ontology of grace and the ontology of the beatific vision, Rahner argued that the relationship of the beatific vision to the *lumen gloriae* might be used as an analogy for the relationship of uncreated and created grace. Just as the beatific vision logically precedes the *lumen gloriae,* which exists as its material cause and *dispositio ultima,* so also God's presence in the soul in uncreated grace logically precedes the created grace that is *its* material cause and *dispositio ultima.* In defining this form of causality exercised by God on man, Rahner rejected the category of efficient causality, arguing instead that it could be understood only as a type of formal causality. I noted, however, that throughout his writings describing this causality he constantly oscillated between the two terms *formal* and *quasi-formal* causality, which verbal distinction, I argued, cannot be interpreted only as a type of shorthand but was rather an indication of Rahner's dialectical way of thinking. In rejecting efficient causality and using formal causality instead, Rahner seemed to be emphasizing the dynamic unity of God and man (in line with the dynamic, unifying side of his thought). But by thereafter adopting the notion of quasi-formal causality, he seemed to presuppose a certain form within the man who receives grace and therefore to be stressing the diversity of God and man (in line with the conceptualizing, distinguishing side of his thought).

In his treatment of the grace/nature problem proper, a similar tension became apparent. Thus, in his reaction against the *nouvelle theologie,* Rahner argued against the direct orientation of nature itself to grace on the grounds that such an orientation would endanger the gratuity of grace. Instead he proposed that man's orientation to grace must be the result of gratuitous grace, constituting, therefore, a supernatural existential. This notion of an existential clearly presupposes a nature that is existentially elevated, and in this context and in line with the static conceptualizing side of his thought Rahner insisted on the existence of pure nature as a *Restbegriff.* This rather static notion of nature stands in contrast however to Rahner's other understanding of nature as dynamism, for in reaction against the extrinsicism of the late Scholastics and in line with the dynamic, unifying side of his thought, he simultaneously asserted that nature was to be "defined" as pure dynamic openness to absolutely everything. In this context, man was the being of pure transcendence, who had a natural desire for the beatific vision and whose nature therefore could not be defined. There is a tension between these two views of nature. If, on the one hand, pure nature constitutes a *Restbegriff,* we must be able to stipulate a natural end for man, which Rahner had difficulty in defining, arguing at times that it was some natural good and at other times that it was a perpetual asymptotic transcendence toward the goal itself. But if, on the other hand, the nature of man is itself pure dynamic transcendence, then it is difficult to see why such a nature would need a supernatural existential in order to orient it to God or indeed how such an existential can ever be distinguished from the pure openness of nature. These tensions are not, I would again maintain, the result of an ambiguity in Rahner's thought but rather the operation of his dialectical analogy, through which he is able to maintain the unity of grace and nature without thereby destroying their distinction.

Finally, the *Schwebe* between the static and the dynamic elements of his thought became apparent again in the development of Rahner's understanding of the operation of grace. In his earlier works, and especially in the first edition of *Hörer,* Rahner seemed to view the operation of grace as raising human subjectivity to enable man to hear the objectively given outer word of revelation. Such a view clearly seems to presuppose the distinction of grace and nature. However, in his later works, we can observe a progressively stronger emphasis on the dynamic unity of grace and nature, and the intrinsic priority of grace only comes to expression in the word of categorical revelation. This later emphasis on the unity of grace and nature is, however, never to the total exclusion of the earlier view, maintaining their distinction, and constitutes another example of Rahner's dialectical structure of thought.

B. Grundkurs

Presupposing the identification of grace and revelation Rahner made in the mid-1960s, in *Grundkurs* he speaks of grace as the self-communication of God. By the term *self-communication,* however, he does not understand that God would say something *about*

himself in some revelation or other.[37] The term really is intended
to signify that God in his own most proper reality makes himself
the innermost constitutive element of man. The Christian message says that man is the event of an absolute and forgiving self-
communication of God. God's self-communication means, therefore, that what is communicated is really God in his own being,
and in this way it is a communication for the sake of knowing and
possessing God in immediate vision and love. Grace and vision of
God are but two phases of God's single self-communication to
man.[38] That the acceptance of God's self-communication must be
and is based on God's offer itself and hence that the acceptance of
grace is once again an event of grace itself follow from the ultimate relationship between human transcendence as knowledge
and freedom and from the term and source by which this transcendence is opened and on which it is based. Divine self-communication means, then, that God can communicate himself in
his own reality to what is not divine without ceasing to be infinite
reality and absolute mystery and without man's ceasing to be a
finite existent different from God.

> In this self-communication God in his absolute being is related to
> the created existent in the mode of *formal* causality, that is, that he
> does not originally cause and produce something different from
> himself in the creature, but rather that he communicates his own
> divine reality and makes it a constitutive element in the fulfillment
> of the creature.[39]

The intrinsic intelligibility and the ontological justification for
understanding the notion of self-communication this way is
found in the transcendental experience. For in transcendence as
such absolute being is the innermost constitutive element by

---

[37] "Zur Frage der Dogmenentwicklung," *Schriften,* 1: 59; *Mysterium Salutis I,*
s.v. "Geschichtlichkeit der Vermittlung," 757, 758, 770; "Zur Geschichtlichkeit
der Theologie," *Schriften,* 8: 91, 93. See also Ratzinger, "Vom Verstehen des
Glaubens," 180.

[38] This affirmation was constant throughout Rahner's treatment of grace:
"Zur scholastischen Begrifflichkeit," *Schriften,* 1: 354; "Natur und Gnade,"
Schriften, 4: 220, 354; "Über den Begriff des Geheimnisses," *Schriften,* 4: 84;
Sacramentum Mundi IV, s.v. "Selbstmitteilung Gottes," 522, 524.

[39] *Grundkurs,* 127–28, my emphasis. Clearly in line with the more dynamic,
unifying perspective of *Grundkurs.*

which this transcendental movement is borne toward itself and is not just the extrinsic term and goal of a movement. "While it is what is innermost in this movement, it also remains absolutely beyond and absolutely untouched by this transcendental movement."[40]

This also means that this kind of self-communication by God to a creature necessarily must be understood as an act of God's highest personal freedom. Christian theology, therefore, understands this self-communication as absolutely gratuitous, prior to any sinful rejection of God by man, and "supernatural."[41] This does not mean that the supernatural "elevation" of a spiritual creature is added extrinsically to its essence, for in the concrete order the spiritual creature is constituted to begin with as the possible addressee of such a divine self-communication.[42] God's creation through efficient causality takes place because God wants to give himself in love.[43] In the concrete order, man's transcendence is willed as the realm of God's self-communication, and only in God does this transcendence find its absolute fulfillment. But precisely for this reason this communication is not to be understood as a natural process.

The statement "man is the event of God's absolute self-communication" does not refer to some reified objectivity in man. It expresses, rather, the subject in the depths of man's subjectivity and hence in the depths of his transcendental experience. It is a

---

[40] *Grundkurs,* 128, 132. Rahner developed this dialectical notion of the term of transcendence being immanent within it by being transcendent earlier: See chapter 4, note 47.

[41] *Grundkurs,* 129, 173–74, 182–83, 311. More in line with Rahner's earlier, more conceptual perspective: *Sacramentum Mundi IV,* s.v. "Trinität," 1014; "Über das Verhältnis," *Schriften,* 1: 337, 339; "Fragen der Kontroverstheologie," *Schriften,* 4: 250, 264–65; "Natur und Gnade," *Schriften,* 4: 234. See chapter 2, note 20.

[42] *Grundkurs,* 291; *Hörer 1,* 24, 192–95, 197, 201, 204, 209, 215, 225; *Sacramentum Mundi II,* s.v. "Jesus Christus," 944; Rahner and Thüsing, *Christologie,* 55, 65.

[43] Creation as the presupposition for grace and the incarnation: "Fragen der Kontroverstheologie," *Schriften,* 4: 266; "Natur und Gnade," *Schriften,* 4: 222; *Sacramentum Mundi IV,* s.v. "Selbstmitteilung Gottes," 523–24; "Buch Gottes— Buch der Menschen," *Schriften,* 16: 279; "Probleme der Christologie," *Schriften,* 1: 185, 205; "Die Christologie innerhalb einer evolutiven Weltanschauung," *Schriften,* 5: 201, 215; *Sendung und Gnade,* 55, 63. See also Ratzinger, "Vom Verstehen des Glaubens," 181.

statement that refers to absolutely all men and that expresses an existential of every person.[44] Such an existential does not become merited and in this sense natural by the fact that it is present in all men as an existential of their concrete existence; it (the existential of grace) is present prior to their freedom, their self-understanding, and their experience. "The gratuity of a reality has nothing to do with the question whether it is present in many or only in a few people."[45]

It follows from this that God's offer of himself belongs to all men and is a characteristic of their transcendence and their transcendentality. Grace therefore cannot be differentiated by simple and individual acts of reflection from those basic structures of human transcendence. The absolutely unlimited transcendence of the natural spirit in knowledge and freedom along with its term, the holy mystery, already implies by itself such an infinity in the subject that the possession of God in absolute self-communication does not fall outside of this infinite possibility of transcendence, although, Rahner insists, it remains gratuitous. Thus, a person who opens himself to his transcendental experience of the holy mystery at all has the experience that this holy mystery is not only the infinitely different horizon but also a hidden closeness, a forgiving intimacy, his real home, that it is a love that shares itself, something familiar that he can approach and turn to from the estrangement of his own perilous and empty life.

The experience appealed to here is not primarily some religious activity but is rather the experience that is given to every person prior to such reflexive religious activity. For if God's self-communication is a radicalizing modification of that very transcendentality of ours by which we are subjects, and if we are such subjects of unlimited transcendentality in the most ordinary affairs of our everyday existence, this means in principle that the original experience of God even in his self-communication can be so universal, so unthematic, and so unreligious that it takes place, unnamed but really, wherever we are living out our existence.[46]

---

[44] Grace as a supernatural existential: see chapter 2, note 38.

[45] *Grundkurs,* 133.

[46] This is clearly continuous with Rahner's earlier understanding of grace as imparting a new formal end to man's transcendental dynamism (see chapter 2, note 35), but again with the stress now on the existential unity of grace and nature.

When a person in theoretical or practical knowledge or in subjective activity confronts the abyss of his existence, which alone is the ground of everything, and when this person has the courage to look into himself and to find in these depths his ultimate truth, there he can also have the experience that this abyss accepts him as his true and forgiving security.[47]

C. Conclusion

A clear continuity is apparent between Rahner's earlier writings on grace and his treatment of it in *Grundkurs*. Thus, in *Grundkurs*, he continues to assert grace and the beatific vision as two phases in one process of divine self-communication, creation as the presupposition for grace and the gratuity of grace and the supernatural existential. In *Grundkurs*, however, there is a development of perspective that is in line with the later development of his thought. He stresses much more than previously the existential unity of grace and nature and defines man as the "event of God's grace." He drops all reference to quasi-formal causality and stresses the operation of grace as effecting its own acceptance. Most significant, he presupposes grace as revelation and, emphasizing the priority of this grace, sees it coming to categorical expression in any categorical experience, even if not specifically Christian or even religious. In all this, we see a progressive emphasis on the dynamic unifying side of his thought, through which emphasis he tried to resolve some of the tensions that had emerged in his earlier work. Nevertheless, some problems remain. In order to maintain the gratuity of grace, Rahner insists on pure nature as at least a limit concept. Yet he cannot define the essential content of this concept; neither can he define a conceivable natural end for man. He similarly insists that the effect of the supernatural existential is a radicalizing of natural human transcendence; yet his definition of man's transcendental experience as "pure openness" to absolutely all seems to leave little room for such a radical elevation. Finally, his emphasis on the intrinsic priority of transcendentally given grace, which he interprets as revelation, makes it difficult to understand how man remains in any sense

---

[47] *Grundkurs*, 138.

really free before God's grace (especially if it is grace that effects its own acceptance) or why the evangelical proclamation of the Gospel is truly necessary. This problem brings us to a consideration of Rahner's understanding of the Christian mystery.

3. THE TRINITY

A. Early Thought

It was in the context of his discussion of the formal/quasi-formal causality of grace upon man that Rahner asserted that the traditional axiom that all works of the Trinity *ad extra* are common to the three persons of the Trinity need no longer apply to the workings of grace; in consequence, the soul's knowledge of God is not just by appropriation but involves a mysterious knowledge of the three persons in relation to the soul itself. This change of perspective enabled Rahner to appeal to man's experience of grace in order to explain the distinctions of the three divine persons as modes of the one divine mystery and to affirm the identity of the economic and immanent Trinity. It is this affirmation that formed the foundational axiom of Rahner's trinitarian theology and that allowed him to argue that the Trinity is no longer proposed to our belief only on the testimony of an external witness, but actually can be experienced by man in grace. Indeed, by studying his own subjectivity under grace, man not only can find the ground for his belief but also can know the truth of God even unto the inner-trinitarian life. In all this, we saw operational the unifying and dynamic tendency of Rahner's thought together with his continually stronger emphasis on the priority of transcendentally given grace.

Notwithstanding his repeated affirmation of the identity of the economic and immanent Trinity and his consequent stress on the unifying relationship between God and the world, we noted how Rahner did seem to make a distinction between the economic and immanent Trinity and therefore simultaneously emphasized the diversity of God and the world. We observed this distinction in his assertion that the (economic) missions of the divine persons are based on and thus distinct from their (immanent) processions;

in his linguistic distinction between the "three (economic) modes of presence" *(drei verschiedenen Gegebenheitsweisen)* and the "three (immanent) manners of subsistence" *(drei distinkten Subsistenzweisen);* in his restriction of a trinitarian "thou" to the economy of salvation; and finally but significantly in his continued use of the two distinct terms *immanent* and *economic* to describe the Trinity, for if they were really identical, there would be no reason to continue to use two words to distinguish between them. Here again, therefore, we saw a tension emerging between Rahner's two views of the Trinity, a tension that is not interpreted correctly as a simple oversight or a contradiction within his theology but is rather, I would maintain, again the consequence of his foundational view of reality as *Schwebe.*

B. Grundkurs

In his later works, Rahner never really returned to the doctrine of the Trinity, notwithstanding his earlier insistence on its importance. In *Grundkurs,* this central Christian mystery receives only a brief four-page summary, which in itself is indicative of the change of emphasis in Rahner's later theology. This later unifying tendency is also apparent in that he reemphasizes the identity of the economic and immanent Trinity, makes no mention of the difference between economic missions and immanent processions, and speaks of only three modes of presence *(Gegebenheitsweisen).*

If we make and hold radically to the presupposition that the Trinity in the history of salvation and revelation is the "immanent" Trinity because in God's self-communication to his creation through grace and incarnation he really gives himself, then we can say in both the collective and individual history of salvation there appears in immediacy to us not some numinous powers or other that represent God, but there appears and is truly present the one God himself. Insofar as he comes as the salvation that divinizes us, we call him really and truly the "Holy Spirit." Insofar as in the concrete historicity of our existence God is present for us in Jesus Christ, we call him "Logos" or the Son in an absolute sense. Insofar as this very God, who comes to us as Spirit and as Logos, is and always remains the ineffable holy mystery, we call him God, the Father. Insofar as in the Spirit, in the Logos, and in the Father we are dealing with a God who gives himself in the strictest sense and not something else, we must say in the strictest sense and equally of the Spirit, of the Logos, and of the Father that they are one and the same God.

Insofar as the modes of God's presence as Spirit, Son, and Father do not signify the same modes of presence *for us,* these three modes of presence for us are to be distinguished strictly. Father, Son, and Spirit are first of all not the same for us, but insofar as these modes of presence of one and the same God for us may not nullify the real self-communication of God, the three modes of presence of one and the same God must belong to him as one and the same God. Hence, the assertions that one and the same God is present for us as Father, Son, and Holy Spirit are to be understood and made in the strict sense as assertions about God as he is in himself, for otherwise they would basically not be assertions about God's self-communication. "In the Trinity in the economy and history of salvation and revelation, we have already experienced the immanent Trinity as it is in itself."[48]

It is only through this doctrine that we can take with radical seriousness the simple statement, so very incomprehensible and so very self-evident, that God himself as the abiding and holy mystery not only is the God of infinite distance but also wants to be the God of absolute closeness in a true self-communication. Here, says Rahner, lies the real meaning of the doctrine of the Trinity.

C. Conclusion

In his earlier trinitarian theology and in that of *Grundkurs,* Rahner maintains both the identity of the immanent and economic Trinity and simultaneously somehow their distinction, simply leaving the tension unresolved. Moreover, another tension also becomes apparent in this context. In light of his own ontology of grace, which, as we saw, assigned to man a permanent supernatural existential, it is difficult to see why a verbal historical revelation of the economic Trinity is absolutely necessary for man. Yet Rahner tries hard to ground man's internal experience of the Trinity in

---

[48] *Grundkurs,* 142.

history and to bind it to God's definitive and irrevocable revelation in Jesus, the absolute bringer of salvation. In doing this, he not only is trying to remain true to the teaching of the church concerning the necessity of revelation but also is remaining true to the structure of his own thought based in the *conversio ad phantasma*. However, the tension remains and once again can be understood only as an example of that structure of thought through which Rahner can change perspectives, emphasizing in turn unity and distinction as required without thereby contradicting himself.

In order to see how Rahner justifies the concrete revelation of Jesus Christ, we must first look at role of history and revelation in his theology.

4. History and Revelation

A. Early Thought

In our analysis of his early theory of revelation, we saw how Rahner unified the whole process of revelation under the one analogous concept of "word of God." From the inner "word" of grace, through the categorical "word" of revelation strictly speaking, to the church and ultimately the sacraments, the whole work of God's self-communication to man can be described as various degrees of the one "word" spoken by God to his spiritual-physical creation. Through this unified approach to revelation in which, true to the basic structure of man (as *Schwebe*), the inner word of grace and the outer word of official revelation are linked intrinsically in a relationship of unity in diversity, Rahner sought to avoid both the immanentism of modernism and a merely extrinsic concept of revelation. But within this theory of revelation, a characteristic tension became apparent, for in analyzing the relationship between the inner and outer words of God's self-communication Rahner seemed to propose a double notion of revelation. On the one hand, he seemed to stress a relationship of mutual priority between the objectively given outer word of revelation to which the graced subjectivity of the individual corresponds, thereby guaranteeing human freedom before the categorical outer word; on the other hand, he seemed to see the inner word of grace as essentially primary within the relationship of mutual causality coming only to expression in the outer word or sacrament, thereby guaranteeing the *ex opere operato* of the church and the sacraments. Once again, then, we are faced with a tension or double emphasis that can be grounded and maintained only in light of Rahner's dialectical analogy. It is this structure of thought that now, in the context of his revelation theory, enables Rahner to explain the relationship of the two words of revelation *both* as a relationship of simultaneous mutual priority in which both words are related through final causality (and in which the distinction within the unity is emphasized) *and simultaneously* as a relationship of formal causality in which the outer word is only an expression of the permanently given inner word (in which the unity is emphasized over the distinction). Furthermore, we noted again a development in Rahner's thought in this matter. In his earlier work (especially in *Hörer 1*), the former emphasis appeared to take precedence with the stress on man's elevated subjectivity as the condition of possibility necessary for him to hear the objectively given external word of revelation. However, from the early 1960s (already clearly noticeable in *Hörer 2*) and progressively more after the Second Vatican Council, Rahner stressed the second aspect.

Regarding the related issue of sacramental causality, we noted the same double emphasis in the relationship between the inner word of grace and the outer sacramental word, noticing how Rahner, true to the foundational structure of his thought, oscillated between the two perspectives. Thus, although in his later works the second (more dynamic and unifying) perspective begins to take precedence, it is never to the exclusion of the first (more static and distinguishing) perspective, and therefore Rahner maintained a balance that his commentators all too often have lost.

Finally, we noted again the important development in Rahner's theory of revelation in which, presupposing the priority of grace and interpreting it now explicitly as supernatural revelation, Rahner argued not only that grace expresses itself in the outer word of official revelation, but also that because grace always occurs in history and therefore always is mediated historically, it can come to categorical expression in any historical word. Thus, any historical mediation, even if not explicitly Christian, can be interpreted as historical revelation (even when categorically false) under the horizon of grace. However, even in this somewhat radical approach to revelation, we noted that the structure of Rahner's dialectical analogy prevented him from losing the balance of his foundational perspective, for even within this heavily dynamic and unifying view of revelation Rahner continued to insist (in line with the conceptualizing, distinguishing side of his thought) on the necessity of the external official word of revelation as the final symbolic cause of all grace and as the hermeneutical key by which categorically correct and incorrect historical mediations of transcendental grace can be distinguished.

B. Grundkurs

In *Grundkurs,* Rahner offers the clearest expression of this radical later approach to revelation. In line with the prevailing emphasis of the book, he approaches the whole issue of revelation from an analysis of the transcendental experience of man. Presupposing the problem of the universal salvific will of God and the particularity of historical Christianity, he poses the question: If from the very beginning God with his absolute reality already has communicated himself in grace as the innermost center of everything that can be, what can still take place in a history of salvation and revelation? The solution to this problem is found in the mutually conditioning relationship of history and transcendence: "man as subject and as person is a historical being in such a way that he is historical precisely *as* a transcendent subject; his subjective essence of unlimited transcendentality is mediated [*vermittelt*] *historically* to him in his knowledge and in his free self-realization."[49] If, on the one hand, the realization of transcendentality takes place historically, and if, on the other hand, true historicity has its ground and the condition of its possibility in the transcendentality of man himself, then the only way to reconcile these two facts is to say that history is ultimately the history of transcendentality itself. This is true not only of the individual history of an individual person but also of the history of social units, of peoples, and of

---

[49] *Grundkurs,* 145.

the one human race. The supernatural existential, therefore, also has a history. If man is always and inescapably and from the very beginning the event of God's absolute self-communication and is at the same time a historical being both individually and collectively, it follows that this ever-present and supernatural existential itself has a history individually and collectively, which is at once the single history of both salvation and redemption.[50]

The universal history of salvation is coexistent with the history of the world and is also and at the same time the history of revelation, for grace as the self-communication of God is in fact nothing other than revelation in its fundamental sense.[51] The justification for such a position is to be found in traditional Catholic dogmatics. According to the Christian view of things, man, despite original sin, always and everywhere has the genuine possibility of encountering God. There is a serious, effective, and universal salvific will of God. But it is a self-evident axiom for the New Testament and for the later teaching of the church that salvation takes place only where there is faith in the Word of God revealing himself.[52] If, then, there can be salvation and hence also faith everywhere in history, then a supernatural revelation of God to mankind must have been at work everywhere in the history of the human race. "In this sense the world is our mediation to God in his self-communication in grace, and in this sense there is for Christianity no sacral and separate realm where alone God is to be found."[53]

Categorical human history indeed can be, in an unthematic way, the historical mediation of the transcendental experience of God as supernatural revelation. But this history of the transcendental revelation of God strives necessarily toward a higher and more comprehensive interpretation of man, and consequently it will be ever more intensely an explicitly religious self-interpreta-

---

[50] See *Sacramentum Mundi III*, s.v. "Offenbarung," 834; Rahner and Ratzinger, *Offenbarung und Überlieferung*, 14.

[51] Rahner developed this idea of grace as revelation, which he heavily stressed in *Grundkurs*, from the mid-1960s onward: see chapter 5, note 29.

[52] *Grundkurs*, 152. Rahner had grounded this assertion earlier: "Was ist Häresie?" *Schriften*, 5: 532; "Der eine Jesus Christus," *Schriften*, 12: 255, 273–74.

[53] *Grundkurs*, 156. Ratzinger, "Vom Verstehen des Glaubens," 183, is critical of Rahner's notion of universal salvific history and especially of his idea of anonymous Christianity.

tion of this supernatural, transcendental, and revelatory experience of God.[54] The attempt is made in every religion, at least on man's part, to mediate the original, unreflexive, and nonobjective revelation historically, to make it reflexive, and to interpret it in propositions. In all religions, there are individual moments when such mediation is, by God's grace, successful. But because of man's guilt these attempts are only partially successful; they are always intermixed with error. Whenever and wherever God himself directs this objectification in the dynamism of his self-communication in such a way that it remains pure, and when this purity of revelation in its objectification is shown to be legitimate for us by what we call signs, then we have what is called public, official, particular, and ecclesially constituted revelation and its history. To be sure, this mode of the history of revelation is only a segment of the universal, categorical history of revelation. It is the most successful instance of the necessary self-interpretation of transcendental revelation, or, better, "it is the full realization of the essence of both revelations and their single history, both transcendental and categorical revelation in the unity and purity of their essence."[55]

Not until the unsurpassable event of the historical self-objectification of God's self-communication to the world in Jesus Christ do we have an eschatological event that absolutely precludes any historical corruption or any distorted interpretation in the further history of categorical revelation and of false religion. In Jesus

---

[54] "Einleitende Bemerkungen," *Schriften*, 10: 402; "Überlegungen zum personalen Vollzug," *Schriften*, 10: 410; "Glaube und Sakrament," *Schriften*, 16: 393, 396; *Sacramentum Mundi III*, s.v. "Offenbarung," 833, 836. See chapter 5, note 33. Here again the operation of Rahner's dialectical analogy is apparent: On the one hand, he insists that grace *necessarily* seeks its highest expression, yet, on the other hand, he maintains that God's act of self-communication in revelation is the act of man's supreme freedom. Moreover, although he maintains that man, under the supernatural existential, is always the event of grace (dynamic view), he nevertheless and simultaneously asserts the necessity of even greater explicitization of this experience (conceptual view).

[55] *Grundkurs*, 159, 138, 149, 162; *Sacramentum Mundi IV*, s.v. "Selbstmitteilung Gottes," 224–5; "Glaubensakt und Glaubensinhalt," *Schriften*, 15: 158; "Zum Verhältnis zwischen Theologie und heutigen Wissenschaften," *Schriften*, 10: 108. Ratzinger, "Vom Verstehen des Glaubens," 182–83, is critical of Rahner's notion of categorical revelation, arguing that it relativizes the importance and unicity of the Old Testament.

Christ, then, we have a criterion for distinguishing, in the concrete history of religion, between what is a human misunderstanding of the transcendental experience of God and what is the
legitimate interpretation of this experience.

> But this means that the event of Christ becomes for us the only
> really tangible *caesura* in the universal history of salvation and reve-
> lation, and it enables us to distinguish a particular and official his-
> tory of revelation within the universal history of revelation before
> Christ.[56]

C. Conclusion

Although Rahner's terminology and method clearly have
changed in *Grundkurs* from those used in his earlier works, the
same fundamental structure is apparent in both: the inner word
of grace exists in a relationship of mutual priority with the outer
categorical word, constituting a characteristic unity in diversity.
However, the change of perspective in his understanding of revelation that began in the mid-1960s comes to its clearest expression
in *Grundkurs*. Moving away from the unity in diversity of the
internal word of grace and the external word of revelation, and
presupposing grace as revelation, Rahner stresses the mutual priority between transcendental grace and any categorical event that
mediates grace to itself. This enables him to assert strongly the
identity of world history and salvation history, the possibility of
salvation through faith in revelation even for those people who
have no knowledge of the Gospel, and his theory of an anonymous Christianity. Yet nevertheless even in this late work,
Rahner continues to insist on the necessity and validity of what
he calls official public revelation as the end to which all grace
tends as its final cause and the hermeneutical key by which correct
and incorrect historical mediations of transcendental grace can be
distinguished. As we have seen, according to Rahner this official
revelation became definitively manifest in Christ. It is to Christ,
therefore, that we must look to see how Rahner tries to explain
the necessity of historical revelation.

---

[56] *Grundkurs,* 177.

5. CHRISTOLOGY

A. Early Thought

(i) Christology from Above

It was in the context of searching for a theological justification for the Catholic practice of adoration of the Sacred Heart of Jesus that Rahner first developed his symbol Christology. Through this symbol theory, he initially was concerned to stress the unity of Christ's human nature with the Logos so that the whole body of Jesus, right down to its individual members (for example, his heart) and all his actions, can be interpreted as real expressions of God in the world and thus worthy of adoration. However, Rahner's symbol theory was nuanced; in his description of the relationship between the symbol and the symbolized, a characteristically twofold structure emerged. This structure was both particularly clear and of great importance in the context of his Christology, for it allowed him not only to stress the unity of the Logos and the humanity of Christ, but also simultaneously and equally to stress the real diversity of the humanity of Christ and the reality of Jesus' human self-consciousness and freedom in relation to God. Through his theory of symbol, therefore, with the equally important assertion that, in the terms of God's relationship with the world, independence and dependence grow in direct and not inverse proportion, Rahner addressed the difficult Christological issues of the immutability of the Logos and the mutability implied in the incarnation (God really becomes in the "other" and yet remains truly God, *actus purus*); the person/nature distinction of the Chalcedonian definition (God's self-utterance—as content—is the man Jesus; the self-utterance—as event—is the Hypostatic Union); and the significance of the death and resurrection of Jesus for all men (God is affected by history, and his salvific will becomes irrevocable in the historical Christ event and yet always remains immutable in himself). We saw Rahner continually oscillating between the two poles of unity and diversity implied in his symbol theory, an oscillation grounded in his foundational thought, but we also saw the tensions inherent in this theology. If the Logos really expressed himself in Jesus' human nature, it is not at all clear how Jesus could ever experience dread, trembling, or forsakenness. Similarly, Rahner, despite all his warnings about Monophysitism and bound to his definition of the nature of symbol, had to assert that the reality of Jesus was God himself, and therefore his Christology from above seemed to tend precisely toward the Monophysitism he had sought to avoid.

(ii) Christology from Below

In his later Christology from below, Rahner did not deny what he had written previously, but he had grown wary of the traditional descent Christology with its mythological overtones. Though maintaining the truth of the traditional "ontic" descent Christology, he tried to develop a new "ontological" Christology. Such an attempt was, he maintained, both necessary in order to make Christology more intelligible and justifiable on the grounds that a translation of either Christology into the terms of the other was both possible and legitimate. Very concerned to preserve the human experience of Christ, he warned against a Monophysite interpretation of the phrase "Jesus is God," and, relying on the real diversity of natures in Christ, he studied the human in Jesus as far as possible. Nevertheless, he aimed at a reconciliation with the traditional descent Christology along two paths: by showing Christ as the culmination of mankind's evolutionary history and by analyzing the historical evidence about Jesus' consciousness of his person and mission, which grounds the later faith of the church.

α. Evolutionary Christology

As we saw in studying Rahner's understanding of matter and spirit, his notion of matter as "frozen spirit" and an evolutionary worldview can be reconciled only on the double precondition that matter exists only for and in view of spirit and that God, as the ground of all inner-worldly becoming, is immanent within the process precisely by being transcendent over it. Thus, true to the dialectical structure of his thought, Rahner maintained both the unity of matter and spirit and of God and the world, within the dynamism of the evolutionary process, and simultaneously the

distinction of each from the other. In his evolutionary Christology, he took this line of thought a stage further, arguing that
God's self-communication in grace and ultimately in the incarnation was logically the final stage and inner rationale of the whole
unified evolutionary process. Thus, within this perspective,
Rahner defined the "savior" as both the unique climax of the
evolutionary process, the point where man accepts God's self-
communication radically and irreversibly, and as the definitive
self-communication of God wherein the Logos, in creating and
accepting his corporeality, expresses himself and lets himself be
present in the world. The Hypostatic Union is the highest possible event within the process of God's self-communication to man
and as such, within a historical evolutionary process that lives
from its end, is the final cause of the grace given to man and the
irrevocable expression of God's salvific will.

β. Consciousness Christology

Taking the event of the incarnation as that point at which God
accepts the world irrevocably and at which the world, through
God's self-bestowal, definitively accepts God's offering of himself,
Rahner defined the "savior" as the *absolute* bringer or mediator
of salvation. Given his foundational assertion that being is presence-to-self, he maintained that it would be inconceivable that
such an absolute savior should not be conscious of his identity
and that it was perfectly legitimate to examine the Scriptures for
evidence about Jesus of Nazareth's understanding of himself. Indeed, when we do so, we find that even before Easter Jesus did
see himself as the absolute bringer of salvation, and this self-consciousness is enough to ground the later Christological definitions
of the church.

Insofar as the historical Jesus did see himself as the absolute
bringer of salvation and was, therefore, aware of his divinity, it
is not at all mythological to assert that Jesus in his human self-
consciousness possessed the *visio beatifica*. Indeed, given that the
incarnation is to be seen as the incommensurable high point of
the Creator-creature relationship, Rahner asserted that the *visio
beatifica* was in fact an intrinsic constitutive element of the Hypostatic Union. However, in order to make room for the genuine

human self-consciousness of Jesus and his feelings of agony and forsakenness (also witnessed to by the Scriptures), Rahner argued in his later writings that it was necessary to reinterpret the *visio beatifica* as a *visio immediata,* which Christ possessed without it thereby having a beatific effect on his human nature. The operation of this *visio immediata* on the human self-consciousness of Jesus was to be considered as similar to the operation of the preapprehension of the horizon of all being in all human consciousness—that is, as an all-pervading, unthematized, subjective condition that is objectified only gradually and conceptually in the course of a man's historical development. We noted that the metaphysical grounding for the distinction Rahner made between the *visio beatifica* and the *visio immediata* was not at all clear (especially because the *visio beatifica* was taken traditionally as signifying precisely an "immediate vision" of God). Neither was it clear why, if the *visio immediata* was the intrinsic constitutive element of the Hypostatic Union, all men did not have an obediential potency for the Hypostatic Union (that is, to become Jesus). Nevertheless, in all this we clearly saw once again that Rahner was only being true to the dialectical structure of his foundational thought. Thus (in line with the dynamic, unifying side of his thought), he asserted that Jesus in the *visio immediata* was conscious of his unity with the Logos, a consciousness that (in line with the conceptualizing, distinguishing side of his thought) when conceptualized was really diverse from that of the Logos and therefore genuinely human and free before God.

B. Grundkurs

In *Grundkurs,* 135 pages are devoted explicitly to Christology, which therefore without exaggeration may be considered as the book's center and culmination: the pages on God, revelation, and salvation history preparing for the section on Christology and the treatments of the church and the sacraments devolving from it. In this Christological center, Rahner deliberately brings together his descent and ascent Christologies. Without claiming that they are unified—they "appear in a somewhat mixed manner"—he nonetheless ascribes a proportionate significance to a descent Christology alongside an ascent Christology and sees an advantage to the "mutual illumination" afforded by the two "aspects and methods."[57]

(i) Christology Within an Evolutionary Worldview

Because the Christian believes that all things are the creation of one and the same God, he also believes that there is an inner similarity in all things despite their variety and consequently that matter and spirit are not to be regarded as absolutely disparate realities. Matter and spirit condition one another reciprocally in a relationship that is not simply static, but that itself has a history. They form a unity in distinction,[58] and if we keep in mind the temporal duration of the relationship between spirit and matter, then without hesitation we can say that it is of the intrinsic nature of matter to develop through a process of active self-transcendence toward spirit.[59]

The specific characteristic of the reality that comes to be in man is his presence to himself and his relationship to the absolute totality of reality, and if this characteristic is seen as the goal of the history of the cosmos itself, it is clear that the world finds itself in man and in him makes itself its own object. "The one material cosmos is the *single* body as it were of a *multiple* self-presence of this very cosmos and its orientation toward its absolute and infinite ground."[60]

These beginnings of the self-presence of the cosmos in the spirit of individual persons has a history that is still ongoing, and this process must have a final result, which according to Christian

---

[57] *Grundkurs,* 177.

[58] The fundamental unity in diversity of matter and spirit is, as we have seen, a fundamental concern for Rahner: Rahner and Overhage, *Das Problem der Hominisation,* 22–23, 49–50; "Die Einheit von Geist und Materie," *Schriften,* 6: 187, 190, 206, 214; "Der Leib in der Heilsordnung," *Schriften,* 12: 415, 423. This unity in diversity is metaphysically grounded in his understanding of sensibility as the being/form of matter: *Geist,* 104, 107, 138, 142, 143, 157, 252, 254; *Hörer 1,* 157, 208. See chapter 4, notes 32 and 33.

[59] *Grundkurs,* 185. Another familiar Rahnerian assertion: Rahner and Overhage, *Das Problem der Hominisation,* 78; "Die Einheit von Geist und Materie," *Schriften,* 6: 213; "Die Christologie innerhalb einer evolutiven Weltanschauung," *Schriften,* 5: 186, 191, 214; "Vom Geheimnis des Lebens," *Schriften,* 6: 182; "Christologie im Rahmen," *Schriften,* 9: 230.

[60] *Grundkurs,* 190.

teaching is not achieved until the cosmos not only is something created but also receives the ultimate self-communication of its own ground in the spiritual creatures that are its goal and its high point. This self-communication takes place in what we call "grace" while it is still in its historical process and "glory" when it reaches fulfillment.[61]

It is only from this perspective that the place of Christology in such an evolutionary worldview can be determined. God's self-communication is a communication to the freedom and inter-communication of the many cosmic subjects, and it can take place only in a *free* acceptance by free subjects and indeed in a *common* history. Hence, the event of this self-communication is to be understood as an event that takes place historically at ever-definite points in space and time, and from there it is addressed to others as a call to their freedom. In a genuine history of a dialogue in freedom between God and the human race, therefore, a point is conceivable at which God's self-communication to the world is not yet concluded, but the fact of this self-communication is given unambiguously already, and the success, the victory, and the irreversibility of this process have become manifest in and in spite of this ongoing dialogue of freedom.[62] This point is precisely what Rahner calls the "absolute savior." And insofar as a historical movement lives by virtue of its end even in its beginnings,[63] it is completely legitimate to understand the whole movement of God's self-communication as borne by this savior even when it is taking place prior to the event of the coming of that savior. Therefore, this savior must be at the same time both the absolute

---

[61] *Grundkurs*, 192;. Grace as the end of the evolutionary process: "Vom Geheimnis des Lebens," *Schriften*, 6: 180, 184; *Sacramentum Mundi II*, s.v. "Jesus Christus," 942; "Christologie im Rahmen," *Schriften*, 9: 238. See chapter 6, note 47.

[62] *Grundkurs*, 195. In Christ is made manifest the irreversible victory of God's self-communication: "Wort und Eucharistie," *Schriften*, 4: 338; "Überlegungen zum personalen Vollzug," *Schriften*, 10: 415; *Sacramentum Mundi III*, s.v. "Offenbarung," 834–35; "Buch Gottes—Buch der Menschen," *Schriften*, 16: 282, 290; "Die Christologie innerhalb einer evolutiven Weltanschauung," *Schriften*, 5: 203. See chapter 6, note 51.

[63] *Grundkurs*, 195. That every historical process lives from its end: "Die Christologie innerhalb einer evolutiven Weltanschauung," *Schriften*, 5: 203; "Der eine Mittler," *Schriften*, 8: 230–31; *Sendung und Gnade*, 61; "Der eine Jesus Christus," *Schriften*, 12: 269.

promise of God to spiritual creatures as a whole and the acceptance of this self-communication by the savior, for otherwise history could not have reached its irreversible phase.

The absolute savior simply cannot be God himself as acting in
the world but must be part of the cosmos, a moment within its
history and indeed its climax. And this is precisely what the Christological dogma expresses: Jesus is truly man, truly a part of the
earth. He is a man who, just like us, receives in his human subjectivity the self-communication of God in grace, but who, in and
through what we call his obedience, his prayer, and freely accepted destiny to die, also lived out perfectly the acceptance of
the grace God bestowed on him. In Jesus, therefore, God did not
somehow disguise himself in human livery. Rather, in Jesus matter is borne by the Logos exactly as the soul is, and this matter is
part of the reality and the history of the cosmos. The Logos himself establishes this corporeal part of the world as his own reality,
both creating and accepting it at the same time. Hence, he establishes it as what is different from himself in such a way that this
very materiality expresses him and allows him to be present in his
world. "His laying hold of this part of the single material and
spiritual reality of the world can rightly be understood as the climax of that dynamism in which the self-transcendence of the
world as a whole is borne by the word of God."[64]

There is perhaps no particular difficulty in conceiving of the
history of the world and of spirit as the history of a self-transcendence into the life of God. But such an ultimate self-transcendence of the spirit into God is to be understood as taking place
in all spiritual subjects, for the realization of this ultimate self-
transcendence cannot be denied to an individual unless he closes
himself to it by his own fault. This presupposes, first, that this self-
transcendence toward the immediacy of God takes place in at
least one person and, second, that all men form one human race
in mutual intercommunication and therefore have a common
goal. Now how can this basic conception be incorporated into
the doctrine about the Hypostatic Union of a particular, individual human nature with the Logos? For Rahner, the incarnation
cannot be understood as the end and the goal of the world's reality without having recourse to the theory that the incarnation

---

[64] *Grundkurs,* 197.

itself is already an intrinsic moment and a condition for the universal bestowal of grace to spiritual creatures.[65] There is a mutual conditioning between the two realities: the intrinsic effect of the Hypostatic Union for the assumed humanity of the Logos consists precisely and really only in the very thing that is ascribed to all men as their goal and their fulfillment—namely, the immediate vision of God that the created, human soul of Christ enjoys.

> When God brings about man's self-transcendence into God through his absolute self-communication to all men in such a way that both elements constitute a promise to all men which is irrevocable and which has already reached fulfillment in one man, then we have precisely what is signified by Hypostatic Union.[66]

Grace in all of us and the Hypostatic Union in the one Jesus Christ can be understood only together, and as a unity they signify the one free decision of God for a supernatural order of salvation, for his self-communication. Every self-expression of God takes place through a finite reality, but as long as this finite mediation of the divine self-expression does not represent a reality of God himself in the strict and real sense, it is still basically provisional and surpassable because it is finite. If, therefore, the reality of Jesus—in whom as offer and as acceptance God's absolute self-communication to the whole human race is present for us—is to be the unsurpassable and definitive offer and acceptance, then we have to say: not only is it established by God, but it is God himself.[67]

(ii) Transcendental Christology

It is clear that a transcendental Christology cannot establish on its own a concrete relationship precisely to Jesus as the Christ, for the historical appearance of the absolute savior is a miracle that encounters us and cannot be deduced.[68] Transcendental Christology rather asks about the a priori possibilities in man that make the coming of the message of Christ possible. The procedure of

---

[65] *Grundkurs,* 199; "Die Christologie innerhalb einer evolutiven Weltanschauung," *Schriften,* 5: 208, 211; "Der eine Mittler," *Schriften,* 8: 230, 232, 235. See chapter 6, note 58.

[66] *Grundkurs,* 201.

[67] *Grundkurs,* 202.

[68] This affirmation stands in a certain tension with the idea that grace *necessarily* seeks its fullest expression.

transcendental Christology consists, therefore, first in an anthropology that asserts that man is understood as the existent of transcendental necessity who in every categorical act always transcends himself and as the categorical object toward the incomprehensible mystery that we call God. Second, man is understood as someone who dares to hope not merely that his existence is borne by this all-pervasive mystery as an asymptotic goal, but rather that this mystery gives itself as the fulfillment of the highest claim of existence. Third, within the unity of transcendentality and historicity in human existence, God's self-communication and the hope for it are necessarily mediated historically. Fourth, this most courageous act of hope searches in history for that self-promise of God that loses its ambivalence for the human race as such, becomes final and irreversible, and is the end in an eschatological sense. And finally, the categoriality of God's irreversible offer of himself to the world as a whole, which allows this irrevocable offer to be present historically and which mediates to us the hope that corresponds to this offer, can only be a man who, on the one hand, surrenders every inner-worldly future in death and who, on the other hand, in this acceptance of death is shown to have been accepted by God finally and definitively.[69]

Transcendental Christology, then, works toward the notion of an absolute savior, but it does not and cannot ask the question whether there has already existed in history a savior as we are understanding the term or who he is concretely. Having, therefore, established the transcendental outline of an absolute savior whom we would expect, it becomes our task to look toward history to see whether we can believe that the event of an absolute mediator of salvation and of the historical concreteness of God's absolute self-communication to the world has taken place precisely and only in Jesus of Nazareth.

(iii) The History of Jesus of Nazareth

Because traditional Christological assertions always have a historical dimension, they also are burdened inevitably with all the dif-

---

[69] Ratzinger, "Vom Verstehen des Glaubens," 185, notes the stronger emphasis in *Grundkurs* on transcendental Christology and criticizes Rahner for making it the "yardstick" against which traditional Christology is measured for its adequacy; H. Meynell, "Rahner's *Grundkurs*," *New Blackfriars* 61 (1980), 87, is also highly critical of Rahner's Christology.

ficulties and uncertainties of knowing an event that lies far back in history. However, a faith that would grasp in Jesus the absolute savior cannot be uninterested a priori in the history of Jesus before the resurrection and in his self-understanding. Otherwise, faith would create the Christ of salvation on the occasion of Jesus of Nazareth, and this Christ would then be mythological. It is true that we cannot write a biography of Jesus, but this inability does not justify the conclusion that we know nothing about Jesus historically. Taking into account, therefore, what a subject is precisely as subject and how and to what extent a subject is capable of verbal self-reflection, we can say that, on the one hand, the self-understanding of the preresurrection Jesus may not contradict the Christian understanding of his person, but also that, on the other hand, it must not be required a priori and with certainty that his preresurrection self-understanding, in itself and especially for us, already coincides positively and unambiguously with the content of Christological faith. In fact, Rahner argues, we really need only to establish that two theses are historically credible in order to establish the grounds of faith for orthodox Christianity's whole Christology. First, that Jesus saw himself not merely as one among many prophets but understood himself rather as the eschatological prophet, as the absolute and definitive savior. Second, that Jesus' claim is credible for us when, from the perspective of our transcendental experience in grace, we look in faith to that event that mediates the savior in his total reality: the resurrection of Jesus. All other assertions about Jesus as the Christ can be left to faith itself as the content of faith.

α. The Self-Understanding of the Preresurrection Jesus

Jesus had a human self-consciousness that stood at a distance from God in freedom, in obedience, and in worship.[70] Without prejudice to the ultimate continuity in his consciousness of a radical and unique closeness to God, Jesus' objectifying and verbalizing

---

[70] Rahner established this idea, as we have seen, in his earlier Christological works: "Probleme der Christologie," *Schriften,* 1: 178; "'Ich glaube an Jesus Christus,'" *Schriften,* 8: 215; *Sacramentum Mundi II,* s.v. "Jesus Christus," 948; "Kirchliche Christologie," *Schriften,* 9: 210–11; Rahner and Thüsing, *Christologie,* 53.

self-consciousness has a history. "It shares the horizons of understanding and the conceptualizations of his milieu, and in regard
to himself, not just in 'condescension' to others. It learns and it
has new and surprising experiences. It is threatened by ultimate
crises of identity."[71]

Whatever else remains unclear about Jesus' self-consciousness,
it is not in doubt that the preresurrection Jesus preached the im-
minence of "God's Kingdom" as the "now" present situation of
an absolute decision for or against salvation. In this sense, it is true
that Jesus proclaimed the Kingdom of God and not himself, but
it is clear that he perceived the closeness of God's kingdom as
inseparably connected with his person. It has to be added immediately that with this closeness of God's kingdom, which Jesus
proclaimed as new and as not yet present until then, we are not
dealing with a merely relatively greater closeness than before.
Such an understanding is impossible just on the grounds of Jesus'
imminent expectation. He clearly perceived himself as the final
call of God; after him, no other call follows or can follow because
of the radical nature in which God, no longer represented by
something else, promises himself. We can conclude from this perception, therefore, that Jesus experienced a relationship to God
that he understood as new and unique in comparison with the
relationship to God held by other humans, but which he nevertheless considered to be exemplary for other humans. At least in
this sense, the preresurrection Jesus already knew himself to be
the absolute and unsurpassable savior.[72]

β. The Resurrection of Jesus

a. Intellectual Presuppositions for Understanding the
   Resurrection

The death and resurrection of Jesus can be understood only if the
intrinsic relationship of the two realities and their unity are kept

---

[71] *Grundkurs,* 246. That Jesus' self-consciousness develops through his historical life has been established already: see chapter 6, note 66. See also "Zum
Theologischen Begriff der Konkupiszenz," *Schriften,* 1: 397 ff., for Rahner's
earlier perspective on Christ's consciousness.

[72] *Grundkurs,* 251. This is consistent with Rahner's earlier thought: *Mysterium*

clearly in mind, for the death of Jesus is such that by its very nature it is subsumed into the resurrection. The resurrection does not mean the beginning of a new period in the life of Jesus; it means rather and precisely the permanent, redeemed, final, and definitive validity of the single and unique life of Jesus, who achieved the permanent and final validity of his life precisely through his death in freedom and obedience.[73] From this perspective, it is also clear that "person" and "cause" ("cause" in the sense of that to which one is dedicated) may not be separated in the discussion of resurrection and in the interpretation of this term. The real "cause" of a person is what is actualized and realized in the concrete existence of the person, and hence "resurrection" is the validity of the cause of the person in the abiding nature of that cause. If, therefore, the resurrection of Jesus is the permanent validity of his person and his cause, and if this person and cause together do not mean the survival of just any person and his history, but rather the *victoriousness* of Jesus' claim to be the absolute savior, then *faith* in his resurrection is an intrinsic element of this resurrection itself, for if there is no faith in the person of Jesus, then his cause has not been victorious. "In *this* sense we not only can but must say that Jesus is risen into the faith of his disciples."[74]

b. Transcendental Hope in the Resurrection as the Horizon for Understanding the Resurrection of Jesus

An act of hope in one's own resurrection is something that takes place in every person by transcendental necessity either in the mode of free acceptance or of free rejection, for every person wants to survive in some final and definitive sense and experiences this claim in his acts of freedom and responsibility. *Resurrection* is, therefore, the term that, in view of man's concrete

---

Salutis II, s.v. "Der dreifaltige Gott," 357; *Sacramentum Mundi II,* s.v. "Jesus Christus," 933, 945; "Kirchliche Christologie," *Schriften,* 9: 214–15, 218; Rahner and Thüsing, *A New Christology,* 9–10; Rahner and Thüsing, *Christologie,* 66.

[73] *Grundkurs,* 262.

[74] *Grundkurs,* 263; Rahner and Thüsing, *A New Christology,* 25; Rahner and Thüsing, *Christologie,* 38. Ratzinger, "Vom Verstehen des Glaubens," 186, rejects this notion of faith as an essential moment of the resurrection.

situation, promises the abiding validity of his single and entire existence. This assertion of a transcendental hope in resurrection does not deny that we are more successful in actually objectifying this self-understanding in the light of the experience of the resurrection of Jesus, for the circle between transcendental and categorical is everywhere operative, according to Rahner's whole understanding of man as *Schwebe*. But this transcendental hope in the resurrection is the horizon of understanding for experiencing the resurrection of Jesus in faith, and we are dependent on the apostolic witness to the resurrection only to the extent that it categorically mediates our transcendental hope to itself.[75]

c. The Resurrection Experience of the First Disciples

Presupposing this transcendental horizon of hope in resurrection, we are now in a position to analyze the apostolic witness itself. Beginning with the simple confessional formula "he is risen," an analysis of the resurrection texts shows that the original witnesses were conscious of the peculiar nature of the Easter experience: this experience is given from without, not produced by oneself, and is different from the visionary experiences that were quite familiar. It is given only in faith, and yet it grounds and justifies this faith. The witness necessarily has to be passed on to others, and hence it bestows a unique task on these witnesses. Witness is being given, then, to an experience that is strictly sui generis. One can refuse to believe these witnesses, but one cannot do so on the grounds that one understands their experience better or because these witnesses have interpreted falsely a religious phenomenon that is familiar to us elsewhere. Furthermore, if by historically accessible facts is understood something that in its own existence belongs to the realm of our normal, empirical world of time and space as a phenomenon that occurs frequently, "then it is obvious that the resurrection of Jesus neither can be nor intends to be a 'historical' event."[76] Finally, in abstract, conceptual theory, an

---

[75] *Grundkurs,* 270–71.

[76] *Grundkurs,* 272. Ratzinger, "Vom Verstehen des Glaubens," 186, is critical of Rahner for undervaluing the historicity of the resurrection; H. Meynell, "Rahner's *Grundkurs,*" *New Blackfriars* 61 (1980), 87, also criticizes Rahner's understanding of the resurrection.

affirmation of our hope in resurrection *and* a rejection of the apostolic experience of this resurrection in Jesus is logically conceivable; consequently, there can be a disbelief in the resurrection of Jesus that does not entail guilt.[77]

What was really experienced, witnessed, and believed with the resurrection was God's acceptance of this Jesus and God's ratification of the permanent validity of his claim: namely, that there was present with Jesus a new and unsurpassable closeness of God that on its part would prevail victoriously and was inseparable from Jesus. By the resurrection, then, Jesus was vindicated as the absolute savior. He was not a "servant" in the ongoing line of the prophets that may never be identified with God; hence, he was "Son." He did not bring *a* word from God; he was *the* Word of God.

d. The Soteriological Significance of the Death and Resurrection of Jesus

At least in the late New Testament soteriological Christology, the death of Jesus obviously is regarded as a cause of our salvation in a true sense, but in what precise sense? Rahner, as we have seen, presupposes that human history is a *single* history and that the destiny of one person has significance for others. If, then, God wills and brings forth a man who in his reality is God's final word, if this offer is grasped in history itself, if this offer is and can be final only if it prevails victoriously, if this acceptance can take place only in and through the single history of this man, a history that becomes final and definitive through death, and if, besides all this, God's word and offer is complete only when man's acceptance and response to that offer become manifest historically as accepted by God in what we call "resurrection," *then* we can and must say that this eschatological word has been actualized in the life of Jesus and is historically present for us in his free acceptance of his death. This death *as* entered into in free obedience and as surrendering life completely to God reaches fulfillment and becomes historically tangible for us only in the resurrection.

---

[77] The problem is, of course, how Rahner can jump to this factual judgment from what is only a possibility.

The life and death of Jesus taken together, then, are the "cause" of God's salvific will . . . insofar as this salvific will establishes itself really and irrevocably in this life and death—in other words, insofar as the life and death of Jesus . . . possess a causality of a quasi-sacramental and real-symbolic nature. In this causality what is signified, in this case God's salvific will, posits the sign, in this case the death of Jesus along with his resurrection, and in and through the sign it causes what is signified.[78]

If the death of Jesus is understood in this way, perhaps it becomes clear that its soteriological significance, when correctly understood, is implied already in the experience of the resurrection of Jesus and moreover that the "late" soteriology in the New Testament, when correctly understood, is a legitimate but nevertheless somewhat secondary and derivative expression of the salvific significance of the death of Jesus. For it works with concepts that are applied extrinsically as a possible but not absolutely indispensable interpretation of the original experience of this salvific significance, which is simply: "we are saved because this man who is one of us has been saved by God, and God has thereby made his salvific will present in the world historically, really and irrevocably."[79]

(iv) The Limits of Classical Christology and Possible New Approaches

The official Christology of the church is a straightforward descending Christology that develops the basic assertion: God in his Logos becomes man. The permanent validity of this classical Christology lies first of all negatively in the fact that when it is presupposed, it prevents Jesus unambiguously from being reduced merely into someone in a line of prophets, and second of all it clarifies positively the fact that God has turned to us in a unique and unsurpassable way in Jesus. It does not contradict, however, the character of an absolutely binding doctrine of the church to

---

[78] *Grundkurs,* 278; Rahner and Thüsing, *Christologie,* 50. Here again the question recurs, On whom does this type of causality work? On the one hand, it appears to be man, but, on the other hand, it appears that God, as he who posits the sign, is also affected by this causality.

[79] *Grundkurs,* 278–79.

call attention to the limits that accompany a particular dogmatic statement.[80] First, the classical Christology seems to jump over the very point that gives us access to the ultimate mystery about Jesus, namely the real humanity of Jesus. Mythological misunderstandings easily follow from this leap, and the humanity of Jesus is thought of all too often as the livery God donned. Second, the Christological "is" formulas that characterize the classical approach are, as we have seen earlier, fraught with the danger of a Monophysite and hence a mythological misunderstanding.[81] Another thing that remains very formal and undetermined in the traditional Christology is the point of unity in the Hypostatic Union. This point of unity can be called *hypostasis* or *person,* but both terms are problematic. If we use the term *hypostasis,* then the assertion remains rather formal and abstract. But if we call this point of unity *person,* the term brings with it from its modern usage the constant danger that the Christological statements will be misunderstood in the sense of Monophysitism or monothelitism,[82] thus overlooking the fact that the man Jesus *in* his human reality existed with a created, active, and existential center of activity vis-à-vis God. Finally, in its explicit formulation, the classical Christology of the incarnation does not give expression in a clear and immediate way to the soteriological significance of the Christ event, and Rahner argues that it would be most desirable today to have a formulation of the Christological dogma that indicated and gave immediate expression to the *salvific* event that Jesus Christ himself *is* and that did so prior to explicit and special soteriological statements.

In discussing possible new approaches to orthodox Christology, Rahner briefly makes a number of suggestions. First, by way of promoting a closer unity between fundamental and dogmatic theology in Christology, he proposes his appeals to a "searching

---

[80] An assertion that was also, as we saw, central to Rahner's understanding of dogma: "Probleme der Christologie," *Schriften,* 1: 183; "Grundsätzliche Bemerkungen," *Schriften,* 10: 246–51; "Zum Begriff der Unfehlbarkeit," *Schriften,* 10: 306, 321; "Lehramt und Theologie," *Schriften,* 13: 75; "Die Theologie und das Römische Lehramt," *Schriften,* 16: 240. See chapter 8, note 9.

[81] *Sacramentum Mundi II,* s.v. "Jesus Christus," 927–28; "Kirchliche Christologie," *Schriften,* 9: 210; Rahner and Thüsing, *Christologie,* 56.

[82] That the concept of "person" has developed away from its original meaning: see chapter 3, note 29.

Christology." He argues that besides what has always been said by way of the traditional grounding of the faith, Christology in fundamental theology *today* can in three ways turn in a kind of appeal to a global understanding of existence that is already "Christian" because of antecedent grace. This global understanding cannot be made reflexive completely, but it nevertheless can be appealed to and would represent a somewhat more reflexive and more complete working out of the content of one part of "transcendental Christology." These three appeals to an absolute love of neighbor, to readiness for death, and to hope in the future have in common the supposition that if a person accepts his existence resolutely, he already is living out in his existence something like a "searching Christology."[83]

Second, Rahner proposes a Christology from below along the lines he has already indicated, which would take the following steps: man is a being with a *desiderium naturale in visionem beatificam*.[84] Because man can experience and actualize his ultimate being only in history, this orientation must come to appearance in history. From this perspective, we can come to the idea of an "absolute event of salvation" and of an "absolute savior," which are two aspects of one and the same event. This unity between the eschatological event of salvation and the absolute savior must be historical because nothing "transcendental" as such can be of final validity. It also at the same time must be the *free* acceptance of God's offer of himself, and this free acceptance is effected by the offer. This salvific event of the absolute savior, moreover, may not be thought of as "absolute" in the sense that it is identical with the fulfillment of the human race, for otherwise history would be complete already. Finally, an absolute and eschatological salvific event must have a really different relationship to God than God's other salvific activity has in a history of salvation that is still open. In an absolute event of salvation, God must live out its

---

[83] *Grundkurs*, 288–91; *Sacramentum Mundi II*, s.v. "Jesus Christus," 924–27; Rahner and Thüsing, *New Christology*, 5–10; Rahner and Thüsing, *Christologie*, 60–63; "Der eine Jesus Christus," *Schriften*, 12: 277–81. P. Young, "Rahner's Searching Christology," *New Blackfriars* 68 (1987), 437–43, is critical of Rahner's later "searching Christology," arguing that it fails to encompass the traditional Christology of the church.

[84] *Grundkurs*, 291; *Sacramentum Mundi II*, s.v. "Jesus Christus," 944; Rahner and Thüsing, *Christologie*, 65.

history and retain it permanently as something done in freedom. Only if this event is God's own history can we speak of an absolute and eschatological event of salvation. And God's very own reality must exist on our side as our own real salvation—that is, on this side of the difference between God and creatures.

Thus, argues Rahner, we have an initial approach toward a Christology from below that is objectively identical with the church's classical Christology from above and that at the same time can clarify the unity between ontic, incarnational, nonrelational Christology (conceptual view) and soteriological, functional, relational Christology (dynamic view).[85]

C. Conclusion

Rahner's approach to Christology in *Grundkurs* is essentially that taken in his later ascending Christology. Nevertheless, a fundamental continuity between his earlier and later works is apparent. Thus, in his evolutionary Christology, he stresses again the immanence of God within the dynamic process of evolution and the unity of spirit and matter, grace and nature, God and the world. In his consciousness Christology, we see again the double emphasis that allows him to assert that, notwithstanding Jesus' dynamic and conscious unity with God, when this consciousness is conceptualized, it develops and has a history. There is a development in *Grundkurs* in that we see, if anything, an even greater emphasis on Jesus' human self-consciousness, his pain and doubt, and even his "crisis of identity." Rahner emphasizes, in the context of his analysis of the resurrection, that Jesus rose into the faith of the apostles and that the resurrection of Jesus is the categorical event that mediates man's transcendental hope for individual resurrection. He continues to maintain that in the death and resurrection of Jesus God's universal salvific will becomes truly irrevocable, thus emphasizing the unity of God and the world and allowing history to affect God, while simultaneously maintaining that God, as *actus purus,* remains immutably what he always is. Finally, in

---

[85] With the insistence on the convertibility of ontic (nonrelational) Christology and ontological (relational, dynamic) Christology here, Rahner's dialectical analogy is again apparent, enabling him to oscillate between conceptual and dynamic perspectives.

Grundkurs, Rahner stresses even more than previously the notion of the convertibility of the statements of classical Christology in modern statements of faith and points the way forward for any future Christology.

Whether Rahner achieves a real reconciliation of his two Christologies, however, is open to question, for many of the tensions that we observed in his earlier thought remain unresolved in *Grundkurs.* Thus, despite his claim to the contrary, it is debatable whether his increased emphasis on the human reality of Jesus really encompasses the traditional Christology of the church. If Jesus' self-consciousness consists in openness to transcendence (through an unthematized *visio immediata*) and in simultaneous orientation to the historical/categorical, then it is difficult to establish how his consciousness was different from any other human being's. And if the Hypostatic Union essentially is constituted by the *visio immediata,* which Rahner distinguishes from the beatific vision, cannot any human being surpass Jesus, whose vision was only immediate and not beatific?[86] Similarly, with regard to the will, because it is theoretically possible for any human being to realize total dedication to God, it does not seem at all clear how Jesus' total acceptance of the will of the Father could be equivalent to the Hypostatic Union, with its unique claim for Jesus as God incarnate. Indeed, as we noted, when Rahner does assert that Jesus accomplishes what we cannot, he never gives a reason for our incapacity.[87] This Arian tendency in his later Christology is reinforced by the fact that he was never able to explain how the Logos can be a real "subject." This is a real dilemma for Rahner, for in his trinitarian theology he asserted that the divine principle of activity was common to all three "ways of subsistence" and that therefore in the immanent Trinity neither the Son nor the Holy Spirit can stand in a certain opposition to the Father to address him as "thou." However, without an inner-

---

[86] Indeed, some of Rahner's interpreters have postulated that every human being is precisely an obediential potency for the Hypostatic Union: see, for example, Hentz, "Anticipating Jesus Christ," in O'Donovan, ed., *A World of Grace,* 115–16.

[87] Except perhaps when Rahner makes the early assertion that Jesus' response to the will of God occurred in first act, as opposed to our response, which occurs in second act ("Zur Theologie der Menschwerdung," *Schriften,* 4: 142 n. 1), an insistence that, in any case, Rahner dropped in his later works.

trinitarian "opposition" it is difficult for Rahner to attribute the humanity to the Logos alone.

Concerning the unity of humanity and divinity in Jesus, further tensions remain unresolved. If, as Rahner maintains, human subjectivity necessarily is influenced by other finite subjects and the environment, it is not clear how the immutable Logos can be said to be one with Jesus' human subject. But, conversely, if the Logos cannot be influenced, what did the incarnation mean to him? Although it is clear that Rahner wishes to join the humanity of Christ to the God of salvation as the perduring mediation between man and God, nevertheless his assertions about God's "becoming in another" (dynamic view) while remaining changeless in himself (conceptual view) appear the height of paradox. As we noted earlier, in the established Christology of the church it is the notion of "person" that traditionally grounded this union in diversity of God and man in Christ, but throughout his Christology, up to and including *Grundkurs,* Rahner fails to develop a fully coherent notion of "person" upon which to ground such a dialectical union. Because of this lack of a notion of "person," he relies instead on the spiritual dynamism that is man (as *Schwebe*) in order to join man to God. Although within such a perspective the two poles might be recognized as somehow diverse, their dynamic relation, each reflecting and somehow encompassing the mysterious reality of the other, renders it impossible for Rahner to distinguish clearly between the two natures.

Thus, the key question remaining unresolved in Rahner's Christology is how the redemptive act achieved in Jesus is simultaneously an act of the Logos as the ontological free subject and also a free, human act. Rahner answers the question by referring it to the unique climax of the Creator-creature relationship, where radical dependence and independence reach their irreversible high point. This is why he defines the *visio immediata* (the peak of the God-man relationship) as the inner constitutive moment of the Hypostatic Union. But here again the central difficulty concerning the lack of a coherent notion of "person" as opposed to "nature" reappears, for the immediate vision of God generally is viewed in the tradition as the highest perfection of human *nature,* and when Rahner understands the Hypostatic Union as the climax of the Creator-creature relationship, his considerations seem to remain entirely on the level of *nature*. The *Aktzentrum* of Jesus seems to be nothing more than Jesus' free, conscious subjectivity on which the Logos exercised an influence no different in essence from that exercised on any other finite subject. Yet, on the other hand, according to Rahner, the Logos also is said to be a subject expressing himself in Jesus Christ. Hence, there seem to be two free, conscious subjects in Jesus, and Rahner's position then seems to be veering dangerously toward Nestorianism.

Rahner's Christology is both brilliant and original and as such represents one of the most comprehensive systems of Catholic theology in the twentieth century. It is unfortunately not entirely consistent: his Christologies from above and from below ultimately do not coalesce. Whereas the former viewpoint displays tendencies that, if unchecked, seem to drive his theology toward Monophysitism, the latter threatens to drift into Arianism. In joining both viewpoints, Rahner, being a careful Catholic thinker, avoided both extremes. However, the dialectical structure of his thought was incapable of attaining a true unity because, as we have seen, throughout his Christology he lacked an adequate notion of "person." His failure to develop such a notion not only prevented him from unifying his Christologies but also led him dangerously close to affirming two independent free subjects in Christ. Thus, having avoided the dangers of both Monophysitism and Arianism, Rahner found himself facing the problem of Nestorianism. His difficulties were complicated by his trinitarian theology, which postulated only one divine subject and three modes of subsistence. The ultimate subject in Christ was therefore unclear, which in turn obfuscated the role of the historical Jesus as the unique mediator of salvation. Rahner's careful use of language fortunately helped him to avoid offending against the canons of orthodoxy, but Rahnerian scholars need to address these unresolved tensions further if the balance of his Christology is not to be endangered or lost.

6. The Church

A. Early Thought

In my analysis of Rahner's ecclesiology, I showed how his notion of the church followed logically and consistently from his understanding of man as *Schwebe,* his doctrine of grace and revelation, and his Christology. It is not, therefore, surprising that the same type of tensions emerge in the context of Rahner's ecclesiology as in the rest of his theology.

Because in Jesus Christ, the Logos-symbol of the Father, God's triumphant grace and his universal salvific will have become definitively and irreversibly present in the world, the whole of humanity has been called to a supernatural destiny and has become the consecrated "people of God." The visible church was not to be understood, therefore, as a "spiritual welfare institution" founded by Christ, but rather as the outer word, the real symbol, of this inner graced reality, the "people of God." The visible church was in fact, according to Rahner, the *Ursakrament* of the eschatologically triumphant mercy of God (in Christ), which categorically expressed its nature in two fundamental directions: word and sacrament. In both directions, the relationship between the inner reality and the outer word or symbol bore the twofold emphasis that we already noted in Rahner's notion of grace and revelation. Thus, the nature of the church is actualized in its historical and social structure. It is, on the one hand, the dynamic expression of a reality whose existence precedes it, in relation to which reality it is relative and changeable (dynamic view), yet, on the other hand, when institutionally determined by the church's free historical decisions, it can become permanent and unchangeable in its concrete form (conceptual view). This duality was the basis of Rahner's remarkably flexible notion of the *ius divinum* and clearly reflected the dialectical structure of his thought. The church also actualizes its nature in its fundamental acts worked for an individual in moments of decisive significance for his salvation, which we call sacraments. These sacraments are seen as both categorical expressions of the grace of God permanently offered to every individual in the supernatural existential and also expressions of the definitive nature of the church, which, when applied to the individual, causes the grace signified *ex opere operato.* Here, in the context of Rahner's understanding of the *ex opere operato,* we observed a tension in his argument, which again is understandable only in the light of the fundamental structure of his thought. On the one hand, Rahner viewed the sacraments as posterior expressions of grace already given to the individual, but, on the other hand, in order to guarantee human freedom before the sacramental sign, he viewed them as infallible causes of grace whose validity is carried by the plural subject of the church even when the individual, on account of personal sin, is not himself in a state of grace. The tension remains unresolved in that Rahner gives no reason why all men cannot fall into mortal sin, thus invalidating the sacraments and their *ex opere operato* causality.

As before in Rahner's understanding of symbol and revelation, so also here in his ecclesiology a development was apparent in his thought, especially in his later works concerning anonymous Christianity. In these later works, presupposing the priority of grace (now, in Christ, irreversibly present in the world), Rahner moved away from a simple unity in diversity between inner grace and its categorical expression in the church and the sacraments, and argued instead that any historical word, whether explicitly Christian or not, can express this grace and mediate it to itself. This does not, he insisted, relativize the importance of the visible church, which, even here in this heavily dynamic approach, is nevertheless necessary as the truest and fullest categorical expression of the inner word of grace, to which all grace tends as its final cause. The church, then, is to be seen as a "vanguard," as the sacramental sign of a grace that goes far beyond the church's sociologically tangible and visible boundaries, without thereby rendering the church unnecessary or superfluous. This is the basis of Rahner's conviction that all individuals who live under the influence of grace are in fact "anonymous Christians," members of the grace-filled "people of God," whether they are conscious of it or not, a conviction that, he asserted (in line with the whole dialectical structure of his thought), undermined neither the uniqueness of the Christ event nor the necessity of the church for salvation.

B. Grundkurs

In *Grundkurs,* Rahner repeats much of what he has written previously on the church. Once again, his approach clearly is that of his later theology, emphasizing the priority of transcendentally given grace coming to categorical expression only in the church and in the consequent historicity of the structures of the church.

But even here the operation of his dialectical analogy is apparent in his insistence on the objectivity of the church as a reality that exists independently of the individual's subjectivity.

(i) The Nature of the Church

Once again and following the whole thrust of his perspective in *Grundkurs,* Rahner begins his ecclesiology from an analysis of man's transcendental experience. If man is a being of interpersonal communication and if salvation touches the whole person, and hence if religion does not concern just some particular sector of human existence, the implication is that the reality of interpersonal relationship belongs intrinsically to the religion of Christianity. But by man's very nature such interpersonal relationships are concretized in society. "If salvation history as the history of God's transcendental self-communication to man is a history which can be experienced in time and space, then it follows from this perspective too that in the Christian understanding religion is necessarily ecclesial religion."[88] Just as Jesus Christ is the absolute mediator of salvation, so also he continues to be present in history in and through the community of those who believe in him, which is what we call the church. It is, therefore, the common conviction of the Christian churches that Jesus "founded" his church, and wherever ecclesial Christianity is found, the conviction is that it has its origins in Christ. But, asks Rahner, what does this "founding" mean?

First of all, the church was founded by the fact that Jesus is the person whom the believers professed to be the absolute savior, and by the fact that he would not be who he is if the offer of himself that God made in him did not continue to remain present in the world. This is true because of the very nature of God's offer. "Abiding faith in Jesus is an intrinsic and constitutive element in God's offer of himself which has become irreversible in Jesus."[89]

Second, this faith may not be regarded as something that hap-

---

[88] *Grundkurs,* 314.
[89] *Grundkurs,* 320; Rahner and Thüsing, *A New Christology,* 25; Rahner and Thüsing, *Christologie,* 38.

pens in the private interiority of an individual, in which case it would never be the continuation of God's offer of himself in Jesus.

Third, the faith that forms community must have a history, and hence so must the church itself because there is a history of salvation. But this historicity includes both change and ongoing identity, and it is inevitable that in an earlier phase of this historical entity free decisions were made that form an irreversible norm for future epochs. If we take the one-directional nature of history seriously, then we see that in the process in which the church comes to be it neither possesses nor has to possess every possibility that was present earlier in the church. In order that a historical decision in one epoch be binding for later epochs, all that can be required seriously is that this decision lay within the genuine possibilities of the church's origins, but it cannot be required that this decision was the only possible one.[90]

Presupposing these principles, and presupposing that the community of those who believe in Jesus is such a historical entity, it follows that this community has its origins in Jesus even if in the course of its development it adopts structures selected from a broad range of genuine possibilities. It is not necessary, therefore, that we trace back to an explicit saying of Jesus the more concrete structures of the constitution of the Catholic Church that the church now declares are always obligatory for it.[91] If a church exists that was brought about by the power of the Spirit and by the power of faith in the risen Jesus, then we cannot grant it just the possibility of free and accidental changes. We also have to grant it the legitimacy of a process of becoming from out of its origins into its full essence.

(ii) The Sacraments

In Jesus Christ and in his presence, which is the church, God offers himself to man in such a way that by his own act of grace

---

[90] The idea that free decisions of the Apostolic church can be normative for future generations was based on Rahner's notion of dialectical analogy, as we have seen, and was stressed heavily in his ecclesiology: *Kirche und Sakramente*, 52; "Über den Episkopat," *Schriften*, 6: 377–78; "Über den Begriff des 'Jus divinum,'" *Schriften*, 5: 262, 268, 271; "Der theologische Ansatzpunkt," *Schriften*, 9: 369; "Grundsätzliche Bemerkungen," *Schriften*, 10: 255; "Was ist ein Sakrament?" *Schriften*, 10: 390; Rahner and Thüsing, *A New Christology*, 26–29.

[91] "Über den Begriff des 'Jus divinum'," *Schriften*, 5: 262, 264, 268, 271.

this offer is bound up definitely with its acceptance by the history of the world's freedom. From this perspective, the church is the sign and the historical manifestation of the victorious success of God's self-communication. When, as the basic sacrament of this victorious grace, the church addresses itself to an individual and involves itself totally in the existentially decisive situations of his life, we have what are called, in traditional Christian terminology, the sacraments. From this perspective of the very essence of the church, the origin or the institution of the sacraments can be understood in a way that is analogous to Jesus' institution of the church itself.[92]

The individual sacraments share in the eschatological finality and certainty of God's redemptive act in Christ, and to this extent we say that a sacrament is an *opus operatum:* an unambiguous and efficacious word of God, which causes grace of itself. But insofar as this sacrament is offered to a person in his individual and still open salvation history, he cannot say with certainty that he accepts absolutely and certainly the word and the offer that comes to him from God. "And insofar as the *opus operatum* of the sacraments encounters the *opus operantis* of the believer or the person who accepts God's act, it is clear that the sacraments are only efficacious in faith, hope and love."[93]

There is present in all the sacraments, moreover, the efficacious word of God, for a sacrament is a tangible word and a tangible response. They also often contain in themselves forms other than words in various ways and in various intensities. These forms are cultic rites, but they do not belong *necessarily,* Rahner maintains, to the essence of the sacrament. This is seen in the fact that in matrimony and in penance, for example, the efficacious word of Christ is present basically only in a human word. To this extent, it is theologically legitimate to understand the sacraments as the most radical and most intensive instance of God's word as a word of the church when this word represents an absolute involvement of the church.[94]

---

[92] "Was ist ein Sakrament?" *Schriften,* 10: 388–90; "Fragen der Sakramententheologie," *Schriften,* 16: 399–400; *Kirche und Sakramente,* 38, 44, 52, 55.

[93] *Grundkurs,* 399.

[94] That the sacraments are the most intense form of God's word is, as we have seen, a central idea in Rahner's understanding of the sacraments: "Wort und Eucharistie," *Schriften,* 4: 320–21; "Überlegungen zur Dogmenentwicklung," *Schriften,* 4: 22–23; *Mysterium Salutis I,* s.v. "Geschichtlichkeit der Vermittlung," 768–69; *Mysterium Salutis I,* s.v. "Kerygma und Dogma," 634, 690–91, 697–98.

It also is to be taken for granted that the whole dialectic between a person as an individual and as a member of the church also is found in the sacraments. It is in a sacramental word that the church addresses God's word to an individual as an individual. But this individual as individual is called through the sacraments into the community of the church, which makes demands upon him as a person of the church and as a member of the community.[95] For this reason, every sacrament has its own quite special ecclesiological aspect.

Finally, *opus operatum* and *opus operantis* are not to be distinguished as an act of God upon man in grace and as a merely free, human act, respectively. Rather, they are distinguished as the official and explicit history of man's salvation becoming manifest in an ecclesial way in the sacraments and as a merely existential salvific act of man in God's grace, respectively.

(iii) Authority in the Church

If religion signifies a call from God, and if the call of a free and personal God cannot be merely a transcendental affair but rather comes in history, then there belongs to the essence of such a religion what we can call the element of the authoritative.[96] The simple question for the religious person is, therefore, whether there is within the realm of his experience and his history a reality that he sees to be established independently of himself and that he can allow to triumph as a power that is not at his disposal, but rather as a power that disposes of him. Of course, religion, in order to be religion, must be taken up and transposed subjectively, but a genuine subjectivity that knows, to begin with, that it has to allow itself to be at the disposal of something objective that it has not established understands what church is within the realm of the religious. "By its very nature, the subjectivity of man, which no one can replace and for which no one can shirk respon-

---

[95] *Grundkurs*, 411–12. Regarding the relationship of mutual causality between individual and community, see "Personale und sakramentale Frömmigkeit," *Schriften*, 2: 129, and *Sendung und Gnade*, 94, 103.

[96] *Grundkurs*, 333; "Über das Ja zur konkreten Kirche," *Schriften*, 9: 494–95. See also Lennan, *Ecclesiology of Karl Rahner*, 179.

sibility, requires that it encounter an objectivity which is the norm for this subjectivity."[97]

Christianity is the religion of a demanding God, who summons the individual's subjectivity out of itself only if it confronts that individual in a church that is authoritative—only if Christ is not only an idea, but a concrete person. If salvation in Christ not only takes place through the communication of an ideology that basically can be reached independently of Jesus and his proclamation, but also depends on the concrete event of his cross, death, and resurrection, then this salvation cannot be found only in and based only on a subjective interiority. The concreteness of Jesus Christ as something that challenges the individual must confront him in what we call the church.

The whole question of the church can be expressed in a simple question: Is man religious merely through his transcendental relation, or does this indubitable and fundamental relation of God to man and man to God in what we call Spirit and grace have a tangible and concrete history? There are only two basic possibilities. Either history itself is of salvific significance, or salvation takes place only in a subjective and ultimately transcendental interiority.

If the first solution is the only really and genuinely human solution, then the church itself belongs to the salvation history of God's grace not only as some useful religious organization, but rather as the categorical concreteness and the mediation of salvation and grace; only this makes the church really church.[98]

C. Conclusion

In Rahner's treatment of the church, once again a clear continuity, including a continuity in unresolved tensions, is apparent between his early and later thought. Just as in his earlier works Rahner defined the whole of humanity as the "people of God," on account of the irreversible presence in Christ of salvific grace

---

[97] *Grundkurs,* 334. That the church cannot absolve the individual from the responsibility of his freedom, see chapter 8, note 51.

[98] *Grundkurs,* 334. This reference of the subject to the historical objectivity of the church reflects Rahner's whole understanding of man as *Schwebe,* but as such stands in a certain tension with his much more dynamic understanding of the church as the categorical expression of grace previously given to the individual.

in the world, and the church as the visible sacrament of this invisible wider reality, so also in *Grundkurs,* from the different starting point of man's experience, he continues to speak of the church as the *Ursakrament,* the sign and historical manifestation of the victorious success of God's self-communication. Just as earlier he saw the church actualizing itself in two directions, in the concrete historical structure of the church and in the sacraments, so too in *Grundkurs* he defends both the ecclesial nature of Christianity as the necessary categorical expression of man's transcendental experience of grace and the sacraments as the actualization of God's grace in the existentially decisive situations of an individual's life. And just as earlier he had developed a remarkably flexible notion of the *ius divinum* that allowed for the structures of the church to be both the dynamic expression of a reality that precedes them and therefore changeable, and yet permanent and unchangeable when institutionally determined, so also in *Grundkurs,* in view of the intrinsic historicity of the community of the church and the unidirectional nature of history, he continues to assert the possibility of structural ecclesial decision making from various legitimate possibilities, which, once decided on, become permanent and binding. In *Grundkurs,* too, we see the unresolved tension between the *ex opere operato* and the *ex opere operantis* of the sacraments in which Rahner holds that the sacraments are both posterior expressions of grace already given and also the infallible causes of grace, whose validity is carried by the plural subject of the church.

However, in *Grundkurs* Rahner stresses more than previously the intrinsic priority of grace coming to expression not just in the church and the sacraments but in any categorical word or event, thus indicating a development in his ecclesiology. Here, too, though, he maintains his balance by insisting on the church's objectivity, which exists independently of the individual's subjectivity, and on its absolute necessity as the truest categorical expression to which all grace naturally tends. But given that what is not ultimately necessary can be dispensed with ultimately, and given that grace already victoriously present in the world and in every individual can come to expression in any categorical word, it remains open to question whether Rahner has grounded sufficiently the church's understanding of itself and its claim to be necessary for salvation.

The tension here between interior grace and the exterior expression of that grace reflects the same tension that we observed in the previous section—namely, how within the terms of Rahner's Christology the human nature of Christ can be regarded as the ultimate, unsurpassable revelation of God. This tension in turn reflects one of the central tensions within the whole of Rahner's system: how the definitive can be found in the finite, in an ongoing historical process to which God is transcendent yet also experienced in interior subjectivity. It is not clear within this system how any exterior expression can ever be absolutely definitive. This problem recurs and is seen perhaps most clearly in Rahner's approach to the issue of the development of dogma, for if it is not possible to make a definitive (dogmatic) statement about the ultimate, unsurpassable revelation in Christ, then the meaning and the definitiveness of Jesus himself will be put into question. It was Rahner's awareness of this unavoidable issue, together with the church's insistence that its dogmatic propositions are true, even in the midst of the history and development of understanding, that forced Rahner to reflect on the meaning, grounding, and definitiveness of true propositions.

7. THE DEVELOPMENT OF DOGMA

A. Early Thought

In his early writings on the development of dogma, Rahner approached the issue from the perspective of his early understanding of grace and revelation. Within this perspective, he saw divine revelation as coming to man from without in the objectively given categorical word of revelation. Yet man is able to recognize this categorical word for what it is, the word of God, only because his human subjectivity is simultaneously elevated by grace. In this early perspective, then, Rahner saw the outer objective word of revelation as existing in a relationship of mutual priority with the inner operation of grace. We noted that this relationship reflects the dynamic *Schwebe* or oscillation revealed in Rahner's original analysis of human being and knowing. Yet this dynamic *Schwebe* constitutes only one part of his understanding of reality, for according to the structure of dialectical analogy there is within the *Schwebe* always and simultaneously a static moment of conceptualization. Within his early theory of revelation, therefore, lest the essential content of revelation dissolve within an unconceptualizable oscillation, Rahner insisted that man necessarily must express the revelation that he has received in a secondary categorical word.

For the apostles, the words of Christ constituted the objectively given outer word of revelation. However, only the operation of grace enabled the apostles to recognize these words as the definitive self-communication of God. The words of Christ existed, therefore, in a objective relationship of mutual priority with inner grace, which enabled the apostles to have a global experience of Christ. True to the structure of dialectical analogy, however, this dynamic experience had to be again expressed in their own categorical words. These words do not exhaust the original experience, but neither can they be entirely lacking. They are in a real sense the theology of the apostles but are also an intrinsic part of the revelation received in Christ. For subsequent generations, an analogous process occurs. The words of the apostles, the Gospels, constitute not a list of propositions but rather a word/*res* unity. They are revealing words that mediate the whole experience of Christ to which they refer. Grace enables subsequent generations to recognize these words for what they are, revealing words of God. True to the structure of man, this dynamic *Schwebe* between the words of the Gospel and the revelatory event they mediate must be reexpressed in the secondary categorical words of doctrinal propositions. These secondary propositions, or dogmas, do not in their turn exhaust the original word/*res* of revelation, but they are legitimate ways of interpreting and passing on the event of revelation. This was the basis for Rahner's justification of an ongoing development of dogma.

Rahner returned to the development of dogma in a series of articles dating from the 1970s. In these later articles, he approached the subject from a different starting point than that of his earlier works. Instead of starting his reflections from the nature of revelation and the relation of the word/*res* to later dogmatic statements, he began from the individual's grace-given experience of a basic trust in the meaningfulness of existence, arguing that this basic attitude had to be expressed in categorical propositions in order to be itself. In this later approach to dogma and its development, Rahner remained true to much of what he had written previously and to the fundamental structure of his thought. From his different existential starting point, he continued to insist on the validity of dogmatic propositions as the necessary expressions of this basic attitude, which mediate it to itself and which never can be entirely lacking. However, here, as elsewhere, the change of perspective that began in Rahner's theology of grace in the early 1960s is apparent. Clearly identifying grace as revelation, Rahner emphasized the priority of the original experience of grace (the attitude of basic trust), which seems to come to subsequent expression not only in revealed or dogmatic propositions but also in nonreligious propositions. He also stressed more than previously the intrinsic limitedness or ambiguity of human statements, which are always open to development and change and which therefore need not be contradicted even by those who cannot accept them.

B. Grundkurs

In *Grundkurs,* Rahner does not address the issue of the development of dogma specifically; however, in a short section on the magisterium and in a highly significant epilogue, he does restate his belief in the validity and necessity of dogmatic propositions of faith. This is important, for even here in the most radical expression of his later theological development, and despite his repeated assertions about the irresolvable pluralism of modern society and the intrinsic limitation of all human propositions, he continues to insist on the necessity of an infallible magisterium and on the validity of dogma and dogmatic creedal formulations.

(i) The Magisterium and the Hierarchy of Truths

In light of the fact that, notwithstanding God's salvific providence in the Old Testament, the absolute authority of a teaching office did not exist before the existence of the church of Christ, we have to recognize that the real reason for this teaching authority must be Christological. It consists ultimately in the fact that Jesus Christ himself is the absolute, irreversible, and invincible climax of salvation history and in the fact that the church is the ongoing presence and the historical tangibility of this ultimate and victorious word of God. As such, the church must participate in the specific characteristic that comes from the fact that God's offer of himself as truth and as love was victorious; that is, ultimately the church as a whole no longer can lose this truth and this love. This is true not because we humans cannot pervert this truth, but rather because in his grace God has also triumphed in Jesus Christ over our human dishonesty and because he will maintain this victory of Christ as an eschatological act of salvation until his (God's) truth will shine upon men from face to face. From this perspective of the eschatological situation, which is the situation of Christ himself, the Catholic understanding of the church says that when the church in its teaching authority really confronts man with an *ultimate* demand in the name of Christ, God's grace and power prevent this teaching authority from losing the truth of Christ.[99] This teaching authority is not an authority through which we receive new revelation from God; it simply interprets, develops, and actualizes the message of Christ in ever new historical concretions.

This fundamental conception still leaves a great deal to be said about the practice of a Catholic Christian. As in the case with every authority, the function of the ecclesial teaching office in the church of Christ has many levels that correspond to the concrete faith situations. The teaching office speaks with all of its authority only in relatively rare instances. Its declarations are usually provisional and limited exercises of the real authority, and, of course, the Catholic Christian's obligation in conscience correspondingly varies a great deal depending on the level of authority exercised.

We may not understand, therefore, the individual statements of the church's teaching in an isolated way. They form part of what the Second Vatican Council called the "hierarchy of truths," and

---

[99] This reflects what we already have seen to be Rahner's notion of dogma and revelation: that is, when the dynamic experience of revelation is conceptualized historically and objectively, it results in infallible propositions of faith.

although all these truths are revealed, they have a quite different relationship to the real core of faith. Faith is not the process of taking a position on a sum of individual propositions; rather, its focus is always on this single totality of truth, and therefore it can understand the individual truth only within a total act of faith. "For a Catholic Christian, then, there is indeed a sum of individual articulated propositions . . . but this sum can be known and appropriated only in an act which does not attain to human propositions of faith, but rather attains to immediacy to God."[100] From this perspective, a Catholic Christian cannot confront a choice among the individual dogmas in the sense that he accepts some as true and rejects others as false. Rather, he can live in the implicit faith of the church even when he is Catholic and accepts the authority of the church absolutely, and he can leave to the church's consciousness of the faith those questions and issues that neither do nor can touch him very closely in his concrete existential situation. "We even have to say that many times it would be better if Christians knew less about certain details of the Catholic catechism but had really grasped the ultimate decisive questions in a genuine and profound way."[101]

(ii) Brief Creedal Statements

In a highly significant final section, Rahner concludes *Grundkurs* by attempting to bring the whole of Christianity into view by way of three brief creedal statements. In a number of articles dating from the late 1960s, he already had argued for the necessity of new creedal formulas and formulated the essentials of the three creeds proposed here.[102] What is significant about these formulas is not so much their novelty or their departure from the traditional Apostles' Creed, but rather the fact that even at the end of his life, despite his acceptance of the irresolvable pluralism of modern thought and the intrinsic limitation of all human propositions, and notwithstanding the emphasis of his later thought on

---

[100] *Grundkurs,* 370.

[101] *Grundkurs,* 371.

[102] "Die Forderung nach einer 'Kurzformel' des christlichen Glaubens," *Schriften,* 8: 153–64; "Reflexionen zur Problematik einer Kurzformel des Glaubens," *Schriften,* 9: 242–56. See also Lennan, *Ecclesiology of Karl Rahner,* 184–86.

the priority of revealing grace, Rahner continued to insist on the validity of the objectively given categorical word of revelation and of dogma.[103] In this sense, his conclusion of *Grundkurs* with a fresh attempt at creedal statements, however strange and impractical that attempt may seem, is important and in itself indicates that even in his later heavily dynamic view of reality he did not lose his balance of perspective, continuing to maintain until the last, in line with the conceptualizing and distinguishing side of his thought, both the necessity and the meaningfulness of the categorical word within the dynamism of revelation.

Very brief formulations of faith are found in the New Testament already, and Rahner argues that they are no less necessary today for retaining what has been learned in instructions for catechumens and for seeing a clear structure in the hierarchy of truths. The effective mission of the church in the face of modern disbelief likewise requires a testimony to the Christian faith in which this message really becomes intelligible for people today. This presupposes a separation of what is essential from everything that is of secondary importance.

Can we reckon with the possibility that a single basic creed can be formulated at least for the whole of Catholic Christianity, or is something like this no longer conceivable to begin with? Rahner argues that we have to answer this question with the second and negative alternative. "There will no longer be any single and universal basic creed of the Christian faith which will be prescribed as authoritative and binding for the whole church; . . . attempts to create a common and universally valid world catechism and to introduce it have collapsed and have met with the unambiguous resistance of both catechists and preachers."[104] Because of this lack, Rahner maintains that we now need *different* basic creeds. The brief creedal statements of the faith that were appropriate for

---

[103] The problem, of course, occurs in attempting to define the essential meaning of these creeds in the light of a situation of intellectual pluralism, which relativizes all propositional statements and renders the legitimate range of their interpretation so wide as to make them practically meaningless. This tension seems to escape many commentators: see, for instance, Lennan, *Ecclesiology of Karl Rahner*, 254, who notes the "dialectic" but fails to see any inherent problem.

[104] *Grundkurs*, 432; "Reflexionen zur Problematik einer Kurzformel des Glaubens," *Schriften*, 9: 244–45.

the Western situation should not merely have been "exported" to the developing world. The fact that they were exported very likely can be explained only by taking into account the strange feeling of superiority that characterized European colonialism. The moment that this theological European imperialism no longer possessed its obviousness and its power, and the moment that the once homogeneous West itself disintegrated into a very deep spiritual and cultural pluralism, it became clear that, in spite of one and the same church and one and the same profession of faith in this church, there no longer could be one and the same homogeneous theology. "The pluralism which is found in the worldwide church . . . is forcing us into a pluralism of theologies which can no longer be integrated."[105] It is Rahner's view that the Second Vatican Council already gave some indication of this situation in that it did not attempt any new and official doctrinal definitions. This is very likely the case because of the perception that a longer doctrinal text that would make a positive statement in a homogeneous theological language and that would be equally intelligible to everyone no longer can be expected so readily today. "However the exercise of the power to make definite doctrinal decisions is not therefore a thing of the past, but rather it can continue to exist in the form of negative anathemas, and even in earlier times this was the predominant mode of these official doctrinal declarations."[106]

Among the fundamental questions that have to be asked about the basic creedal statements belongs the question as to what really has to be expressed in this type of creed and what can be left out. Rahner's response is that such basic creeds would have to contain only what is of fundamental importance. They also can vary a great deal in their content, which should consist primarily and especially in what constitutes for the listeners in question an initial and hopefully successful point of departure for reaching an under-

---

[105] *Grundkurs*, 433; "Reflexionen zur Problematik einer Kurzformel des Glaubens," *Schriften*, 9: 246. The irresolvable pluralism in the contemporary theology of the church is also an important theme in Rahner's later works (see chapter 8, note 108) and begs the question of the meaning and role of the infallible magisterium, which, as we have seen, Rahner simultaneously asserts is necessary.

[106] *Grundkurs*, 433.

standing of the whole of Christian faith. For this kind of creed really to be a profession of Christian faith, therefore, it has to give expression to our faith in the historical Jesus as our Lord and as the absolute savior, and it has to be related to this historical facticity.[107] There is, of course, something like an anonymous Christianity, in which grace takes place without the person in question being related explicitly in his objectified consciousness to the historical Jesus, but it is to be taken for granted that even a merely basic creedal statement of explicit Christian faith has to express explicitly the relationship of the other elements to Christ. Rahner presents three brief theological creeds and explains his understanding of them in order to make what he has said more concrete.

α. A Brief Theological Creed

The incomprehensible term of human transcendence, which takes place in man's existential and original being and not only in theoretical or merely conceptual reflection, is called God, and he communicates himself in forgiving love to man both existentially and historically as man's own fulfillment. The eschatological climax of God's historical self-communication, in which this self-communication becomes manifest as irreversible and victorious, is called Jesus Christ.[108]

This creed contains three fundamental statements. The first has to do with what we mean by God, characterizing him as the term of human transcendence and hence precisely as a mystery. The experience of God is not found in the first instance in theoretical reflection, but rather takes place basically and originally in our everyday acts of knowledge and freedom. This experience of God is, therefore, both inescapable and also very anonymous and preconceptual. This first creed not only says that God exists but also tries to indicate how we reach an understanding of what God really means.

The second statement explains that God is not merely man's

---

[107] "Reflexionen zur Problematik einer Kurzformel des Glaubens," *Schriften*, 9: 248–49.

[108] *Grundkurs*, 435–36; "Reflexionen zur Problematik einer Kurzformel des Glaubens," *Schriften*, 9: 250.

eternally asymptotic goal, but rather he gives himself in his own reality in self-communication to man. Indeed, he does so on the presupposition that man is a sinner and hence does so in forgiving love. He gives himself both existentially and historically at the same time. This expresses two elements in their relationship of mutual conditioning: the existential self-communication of God in the Holy Spirit and also the history of salvation. "The latter is nothing else than the historical self-mediation and the historical and historically ongoing objectification of God's self-communication in grace."[109] This statement about God's twofold self-communication, the existential mission of the Spirit and the historical mission of the Logos—along with the fact that the original, incomprehensible, and abiding mystery of God as Father has already been mentioned—gives us first of all the Trinity in the economy of salvation. And it also gives us the immanent Trinity because if there were no immanent Trinity, the former would not really be God's self-communication.

The third basic statement says that this historical self-communication of God has its eschatological climax in Jesus of Nazareth, for when God's historical self-communication is not merely present as offered but also has been accepted, then we have precisely what is called the God-man or the Hypostatic Union, which includes the death and resurrection of the God-man.

β. Brief Anthropological Creed

A person really discovers his true self in a genuine act of self-realization only if he risks himself radically for another. If he does this, he grasps unthematically or explicitly what we mean by God as the horizon, the guarantor, and the radical depths of this love, the God who in his existential and historical self-communication made himself the realm within which such love is possible. This love is meant in both an interpersonal and a social sense, and in the radical unity of both these elements it is the ground and essence of the church.[110]

There are three statements here, too. The first says that in the existential self-transcendence that takes place in the act of loving

---

[109] *Grundkurs,* 436.

[110] *Grundkurs,* 437; "Reflexionen zur Problematik einer Kurzformel des Glaubens," *Schriften,* 9: 252.

one's neighbor, a person has an experience of God at least implicitly. Again this statement makes clear and concrete that the basic
actualization of human transcendence does not take place in theoretical reflection. This first statement is established theologically
also by the truth about the unity of love of God and love of
neighbor.

The second statement of this creed says that it is precisely
through his self-communication that God creates the possibility
for the interpersonal love that in the concrete is possible for us
and is our task. If a person reflects on Matthew 25, he certainly
does not have to deny a priori that the entire salvific relationship
between man and God and between man and Christ already is
found implicitly in a radical love for one's neighbor, which has
been realized in practice.

The third statement of this second creed says that this love in
which God is loved in our neighbor has two dimensions: an existential dimension of intimacy and a historical and social dimension. These two dimensions correspond to the two aspects of
God's self-communication. When this love reaches its high point,
and indeed in the unity of both these aspects, then we have in
fact what we call a church.

γ. A Brief Future-Oriented Creed

> Christianity is the religion which keeps open the question about
> the absolute future, which wills to give itself in its own reality by
> self-communication and which has established this will as eschato-
> logically irreversible in Jesus Christ, and this future is called God.[111]

This shortest of the creedal statements transposes the statement
about man's transcendentality in the first creed by interpreting
this transcendentality as an orientation toward the future, as man's
futurity. The creedal statement says of the future that it is not the
asymptotic goal of history that keeps this history in motion but is
never reached in its own reality. Rather, this future wills to give
itself through its own self-communication. This self-communication that is always existential also has a historical aspect, and in

---

[111] *Grundkurs,* 439; "Reflexionen zur Problematik einer Kurzformel des
Glaubens," *Schriften,* 9: 254.

this aspect it has reached an eschatological irreversibility in Jesus Christ. Now, a divine self-communication to the world that has become eschatologically irreversible in Jesus Christ already contains implicitly what the doctrines of the Trinity and Christology say more explicitly, and in the experience of our orientation toward an absolute future God is experienced as mystery in the absolute sense. Insofar as Christianity is the worship of the one true God as opposed to all the idols that absolutize finite powers and dimensions of man, it is the religion that keeps man open for the absolute future.

C. Conclusion

Others have noted elsewhere the evolution in Rahner's theory of dogma, arguing that in consequence of the change in his view the future history of dogma would be transformed into a history where plural and inculturalized formulations of faith would play an increasingly secondary role to concrete action on behalf of one's neighbor and contemplation of the silent mystery. It is my contention, however, that such an interpretation of the change in Rahner's theory of the development of dogma has failed to do justice to the subtlety and complexity of his thought. I maintain that this change of emphasis is consistent with the development in the rest of Rahner's theology and can be interpreted correctly only in light of the foundational structure of his thought as dialectical analogy. Thus, although it is undoubtedly true that in his later works the more dynamic and unifying side of Rahner's thought began to take precedence in his theology in general and specifically in his theory of dogmatic development, it is equally true that this dynamic side never totally excluded the other more conceptualizing side of his thought, for Rahner always remained true to the structure of dialectical analogy. So just as in his foundational epistemology Rahner insisted on the necessity of the concept within the dynamism of human knowing and on its validity on the ground that being is conceptualizable, so also he continued to insist right up to the end of his life on the necessity and the validity of dogma within the dynamism of faith. This insistence on the necessity of the categorical word is fundamental to his understanding of revelation and of the development of dogma, and it is the basis of his trenchant and oft-repeated rejection of modernism. The suggestion, therefore, that in his later works he somehow moved away from the necessity of the categorical word toward a "dogma-free" retreat into mystery is a misunderstanding not only of his theory of the development of dogma but also of the whole structure of his thought and understanding of reality.

The real problem with Rahner's understanding of dogma and its development is not then that he abandoned the necessity of categorical, propositional words within the process of development but rather that, despite his repeated insistence on their existence and validity, the essential content of such propositions seems to be incapable of clear definition. This incapacity clearly is grounded in Rahner's own foundational epistemology, where, as we saw, despite his affirmation of its existence, the concept also is relativized and incapable of complete essential definition. By his insistence on the necessity of categorical propositions within the process of revelation, Rahner sought to affirm the existence and the validity of dogma and an infallible magisterium. But by his equally dogged insistence on the irresolvable intellectual pluralism of the modern world and the limitedness of all human concepts, even when infallibly defined, he sought to achieve flexibility in the interpretation of dogma and openness to a possible future of development that might include new, different, and even contradictory formulations of a particular dogma, without thereby denying the infallibility of earlier propositions. In light of this flexibility of interpretation and of the contemporary pluralism that became a central theme in his later writings, Rahner was able to assert the existence of a new and legitimate type of theological pluralism within the church, inconceivable before the Second Vatican Council, which makes the absolute contradiction of a given dogma by a believing Christian both unnecessary and meaningless. Instead of contradicting a dogmatic teaching that he finds difficult, a Christian simply can ignore it while waiting for a new and better formulation. This is the nub of the problem, for, on the one hand and in line with the conceptualizing side of his thought, Rahner clearly wanted to maintain, right up to the end of his theological career, the necessity and validity of dogma and the meaningfulness of an infallible magisterium. However, on the other hand and in line with the more dynamic side of his thought, his stress on the intrinsic and irresolvable intellectual pluralism of modern society and his insistence on the limitedness and relativity of all propositions seem to render the essential content of any dogmatic formulation so vague that the actual meaning of both dogma and also an infallible magisterium becomes almost vacuous. This is the dialectic that we face in Rahner's later theology of the development of dogma, but it is a dialectic that was set up in his very first philosophical works on the process of human knowing and that formed the background to his whole theological project. It is a dialectic that raises a number of serious problems, but it is also a structure of thought through which Rahner was able to hold and maintain an admirable theological balance that his theological disciples all too often have lost.

FINAL WORD

KARL RAHNER was one of the great synthetic thinkers of the twentieth century, and the theological system he developed was and remains an outstanding achievement whose influence, especially in the development of postconciliar Catholic thought, scarcely can be overestimated. Throughout this analysis of his thought, I have attempted to show that the inner coherence of this theological system is grounded in his highly complex and subtle understanding of dialectical analogy. Not a static structure encapsulated once and for all in concepts, Rahner's analogy is rather a dynamic movement whose constant oscillation draws together concept and judgment, the sensible *Diesda* and the horizon of being, nature and grace, God and the world. Precisely because it oscillates between polar extremes, it does not destroy the distinctions necessary to orthodox Christianity but rather preserves them in its movement. It is this structure of dialectical analogy that enables Rahner in his theology constantly to change perspective, emphasizing in turn both unity and diversity in his vision of reality, and as such it is this structure that provides the hermeneutical key to the correct interpretation of his whole theological project. It is my contention that in maintaining this complex, flexible, and profound understanding of analogy, Rahner ultimately was trying to be true to the sacramental awareness that is fundamental to any truly Christian view of reality, in which the finite realities of this world can be neither absolutized nor totally deprived of meaning and intelligibility. However, it is also my contention that, notwithstanding its inner coherence and its compatibility with the truths of the Christian faith, Rahner's dialectical analogy, and with it his entire system, fails to ground itself fully. It is valid insofar as it reflects the tensions within the Catholic vision of reality, but as such it neither explains itself nor resolves the tensions it exposes. This problem, which is intrinsic to Rahner's theological system, has its origins in his foundational metaphysics. It is a problem that deserves greater attention from Rahnerian scholars if the magnificent balance of Rahner's thought is not to be endangered or even lost.

SELECTED BIBLIOGRAPHY

A. KARL RAHNER

1. Books

Geist in Welt. 2d ed. Edited by Johannes Baptist Metz. Munich: Kösel KG, 1957.

Grundkurs des Glaubens: Einführung in den Begriff des Christentums. 6th ed. Freiburg, Basel, Vienna: Herder, 1984.

Hörer des Wortes. Munich: Kösel-Pustet, 1941.

Hörer des Wortes. 2d ed. Edited by Johannes Baptist Metz. Munich: Kösel KG, 1963.

Karl Rahner in Dialogue: Conversations and Interviews, 1965–1982. Edited and translated by H. Egan. New York: Crossroad, 1986.

Sendung und Gnade. Innsbruck, Vienna, Munich: Tyrolia, 1959.

Rahner, Karl, and W. Thüsing. *A New Christology.* Translated by D. Smith and V. Green. London: Burns and Oates, 1980.

2. Collected Articles

Schriften zur Theologie. Vol. 1. Einsiedeln, Zürich, Cologne: Benziger, 1954.

Schriften zur Theologie. Vol. 2. Einsiedeln, Zürich, Cologne: Benziger, 1955.

Schriften zur Theologie. Vol. 3, *Zur Theologie des geistlichen Lebens.* Einsiedeln, Zürich, Cologne: Benziger, 1956.

Schriften zur Theologie. Vol. 4, *Neuere Schriften.* Einsiedeln, Zürich, Cologne: Benziger, 1960.

Schriften zur Theologie. Vol. 5, *Neuere Schriften.* Einsiedeln, Zürich, Cologne: Benziger, 1962.

Schriften zur Theologie. Vol. 6, *Neuere Schriften.* Einsiedeln, Zürich, Cologne: Benziger, 1965.

Schriften zur Theologie. Vol. 7, *Zur Theologie des geistlichen Lebens.* Einsiedeln, Zürich, Cologne: Benziger, 1966.

Schriften zur Theologie. Vol. 8, Einsiedeln, Zürich, Cologne: Benziger, 1967.

Schriften zur Theologie. Vol. 9, Einsiedeln, Zürich, Cologne: Benziger, 1970.

Schriften zur Theologie. Vol. 10, Zürich, Einsiedeln, Cologne: Benziger, 1972.

Schriften zur Theologie. Vol. 11, *Frühe Bussgeschichte in Einzeluntersuchungen.* Zürich, Einsiedeln, Cologne: Benziger, 1973.

Schriften zur Theologie. Vol. 12, *Theologie aus Erfahrung des Geistes.* Zürich, Einsiedeln, Cologne: Benziger, 1975.

Schriften zur Theologie. Vol. 13, *Gott und Offenbarung.* Zürich, Einsiedeln, Cologne: Benziger, 1978.

Schriften zur Theologie. Vol. 14, *In Sorge um die Kirche.* Zürich, Einsiedeln, Cologne: Benziger, 1980.

Schriften zur Theologie. Vol. 15, *Wissenschaft und christlicher Glaube.* Zürich, Einsiedeln, Cologne: Benziger, 1983.

Schriften zur Theologie. Vol. 16, *Humane Gesellschaft und Kirche von Morgen.* Zürich, Einsiedeln, Cologne: Benziger, 1984

3. Encyclopedia Articles

Kleines Theologisches Wörterbuch. 1961 ed. S.v. "Glaube," "Hypostatische Union," and "Praeambula Fidei" by Karl Rahner and Herbert Vorgrimler.

Lexikon für Theologie und Kirche. 1986 ed. S.v. "Jesus Christus."

Mysterium Salutis I. 1965 ed. S.v. "Kerygma und Dogma," and "Geschichtlichkeit der Vermittlung," by Karl Rahner and Karl Lehmann.

Mysterium Salutis II. 1967 ed. S.v. "Der dreifaltige Gott als transzendenter Urgrund der Heilsgeschichte."

Sacramentum Mundi II. 1968 ed. S.v. "Jesus Christus."

Sacramentum Mundi III. 1969 ed. S.v. "Offenbarung."

Sacramentum Mundi IV. 1969 ed. S.v. "Selbstmitteilung Gottes," "Trinität," and "Trinitätstheologie."

4. Quaestiones Disputatae

Das Dynamische in der Kirche. Quaestiones Disputatae no. 5. Freiburg, Basel, Vienna: Herder, 1958.

Kirche und Sakramente. Quaestiones Disputatae no. 10. Freiburg, Basel, Vienna: Herder, 1960.

Zur Theologie des Todes. Quaestiones Disputatae no. 2. Freiburg, Basel, Vienna: Herder, 1958.

Rahner, K., and P. Overhage. *Das Problem der Hominisation.* Quaestiones Disputatae nos. 12–13. Freiburg, Basel, Vienna: Herder, 1961.

Rahner, K., and J. Ratzinger. *Episkopat und Primat.* Quaestiones Disputatae no. 11. Freiburg, Basel, Vienna: Herder, 1961.

———. *Offenbarung und Überlieferung.* Quaestiones Disputatae no. 25. Freiburg, Basel, Vienna: Herder, 1965.

Rahner, K., and W. Thüsing. *Christologie: Systematisch und Exegetisch.* Quaestiones Disputatae no. 55. Freiburg, Basel, Vienna: Herder, 1972.

5. Other Articles

"Kritik an Hans Küng." *Stimmen der Zeit* 186 (1970): 361–77.
"Replik." *Stimmen der Zeit.* 187 (1971): 145–60.

6. Translations of Rahner's Work

The Church and the Sacraments. Translated by W. O'Hara. London: Burns and Oates, 1974.

The Dynamic Element in the Church. Translated by W. O'Hara. London: Burns and Oates, 1964.

The Episcopate and the Primacy. Translated by K. Barker, P. Kearns, R. Ochs, and R. Strachan. Edinburgh and London: Nelson, 1962.

Foundations of Christian Faith: An Introduction to the Idea of Christianity. Translated by W. Dych. New York: Crossroad, 1978.

Hearer of the Word. Translated by J. Donceel. New York: Continuum, 1994.

Hearers of the Word. Revised by J. B. Metz, translated by Ronald Walls. London: Sheed and Ward, 1969.

Hominisation. Translated by W. O'Hara. London: Burns and Oates, 1965.

Revelation and Tradition. Translated by W. O'Hara. London: Burns and Oates, 1966.

Spirit in the World. Revised by J. B. Metz, translated by William Dych. London: Sheed and Ward, 1968.

Theological Investigations. 23 vols. Translated by C. Ernst, K. H. Kruger, B. Kruger, K. Smith, D. Bourke, D. Morland, E. Quinn, H. Riley, and Joseph Donceel. Vols. 1–6, Baltimore: Helicon, 1961–69. Vols. 7–10, New York: Herder and Herder, 1970–73. Vols.11–14, New York: Seabury, 1974–76. Vols 15–21, New York: Crossroad, 1979–88. Vols. 22–23, London: Darton, Longman and Todd, 1991–92.

B. Secondary Literature

1. Books

Altmann, W. *Der Begriff der Tradition bei Karl Rahner.* Berne: Lang, 1974.

Balthasar, H. U. von. *Cordula oder Ernstfall.* Einsiedeln: Johannes, 1966.

Boff, L. *Die Kirche als Sakrament.* Paderborn: Bonifacius Druckerei, 1972.

Bonsor, J. *Rahner, Heidegger, and Truth: Karl Rahner's Notion of Christian Truth—The Influence of Martin Heidegger.* Lanham, Md.: University Press of America, 1987.

Carr, A. *The Theological Method of Karl Rahner.* Missoula, Mont.: Scholars Press, 1977.

Denzinger, Heinrich, and Adolf Schönmetzer, eds. *Enchiridion Symbolorum Definitionum et Declarationum de Rebus Fidei et Morum.* Freiburg: Herder, 1965.

Donceel, J. *The Philosophy of Karl Rahner.* Albany: Magi, 1969.

Duffy, S. *The Graced Horizon: Nature and Grace in Modern Catholic Thought.* Collegeville, Minn.: Liturgical Press, 1992.

Dulles, A. *A Church to Believe In: Discipleship and the Dynamics of Freedom.* New York: Crossroad, 1982.

———. *Models of the Church.* New York: Doubleday, 1974.

Dych, W. *Karl Rahner.* London: Geoffrey Chapmann, 1992.

Eicher, P. *Die Anthropologische Wende.* Freiburg: Universitätsverlag, 1970.

Fabro, C. *La Svolta antropologica di Karl Rahner.* Milan: Rusconi, 1974.

Farrugia, E. *Aussage und Zusage: Zur Indirektheit der Methode Karl Rahners veranschaulicht an seiner Christologie.* Rome: Editrice Pontificia Universitá Gregoriana, 1985.

Fischer, Klaus. *Der Mensch als Geheimnis.* Freiburg, Basel, Vienna: Herder, 1974.

Hill, W. *The Three-Personed God: The Trinity as a Mystery of Salvation.* Washington, D.C.: Catholic University of America Press, 1982.

Hines, M. *The Transformation of Dogma: An Introduction to Karl Rahner on Doctrine.* New York: Paulist Press, 1989.

Kehl, M. *Die Kirche als Institution: Zur theologischen Begründung des institutionellen Charakters der Kirche in der neuen deutschsprachigen katholischen Ekklesiologie.* Frankfurt: Knecht, 1976.

Kress, R. *The Church: Communion, Sacrament, Communication.* New York: Paulist Press, 1985.

Kull, D. *Karl Rahner's Theology of Revelation.* Manila: Loyola, 1979.

Küng, H. *Rechtfertigung: Die Lehre Karl Barths und eine katholische Besinnung.* Einsiedeln: Benziger, 1957.

———. *Unfehlbar? Eine Anfrage.* Zürich: Benziger, 1970.

Lakebrink, B. *Klassische Metaphysik: Eine Auseinandersetzung mit der existentialen Anthropozentrik.* Freiburg: Rombach, 1967.

Lennan, R. *The Ecclesiology of Karl Rahner.* Oxford: Clarendon, 1995.

Lonergan, B. *De Verbo Incarnato.* Rome: Gregoriana, 1964.

Lubac, H. de. *Paradoxe et mystere de l'église.* Paris: Aubier-Montaigne, 1967.

Marshall, B. *Christology in Conflict: The Identity of a Saviour in Rahner and Barth.* Oxford: Blackwell, 1987.

Metz, J. B., W. Kern, A. Darlap, and H. Vorgrimler, eds. *Gott in Welt: Festgabe für Karl Rahner zum 60. Geburtstag.* Freiburg: Herder, 1964.

Muck, O. *The Transcendental Method.* Translated from German by W. Seidensticker. New York: Herder, 1968.

Nichols, A. *From Newman to Congar: The Idea of Doctrinal Development from the Victorians to the Second Vatican Council.* Edinburgh: T&T Clark, 1990.

O'Donovan, L., ed. *A World of Grace: An Introduction to the Themes and Foundations of Karl Rahner's Theology.* New York: Crossroad, 1981.

Puntel, A. *Analogie und Geschichtlichkeit.* Freiburg: Herder, 1969.

Roberts, L. *The Achievement of Karl Rahner.* New York: Herder, 1967.

Sanna, I. *La cristologia antropologica di Karl Rahner.* Milan: Rusconi, 1974.

Schnell, U. *Das Verhältnis von Amt und Gemeinde im neueren Katholizismus.* Berlin: W. de Gruyter, 1977.

Schwerdtfeger, N. *Gnade und Welt: Zum Grundgefüge von Karl Rahners Theorie der "anonymen Christen."* Freiburg: Herder, 1982.

Semmelroth, O. *Die Kirche als Ursakrament.* Frankfurt: Knecht, 1953.

Sheehan, T. *Karl Rahner: The Philosophical Foundations.* Athens: Ohio University Press, 1987.

Simons, E. *Philosophie der Offenbarung.* Stuttgart: Kohlhammer, 1966.

Speck, J. *Karl Rahners theologische Anthropologie.* Munich: Kösel, 1967.

Tremblay, Jacynthe. *Finitude et devenir.* Montreal: Fides, 1992.

Van Der Heijden, L. *Karl Rahner: Darlegung und Kritik seiner Grundposition.* Einsiedeln: Johannes, 1973.

Vass, George. *A Theologian in Search of a Philosophy.* Vol. 1 of *Understanding Karl Rahner.* London: Christian Classics, Sheed and Ward, 1985.

―――. *The Mystery of Man and the Foundations of a Theological System.* Vol. 2 of *Understanding Karl Rahner.* London: Christian Classics, Sheed and Ward, 1985.

Vorgrimler, H., ed. *Wagnis Theologie: Erfahrungen mit der Theologie Karl Rahners.* Freiburg, Basel, Vienna: Herder, 1979.

Walsh, M. *The Heart of Christ in the Writings of Karl Rahner.* Rome: Gregorian University Press, 1977.

Weger, K-H. *Karl Rahner: An Introduction to His Theology.* Translated from German by D. Smith. New York: Seabury, 1980.

Wong, J. H-P. *Logos-Symbol in the Christology of Karl Rahner.* Rome: LAS, 1984.

2. Articles

Allik, T. "Karl Rahner on Materiality and Human Knowledge." *The Thomist* 49 (1985): 367–86.

Balthasar, H. U. von. "Grösse und Last der Theologie heute." *Wort und Wahrheit* 10 (1955): 531–33.

Baum, G. "Truth in the Church: Küng, Rahner, and Beyond." *The Ecumenist* 9 (1971): 33–48.

Bracken, J. A. "The Holy Trinity as a Community of Divine Persons. II. Person and Nature in the Doctrine of God." *Heythrop Journal* 15 (1974): 257–70.

Bradley, D. "Rahner's *Spirit in the World:* Aquinas or Hegel?" *The Thomist* 41 (1977): 167–99.

———. "Religious Faith and the Mediation of Being: The Hegelian Problem in *Hearers of the Word.*" *Modern Schoolman* 55 (1978): 127–46.

Bresnahan, J. "Rahner's Ethics: Critical Natural Law in Relation to Contemporary Ethical Methodology." *Journal of Religion* 56 (1976): 36–60.

Brooke, O. "Natural Religion and the Supernatural Existential." *Downside Review* 83 (1965): 201–12.

Buckley, J. "On Being a Symbol: An Appraisal of Karl Rahner." *Theological Studies* 40 (1979): 453–73.

Burke, P. "Conceptual Thought in Karl Rahner." *Gregorianum* 75 (1994): 65–93.

Burns, R. "The Agent and the Intellect in Rahner and Aquinas." *Heythrop Journal* 29 (1988): 423–49.

Callahan, A. "Karl Rahner's Theology of Symbol: Basis for His Theology of the Church and the Sacraments." *Irish Theological Quarterly* 49 (1982): 195–205.

Carmody, D., and J. Carmody. "Christology in Karl Rahner's Evolutionary World View." *Religion in Life* 49 (1980): 195–210.

Cawte, J. "Karl Rahner's Conception of God's Self-Communication to Man." *Heythrop Journal* 25 (1984): 260–71.

Clarke, W. N. "What Is Most and Least Relevant in the Metaphysics of St. Thomas Today?" *International Philosophical Quarterly* 14 (1974): 411–34.

Conlon, J. "Karl Rahner's Theory of Sensation." *The Thomist* 41 (1977): 400–417.

[D.] "Ein Weg zur Bestimmung des Verhältnisses von Natur und Gnade." *Orientierung* 14 (1950): 138–41.

De h-Ide, S. "Rahner and Lonergan." *Studies* 65 (1976): 63–67.

Donceel, J. "A Thomistic Misapprehension?" *Thought* 32 (1957): 189–98.

———. "Transcendental Thomism." *The Monist* 58 (1974): 67–85.

Doud, R. "Sensibility in Rahner and Merleau-Ponty." *The Thomist* 44 (1980): 372–89.

Eberhard, K. "Karl Rahner and the Supernatural Existential." *Thought* 46 (1971): 537–61.

Ernst, C. "Some Themes in the Theology of Karl Rahner." *Irish Theological Quarterly* 32 (1965): 251–57.

Fabro, C. "Review of *Geist in Welt.*" *Divus Thomas* 43 (1940): 168–71.

———. "Karl Rahner e l'ermeneutica tomistica." *Divus Thomas* 74 (1971): 287–338, 423–65.

Falk, H. "Can Spirit Come from Matter?" *International Philosophical Quarterly* 7 (1967): 541–55.

Girotto, B. "Il problema dell'essere nel pensiero di K. Rahner." *Filosofia* 30 (1979): 555–84.

Hill, W. "Uncreated Grace: A Critique of Karl Rahner." *The Thomist* 27 (1963): 333–56.

Honner, J. "Unity-in-Difference: Karl Rahner and Niels Bohr." *Theological Studies* 46 (1985): 480–506.

Hoye, W. "A Critical Remark on Karl Rahner's *Hearers of the Word.*" *Antonianum* 48 (1973): 508–32.

Hughes, J. "Infallible? An Inquiry Considered." *Theological Studies* 32 (1971): 183–207.

Hurd, R. "Being Is Being-Present-to-Itself: Rahner's Reading of Aquinas' Metaphysics." *The Thomist* 52 (1988): 63–78.

———. "Heidegger and Aquinas: A Rahnerian Bridge." *Philosophy Today* 28 (1984): 105–37.

Jüngel, E. "Das Verhältnis von 'ökonomischer' und 'immanenter' Trinität." *Zeitschrift für Theologie und Kirche* 72 (1975): 353–64.

Kenny, J. "Reflections on Human Nature and the Supernatural." *Theological Studies* 14 (1953): 280–87.

Kerr, F. "Rahner's 'Grundkurs' Revisited." *New Blackfriars* 719 (1980): 148–57.

Knasas, J. "'Esse' as the Target of Judgement in Rahner and Aquinas." *The Thomist* 51 (1987): 222–45.

Küng, H. "Anonyme Christen—Wozu?" *Orientierung* 39 (1975): 214–16.

———. "Im Interesse der Sache." *Stimmen der Zeit* 187 (1971): 43–64, 105–22.

Lotz, J. B. "Zur Thomas-Rezeption in der Marechal-Schule." *Theologie und Philosophie* 49 (1974): 375–91.

Macquarrie, J. "Karl Rahner: The Anthropological Approach to Theology." *Heythrop Journal* 25 (1984): 272–87.

Mansini, G. "Quasi-formal Causality and Change in the Other: A Note on Karl Rahner's Christology." *The Thomist* 52 (1988): 293–306.

Mascall, E. "Thomism, Traditional or Transcendental?" *Tijdschrift voor Filosofie* 36 (1974): 323–41.

McCool, G. "Is St. Thomas's 'Science of God' Still Relevant Today?" *International Philosophical Quarterly* 14 (1974): 435–54.

———. "Neo-Thomism and the Tradition of St. Thomas." *Thought* 62 (1987) : 131–46.

———. "The Philosophy of the Human Person in Karl Rahner's Theology." *Theological Studies* 22 (1961): 537–62.

McDermott, J. "The Analogy of Knowing in Karl Rahner." *International Philosophical Quarterly* 36 (1996): 201–16.

———. "The Christologies of Karl Rahner." *Gregorianum* 67 (1986): 86–123, 297–327.

———. "Dialectical Analogy: The Oscillating Center of Rahner's Thought." *Gregorianum* 75 (1994) : 675–703.

———. "Karl Rahner on Two Infinities." *International Philosophical Quarterly* 28 (1988): 439–57.

———. "Metaphysical Conundrums at the Root of Moral Disagreement." *Gregorianum* 71 (1990): 713–42.

———. "A New Approach to God's Existence." *The Thomist* 44 (1980): 219–50.

Meynell, H. "Rahner's *Grundkurs.*" *New Blackfriars* 61 (1980): 77–89.

Modras, R. "Implications of Rahner's Anthropology for Fundamental Moral Theology." *Horizons* 12 (1985): 70–90.

Molnar, P. "Can We Know God Directly? Rahner's Solution from Experience." *Theological Studies* 46 (1985): 228–71.

———. "The Function of the Immanent Trinity in the Theology of Karl Barth: Implications for Today." *Scottish Journal of Theology* 42 (1989): 367–99.

———. "Is God Essentially Different from His Creatures?" *The Thomist* 51 (1987): 575–631.

Moloney, R. "The Mind of Christ in Transcendental Theology: Rahner, Lonergan, and Crowe." *Heythrop Journal* 25 (1984): 288–300.

———. "Seeing and Knowing: Some Reflections on Karl Rahner's Theory of Knowledge." *Heythrop Journal* 18 (1977): 399–419.

Pearl, T. "Dialectical Panentheism: On the Hegelian Character of Karl Rahner's Key Christological Writings." *Irish Theological Quarterly* 42 (1975): 119–37.

Race, A. "The Christologies of Karl Rahner." *Theology* 89 (1986): 178–86.

Ratzinger, J. "Vom Verstehen des Glaubens: Anmerkungen zu Rahners *Grundkurs des Glaubens*." *Theologische Revue* 74 (1978): 177–86.

Reichmann, J. "The Transcendental Method and the Psychogenesis of Being." *The Thomist* 32 (1968): 499–508.

Richard, R. "Rahner's Theory of Doctrinal Development." *Proceedings of the Catholic Theological Society of America* 18 (1963): 157–89.

Sheehan, T. "Metaphysics and Bivalence: On Karl Rahner's *Geist in Welt*." *Modern Schoolman* 63 (1985): 21–43.

Sobosan, J. B. "Anonymity and Christianity." *Homiletic and Pastoral Review* 76 (1976): 62–69.

Surlis, P. "Rahner and Lonergan on Method in Theology." *Irish Theological Quarterly* 39 (1972): 23–42.

Tallon, A. "Getting to the Heart of the Matter: Spirit." *Louvain Studies* 11 (1969): 277–81.

———. "Personal Becoming: Karl Rahner's Metaphysical Anthropology." *The Thomist* 43 (1979): 1–177.

———. "Spirit, Freedom, History: Karl Rahner's *Hörer des Wortes*." *The Thomist* 38 (1974): 908–36.

————. "Spirit, Matter, Becoming: Karl Rahner's *Spirit in the World.*" *The Modern Schoolman* 48 (1971): 151–65.

Tappeiner, D. "Sacramental Causality in Aquinas and Rahner." *Scottish Journal of Theology* 28 (1975): 243–57.

Teske, R. "Rahner on the Relation of Nature and Grace." *Philosophy and Theology* 3 (1989): 109–22.

Torrance, T. "Towards an Ecumenical Consensus of the Trinity." *Theologische Zeitschrift* 31 (1975): 227–350.

Van Roo, W. "Reflection on Karl Rahner's *Kirche und Sakramente.*" *Gregorianum* 44 (1963): 465–500.

Viladesau, R. "How Is Christ Absolute? Rahner's Christology and the Encounter of World Religions." *Philosophy and Theology* 2 (1988): 220–40.

Vogels, H. "Erreicht Karl Rahners Theologie den kirchlichen Glauben? Kritik der Christologie und Trinitätslehre Karl Rahners." *Wissenschaft und Weisheit* 52 (1989): 21–62.

Weger, K. "Das 'anonyme' Christentum in der heutigen Theologie." *Stimmen der Zeit* 194 (1976): 319–32.

————. "Können Nicht-Christen jetzt auch Christen sein? Überlegungen zum 'anonymen Christentum.'" *Erbe und Auftrag* 63 (1987): 441–53.

Wilhelmsen, F. "The Priority of Judgment over Question: Reflections on Transcendental Thomism." *International Philosophical Quarterly* 14 (1974): 475–93.

Young, P. "Rahner's Searching Christology." *New Blackfriars* 68 (1987): 437–43.

INDEX